Political Lives

Political historian Dr CHRIS WALLACE is a professor at the Faculty of Business Government and Law, University of Canberra. Her previous book, *How To Win An Election* (NewSouth, 2020), drew important lessons for Labor from its shock 2019 election loss against the backdrop of the last half century of Australian federal elections. Wallace was formerly a longstanding member of the Canberra Press Gallery, and her political analysis and commentary currently appears in *Nikkei Asia*, *The Sydney Morning Herald*, *The Age*, *The Saturday Paper* and *The Conversation*. Twitter: @c_s_wallace

For years there has been no shrewder or sharper commentator on Canberra politics than Chris Wallace. In this compelling, typically acute and unique study she contrives to illuminate all at once – and often as if for the first time – both the character of Australia's prime ministers and the way Australian political history has been made.
Don Watson

Original, compelling and provocative. Every page offers fresh insights. *Political Lives* provides a genuinely new way of looking at Australian politics and political biography. Wallace has written a series of brilliant mini biographical essays on prime ministers and their biographers, exploring their backgrounds, relationships, motivations and political impact. The result is a biography of prime ministerial biography, the like of which we have not seen before.
Mark McKenna

Politicians' log cabin stories have become such an important part of politics. But it has not always been so. Chris Wallace traces the intriguing role biography has played in framing our views of our leaders past and present, and examines how it has become such a potent force in the political contest.
Laura Tingle

Chris Wallace, scholar–journalist, has written this superb and fascinating analysis of political biography since federation. Everyone interested in political history will love it. It concludes with a vital oath all her colleagues should observe: 'First do no harm – unless it's deserved and intentional'.
Kim Beazley

Political Lives

Australian prime ministers
and their biographers

CHRIS WALLACE

UNSW PRESS

A UNSW Press book

Published by
NewSouth Publishing
University of New South Wales Press Ltd
University of New South Wales
Sydney NSW 2052
AUSTRALIA
https://unsw.press/

© Chris Wallace 2023
First published 2023

10 9 8 7 6 5 4 3 2 1

This book is copyright. Apart from any fair dealing for the purpose of private study, research, criticism or review, as permitted under the *Copyright Act*, no part of this book may be reproduced by any process without written permission. Inquiries should be addressed to the publisher.

A catalogue record for this book is available from the National Library of Australia

ISBN   9781742237497 (paperback)
        9781742238562 (ebook)
        9781742239477 (ePDF)

Internal design Josephine Pajor-Markus
Cover design Lisa White
Cover image February 24, 1995: Sydney, NSW. Former Prime Minister Bob Hawke & girlfriend Blanche D'Alpuget drink tea while giving evidence to Senate Inquiry, Parliament House, Sydney. Verity Chambers / Newspix

All reasonable efforts were taken to obtain permission to use copyright material reproduced in this book, but in some cases copyright could not be traced. The author welcomes information in this regard.

Contents

Preface: Wait. What?	vii
1 Absent fathers	1
2 The Great War to the Great Depression	27
3 Menzies biography mystery	56
4 World War II to the end of the Menzies line	94
5 The modern era begins	119
6 Bob Hawke, writ large	167
7 Polaroids of a busy life	222
8 Political biography as political intervention	256
Notes	264
Bibliography	294
Index	302

For Arch

Preface

Wait. What?

Writers rarely spike a book and return a publishing advance. I did several years ago with a biography of Australia's then prime minister Julia Gillard. Countless times since I've been asked why.

When the book was conceived, Gillard was deputy prime minister and a parliamentary performer of power and flair in the majority Rudd Labor government. She was on an upward trajectory to become Australia's first woman prime minister but her ascension was faster than she or anyone else anticipated, or wanted.

Prime Minister Kevin Rudd was intelligent, media savvy and immensely popular, those three things obviously entwined. Rudd's declaration of climate change as the 'moral challenge of our generation' in the run up to the 2007 election, and early moves after winning office like the Apology to Australia's Indigenous Peoples, justly attracted strong support. When the global financial crisis hit in 2008, the government handled it superbly. Treasurer Wayne Swan became only the second Australian to be recognised internationally for the calibre of his economic management when named Euromoney Finance Minister of the Year for, uniquely among industrialised countries, leading Australia through the crisis without a recession. The government was seen to be achieving on multiple fronts.

So to the outside world the Rudd Government was a high performing one – and while this was true, the picture inside the government was far from pretty. Dictatorial, capricious and rude to colleagues and public servants alike behind the scenes, Rudd did not govern according to the robust but orderly cabinet process the Hawke and

Keating governments did to great effect when Labor was last in office. Instead Rudd was a crisis manager, himself perpetually generating the crises through unpredictable and provocative behaviour about which colleagues and public servants remained loyally silent. Public servants traditionally have to remain silent, of course, but Labor ministers within the confines of cabinet do not. The gap between Rudd's positive public standing and his unreasonable behaviour behind the scenes was so big it was judged wiser to manage and contain the situation to keep the government on an even keel. In any case, even if there was the will to do so, how could the internal dysfunction caused by Rudd be explained to his adoring public without Labor taking a terminal hit in the polls?

So Gillard, Swan and other senior ministers like Jenny Macklin and Stephen Conroy led internal efforts to make the government function as effectively as it could around the dysfunction Rudd created. They hoped and expected Rudd could and would deliver Labor at least one more election before that internal dysfunction broke into public view and damaged the government – something they would deal with when it happened after pocketing another election win in 2010.

Rudd charged on. Against the backdrop of his inspiring public declaration of climate policy as the 'moral challenge of our generation', he had high hopes of having a global impact at the Copenhagen Climate Change Conference (COP 15) in December 2009. He saw the Copenhagen summit, where more than a hundred world leaders would gather to make a decisive, binding treaty to avert global climate catastrophe, as his moment on the world stage. But Rudd had an unrealistically high estimation of his ability to get his fellow leaders to conclude such a treaty – a manifestation of the grandiose narcissism insiders had concluded was the essential flaw in his temperament. The Copenhagen summit failed, with world leaders kicking the climate change policy can down the road again as had happened at the previous fourteen COP meetings. Rudd was uncomprehending and, personally, devastated.

Wait. What?

In the wake of the Copenhagen summit's failure, colleagues urged Rudd to call an election immediately to capitalise on the high tide of climate policy concern in Australia, and give Labor a second term in office to take decisive action on it at home. Instead Rudd entered a protracted political paralysis. Supportive friends unsuccessfully tried to coax him from his post-Copenhagen malaise. The government's standing in the polls slid. By the winter of 2010 restless and increasingly desperate Labor backbenchers, sensing the vacuum and knowing an election had to be held that year, agitated for change. Never one to miss a power play, factional warrior Bill Shorten got involved, and Rudd's demise was inevitable. The preference of Labor elders, including Gillard, for Rudd to take Labor to the polls again early in 2010 and get another win was foreclosed by the slump in Rudd's polling and backbencher agitation reinforced by Shorten. The prime ministership fell to Gillard with only a minimal 'assist' from her right at the end.

Rudd and his caucus allies characterised Gillard's ultimately uncontested succession to the prime ministership as the act of a ruthlessly ambitious political killer. It's true that Gillard, a faction boss in her own right, was no saint. She had made thuggish moves in the past. They included throwing her numbers behind Mark Latham to oust opposition leader Kim Beazley in the run up to the 2004 election, and to oust Kim Beazley again as opposition leader in favour of Rudd in the run up to the 2007 election. When doing biographical research into Gillard while she was deputy prime minister, the guarded off-the-record comment of one junior female minister stuck in my mind: Gillard was supportive once she had broken you to her will, and you fell into line, but she wasn't supportive until then. This contrasted with the ethos among most women in the Labor caucus at the time, inculcated by the inclusive and collegiate Jenny Macklin, among others: one of mutual solidarity. Yet the idea Gillard had done for Rudd in the Lady Macbeth–like manner alleged by the Ruddites was far from the truth. It was for Rudd a self-serving trope, and for Gillard an unfair and damaging one that the Tony Abbott–led opposition seized on and exploited with relish.

So my Gillard biography began in apparently normal political times when she was a successful deputy prime minister. During the research and writing Gillard deposed Rudd and became Australia's first woman prime minister, leading a majority government operating in a fairly normal political environment. Then at the 2010 election, after a successful first week of campaigning, she was hit by guerrilla-style interventions from Labor's bitter ex-leaders Rudd and Latham and, under pressure, missteps of her own, memorably the 'real Julia' gambit where she promised to share with voters her authentic self.

The election reduced Labor from majority to minority government. By the time the biography neared completion, Gillard was besieged by a viciously misogynist campaign led by Abbott and backed by his colleagues and the right-wing media claque, while simultaneously being undermined within Labor's own ranks by an embittered Rudd and his caucus coterie. The atmosphere was toxic. Under sustained pressure from within and without, Gillard, with help from constructive colleagues, managed a large and effective legislative agenda and several significant reforms including carbon pricing, fairer school funding and the National Disability Insurance Scheme (NDIS), much of it negotiated through parliament by Anthony Albanese in his capacity as the Leader of the House. Under the dual political assault from within and without though, Gillard became a wooden performer, with brief exceptions like her spectacular misogyny speech which garnered global praise in 2012. Both Rudd and Abbott were coming for her. Labor's agony at the unprecedented tearing down of a serving Labor prime minister was palpable.

Anticipation surrounding the book's release was intense and the head publicist at my publisher, Allen & Unwin, alerted me to a looming media frenzy. At the end of one last research trip to pin down some final details, I sat contemplating this at a desk where I was staying: Melbourne's University College, motto *Frappe Fort*. The college

Wait. What?

translated this mildly as, 'What you do, do with a will'. A good sub-editor would have made it the snappier Anglo-Saxon, 'Hit Hard'.

As I looked out at the cool wintry afternoon light it became clear to me that my biography could be used to do just that to Gillard. It could hit her hard when she and her generally meritorious government were suffering an onslaught unparalleled, in the dual internal and external nature of the attack, in Australian postwar political history – and one certainly unmatched for sheer nastiness. It could hit Gillard hard because no biography of a human being, other than the worst pabulum from partisan supporters, could fail to include unattractive or critical elements. Human beings are flawed. They are fallible. Even the best have their lesser side. Good biographers strive to present their subjects in the round, the good and bad portrayed fairly, in context, with necessary nuance.

Gillard's life story contained its share of lesser elements. Enemies in the opposition, the government and the media were poised to cherrypick my biography for exploitable stories. In the fevered political atmosphere of that moment, the biography could damage her, and through her the government, no matter the nuance or context or, in less fevered political times, the essential triviality of the matters concerned. Was this right? Whatever one's view of Gillard, her prime ministerial performance and her government, was this fair? Was this, I asked myself, what a biography should do?

I flew home to Canberra and wrote to my publisher to say I had decided to put the biography aside and return my advance.

> In the current extraordinarily fetid political environment, every crazed coalition politician and shock jock will comb the text for bullets to fire at a prime minister who – while human and therefore, like us, flawed – is doing a fair job stabilising federal Labor and getting it back onto some sort of strategic track after the Rudd disaster. ... After much soul-searching and lost sleep, I've concluded I don't want on my conscience a destabilisation

of the Gillard Government just as it rights itself – and that's what's likely in this toxic political environment. The potential consequences are horrendous. Do I – do you? – want to contribute (however unfair the use of the material may be) to an Abbott Government? I don't.

The circumstance – a fragile minority Gillard Government facing enemies within and without, with an especially excoriating Opposition and a media in which significant parts are behaving like jihadists – was not foreseen when the book was contracted. I think I should leave the scene of battle now lest I inadvertently aid the black hats. The alternative is a compromised, eviscerated book and I don't think that's a choice I could live with – and I don't think that's the book you're interested in either.[1]

I closed saying I was 'deeply sorry about this decision, but I feel I have no other moral choice'. Allen & Unwin were disappointed but understanding, and also amazed an author would voluntarily return an advance. They supported my proposed response to questions, that 'I have made this decision for what I consider to be good reasons and I have nothing further to say'.

The Gillard biography would have been my fourth book. None of the earlier ones was without its own challenges and, at times, controversy. An old friend commented while I wrote my first biography that doing so was 'a kind of sorcery', an observation I could have profitably reflected upon earlier than I did. My experience with the Gillard biography spurred me to contemplate it in earnest. This book is the result.

I did not intend the Gillard biography to help or hurt Gillard's political fortunes. When I conceived it, I did not foresee its potential exploitation by 'bad actors' in the supercharged political environment which developed – something well beyond the normal thrust and parry of national politics. That is why I did not proceed with the book.

Wait. What?

What about contemporary political biographers before me? Who were they, what motivated them, and what challenges did they face? Were they alert to the risk I perceived only late in the writing of the Gillard biography, that nuanced elements of a politician's life story could be used crudely to damage them in real time? Or did they deliberately practise a 'kind of sorcery' to influence their subject's political trajectory? Did they practise political biography as political intervention?

To gain the benefits of historical distance I decided to confine the study to the first hundred years since Federation. I found, read and researched every biography written in the lead up to, or during, the active political careers of Australia's twentieth century prime ministers – books that could actually affect their careers. I interviewed every living Australian prime minister and every living prime ministerial biographer for that period to explore the heart of the relationship and exchange between them. Reputational capital has value. What was the biographer's motivation? What was the subject's motivation? What was the biography's immediate effect? This is an intimate history of biographers' image-making and image-breaking in Australian national politics, from the vantage point of the prime ministers and the biographers themselves.

Chapter 1
Absent fathers

No publicist or writer who was their contemporary has displayed any wish to breathe life into this cold clay ...

Herbert Campbell-Jones

Federation joined Britain's six antipodean colonies into one nation in 1901 when New South Wales, Victoria, Queensland, Tasmania, South Australia and Western Australia became the Commonwealth of Australia. Six years later in *The Real Australia,* journalist and writer Alfred Buchanan could, as a contemporary observer, already write about four prime ministers: Edmund Barton, Alfred Deakin, Chris Watson and George Reid.[1] In Australia's first dozen years, they and two others – Joseph Cook and Andrew Fisher – formed Australia's first ten governments. Deakin and Fisher were each prime minister three times, and Barton, Watson, Reid and Cook were each prime minister once.[2] Four were non-Labor governments: those of Barton (Protectionist), Deakin (Protectionist, Commonwealth Liberal), Reid (Free Trade) and Cook (Commonwealth Liberal). Two governments, those of Watson and Fisher, were Labor. New South Wales seemed to have a stranglehold on the prime ministership with four of those six leaders – Barton, Reid, Watson and Cook – hailing from there. The two who did not, however, formed six of those first ten governments: Deakin from Melbourne, and Fisher from the rural Queensland town of Gympie.

These are the absent fathers of Australian politics. None of our first half dozen prime ministers was the subject of a published biography in the lead up to, or during, their prime ministership. The first biography of Barton was not published until 45 years after his prime ministership; Deakin's was 13 years after his prime ministership, Watson's 95 years, Reid's 84 years, Fisher's 93 years and Cook's 74 years. All these biographies were posthumous.[3] Deakin later became the focus of scholarly attention, stimulated by JA La Nauze's *Alfred Deakin: A Biography* published in 1965, nearly half a century after Walter Murdoch's posthumous *Alfred Deakin: A sketch*; and most recently with Judith Brett's *The Enigmatic Mr Deakin*.[4]

Generally, however, the biographical neglect of Australia's first half dozen prime ministers is striking. Most Australians would struggle even to conjure an image of them in their minds. Few biographies of Australians of any kind were published at the time, of course; there was little to no local book-publishing industry. The biography of prime ministers in the 'mother of parliaments', Westminster, was sparse at the time too, so Australian practice was not so different from Britain. Both contrasted strongly with practices in the United States where campaign politics from its inception featured political biography that, whether true or not, often underlined the 'log cabin' roots of presidential candidates.

The Australia these early prime ministers governed emerged from the turbulent late-colonial period marked by boom and bust, which took many banks and individual fortunes down with it, and the great maritime and shearers' strikes of the 1890s which arose from and heightened working-class consciousness, spurring the development of the labour movement's industrial and political wings. Australians numbered fewer than four million people. 'Imponderable psychological forces molded the Parliament' in its earliest years contemporary *Argus* reporter, Herbert Campbell-Jones, later wrote.

> It is desirable to recall ... that motor cars were then practically unknown; that electric light had only just crept into use ... that the world famous beaches of Bondi and Coogee were ugly shores covered by bracken where boys went shooting within three miles of the heart of the city; that the banks of the Yarra were public tips ... that men went abroad in tropical heat in bowler hats, thick suits, starched shirts and 2½ inch collars; that the word 'Damn' was not permitted on the stage ... [and] that sports of any kind were forbidden on the Day of Rest; that aviation was still the dream of Jules Verne; that wireless had only been suspected ... that cable messages cost about 9/- a word ... that Victor Trumper was giving class bowlers heartache; and that aristocratic yearlings were selling for an hundred guineas.[5]

If this sounds small, distant and alien from today's vantage point, consider the colonial environment in which Australia's early prime ministers grew up. Buchanan points out that the first, Barton, was born into a 'greater Sydney' of just 53 000 people, growing fast but in absolute terms smaller than contemporary Wagga Wagga in New South Wales or Shepparton in Victoria, and much smaller than today's Bunbury in Western Australia or Bundaberg in Queensland.

These early prime ministers, of course, were themselves part of the continuing violent dispossession of First Nations peoples from their continent occupied for at least 65 000 years before British colonisation. One only has to look at 'Colonial Frontier Massacres, Australia, 1788 to 1930', the map created by historian Lyndall Ryan and her research team at the University of Newcastle, to take in this profound truth: massacres of Indigenous Australians by white colonisers proliferated up to and beyond Federation.[6] Julianne Schultz in *The Idea of Australia* underlines how 'forgetting is essential' in a country awash in the blood of brutal colonial conquest. It makes a mockery of Australia's most celebrated epigram, 'Lest we forget', Schultz said: *'Best we forget* would be more honest'.

> By rarely going back to first principles and examining the past, a terra nullius of the mind has prevailed. Unchallenged tendrils of memory are easily twisted to gird myths.[7]

How much easier this is when Australia's founding fathers are largely absent from the community's historical memory.

Relatively well remembered is the rise of the Australian Labor Party, but not so much its leaders. Labor's rise was a marked phenomenon of the early federation period – in Colin Clark's view 'earlier, stronger, and much better organized than the British Labour Party'.[8] While its significance was clear in retrospect, this was not immediately so. In *The First Decade of the Australian Commonwealth: A Chronicle of Contemporary Politics, 1901–1910*, published at that decade's end, Henry Gyles Turner portrayed a Labor ascendancy initially obscured by the 'triad of parties' – Labor, Protectionist and Free Trade – none of which commanded a clear majority during those years. 'At many festive boards, when Mr Deakin poured forth his oratory', he wrote, 'it was often mingled with the plaintive admission that he could not play the game while there were three elevens in the field, and the humorous definition passed into common parlance'.[9] The joining, breaking and remaking of administrations at frequent intervals distracted attention, Turner argued, from the near trebling of the federal Labor caucus to 65 members and senators by the end of the Australian parliament's first decade. Labor has cohered as a party ever since. On the conservative side of politics, the original Protectionists and Free Traders grouped and regrouped in various forms over the course of the twentieth century until emerging as the relatively stable Liberal Party and National Party of today. The Coalition has governed Australia for twice as long in the post–World War II period (51 years) as Labor (26 years).

In this fluid situation where party identities, allegiances and appeals were yet to be settled in all their particulars, the personal identity and individual appeal of specific party leaders could be at a premium, conferring a competitive advantage significant even measured against the impact of party identity. Was biography or autobiography an instrument to be deployed in the pursuit of that advantage, positively or negatively? Given two-thirds of the leaders who became prime minister in Australia's first dozen years had publishing and press connections, this would seem possible, even probable. Deakin, Watson, Reid and Fisher each in their way had ink in their veins, or at least on their hands. Deakin and Reid were in their different ways both writers, Watson was a compositor, and Fisher had co-founded, and for a time in the late 1890s wrote for and edited, a regional newspaper. Yet no contemporary biography of them, or autobiography by them, was published. This was also the case for the other two but more understandably so: Barton was a lawyer and Cook was a miner. One, George Reid, wrote a memoir but long after he left Australian politics, when he had become a member of Britain's House of Commons.[10] It seems that book-length biography was *not* an instrument deployed in the pursuit of political advantage by prime ministers in the early post-federation period, on any of the three sides of politics. The *Argus'* Herbert Campbell-Jones, for example, commented on the 'surging tide' of Labor politics that 'threatened to inundate the Federal Parliament' in these early years, but noted too that, 'Many have speculated upon the origin of the natural forces which caused this new phenomenon; but few stop to puzzle over the personnel of the third party'.[11]

Australia's founding prime minister, Edmund 'Toby' Barton, was a Protectionist who held office from January 1901 to September 1903. Barton's political capital relied more on presence than personal narrative. Buchanan's near contemporary sketch of Barton in *The Real Australia*, just four years after he resigned the prime ministership to join the High Court, suggests Barton had a vote-winning style without needing to utter even a syllable.

> Some of his critics said that he travelled the country on his hair. The statement was at best a half truth, and at worst a trifle libelous. For the Goddess ... gave him something more than an idealistic head of hair, useful asset though that has been. It gave him a large skull-index, a massive forehead, an impressive set of features that look their best when on a platform surmounting a vast concourse of people. It gave him a certain faculty for looking like a great man. To ... watch him closing his lips firmly and looking out with the Roscius-like gaze over the heads of the audience, is to experience an unreasonable desire to rise up in the middle of the hall and cheer.[12]

Like a good thespian preserving the integrity of his public role, the clubbable Barton kept his life off the political stage to himself. Buchanan would write two generations after Barton's prime ministership that 'the man himself has had no biographer and to the younger generation his fame and his achievements are but a vague memory'.[13] Geoffrey Bolton found a conscious 'guarding' of privacy by Barton and his wife, including the destruction of almost all personal and family material which might have illuminated it: 'they were good at minding their own business'.[14]

Barton's prime ministership was relatively short. A month after he resigned in 1903 to join the High Court, he wrote to Tom Bavin, who had been his prime ministerial private secretary, about his profound caution concerning 'that life story business'. He referred to a claim by 'the Sunday *Times* man in Melbourne, McKinney' that he had made a 'semi-promise' to talk to him, and asked Bavin whether there was any paperwork to sustain the claim. 'I don't recollect making any "semi-promise" or even demi-semi-promise ... so I want to find out whether we wrote anything on which he can base his aspertions [sic]', Barton said.[15] It was not that he did not care about posterity, however. When Barton sailed for Britain in 1915 he wrote detailed instructions to Bavin regarding his papers – 'especially about the Federal struggle' – should misfortune befall him on the trip. 'I am not referring particularly to German assassins but to the ordinary chances of life', Barton wrote, adding that Bavin 'may want to refer to some of them' in future writings.[16]

Barton's fellow Protectionist and successor, Alfred Deakin, was prime minister three times between September 1903 and April 1910. While briefly a practising barrister at the outset of his career, Deakin was a journalist by profession, published author, poet and sometime playwright. Deakin was the Australian prime minister whom one might most expect to have been the subject of contemporary biography or autobiography given his intense literary industry and reflexivity. 'He was a *writer*', JA La Nauze observed, 'one who used words exactly'.[17] He nevertheless did not stimulate the production of a contemporary biography nor publish an autobiography himself.

Deakin's papers yield insights into his relationship with biography, revealing, for example, his 'persistent search for gallant heroes' as a boy. He purloined from his older sister 'Mrs Markham's History' – *A history of England: from the first invasion by the Romans to the 14th year of the reign of Queen Victoria* by Elizabeth Penrose under the pseudonym 'Mrs Markham'. From it the youthful Deakin playfully adopted 'the style and title of that most unheroic and unpicturesque sovereign, King George III, when presiding over a triple alliance of my mates in which the other two members, for reasons best known to themselves, represented respectively Napoleon Bonaparte and the King of the Sandwich Islands'. As a teenager his voracious reading included only 'a smattering of history and biography, Boswell sipped and put aside till later'.[18]

In his twenties, however, as a young member of the Victorian parliament, Deakin clipped out newspaper accounts of prominent biographies and pasted them into notebooks. One notebook included long reviews of biographies of Byron, Emerson, Mazzini, Sheridan and Cromwell as well as one of James Froude's edited collection of Jane Welsh Carlyle's letters, which canvassed Froude's controversial biography of Carlyle.[19] Deakin's literary correspondence shows that he read biographies while prime minister. 'Since the House rose', he wrote to Walter Murdoch in 1906, for example, 'I have had a little relaxation with *Ten Tudor Statesmen* [and] the biography of WT Arnold prefixed to his *Roman Imperialism*'.[20] At his death, Deakin's library included eighty-one biographies as well as a twenty-volume series, *English Men of Letters,* and the nine-volume *Great Writer* series.[21]

Deakin was, in fact, a lifelong memoirist – just not for publication. In a biography published half a century after Deakin left politics, La Nauze posed the question, 'To whom was his life-long commentary on "myself in Protean shapes" addressed?' He noted Deakin's 1888 comment in his private papers that, 'I write it is true to an imaginary reader', and how in December 1902, when attorney-general in the Barton Government, Deakin foreshadowed, again in his private papers, a possible autobiography: 'a testament so to speak [with] some memorials ... of matters of fact'. La Nauze comments that the 'self-analyses' of Deakin's later years 'might be regarded as rough drafts to be drawn on when he came to compose it', and that by 1911 he seemed for the first time to be addressing 'some real reader other than himself'.[22]

Whether this was so or not, Deakin did not write an autobiography for publication. Nor did any of the journalists with whom he shared professional roots write a biography of him during his years in the Australian parliament. Buchanan, who as a journalist knew and reported on Deakin, says his attitude to the press differed from most Australian politicians. 'He had been on a daily paper himself, and never quite lost a feeling of camaraderie for those whose duty it was to call on him for information', Buchanan says. 'With many of them he had a personal friendship, a friendship that did not affect his statesman's reticence in regard to matters that had not reached the publicity stage'.[23]

This perhaps makes the lack of a contemporary Deakin biography even more surprising.

Stuart Macintyre argued that while the 'literary output of our twentieth-century national leaders is unimpressive', Deakin's 'inner history of the Federal Cause' is the exception to that 'threadbare list'.[24] It was not published until twenty-five years after Deakin's death, however, and in any case 'minimizes his part in the events it relates' – evidence of a modesty in Deakin that may have severely circumscribed a published autobiography even had he not suffered early mental decline and death in 1919 at just 63 years old.[25] Buchanan described him without irony in *The Real Australia* as 'belauded impartially and comprehensively as an Adonis and a Demosthenes, as a Caius Gracchus and a Marcus Aurelius, as a Beau Brummell and a William Pitt'.[26] Yet Deakin remained unsung in biography until Walter Murdoch's *Alfred Deakin: A Sketch* was published thirteen years after he left the prime ministership and four years after his death.

―――

John Christian 'Chris' Watson, Deakin's successor and the world's first social democratic prime minister, held office from April to August 1904. Watson was born Johan Cristian Tanck in Chile to a Chilean-born father of German parentage, who was an officer in the merchant marine, and an Irish mother who had emigrated to New Zealand. They met and married when Tanck's ship, the *Julia*, visited Port Chalmers in New Zealand, and went to Chile together on the return voyage. After Tanck disappeared or died – the historical record is unclear – Watson's mother repatriated from Chile to New Zealand and married George Watson, whose surname her infant son later took, becoming John Christian Watson. Watson grew up in New Zealand, and emigrated to Australia aged 19 in search of work as a compositor. There was no contemporary biography of Watson – indeed, no biography at all until 1999 when *The Man Time Forgot: The life and times of John Christian*

Watson, Australia's first Labor Prime Minister by Al Grassby and Silvia Ordonez was published.[27]

Grassby and Ordonez contextualised Watson's life story in the times, when reinvention to enhance respectability and 'Britishness' was far from uncommon. While, according to Grassby and Ordonez, no party leader in the Australian parliament has been 'as evasive or contradictory' on the details of their early life as Watson, this did not impede his political progress. Without British citizenship, Watson was ineligible to sit in the Australian parliament: 'How was the Chilean-born man, of German stock, who had grown up in New Zealand', they ask, 'able to achieve this?'[28] Grassby and Ordonez compare Watson's evasions with those of others like his fellow parliamentarian, American-born King O'Malley, a minister in the later Fisher and Hughes governments who, like Watson, lacked the British citizenship requisite for Australian MPs. They point out that evasions and fabrications were not the exclusive preserve of politicians, citing as an example, prominent University of Melbourne historian, Professor Ernest Scott, whose re-engineered life story concealed his illegitimacy.[29]

Personal edits, reinventions and biographical lacunae eased the passages of people like Watson, O'Malley and Scott through public life in the antipodes. That Watson did a good job of obfuscating his origins and avoiding disqualification from parliament is shown, for example, in Buchanan's pen portrait of him in an unpublished collective biography of Australia's first eleven prime ministers. Buchanan names Watson's stepfather as his father thereby establishing the necessary Britishness; has his parents' marriage taking place in England; and explains Watson's Chilean birth as incidental to the sea journey on which the Watson family allegedly 'emigrated' to New Zealand, which included a South American stopover, all of which is false.[30]

George Reid, Watson's successor, was Australia's first Free Trade prime minister and held office from August 1904 to July 1905. Reid was a public servant turned lawyer–politician, and the author of four books and one published poem all of which were aimed at career advancement. This was arguably true even of the memoir published in 1917, twelve years after his prime ministership and eight years after leaving the Australian parliament, since Reid was by then serving as the member for St George's, Hanover Square in the House of Commons.

Reid was a man mindful of his audience. 'Bores are in a class of infinite variety', Reid reminisced. 'But the worst are those who occupy public time'.[31] From an early age he exploited the power of writing to shape and advance his position, letting the texts build his public persona by inference. His first three books were written in consecutive years when he was a young Colonial Treasury official in New South Wales. The first, at sixteen pages more pamphlet than book, put Reid on the political map. *The Diplomacy of Victoria on the Postal Question, and the True Policy of New South Wales*, published in 1873, was about mail steamer services to Australia – an important public policy issue given Australia's geographical isolation and the state of communications technology at the time.[32] It led NSW postmaster-general Saul Samuel to request Reid's secondment from Treasury, to act as his private secretary on a mission overseas concerning postal links with Britain and the United States. NSW governor Hercules Robinson supported the idea and offered letters of introduction to friends in Britain but the Treasury under-secretary scotched the secondment, Reid said in his memoir, out of rivalry with Saul Samuel.[33]

At the end of his life Reid described writing *The Diplomacy of Victoria on the Postal Question* as part of his conscious 'efforts to get "out of the ruck"' as a young man.[34] A copy of the pamphlet in the National Library of Australia's collection, hand-inscribed to 'The Revd [J]D Lang with GH Reid's Compliments ... 12th June 1873', shows Reid making the most of its potential to impress influential colonists.[35] In this case it was through the dispatch of a copy to the prominent

Presbyterian 'divine and politician' John Dunmore Lang.[36] Reid was 28 years old. Disappointment at the publication's favourable notice not translating into the Samuel secondment fuelled his next endeavour since, 'if there is one lesson which a young man should take to heart more than another it is this: make failure in one direction the starting point for success in another'.

> I set about writing *Five Essays on Free Trade*. Free Trade was a subject on which I had often spoken in debating clubs. New South Wales had always based her fiscal policy upon Free Trade; Victoria had just entered upon a Protective policy. I believed in the former view with all the ardour which beginners sometimes share with experts. Since there was nobody to convince in New South Wales I addressed my essays to the electors of Victoria, with a degree of confidence which must have seemed amusing, if not disgusting, to an adverse critic. Although confidence may be 'a plant of slow growth in an aged bosom', it flourishes luxuriantly between young shoulders.[37]

If Reid's first effort made an impression, this second book was successful beyond any reasonable prediction. After an indifferent school record, and beginning work as the most junior of clerks in a merchant's office aged thirteen, Reid was a 30-year-old public servant and author of note – and a correspondent of leading British Liberal politician William Gladstone. In 1875, Reid sent *Five Essays on Free Trade* to Gladstone at his Carlton House Terrace home in London.[38] Gladstone's first prime ministership had ended the year before when he lost the 1874 general election to Disraeli. Reid received a warm, handwritten note from Gladstone for his initiative. 'You are at liberty to make such use of this letter as you may think proper and I shall be glad if I can find any opportunity of drawing attention or causing it to be drawn to the subject of your Essays', Gladstone wrote.[39] Honorary membership of the Cobden Club in London, a leading Free Trade dining group whose leading lights included John Stuart Mill and Gladstone himself, followed.⁴⁰ Equally important for Reid's immediate prospects, *Five Essays on Free Trade* brought him to the favourable notice of politicians in New South Wales, including Henry Parkes.⁴¹

Reid followed this the next year with *An Essay on New South Wales, The Mother Colony of the Australias*, printed by the NSW Government for use at the US Centennial Exposition.⁴² Reid generated momentum entirely with words – ostensibly through matters of policy, not biography, yet by inference steadily building public perceptions of him. Strong early returns on this strategy drove him on to even more ambitious heights. He not only dispatched *An Essay on New South Wales* to Lord Salisbury, then a minister in the Disraeli Government, at his Arlington Street home – again receiving a handwritten note in reply – but even to Queen Victoria, whose secretary wrote from Windsor Castle that 'in compliance with your request I have laid [it] before the Queen'; he relayed her thanks.⁴³ Another testament to Reid's self-publicising drive is a 12-page pamphlet titled 'Opinions of the Press' in which he compiled glowing quotes about *An Essay on New South Wales* from book reviews in the *Sydney Morning Herald*, *Warrnambool Examiner*, *Taranaki News*, *Manchester Guardian* and another 146 newspapers across Australia, Britain, Ireland and New Zealand.⁴⁴

Over the next two decades Reid was admitted to the bar, entered the NSW parliament, was elected premier and became deeply engaged in the campaign for an Australian nation. As Federation became increasingly likely, an unknown author began a biography. The handwritten 241-page manuscript begins with Reid's parentage and 'Place of Nativity in Scotland', and ends with the proroguing of the NSW parliament on 16 November 1896. Though unpublished, it is likely the first contemporary biography of a serving politician who achieved the Australian prime ministership. A Carlylesque paean of praise, it burnished Reid and his record with vigour.⁴⁵

The manuscript was a work in progress. The contents page points to a page 242 absent from the manuscript – either missing or, more likely, pointing to the next section the author planned to write since the contents refer to the 'Banquet to Mr Reid in 1897 &c &c' on that page.[46] Elements of the biography provide clues about the anonymous author. That the manuscript is part of the Reid Papers held at the National Library of Australia (NLA) suggests it was a friendly enterprise by someone known to Reid. However, the author does not appear to be Reid, a family member or intimate. Several things point to an outsider. There is the misspelling of Reid's middle name, Houstoun, which in the decorative heading at the beginning of the manuscript is spelled 'Houston'. There is a blank space after the word 'Miss' in the sentence where Reid's father becomes acquainted with, and subsequently marries, Reid's mother; Reid or someone close to him would have known, or at least been in a position to ask and fill in Reid's mother's maiden name before producing a fair copy of the biography like this.[47] A gap is also left in the manuscript for the year of Reid's mother's decline and death in another sign the author was acquainted, but not closely, with Reid.

The author provides personal observations of Reid's father, minister at the Mariners' Church in Sydney's The Rocks, including scenes from Reverend Reid's induction there on 24 June 1862. The author writes that he was a 14-year-old chorister in Mr J McCormick's Choir which sang hymns at the induction, making him male, almost certainly Presbyterian, and born between 25 June 1847 and 24 June 1848.[48] The author was thus a few years younger than George Reid himself. Later in the manuscript, recounting Reid's involvement in the NSW Cricketers' Association, the author reveals himself as a one-time journalist who had reported on its meetings and matches 'when connected with the daily press'.[49]

After thirty pages describing Reid's antecedents and eulogising Reid's father, the anonymous biographer begins the story of Reid himself with a charming statement of the late Victorian biographical sensibility which permeates the manuscript.

> If it is true that history is sure to please, biography has higher claims on the human heart. In history events are the chief cause of attraction while in Biography it is the man that attaches and we identify ourselves with his career, or in other words we enter into all his views, delight in his successes (provided he is not the most worthless and corrupt of his species) and feel mortified at his disappointments. Contemporary biography has a strong hold on our sensibilities, especially when we know the subject of the book or of the persons with which he has been in relation. To revive old associations, renew deceased friendships, recall forgotten adventures, renovate old habits and feelings, a tender interest steals over the mind quite unconnected with the merits of the hero of the reminiscences.[50]

Of course, that tenderness melds with perceptions of 'the hero' by the time the reader finishes such a biography, and that is its very point.

When the anonymous author declares himself a 'willing victim' in traversing Reid's life and career, the reader can be under no misapprehension that a critical evaluation is about to unfold. It takes only another two pages for the first significant omission arguably helpful to Reid's career to appear. 'Although the affairs of private life may not generally be considered subjects suitable for public notice', the author writes, 'yet it is but right and just to remark that owing to his circumstances, [Reverend Reid] was compelled to send his children into the world to gain their livelihood, rather than to a college for future admission to one of the learned professions'. The author then asserts that Reid was 'destined' for the public service and 'received his first appointment' in 1864 at the Treasury. This was strictly true but misleads readers to believe it was the first job of Reid, by then 19 years old.[51] In fact, Reid started work as a junior clerk in a merchant's counting house when he was 13.[52] It enabled the anonymous biographer to be candid about the Reid family's limited means, but to avoid disclosing that George had no formal education as a teenager. Reid himself remedies this gap years later, at the end of his life, in *My Reminiscences*.[53] However, it was likely to be a liability in late colonial New South Wales for an ambitious non-Labor premier competing with well-educated rivals like Barton in New South Wales and, on the federation stage, Deakin from Victoria.

Later in the manuscript the anonymous biographer gilded Reid with Richard Cobden's free trade glow. Cobden 'became "the apostle of Free Trade" in Great Britain', the biographer writes, 'and the mantle has fallen from his shoulders on to those of our young Australian Premier as 'the apostle of Free Trade in Australia'.[54] Three pages later a small newspaper clipping is attached, apparently from the Vancouver newspaper the *British Colonist*, which had asked readers to nominate 'the fifty most illustrious names in British history'.[55] The cutting shows the Prince of Wales topping the list of results for 'LIVING MEN ONLY', followed by the Dukes of Cambridge, Argyle, Devonshire, Salisbury, Rosebery, Curzon and so on before Lord Kitchener appears at No 14 and Cecil Rhodes at No 17, followed by Balfour, Chamberlain and then, astonishingly, at No 20, 'Mr Reid, NSW'. Asquith comes in at No 21, Rudyard Kipling at No 37, followed by Herbert Spencer and John Ruskin and, at No 46, the Archbishop of Canterbury. It is faintly possible that the anonymous biographer's laying of Cobden's mantle on Reid's shoulders is not merely puff but merited, that his standing was far higher in the late nineteenth century than posterity makes credible. More likely is that Reid had the political wit to organise a writing campaign to the *British Colonist* propelling his name onto and up that list. If the latter, Reid was far ahead of his time in terms of political self-promotion.

WG McMinn's biography *George Reid* was published nearly a century after the anonymous biographer wrote, and remains the only one. McMinn noted that Reid was famously casual about his papers and that, given he left virtually none, posterity's judgment of him rests mainly on caricatures of him by political rivals like Barton and Deakin, and by newspaper sketch writers and cartoonists who exploited for their own purposes his large girth, moustachioed, walrus-like visage, and tendency to forty winks during tedious parliamentary debates.[56] McMinn made a good fist of historical recovery in *George Reid* but further serious scholarship did not follow. Interestingly, despite more than two dozen footnotes to the anonymous biographer's manuscript (in the form 'MS biog.'), McMinn does not mention its existence, discuss it or explore its authorship, but merely makes a minimalist listing of it under 'Reid Papers' in his select bibliography. That listing inaccurately refers to 'Mss 242', an erroneous citation of MS 2242, the National Library of Australia call number for 'special collections relating to Sir George Reid' – only discoverable by an especially close reading of the listing for MS 7842 which constitutes the main and more visible 'Papers of Sir George Reid'.[57]

Thus one of the least known biographically significant documents concerning an early Australian prime minister has lain in the shadows for over a century. While the manuscript's provenance is uncertain, it is likely another layer in Reid's powerful self-making through words – in this case, through his own life story in a friendly biography by a sympathetic contemporary journalist. Notwithstanding its Victorian biographical style – short on private disclosure, long on public achievements – completed and published it might have hastened Reid's progress to the prime ministership or helped him hold onto to it for longer by providing a biographical context that gave antipathetic characterisations of him less purchase. It could have added nuance to, if not defeated, the stereotype that bedevilled Reid even before he moved onto the national political stage. That this was at least partly the biography's intention is suggested by ripostes in it to slurs like the 'Reid the Wriggler' epithet with which he was branded as NSW premier, implying he was less than wholly committed to Free Trade.[58] 'It may be stated that Mr Reid has ever entertained but one set of opinions since he became a candidate for public life', wrote the biographer, 'and they were those laid down by the great apostle of Free Trade, Richard Cobden'.[59]

The 'Reid the Wriggler' slur fed into the 'Yes–No Reid' stereotype foisted upon Reid in the federation campaign. A Buchanan anecdote provides insight into how completely the caricature came to dominate perceptions of the man. Buchanan describes a Labor deputation to Reid in August 1897 which several reporters also attended. They waited in the premier's 'official room' for Reid to arrive.

> After a few minutes, a door was opened within. The man who entered was a surprise, almost a shock, to one who, like myself, was seeing the much-caricatured Premier of New South Wales for the first time. Erect, frock-coated, serious of mien, he seemed as much like a figure of fun as the statue of Jupiter Ammon is like Mr Punch.
>
> The man who came into the room had the look of a general surveying a battle front. The dominant forehead and clear blue eyes made other features unnoticeable. There was no hint of arrogance nor yet a trace of anxiety; the whole manner and bearing, as he advanced to the table, betokened confidence, decision and intellectual grip.[60]

Reid was 52 years old at the time and, Buchanan writes, at the height of his mental powers: '[D]espite his heavy physical frame and lack of forethought in health matters, his mental and physical fitness remained with him, but little impaired, to the end of a life that took him three years past the allotted span'.[61]

Buchanan was not alone in thinking the stereotype of Reid unfair. 'The political leader is dissected while he still lives', observed Herbert Campbell-Jones, who covered the first Australian parliaments for the Melbourne *Argus*. 'Vivisection has become a fine art in Australia, and Sir George Reid suffered much by it'.[62] Campbell-Jones then proved his own point with the observation that, 'Spectacles made him look like a cross between a fat German professor and a Japanese wrestler'.[63]

Absent fathers

The anonymous biographer put down his pen the same year as Buchanan had his stereotype-shattering encounter with Reid. Had he instead brought his project to fruition, a more balanced view of Reid may have prevailed, or at least been juxtaposed against the buffoonish, cartoonish orthodoxy which prevailed then and continues still.

Labor prime minister Andrew Fisher held office three times between November 1908 and October 1915. Fisher was a Scottish-born miner from Queensland. He felt the power of the press early in his political career when the *Gympie Times* campaigned against his re-election to the Queensland Legislative Assembly in 1896, and he lost his seat. Fisher's response was to establish the rival *Gympie Truth* which, with two political allies, he largely wrote and edited until a bout of illness in 1897 restricted him to financial management of the paper. Fisher was returned to the Queensland parliament at the next election and, upon Federation, to the Australian parliament.[64] Fisher's surviving library does not suggest much interest in biography.[65] A biography was a long time coming, too, with Fisher's papers held until relatively recently in Britain, and with two biographers – Denis Murphy and Clem Lloyd – dying before their respective works on him could be completed.[66] David Day's biography *Andrew Fisher, Prime Minister of Australia* and Peter Bastian's *Andrew Fisher: An underestimated man* eventually appeared a century after Fisher's prime ministership.[67] Much as with George Reid, Fisher's reputation during and after his prime ministerial career is, in Day's view, 'refracted through the jaundiced eyes of his political opponents'. Fisher's stature 'steadily diminished as sympathetic biographies of Alfred Deakin and Billy Hughes exaggerated the achievements of their subjects and cast Fisher's achievements into the shade', he writes. 'They set the tone for historians writing about the early years of the Australian nation. In the absence of a biography of Fisher it was difficult for a more balanced view to take hold'.[68]

Joseph 'Joe' Cook was a Commonwealth Liberal prime minister between June 1913 and September 1914. Cook was by origin an English miner and founding member of the NSW Labor Party, who parted company with his party over the 'Pledge' binding Labor MPs to accept party discipline. He ended up a conservative in the Australian parliament allied successively with Reid, Deakin and Billy Hughes. His prime ministership was short and there was no contemporary biography of him.

All six Australian prime ministers to this point – the beginning of World War I – were without biographies, contemporary or otherwise. Two journalists, Herbert Campbell-Jones and Alfred Buchanan, attempted to fill the vacuum. Campbell-Jones made detailed contemporary notes of the first Australian parliament in which all six of these foundation prime ministers served and later wrote a collective biography based on those notes; it was never published. Buchanan wrote brief contemporary sketches of the first four prime ministers, publishing them in *The Real Australia* (1907), as well as writing an unpublished work with biographical profiles of the first eleven prime ministers.

From Federation to 1911, Herbert Campbell-Jones was a reporter and chief of staff of the Melbourne *Argus* from which, given the Australian parliament met in Melbourne for its first quarter of a century, he had an intimate vantage point. By the time his unpublished manuscript 'The Cabinet of Captains: the romance of Australia's first Federal Parliament' was finished around 1935, only a few members of that first parliament remained. 'Each of the survivors – active and passive – has been asked to write a personal story of that remarkable gathering of Australian legislators and each has paused and promised, prepared and postponed', Campbell-Jones wrote in his preface. 'There is danger of all of them returning to dust without placing on record the salient facts which will help posterity to understand why this Act was placed on the Statute Books and why that thing was not done'. Campbell-Jones decided to fill the breach.

> No publicist or writer who was their contemporary has displayed any wish to breathe life into this cold clay and so having been in almost daily contact with every Federal Minister and each Federal Department from the day that they commenced to function for more than ten years continuously, the writer offers these brief and rough outlines of the political characters of the principal personages of that first National Parliament as possible foundation for the fuller narrative which must some day find its way to the printing presses.
>
> They do not profess to be more than crude thumbnail sketches nor is the reader asked to believe that they are irrebuttably accurate. Each of us forms his own evaluation of the parts and idiosyncrasies of his fellows and often they differ. But this claim is made, that they are honest and that the notes upon which they are based were made when the several incidents occurred, and that though some phases of the subjects' lives may have been extenuated – for which of us could survive a truly impartial investigation – naught has been set down in malice.[69]

Campbell-Jones was modest about his collective biography of that first parliament. Vivid, witty, sharply observed, dense with telling detail, 'The Cabinet of Captains' is an unpublished jewel of Australian political history – and though retrospective, that Campbell-Jones wrote it based on contemporary notes makes it especially valuable for historians.

Alfred Buchanan was born in England around 1874, and emigrated at nine years old with his family to New Zealand. After taking his MA there in the 1890s, Buchanan emigrated to Australia and became drama critic and 'special writer' at Deakin's old paper, the Melbourne *Age*.[70] From 1903 to 1906, as the *West Australian*'s leader writer in Perth, he was the protégé of politician and newspaper proprietor Winthrop Hackett; the Perth *Sunday Times* later commented that Buchanan 'brought a deal of scholarship to his editorials' at the *West Australian*.[71] It was then that his first novel, *Bubble Reputation: A Story of Modern Life*, was published, which dealt with 'the inner working of Australian politics and throws many side-lights on journalistic life'.[72] Buchanan was an innovator. 'This book does what hardly another Australian novel has done', said a review in the *Argus*. 'It presents to the world present-day Australian life in the town – the life of the majority of the people'.[73]

Good notices for *Bubble Reputation*, reinforced by the successful publication of Buchanan's *The Real Australia* around the same time, led him to move from Perth to England briefly before returning to Australia, journalism and two more novels: *She Loved Much* (1907) and *Where the Day Begins* (1911). The latter's protagonist is a politician. Buchanan was now chief parliamentary reporter for the *Age*, giving him direct exposure to the Australian parliament and its members. During this time he also did a law degree and wrote a play, *The Image Breaker*, which was produced by Australian theatre pioneer Gregan McMahon for Melbourne's Repertory Theatre to a sell-out crowd in April 1914. *The Image Breaker*'s protagonist is 'a young Socialist, who comes before the audience first as a rough crude agitator, is later arrested for sedition, and eventually rises to the position of boss of Australian unionism', a review in the Adelaide *Advertiser* recounted. 'Industrial life and problems, and the positions occupied in the general scheme of things by the working poor, and the idle rich, are the main phases of the play which was well received'.[74]

In 1915 Buchanan quit the *Age* to become editor of the John Wren-owned *Daily Mail* in Brisbane.[75] After a few years at the helm, however, 'press life and he … parted for ever', declared Melbourne's *Punch*, when Buchanan returned to Melbourne and permanently entered the law.⁷⁶ In between he squeezed in a stint as press secretary for Prime Minister Billy Hughes, during Hughes' successful 1919 federal election campaign.⁷⁷

Why so much detail on Buchanan who, after all, did not succeed in publishing any contemporary prime ministerial biography except the briefest of sketches about the first few? It is because Buchanan typifies a particular type of prime ministerial biographer: the 'scholar–journalist' or 'writer–journalist'. Buchanan was better educated than many of his journalistic colleagues who mostly had craft-based, apprenticeship-style training through the cadetship system. He already had an MA before emigrating from New Zealand and later, while working as a journalist and writer in Australia, gained a Bachelor of Laws. Buchanan had, and acted upon, serious literary aspirations. With several books published at home and abroad, and a play produced to good notices, he would have to be judged a successful professional writer in a broader sense than covered by the term 'journalist'.

While Buchanan devoted the last two decades of his life to the law, the unpublished manuscript of prime ministerial profiles completed the year before his death shows that politics still had its hooks in him. He was multifarious in his interests and activities – journalist, novelist, non-fiction writer, playwright, lawyer and, briefly, political staffer – all pursued with aplomb. Buchanan's reflections on the nature of those drawn to journalism are relevant.

> They are a motley crowd; they number in their ranks representatives of all the professions, and of no profession at all. They embrace men and women of good social position, and men and women who are distinctly outside the pale. They have no definite organization, no professional status, no formal rules of etiquette, no exclusive caste, no artificial barriers against membership. They have one standard of living, unorthodoxy; one bond of fellowship, Bohemianism; one passport to success, ability; one aversion, dullness; one insidious enemy, human nature; one unreliable friend – the world.⁷⁸

The problem with being one of this 'motley crowd' is obvious. Accomplished polymaths like Buchanan tend to be lost to history; assembling the foregoing sketch required the diligent trawling and piecing together of usually brief newspaper allusions to him. In contrast, peers who concentrated their professional efforts in one field rather than the several Buchanan pursued had a better chance of winning the notice of posterity, not least because of the advantages conferred by an unambiguous professional identity.

Perhaps the price paid by the scholar–journalist and writer–journalist is worthwhile, in the public interest, Buchanan seemed to suggest. '[I]f the would-be journalist possesses certain qualifications, in addition to literary skills, he may be recommended to join the ranks of the unlisted legion', he writes.

> If he has a saving sense of self-restraint; if he has the faculty for seeing ahead; if he has a definite amount of moral stamina; if he can treat the profession, not as an end, but as a means to an end; if he can live through it and eventually rise above it – if he can do this, the press is his most perfect and his ideal medium. The monetary test is not the final one. The working journalists can at least take to themselves one or two reflections. The ways of the grocer and of the apothecary, of the lawyer and the bill-discounter, are not their ways. Government House may not know them, and the drawing-rooms of Toorak and Potts Point may forget their feet. But they have their consolations. They are the rebels and the outlaws, and yet a strange paradox – the entertainers, the instructors, the beacons of the whole reading world.[79]

While Buchanan makes a large claim in this last sentence, the critical insights of those with the diverse backgrounds he alludes to would almost certainly be of value. In *The Real Australia* Buchanan included biographical sketches of Barton, Reid, Deakin and Watson who were still serving in the Australian parliament, and whom he knew as a journalist. His manuscript 'The Prime Ministers of Australia' (1940) may have been completed two decades after leaving journalism and entering the law, yet it reads as freshly as if Buchanan wrote it during the prime ministerships concerned. Of course, he may well have, or, like Campbell-Jones, written it later from retained contemporary notes.

In his writer–journalist persona Buchanan produced insightful, balanced accounts of Australia's first eleven prime ministers apparently unjaundiced by any particular political motivation or obvious personal slant. His death the year after the manuscript was completed disrupted its possible publication. Buchanan's son, Captain AE Buchanan, who inherited the manuscript, was director of naval operations in Melbourne at the time of his father's death. World War II was in train. Captain Buchanan joined the planning staff of the Chief of Combined Operations in London and later commanded HMAS *Arunta*, so neglect of his late father's manuscript is understandable.[80] Not donated to the National Library of Australia until thirty years after his father's death, 'The Prime Ministers of Australia' was denied the readership it deserved. Given the sparseness of publications on Australian prime ministers in the first half of the twentieth century, the fact that postwar politicians, pundits and the public were denied Buchanan's account of Australia's 'first eleven' is a loss.

The National Library missed a chance to remedy this in 1973 when National Librarian AP Fleming decided that, 'though very well written, [it] may be outdated by the La Nauze study', likely a reference to JA La Nauze's two-volume posthumous biography of Alfred Deakin.[81] Whether or not this was the case, La Nauze had written a biography of only Deakin; Fleming does not consider the other ten prime ministers covered in Buchanan's manuscript, of whom Barton, Watson, Reid, Fisher and Cook were yet to be the subject of political biographies. The memo was copied to Alec Bolton, then in charge of the National Library's publishing program, who agreed with Fleming.[82]

This showed a lack of understanding of the fresh perspective a writer–journalist who observed and knew their subjects directly could bring to prime ministerial biography, compared to an academic historian working well after the event: not better, not worse, simply different and complementary. The diplomat Malcolm Booker commented that in relation to 'particular events in Australian history with which I have had personal contact I have sometimes been surprised at how different they have appeared to historians compared with what seemed to me to be happening at the time'. Booker was correct that 'no one sees more than part of the truth'.[83] Accounts like Buchanan's as well as those like La Nauze's together give a fuller picture.

Chapter 2
The Great War to the Great Depression

*We enshrine the great personalities of our day
in pyramids of printed comment ...*

Douglas Sladen

William Morris 'Billy' Hughes was a Labor, then Nationalist, prime minister from October 1915 to February 1923. Hughes represents a break in the pattern of prime ministerial projection in Australia to that point, both as an inveterate storyteller and shaper of his own image, and as the subject of the first contemporary political biographies of an Australian prime minister.

Hughes' first public speaking success came at an eisteddfod in Sydney in 1890 where he won the prize for an impromptu speech on the topic 'Myself', a performance some would argue did not end during his lifetime.[1] Hughes was closely connected to the worlds of journalism and writing and was active in them, including writing 'snappy sketches of ... his contemporaries'.[2] On at least one occasion, in between terms as attorney-general in 1914, Hughes provided industrial advice to the Australian Journalists' Association (AJA).[3] In 1918, as prime minister, he established the first Commonwealth publicity bureau. In 1923, ten weeks after losing the prime ministership but continuing as an MP, he joined the AJA and resumed writing the newspaper columns through which he had built much political capital during his career, but now as a card-carrying journalist.⁴ Hughes wrote several books. Some, notably *The Case for Labor,* were compilations of his newspaper columns but others, including *Crusts and Crusades: Tales of Bygone Days,* were memoir.⁵

Like his British wartime counterpart, Welsh-born prime minister David Lloyd George, Hughes used words as the kindling of an extraordinarily long political life. Hughes served in the NSW parliament for seven years and then continuously as a federal MP from the first Australian parliament in 1901 until his death in 1952. He was the subject of three contemporary biographies during his active political career. The first two were written by Britons and published in Britain in 1916 for a domestic British audience.⁶ A third was published much later, in 1946, three years after Hughes, aged 78 years, narrowly lost the conservative United Australia Party (UAP) leadership to Robert Menzies, 23 votes to 19.⁷ In an interesting reflection on internal party attitudes to Menzies in the 1940s, Cameron Hazlehurst points out that Hughes had more House of Representatives votes from his UAP colleagues than Menzies, and only lost on the votes of senators, a majority of whom backed Menzies.⁸

Stanhope W Sprigg's *WM Hughes: The Strong Man of Australia,* and Douglas Sladen's *From Boundary-Rider to Prime Minister: Hughes of Australia, The Man of the Hour,* were both prompted by Hughes' high profile forays into the public life of wartime Britain.⁹ They were unequivocally, as Donald Horne put it, 'glamorising'.¹⁰ Different kinds of books by two very different authors, both were politically motivated biographies. Rather than in the service of individual political ambition, however, they were written in the service of Empire. As Sprigg put it, 'In the case of Mr Hughes his faith can certainly be relied upon to produce results of the highest importance and usefulness to all who live under the British flag'.¹¹

A second-generation journalist, Stanhope Sprigg was literary editor of the London *Daily Express* when he wrote *WM Hughes:*

The Strong Man of Australia. His book is a chronologically orthodox, compact 96-page paperback featuring a photograph of 'The Strong Man of Australia' on its cover; an underlined strap in italics across the top announces the book contains 'a Stirring Message to the Young People of the Empire from MR HUGHES'. Sprigg opens saying it was his 'privilege to meet Mr Hughes for a few minutes during his recent stay in London', and that he had 'kindly acceded' to Sprigg's request for 'a message to the young people of the Empire'. The reader is in no doubt about the author's view of his subject.

WM Hughes: The Strong Man of Australia was one of London publisher C Arthur Pearson's series 'Books for War Time' which sold for a shilling in paperback (cloth boards sixpence extra, postage another threepence on top); others included Horace G Groser's *Lord Kitchener: The Story of his Life* and Charles White's *Our Regiments and Their Glorious Deeds*. Sprigg explains to British readers that, 'The Australian working man, of course, is a very different type of politician to his brother labourer in England, who believes it is bad form to discuss politics in public, except at elections'. Politics is 'usually an absorbing passion' among Australia working men, Sprigg writes: 'He counts himself ignorant if he be not acquainted with all the latest developments in the political arena. And, most of all, he reads, and studies, and loves political speeches'.[12]

Demographers have since documented a positive relationship between migration and literacy which supports Sprigg's claim. James Jupp refers to remarkably high literacy levels among assisted migrants to Australia in the mid-nineteenth century: '81 per cent of the Scots, 72 per cent of the English and Welsh and 49 per cent of the Irish could both read and write'.[13] Similarly, mapping nineteenth century British and Irish literacy and comparing it to that of emigrants to Australia, Eric Richards found emigrants 'consistently more literate than the home … populations'.[14]

Both Sprigg's newspaper, the *Daily Express,* and his publisher, C Arthur Pearson, were then owned by (Cyril) Arthur Pearson, a Liberal-leaning British media proprietor who, like Hughes, supported an 'Imperial Preference' tariff policy. The year Sprigg's book was published, Pearson, suffering glaucoma and losing his eyesight, sold the *Daily Express* to Lord Beaverbrook. Five years later Sprigg was retrenched and, under financial pressure, withdrew his 14-year-old son Christopher from Ealing Priory School.[15] They moved to Bradford where Sprigg became literary editor of the *Yorkshire Observer* and Christopher a cub reporter on the same paper – a third generation journalist.[16]

Christopher became a Marxist and died in 1937 fighting with the International Brigades in the Spanish Civil War. He left behind manuscripts written under the pen name Christopher Caudwell, posthumously published as *Studies in a Dying Culture* and *Romance and Realism: A Study in English Bourgeois Literature*. They were obliquely but distinctly influential in the development of Marxist aesthetics; EP Thompson described him as 'an extraordinary shooting-star crossing England's empirical night [and] a premonitory sign of a more sophisticated Marxism'.[17] With this family experience of unemployment and geographical dislocation in the 1920s, and of economic crisis in the 1930s, the arc from the older Sprigg writing popular political biography in the service of Empire to his offspring writing radical Marxist cultural tracts was just one generation long.

Like Sprigg's book, Douglas Sladen's *From Boundary-Rider to Prime Minister: Hughes of Australia, The Man of the Hour* is a polemic designed to rally domestic support in Britain for the war, though his authorial motives were almost certainly different. Sprigg is likely to have been acting as authorial gun for hire, servicing the political agenda of the Pearson media stable for which he worked – either on their time or after hours for additional pay. While Sprigg had two other war-related publications around the time his Hughes biography appeared, the rest of his publishing record consists of editing several editions of *Louis Wain's Annual* showcasing big-eyed, anthropomorphised feline art. Sprigg's oeuvre reeks of financial necessity rather than personal politics. In contrast, Sladen initiated the polemic that is *From Boundary-Rider to*

Prime Minister himself; it reflected his own political agenda and was prompted by a conscious desire to promote it.

Sladen's *From Boundary-Rider to Prime Minister* was described by KJ Cable as 'his edition of Billy Hughes' pamphlets and speeches'.[18] Sladen's own memoir, in which he says, 'I edited a little book about him', provides some comfort to this characterisation.[19] However, *From Boundary-Rider to Prime Minister* is more than that, structurally prefiguring the kind of biographical pastiche familiar online today, and no less biographical for it. Sladen is notable, too, as an academic turned writer rather than a journalist – the first and, as it turns out one of the few, non-journalists to write a contemporary Australian prime ministerial biography.

Douglas Sladen was born in 1856 and educated at Cheltenham College, before reading history at Oxford. The *Cosmopolitan* of 1888, profiling Sladen in his early thirties, provides colourful detail on his early years. The smart and sporty Sladen was a footballer and champion shot at Oxford from which, upon graduating in 1879 with a First in History, he emigrated for four short but influential years to Australia where his uncle, Charles Sladen, was a long-serving conservative politician and, briefly, premier of Victoria. There Sladen married Margaret Muirhead, the daughter of a Western District grazier, took a law degree at the University of Melbourne, and in 1883 became the founding lecturer in modern history at the University of Sydney. Disinclined to academic life, however, Douglas returned to London with Margaret and began a long career as a poet, writer and man about town, consciously identifying himself with Australia to which, he declared at the end of his life, he owed everything.[20] Sladen initially came to notice as a poet of the antipodes. '[T]hat weird and melancholy country proved the inspiration of some of his happiest efforts', *Cosmopolitan* reported. Sladen 'always thinks and writes like an Australian upon all Australian subjects and prides himself very much on being a colonist', it added.[21]

This is surprising given he lived all but four years of his life in England, but is proved out in his own poems and, later, novels, as well as in the anthologies of Australian poems and songs he published in Britain. An admirer of poet Adam Lindsay Gordon, he was the behind-the-scenes driver in Gordon's bust being installed in Westminster Abbey. Sladen was also notable for designing and launching *Who's Who* in London at the invitation of publisher Adam Black who purchased the copyright of the idea in its nascent form. 'Can you do anything with this?' Sladen recounts Black asking. 'We want to make a sort of annual biographical dictionary of it'. Sladen took the idea and developed it into the template *Who's Who* uses to this day.[22]

It is true that *From Boundary-Rider to Prime Minister* is larded with direct quotes from Hughes' writings and speeches, including entire chapters that contain Hughes quotes thematically arranged and, towards the end, entire speeches and articles by him. The first third of the book, however, is substantially Sladen, and his immoderate claims about Hughes' talents and life story – 'Never in the history of the world has a man triumphed over greater obstacles in his rise to power' – make it a classic of contemporary 'B grade' point-of-view political biography.[23] Australia's high commissioner to London, former prime minister Andrew Fisher, wrote the introduction, after which Sladen's hyperbole is unleashed.

Chapter I, 'Advance Australia!', begins with a quote from Shakespeare's *Henry V*: 'Though it appear a little out of fashion / There is much care and valour in this Welshman'.[24] Sladen then canvasses a concept which in the early twentieth century was still a relatively novel concept in politics: personality.

> Hughes of Australia may be summed up in a single word – PERSONALITY. Personality counts for as much now as it did in the days of ancient Egypt, where the immortal personality – the *Ka* – was so peculiarly honoured. The Pyramids were built to be the dwelling-places of these *personalities* of the dead Pharaohs, who inhabited mud-brick palaces in their lifetimes.

The Great War to the Great Depression

> We enshrine the great personalities of our day in pyramids of printed comment, and Mr Hughes's pyramid is already looming large on the horizon.[25]

The ensuing fifty pages leaves no excess in praise of Hughes unuttered. He is 'one of the men who move mountains', declares Sladen, 'a Nelson of politics', 'lithe, muscular, watchful, intrepid' with 'the ideal build for a light cavalryman', 'lion-hearted', 'a brilliant writer' and 'one of the greatest Labour Leaders in history'.[26] An entire chapter is devoted to building the image of Hughes as 'An Australian Abraham Lincoln', in which Sladen compares 'Mr Hughes' Address to the Heroes of Anzac' to the Gettysburg Address.[27] 'Where Lincoln fought for the United States and the slaves', Sladen writes, 'Mr Hughes has fought and fights for the Empire and Labour'.[28] It is England's folly 'that at such a moment fails to send him to the House of Commons to sound the bugle which shall awaken our sleeping sentries from their bivouac and make victory possible'.[29] What is more, Sladen argues, Hughes' power as a speaker was peerless: 'No man living surpasses him in the highest flights of his great orations. He can sweep any audience, from Oxford and Cambridge and the House of Commons to the hard-headed rank and file of the Australian Army, right off their feet'.[30]

The extravagance of this last claim is underlined by Sladen's account in his memoirs of his sole meeting with Hughes for the purposes of researching the book. Sladen had attended the function held for Hughes upon his arrival in London, 'which produced wild cheers of welcome'.[31] He believed no-one had done more than Hughes to turn 'The People' into 'Patriots' and was impressed by his practical ideas for winning the war – so impressed he told English publisher Sir George Hutchinson, 'we ought to bring out a book in a popular form about Hughes'. Hutchinson commissioned him to write one.

At Sladen's request, London-based Australian newspaperman Keith Murdoch introduced him to Hughes who 'invited me down to spend the day with him at a great house in Kent which had been lent to him by an admirer, a famous peeress'. When the day came Hughes did not want to talk before lunch and instead showed Sladen around the house and 'gave me a very fine lunch with plenty of choice things to drink, wishing perhaps to put me into an enthusiastic frame of mind'. At two o'clock, work began. 'He gave me various valuable printed matter, speeches, essays, a list of dates, and comments of the Press', recounts Sladen, and then 'started one of his great outbursts', looking away from him to some imaginary crowd.

> He did not know his man. When he had been going for a few minutes I looked at my watch and saw it was just three o'clock, and after that, as I always do when I am listening to a sermon, I fell asleep.

> When I woke, refreshed and able to keep awake, it was half-past three and he was still addressing that audience. He had not noticed me, so I did not apologize, but when he had finished orating I asked him some more questions and took care to make the best possible use of my materials for impressing the British public with the value of the Prime Minister who had come all the way from Australia to help.[32]

The excesses of Sprigg and, especially, Sladen concerning Hughes have to be set in the context of Hughes' impact in World War I Britain. In Britain, as in Australia, Hughes was exceptional at winning press coverage, and he had a strong bond with fellow Welshman David Lloyd George; they were close even before Lloyd George became prime minister.

Robust notices were not confined to the press. In 1916, the same year the Sprigg and Sladen biographies appeared, journals like *Empire Review* ran editorials extolling Hughes' wisdom and reprinting his speeches.[33] Vyrnwy Morgan in *The War and Wales*, also published in 1916, declared Hughes 'one of the most trenchant champions of freedom' the war had brought to light, and quotes Lloyd George's assessment that, after arriving in Britain virtually unknown that year, Hughes 'is not merely a household word throughout the British Empire, but his speeches have been ringing through Europe ... a source of inspiration to the Allies'. Hughes and Lloyd George, Morgan declared, 'have been thought of as the "Castor and Pollux" in the Imperial firmament of this period – shining with equal lustre'.[34]

Hughes' impact was strong enough to spur an anonymous book-length attack on him as well: *Mr Hughes: A Study*, published by T Fisher Unwin Ltd in London in 1918.[35] Written by a free trader outraged by Hughes' advocacy of Imperial Preference tariffs, it suggested Hughes 'ought properly to be attending to ... affairs at home' instead of promoting 'tariffist' interests in Britain: 'It is for the people of Australia to pronounce whether he is theirs, and whether they approve of his taking a vacation in Britain for the express purpose of playing firebrand for the profiteering interests.'[36]

Even decades later, Hughes' presence and profile in World War I Britain and its aftermath lingered on in biographies of Lloyd George. Frank Owen's *Tempestuous Journey: Lloyd George, His Life and Times*, published in 1954, for example, refers to that 'formidable fellow' with the 'heart of a fighting bull', the 'most extraordinary of them all' amongst the colonial leaders attending the War cabinet in London in 1916, 'the astounding "Billy" Hughes'.[37] The significance of the Sprigg and Sladen biographies, though, lies in their nature as polemics in service of a purpose for which the subject was merely instrumental. It was not Hughes' profile or his career that mattered, but how spreading his message could help them mobilise British opinion behind the war.

Frank C Browne's *They Called Him Billy*, published thirty years after the Sprigg and Sladen biographies, overreaches even on the flyleaf. 'Few men become a legend in their own lifetime', it says. 'Perhaps only three such men have graced the world scene in the last eighty years. They are Winston Churchill, George Bernard Shaw, and William Morris Hughes'.[38] Donald Horne later dismissed Browne's book as 'little more than a collection of unassessed Hughes anecdotes'.[39] Browne did indeed acknowledge 'close contact' with, and cooperation from, Hughes during its writing.[40] He also declared an earnest intention to help fill the vacuum in contemporary Australian political biography. 'A review of extant Australian biography would almost convince one that few figures of any permanent significance graced the Australian scene after about 1870', he wrote in a note at the end of the book.

> We seem to have chronicled almost every clank of a convict leg iron – every gesture of the early Military and Naval autocrats. After that – silence. The great figures of the last eighty years, the men largely responsible for Australia's social, economic and political development have been largely neglected.[41]

Along with other serious omissions, this was true.

Hughes may have been 84 years old by the time Browne's book was published in 1946 but he was still an MP and, in his own mind, his career was not over. The same year, Hughes wrote that biography should hold a 'mirror up to nature, and so portray the man in all his moods and in all the vicissitudes of his life' so that readers could know what sort of person he was.

> Boswell's *Johnson* does this. So do Plutarch's *Lives*. I have few illusions about myself, for I have served too long the ruthless purposes of the caricaturist and his blood brother on the press. But my most venomous critic has never charged me with stodginess. In the darkest hours I have contrived to smile. And I like to think that, had perverse Fate not flung me into public life, I should have made a quite good Evangelist. Think of these things, I pray you.[42]

Enfolding himself with Samuel Johnson and the noble Greeks and Romans of Plutarch's *Lives*, then cloaking himself with an evangelical mantle as the alternative to the life obsessed with temporal power he actually led, is an aggrandising biographical elision typical of Hughes. He may, as he said here, have had few illusions about himself, but that did not stop him being a master 'illusionist' with an 'itch for an audience', as Horne puts it, whose 'gargantuan appetite for lying' made him 'in a sense ... mad, living out his own unrealities'.[43] In his Canberra Press Gallery memoir, Don Whitington describes Hughes as the 'cunning little gnome who had been the arch conspirator of Australian politics for two generations and who continued to be a force, if only a negative force, for another ten years'.[44]

Less pejorative than Horne and Whitington, but equally, Malcolm Booker describes Hughes as 'the deliberate creator of his own caricature [which] was of great political value ... and had its own important political effects'.

> When I was WM Hughes' private secretary in 1940–41, he told me, as I am sure he told others, of the kind of book he wanted written about him: one which demonstrated that he was the prime mover in all the important political and social developments which have formed modern Australia. It was in his view an extensive list ... He regarded his book, *Australia and the War Today*, published in 1935, as being vastly influential among the people if not among the politicians ... [H]e concluded that the only author who could write a suitable book about him was himself. In a 'preliminary canter' (as he spoke of it), he wrote two books of anecdotes [but] concluded, rather despairingly, that he would have to leave the major work to someone else.[45]

During this, his last decade of life, Hughes' efforts to secure more and better biographies of himself were as energetic as ever. As outlined earlier, in 1943, just three years before the publication of Browne's *They Call Him Billy*, Hughes lost a UAP leadership ballot to Menzies by just four votes, so his self-perception as a continuing political player was not completely without basis.[46]

However, Browne was a poor choice as one of Hughes' 'biographers-elect', as LF Fitzhardinge later described them.[47] Browne wrote and published a typewritten gossip sheet called *Things I Hear* from an office in York Street, Sydney, which the then Senator John Gorton used to refer to, with some justification, as 'Things I Smear'.[48] Five years after the publication of *They Called Him Billy*, Browne was jailed for breaching parliamentary privilege in the notorious 'Browne and Fitzpatrick Case' of 1955. Liberal Party whip Henry 'Jo' Gullett, who knew Browne well, described him as 'a thug' and 'a fistman'.[49] Historian and journalist Clem Lloyd's account of the episode notes that Browne's reputation 'lacked fragrance', that his writings were often 'scabrous', and that MPs described Browne variously as a 'character assassin', 'arrogant rat' and 'blackmailer'.[50]

Browne was, in short, 'a hated journalist'.[51] He was also a failed UAP candidate, running unsuccessfully against Labor's HV 'Doc' Evatt in the seat of Barton at the 1943 election. A contemporary political biography penned by a journalist despised by politicians and fellow journalists alike is unlikely to bring its subject credit. Fitzhardinge describes Browne, along with another journalist, W Farmer Whyte who began a biography of the living Hughes not published until after Hughes' death, as two biographers who 'persevered long enough to produce books which Hughes disowned' but does not elucidate how or why this alleged disowning occurred.[52]

Variously during the first half of the 1940s, Hughes had three people working on separate biographies – Browne, Whyte and Fitzhardinge. Fitzhardinge's accounts of his first period working on what would eventually be a scholarly two-volume posthumous biography of Hughes suggests he did not know Browne and Whyte were also working on biographies. Correspondence between Hughes and Whyte suggests that Whyte was ignorant of the other projects too.

Hughes wrote to Whyte on 3 March 1944 that the idea, suggested by a mutual acquaintance, of Whyte writing his biography 'appeals to me very strongly', and he wonders whether they could come to a mutually satisfactory arrangement. 'We have known one another for many years, you are familiar with the background [and] with your literary gifts are equipped to do justice to what after all is part of the history of Australia for the past half century'. Hughes signed off, 'What about it?'[53] There is no mention of a biography by Browne.

Nearly two years later, on 4 January 1946, Hughes writes Whyte a letter of a very different kind about publicity for Browne's *They Called Him Billy*.[54] Hughes placates Whyte in advance over a Christmas card Hughes sent Browne which was reproduced 'in the *Sun* [Sydney] over a "puff" for his "book" on me – a scurvy trick'. Hughes hoped Whyte would ignore it. 'I can't do anything effective because whatever I said would be used to boost the "book"', Hughes wrote, the inverted commas around "book" showing Hughes distancing himself from the biography, at least to Whyte. 'At the best it will be a bar counter snack. What you are doing is at worst a decent sit-down meal & at best a banquet'.[55]

Fitzhardinge's two-volume political biography published after Hughes' death places it beyond the scope of this book. However, Fitzhardinge began work on it in 1940, twelve years before Hughes' death, and left valuable accounts of his dealings with Hughes which throw light on the dynamic between a biographer and contemporary political subject.[56] The first account is in the preface to the biography's first volume, *That Fiery Particle*, where Fitzhardinge declares that 'neutrality is impossible' with Hughes: 'He exercised strong attraction and strong repulsion – often (as in my own case) alternately on the same person'.[57] The second is in an interview with Tom Molomby upon publication of the second volume, *The Little Digger 1914–1952*, in 1979.[58]

In the interview Fitzhardinge recalled he was finishing a biography of Littleton Groom, commissioned by Groom's widow, with the help and advice of solicitor-general George Knowles, when the prospect of a Hughes biography arose. 'Billy was Attorney-General, and so Sir George's Minister, and he was casting around – I think that this was the first of a number of long series of searches for someone who would do his biography while he was still around to make sure it was done the way he wanted it done – and Sir George suggested me to him'.

Fitzhardinge described himself as then a 'young and ... ambitious fellow involved in Australian history' who thought 'this would be one of the best ways to see how the wheels really went round'; as an historian, he was keen to 'get hold of his papers'. Hughes, however, kept them from him, saying repeatedly, 'We're not ready for that yet'. This continued for a year.

> I had a contract with Billy, thirty shillings a thousand words, half on delivery of manuscript and half on publication, and I delivered a few drafts, sections on his early career, as a basis for discussion in these interviews with him. With some difficulty I got the fifteen bob from him for those. Whenever he wanted another draft he'd suddenly remember that he owed me a pound or two for the previous one. But we quite clearly were not getting anywhere and so after a time ... I decided to cut my losses and let the whole thing drift.[59]

Messages were relayed from Hughes 'demanding to know where I was', which intensified Fitzhardinge's disappearing act, and '[e]ventually things quietened down'.

In 1950, Fitzhardinge was appointed Reader in History at ANU and presented a paper on Hughes' early career to the Royal Australian Historical Society (RAHS). Unbeknown to Fitzhardinge, the society had invited Hughes to give the vote of thanks. 'By the time he'd finished', said Fitzhardinge, 'nobody in the room even remembered that I'd been there'. Hughes sent comments on his presentation, some of which Fitzhardinge took up and others – including those which 'were blatantly contrary to Hansard' – he ignored.

When a year later the paper appeared in the RAHS journal, Fitzhardinge sent a copy to Hughes at Parliament House as a courtesy. 'Immediately the telephone started to run hot with imperious demands that Mr Fitzhardinge must go and see Mr Hughes immediately, with no delay whatever', he recalls, revealing he 'wasn't at all sure whether he'd be behind the door with a meat axe or what' given the cursory treatment he had given to Hughes' comments on his draft paper.

> I went rather nervously over to his room in Parliament House and found, on the contrary, if he could have reached me I think he would have kissed me on both cheeks, but he couldn't fortunately. But I had a most cordial reception and I was told that this was absolutely marvelous, this paper, and I must drop everything immediately, whatever I was doing, and come down to Lindfield and devote myself to doing his biography in full.[60]

But Fitzhardinge did not want to resume the project and fobbed Hughes off, raising his new job at the ANU as an obstacle and saying he would have to take it up with the vice chancellor, 'never thinking for a moment that [Douglas] Copland, who was supposed to be a fairly hard man, would fall for it'.

As it turned out, Hughes was 'one of Copland's secret passions'. Fitzhardinge was summoned and told the ANU had 'signed up with Billy ... to provide my services to write his biography'. In the year between this development and Hughes' death in 1952, Fitzhardinge would occasionally go to Hughes' home where they would 'have a pleasant little chat' during which Hughes would 'side-step any questions that I had thought up to ask him'.

> At a certain point in these interviews Billy would take me down to the billiard room in his basement of his house at Lindfield which was a great cavernous place with cartoons and testimonials and whatnot round the walls. He'd show me some of these and then he'd point to a dark corner with his long bony finger. He'd wave at a dark corner where you could dimly see a heap of trunks and boxes and things and say: 'It's all in there, Fitzhardinge. It's all in

there. Nobody can do it without that. Here, come up and have a cup of tea'. And that was as near as I got to the papers during his lifetime.[61]

When the papers finally did come to Fitzhardinge after Hughes' death they were chaotic, 'looking as if a demented hen had been scratching around'; worse, they were disappointing in substance. One highlight, in a folder marked 'Speeches, Notes, etc' – 'they were all labelled that' – was a set of Hughes' false teeth, demonstrating, Fitzhardinge said, the hazards of archival work.

While this shook its discoverer, a newly minted history graduate – one of several research assistants who worked with Fitzhardinge on the project over the years – it was documentary shocks like the revelation of Hughes' birth certificate that shook the biographer himself. It showed a different date and different place of birth to those Hughes had always claimed. 'At this point I rang up [journalist and friend] Alec Chisholm and said: "I cannot do this life. There is nothing I know about this man. He was such an unmitigated liar that you can't believe anything about him. There's just no ground to stand on." At that point I nearly gave up, but not quite'.[62]

Hughes' successor as prime minister, Stanley Melbourne Bruce, also a Nationalist, was in office from February 1923 to October 1929. With him, the contemporary political biography of Australian prime ministers returned to the norm: there was no contemporary biography of Bruce. However, Cecil Edwards eventually wrote one. As a young reporter Edwards had covered his prime ministership and was seconded by Keith Murdoch at Bruce's request to be his press officer in the 1925 general election campaign.[63] When he wrote the book, Edwards was editor of the Melbourne *Herald* and on the verge of retirement. While published well after Bruce's departure from parliamentary politics, it yields insights into the negotiations involved in such a venture, comparable to those between a journalist and a serving political leader negotiating a biographical project. It is included here because of examples Edwards provides reflecting on the writing of the biography – difficulties which point to the contrasting benefits of writing such biographies contemporaneously with a political leader's career.

Writing to Bruce in 1962, Edwards said he had thought for years that someone ought to write a biography of him but that 'every rung climbed in newspaper work has meant less time for me to do anything about it'.[64] Edwards told him that, as one 'who knew you fairly well in the earlier stages of your political career, and who has had close association with Australian politics then and since, I feel I could make a good fist of it'. Some of Bruce's attitudes to biography emerge in this correspondence. Bruce considered his past 'streaky' and was himself disinclined to write a memoir, he told Edwards.[65] In subsequent letters further diffidence, but also a degree of acceptance, was communicated. 'Nor am I prepared to invite someone to do it – with the implication behind my doing so that I am inspiring the life to be written', he told Edwards. 'On the other hand, if any misguided person decided they wanted to write it – provided it was a responsible person and someone about whom I felt happy at his undertaking the job – I would be prepared to co-operate to the maximum extent'.[66]

Edwards would later find that Bruce had perhaps been somewhat disingenuous in their correspondence over the course of 1962 and 1963, in which Edwards played the biographer–suitor having to persuade a reluctant Bruce to agree. In 1959, when Bruce was 76, he began summarising the wartime files from his papers, the kind of activity one might undertake with a future biography, if not autobiography, in mind. In 1961 Bruce wrote to Keith Hancock at the ANU, of which Bruce was chancellor, and asked, since he felt 'too lazy at my advanced age', whether he might have 'some young gentleman' who could continue the summaries, enclosing one of his files as a sample.[67] Hancock replied that they were too historically significant to let 'some junior person rummage around in them' and advised Bruce to send all his wartime papers from London to Australia. Bruce began to send sections of them to the Department of External Affairs, only stopping when he reached agreement with Edwards in mid-1963 about the writing of a biography.[68]

After striking an agreement, Bruce and Edwards began a third round of letters which discussed a *modus operandi*. At Edwards' prompting, Bruce read Earle Page's memoir, *Truant Surgeon,* and commented that Page 'appears to me to go into far too much detail, with the result the book becomes somewhat boring'.[69] Edwards agreed that excessive detail should be avoided. 'I have no desire to write a definitive work in 10 volumes ... which no-one except our friends the professors (and their unfortunate students) would read', he told Bruce. 'On the other hand, an expanded gossip column would be equally inappropriate. I have in mind something which will not entirely repel the professors by its lightness or the ordinary reader by its dullness'.[70] Edwards continues in this letter to set out ground rules establishing his control of the text while benefiting from Bruce's cooperation.

> It will be, of course, my book about you and your times. You will not be responsible for any judgments I pass in it, on the strength of the information assembled. In fact, I hope you will disagree with some of the conclusions I reach.

> May I say frankly that one of the difficulties I face is that I have always admired you and your work? I shall therefore have to be on my guard to keep this side of idolatry. You should be painted 'warts and all' (which doesn't mean 'all warts') and, therefore, I hope you will not mind if I ask embarrassing questions in the attempt to get a full picture. My training over the years has inclined me always to seek the motive behind the action – my own included. It is difficult, with the best will in the world, to be frank with oneself, not to speak of being frank with other people. In

other words, I should like to take you through the events of your life almost as if I were a cross-examining barrister – not because I necessarily agree with the questions I put but because they are necessary to get a clear view.[71]

Here Edwards exemplifies the aspirations of the scholar–journalist or writer–journalist in a biography of an admired subject: substantial but accessible, sympathetic but not 'captured' or hagiographical, and reflective about the task. Edwards' use of flattery to ease Bruce into accepting this approach is unexceptional in the circumstances, and balanced by his declared interest in 'warts'. Though this biography was not contemporary, it is reasonable to think that if it were – and providing it was not a consciously political exercise – Edwards would have taken the same approach.

Writing later about the writing of this book, Edwards refers to, 'That little bell that rings … known to all newspapermen', invoking scepticism about unconfirmed assertions. 'It continued to ring for me after I had left journalism and become an author', he said, going on to recount four instances in relation to the Bruce biography. The finished manuscript included the assertion, repeated ubiquitously over four decades, that Bruce had been Australia's youngest prime minister. Upon checking Edwards found Chris Watson became prime minister at 37 years old whereas Bruce was 39.

Another apparently trivial, but given Bruce's toff image highly symbolic, commonplace was that he had won the Royal Canberra Golf Club championship in 1929, the year he lost office and his own seat. It survived as far as the galley stage of *Bruce of Melbourne* but, while proofreading, Edwards decided to check it. The claim was untrue; Bruce was not even a member of the club and therefore ineligible to compete in the club championship: 'Every member of Royal Canberra would have laughed at the story, which the honor roll of champions in the clubhouse disproved, and would have judged the accuracy of the rest of the book on that error'.[72]

A third example concerns what would have been a major error in relation to a vitally important point of twentieth century history. Bruce told Edwards that in October 1938, at a private meeting in the House of Commons where Bruce was offered the chair of the British Broadcasting Corporation (BBC) by British prime minister Neville Chamberlain, Chamberlain told him he believed war inevitable. Since this was just a month after Chamberlain concluded the Munich Agreement with Adolf Hitler, returning to England and declaring 'peace for our time', if true it meant the history books would have had to be rewritten. Bruce told Edwards he had declined the offer of the BBC chair, telling Chamberlain he agreed war was coming and, on that basis, had just had his term as High Commissioner in London extended by Australian prime minister Joseph Lyons.

> Bruce was meticulous about dates and, in general, his memory was very good. Yet the story must be checked, particularly because it flew in the face of accepted knowledge. How? Chamberlain was dead; his relatives searched his papers for me without finding anything that bore on the incident. Bruce could not find any note of the episode, although his habit was to keep notes of important conversations – of which this was clearly one.

> The little bell kept ringing. Uneasily I hunted through the newspaper files and came across this: Lyons had announced, in December *1937*, that Bruce had agreed to extend his term when it expired at the end of 1938. So the conversation had been in 1937, not 1938; before, not after, Munich. Bruce, in some bewilderment, was forced to conclude that, although his memory of the facts was correct, he was a year out in the time. Later he found a note that confirmed this, and wrote to tell me so.[73]

It is terrifying near misses like this that underline the value of well executed contemporary biography, in which such a conflation would be far less likely to find its way erroneously into print. It is also a credit to Edwards that his professional training and instincts as a journalist led to fact-checking of the same high order one would expect in a trained historian presented with the same problem. In a memoir written a decade after *Bruce of Melbourne*'s publication, Edwards reflects at length about its writing and reception, including on the snobbish put downs by academic reviewers that 'it was really remarkably good – considering that its author was a newspaperman'. He makes a not unreasonable plea for reviewers to 'deal with a book as it is'.[74]

The 'streaky' past Bruce referred to at the outset of his correspondence with Edwards likely reflected the fact that all was not as it seemed in his family. As a public figure Bruce, who went on to become Viscount Bruce of Melbourne, was quintessentially rich, British and Oxbridge. Edwards, however, 'disposed of so many fables and accretions to the Bruce legend that he good-humoredly grumbled that I was spoiling all the stories he had been dining out on for decades'. A key one concerned Bruce's father who reputedly attended a Scottish university; Edwards' diligent inquiries revealed instead that he left school in Scotland at 13 years old and worked in the drapery trade in Ireland before emigrating to Australia as an apprentice.[75] There is no sign, however, that he discovered the tragic suicides of Bruce's father and two brothers, disclosed long after Bruce's death in David Lee's 2010 biography, *Stanley Melbourne Bruce: Australia's Internationalist*.[76]

James 'Jim' Scullin, Bruce's successor, served as a Labor prime minister from October 1929 to January 1932. As his posthumous biographer John Robertson notes, Scullin was the only person between 1914 and 1972 to lead a victorious election campaign against a conservative prime minister.[77] Scullin's win over Bruce, whose plan to abolish the Commonwealth Arbitration Court saw him lose even his own seat, could not have come at a worse time: the onset of the Great Depression.[78]

Scullin, a journalist and former editor of the Ballarat *Evening Echo*, was regarded in a 'fraternal light' by Canberra Press Gallery reporters. At a gallery dinner soon after his election journalists sang boisterously, to the tune of 'John Brown's Body', a song to their 'fellow scribe' in his presence: 'When we shivering scribes are standing outside the pearly gates / And press passes won't bluff Peter well we won't have long to wait / For Jimmy's in his office, he won't forget a mate / And we'll all go marching in!'[79] While suggesting Scullin would ensure their entry to heaven, neither they nor anyone else immortalised him in the temporal world with a contemporary biography.

However, the story of Scullin's ill-fated government, with him as tragic protagonist, was the focus of the first book to emerge from the Canberra Press Gallery. Warren Denning's *Caucus Crisis: The rise & fall of the Scullin Government* was published in 1937 by the Parramatta-based *Cumberland Argus* newspaper, five years after the events described in the book.[80] Denning was a key figure in the history of federal political journalism, joining the Canberra Press Gallery in 1928 with the *Argus* and later becoming the ABC's founding federal political correspondent, establishing its Canberra bureau in 1939.

Contemporary history rather than contemporary biography, *Caucus Crisis* nevertheless relies heavily in its account of the government's rise and dramatic fall on brief evocative portraits of key political players including Jack Lang, EG 'Red Ted' Theodore, 'Stabber Jack' Beasley and Scullin himself. 'Personal sketches and inside stories enable us to live again through days of anxiety and national peril', as the *Canberra Times* review put it upon the book's publication, as though those events were decades, not just five years, earlier.[81] The anonymous reviewer noted that Denning's work 'is of value in recording incidents which hitherto have escaped mention in the annals of years now receding fast as prosperity's comforts spread'.

Caucus Crisis was something of a 'wholesale' classic, notable in the political confines of Canberra because of its continuing reputation and availability to politicians and journalists through the Parliamentary

Library, but not widely known to the public. It got a brief second life beyond Parliament House in 1982 when Hale & Iremonger republished it, adding as a preface a memoir of Denning by journalist Alan Reid. Reid came to Canberra as a junior reporter in 1937 when Denning was a dominant press gallery figure, and over the course of his career became the next 'Warren Denning'. *Caucus Crisis* gained a third life under the title *James Scullin* when Black Inc. republished it in 2000 with an introduction on Scullin by novelist Frank Moorhouse.[82] The book's latent life is such that, sixty years after its first publication in 1937, the recently fallen prime minister Paul Keating counselled a gallery journalist not to accept a commission to write a history of his just defeated government but rather to 'write a book like *Caucus Crisis*'.[83]

Denning concerned himself 'with causes and consequences, rather than with events' in *Caucus Crisis*.[84] He repeatedly advised Reid as a junior reporter in the late 1930s, 'Don't get obsessed with details, my boy – always try to take the broad view'.[85] Denning's account is innovative in several ways, not least in making the presence, role and anxieties of Depression-era political journalists explicit.

> Newspapermen found the responsibility of telling the people of Australia the story of what was happening at Canberra, so that on the one hand incompetence might not be cloaked, and on the other, grave national difficulties not intensified by hysteria or panic, was a heavy one. It was increased by the reticence of the Scullin Government, and its fear or dislike of publicity and criticism. Soon it was realised, however, that Ministers, public servants, financial experts, economic advisers, bankers, and business men were all equally adrift in a vast ocean of uncertainty.[86]

Denning lets readers in, too, on behind-the-scenes interactions between journalists and politicians. For example, he first hears about a '"mystery man" … now actually on the water, en route to Australia', sent 'to take charge of Australia on behalf of the banks' when 'I was called to the roof of Parliament House by a Labor member who was in a great state of perturbation'.[87] Scullin's cabinet knew but caucus had not been told. The 'mystery man' was Bank of England adviser, Sir Otto Niemeyer, the enduring villain of Australia's Depression narrative. Another behind-the-scenes glimpse was set 'early one warm, sunny morning, when Canberra seemed at its brightest, and the city with its quiet pastoral background held no brooding sense of tragedy', when word began to circulate that a royal commission in Queensland had found Scullin Government treasurer Ted Theodore corrupt. 'The warm, quiet terrain suddenly seemed charged with drama, when I walked towards Parliament house with Mr Curtin', Denning wrote, 'discussing the possibility of the story being true, and the consequences which it must entail'.[88]

One of the best sections of *Caucus Crisis* is an extended description of caucus meetings where the 'tumult' was so terrific that it 'was no uncommon spectacle to see Mr Scullin walk out ... profoundly distressed'. Far from attempting to listen in to a forum forbidden them, journalists 'were embarrassed in their efforts to get far enough away from the disturbance to be able to proclaim that they were making no effort to hear it'.[89] Before Denning, no Australian journalist had let readers in to the private interactions between them and the politicians they reported on in this way. It remains rare.

The Hale & Iremonger edition of *Caucus Crisis* in 1982 was welcomed by political aficionados, many of whom had been grappling for several years with the challenges of stagflation in the late 1970s and recession in the early 1980s.[90] The book's appeal lies significantly in Denning's use of evocative biographical detail to make a political and economic drama palatable to readers who knew little about economics. The contrasting pictures Denning draws of Scullin and Theodore is an example. Scullin's life was 'careful and ... of almost Spartan simplicity', resident with Mrs Scullin at the Hotel Canberra to save the nation the expense of running The Lodge. 'Had he permitted himself a little more healthy amusement (an occasional game of bowls was his only relaxation at Canberra), perhaps he would have survived the trying years better', Denning wrote.[91] Whereas Theodore had shaken 'the dust of Queensland from his feet' from early years spent 'in the crudity of the mining camps', in contrast to Scullin's early years 'in the quieter spheres of business and journalism'.

> The consequence was that Mr Theodore was much more of a realist than the little Victorian, whose more delicate character seemed to shrink amid the blatancies of his movement. Mr Scullin's heart was in the regeneration of society on behalf of the common people, but he could not easily submerge himself in their daily trials and troubles. Mr Theodore accepted the crudities as implicit in the career he had chosen, and his unequivocal temperament brushed through them, as of little consequence. ... Mr Scullin talked politics to the miners in pleasant but rather strained gatherings in hotel parlours; Mr Theodore sat outside with them on the roadside and talking mining, and life, and politics just incidentally.[92]

The 1982 republication of *Caucus Crisis* prompted Clem Lloyd to write that Denning 'possessed the most luminous pen ever to grace the Commonwealth parliamentary press gallery', with a 'concise literary style that is only just below the top rank'.

> There is no other book in the limited genre of Australian political history even remotely like it. Until Don Whitington and Alan Reid began to write political books in the 1950s and 1960s it was the only work of substance produced by an Australian political journalist in the first half-century of Federation.[93]

Michael Easson was critical of one aspect of *Caucus Crisis*, namely the economics of Denning's account which 'crumbles on close inspection'. The broad view, Easson commented, 'can also be a shallow view'.[94]

In Denning's defence, most press gallery journalists were ignorant of anything beyond basic economics until the 1980s when economic crisis and the new permeability of journalistic ranks to expert writers led many media outlets to hire specialist economic reporters. Denning's use of biographical detail to make an economic as well as political story lucid to a wide readership prefigured something of the economic journalism written for wider audiences in the 1980s. Even a critic like Easson acknowledged that *Caucus Crisis* 'deserves to be read' because of its 'penetrating pen-portraits and acute comments'.[95]

Denning was, in fact, fourth in an ill-fated line of writer–journalists or scholar–journalists producing contemporary prime ministerial biography that was not published. First was the unidentified author of the manuscript on George Reid while Federation was being put together, then Alfred Buchanan and Herbert Campbell-Jones writing in the first decades after Federation.

Denning was born to a boot salesman and his wife in 1906, and grew up in Sydney where, according to historian Ian Hancock, dreams of 'boarding-school and Oxford' morphed into the prosaic reality of a cadetship, at the age of 16, on the *Cumberland Times* in Parramatta.[96] Reid argues Denning was more complex than his Canberra Press Gallery origins as a *Labor Daily* reporter, arriving in 1927, suggest. Denning wrote for a range of papers during the course of his career, including the conservative *Argus*. He did more than report politics, says Reid, who in a description of Denning which applied equally to himself, says 'Denning took part'.

> He was a born intriguer; he could not help himself. It was part of the nature of the man, though his intrigues were usually directed toward shaping future events and rarely against an individual.
> And he had connections, powerful connections.[97]

Those connections ranged from John Curtin, whom Denning more than once helped to the Hotel Kurrajong when, as a dispirited backbencher, 'he stumbled to his bed ... after a drinking session', to fearsome conservative politician Archie Cameron who as the Lyons Government's postmaster-general induced Denning to become the Australian Broadcasting Commission's founding Canberra correspondent.[98]

Denning 'lamented his lack of formal higher education' and 'admired those with high academic attainments', notes Reid.[99] His only testamur would be a Diploma of Journalism from the University of Melbourne in 1935, and the several published books he wrote on politics and Canberra, both of which he loved. Denning's papers contain the unrealised parts of his writerly ambitions: several substantial, chapter-length prime ministerial profiles, a manuscript collating them around 1957 into a book-length work covering prime ministers from Barton to Menzies (then still in office), as well as a standalone book-length biography of Menzies completed around 1973, none of which were published during his lifetime.[100] The profiles were 'composed in the mid-1940s', according to Hancock who describes them as 'balanced, shrewd and sympathetic'.[101] The fact that the book-length collation of prime ministerial profiles extended to, and covered, Menzies' prime ministership to 1957 shows that contemporary political biography was a continuing project for Denning well beyond the 1940s, as was the book-length biography of Menzies finished in the early 1970s.

There are two reasons to rue the fact that Denning's contemporary biographical works remained unpublished. One is that Denning worked in the pre-1949 era when there were only seventy-four House of Representatives members and just thirty senators – just under half the current numbers and easily small enough to get to know individual politicians well and draw informed conclusions on them. '[I]n those days relationships between Parliamentarians and individual pressmen were much closer', Reid notes, an almost inevitable result of a small number of politicians and reporters enclosed in one building in the then small capital, Canberra.[102] The other reason is that Denning really did have a sense of the big sweep of Australian political history in the first half of the twentieth century. 'The difficulty in estimating their relative importance is that each has to be considered against his own background and the times have changed so dynamically in Australia', Denning wrote in the 1940s, for example, reflecting on the first sixteen prime ministers since Federation in 1900.

> A world war, a depression, and another world war; each has done something more than mark a period of change; they have marked the beginning point of new epochs in the values and the emphasis of Australian life.
>
> Only fourteen years, in the deceptive measurement of the calendar, separated Alfred Deakin from Mr Bruce; less than fourteen years separate SM Bruce from John Curtin. But in significance each of the three periods could be a century apart.
>
> Australian development has been telescoped by the rapidity of the modern world into years where older countries dealt in decades, and decades where older countries dealt in centuries.[103]

Why Denning's contemporary prime ministerial biographies remained unpublished is a mystery, although correspondence with *Meanjin* editor, Clem Christesen, hints at one possible explanation. Denning submitted three pieces for publication to *Meanjin* in the early 1950s; one on Chicago architect Walter Burley Griffin, who designed Australia's capital, was accepted. The other two were rejected including Denning's profile of John Curtin who had died eight years earlier. 'The only script I did not like', wrote Christesen, 'was that on Curtin. It seemed to me to be far too "superficial", though obviously sympathetic'.[104] Denning may have fallen victim to the very disjunctures in time that he wrote about in the 1940s. His pre–World War II observational and writing style may have seemed as distant to editors and publishers in the 1950s as those of the late colonial period were to editors and publishers of the early federation period, a new 'modern' regularly, and sometimes roughly, displacing the old.

No contemporary biography was written about Scullin's successor Joseph Lyons, originally a Tasmanian schoolteacher and Scullin Government minister who broke with Labor during the Depression and forged a new conservative grouping, the United Australia Party. As head of the UAP, Lyons was prime minister from January 1932 to April 1939.

The lack of a biography was a striking omission given Lyons' electoral success: he was the first Australian prime minister to win three consecutive elections (1931, 1934 and 1937). Who was there to champion Lyons' story though? Like Hughes, he was a Labor 'rat', in Lyons' case deserting and bringing down the Scullin Government during the Depression to make common cause with conservatives in the interest of pursuing a conservative economic policy. History has judged that approach wrong for the times; the modern expert consensus backs what later came to be known as a Keynesian approach. Further, the UAP did not long survive Lyons' death.

So as a Labor rat, champion of a discredited approach to economic policy, and the creator of a political party that lasted only fourteen years, the lack of a Lyons biography is perhaps understandable. On the other hand, it was a loss to history. As the second senior Labor figure in a generation to defect and find electoral success as a conservative prime minister, a Lyons biography may have provided pause for reflection in Labor ranks.

Country Party leader Earle Page who, upon Lyons' death in April 1939, served as acting prime minister for nineteen days, had no biography either. Denning's substantial biographical profiles of Lyons and Page, languishing unpublished, could have provided value and insight for interested readers – including voters – of the day. However, a contemporary biography well beyond the ambit of Denning's unpublished chapter-length profile was very nearly written on the man conservatives then reluctantly chose to become the next UAP prime minister: Robert Menzies.

Chapter 3
Menzies biography mystery

*It is the fashion, and no doubt always was, to over-praise
or over-blame the statesman while they are alive, and
to forget them or forgive them when they are dead.*

Robert Menzies

Robert Gordon Menzies was twice prime minister of Australia. From April 1939 to August 1941, he led a United Australia Party (UAP) and then coalition government. In 1944 he founded the UAP's successor, the Liberal Party, which he led to victory in coalition with the Country Party in December 1949. He remained as prime minister until he retired in January 1966.

His two prime ministerships differed sharply. The first was relatively brief and unhappy, and ended with what the author of his posthumous biography, Allan Martin, calls 'the most humiliating personal collapse in the history of federal politics' in Australia. Menzies had the 'galling' experience, as Martin describes it, of losing the support of his cabinet, forcing his resignation as leader of the United Australia Party and thus the prime ministership.[1] The conservative government led by his successor, Country Party leader Arthur Fadden, lost the confidence of the House of Representatives several weeks later, and was replaced by the John Curtin–led Labor government which saw Australia safely through World War II.

That Menzies later returned to the prime ministership and became Australia's most electorally successful politician is remarkable, and obviously involved not just changed political circumstances and more than the usual amount of political skill but also a reworking of his image. Press gallery journalist Don Whitington, who covered Menzies in office, notes that the popular conception of him as the 'silver-haired orator, the father figure who wooed and won the Australian electorate after 1949' was at odds with the earlier 'supercilious, acidulous' version: 'The cloak of urbanity he wore with such distinction in later life was then only on the drawing board, to be designed and fashioned and completed in the years of travail he spent in the political wilderness after he was deposed'.[2]

Whitington's characterisation of the changed public Menzies being the result of a '*cloak* of urbanity' is apt. Martin cautions that while differences between the two parts of Menzies' federal political career require exploration, 'we are dealing with a man who ... changed little in essential ways'.[3] Martin adds that the 'old saying that "the Liberals can never win with Menzies" rumbled on' and that in 1946 Menzies came close to leaving politics. 'In a bleak conversation over dinner in their club he told his legal mentor and friend, Owen Dixon, that he was returning to the Bar', Martin wrote. 'He knew he was "the subject of dislike and hostility throughout the community" and that the Liberal Party "could not win under his leadership"'.[4] Menzies was 'on the outer both within his party and with Empire allies' notes Anne Henderson in her study of Menzies in this trough between his prime ministerships.[5] So deep was his pessimism about the prospects for personal political resurrection that he pursued but 'failed to find an overseas posting on some three occasions', according to Henderson; and in 1944 he allowed his name to go forward, unsuccessfully, for the position of Victorian chief justice.[6]

Menzies' unpopularity was entrenched, even among his own party's supporters. Cameron Hazlehurst's detailed analysis incorporating Gallup Poll data shows that as late as the middle of 1947 'Menzies and the

Liberal Party were failing to make significant gains in public support'. Hazlehurst noted that both the Liberal Party's NSW and Queensland branches asked Menzies not to campaign in their state elections that year. Some 165 out of 172 members of a Liberal Party branch in Nhill, squarely in the conservative stronghold of Victoria's Western District, supported a motion for a change of federal leader, forwarding it for consideration at the Victorian state council meeting on 17 April 1947: 'Some respondents said Menzies was "too conceited", others that he was "too up in the clouds"'.[7]

A contemporary political biography could potentially have helped change this. However, none appeared, for an adult audience at least. A profile in the American annual *Current Biography* in 1941, revised and updated in 1950, and a short biography for young readers by Ronald Seth in 1960, were the only contemporary biographical works while Menzies was in politics.[8] The spectrum of perceptions about him early in the second part of his prime ministerial career can perhaps best be conveyed by two eight-page booklets.

The first, a passport-sized pamphlet published in the run up to the 1949 election, had the title *How Well Do You Know This Man?* You have to open it to find out Menzies is the subject and recognise the address of the party's NSW office – 30 Ash Street, Sydney – which appears in tiny type on the bottom of the back page to know it is a Liberal Party publication. 'RG Menzies is a man of the people' it begins, amusingly failing to divine that a man of the people would normally use his first name rather than his initials.[9] 'He is a fighter ... He has never "squibbed" an issue', is juxtaposed with a smiling picture of him standing with coalminers, leading the reader's mind away from the politically problematic conflicts of World War I, in which Menzies did not serve, and World War II, during which his first prime ministership failed, to the Cold War. 'He is pledged to ban the Communist Party, in sharp contrast to the Socialists' policy of private encouragement of the Communists while publicly denouncing them', the pamphlet continued.

Menzies biography mystery

At the other end of the spectrum is the cartoon booklet *The Calamitous Career of Dictator Bob,* published in 1951 by the Communist Party of Australia, though, as with the Liberal Party pamphlet, this is not disclosed. If *How Well Do You Know This Man?* judiciously dodges the negative aspects of Menzies' record, *The Calamitous Career of Dictator Bob* is a graphic character assassination which takes the reader from 1914 – 'Resigned from the army to avoid going to war' – via several inglorious episodes to 1950 when 'Menzies introduced his infamous Communist Party Dissolution Act ... to smash all opposition to his policies' and seek 'the powers of a dictator'.[10] 'We don't want fascism here!' is the kicker on the back page, urging readers to 'Vote NO', in the 1951 anti-communist referendum. Thus Menzies' life and character were dramatically contested territory early in his comeback as prime minister.

Ronald Seth's *RG Menzies* was part of Cassell's 'Red Lion Lives' series, 'intended for young people who are of an age to be thinking of their future careers'. Explicitly inspirational, each biography portrayed 'one of the most famous men or women of modern times, all of them at the top of their particular professions'; aristocrat Lord Louis Mountbatten, Conservative British prime minister, Harold Macmillan, cricketer Don Bradman, industrialist Lord Nuffield and contralto Kathleen Ferrier are among the series' other subjects. 'It is [his] tenacious, fight-back quality, and not luck, that has made Menzies what he is', proclaims the flyleaf. Cassell's choice of Ronald Seth to write the book is interesting.[11] Seth wrote sex advice books under the pseudonym Robert Chartham and, under his own name, a plethora of non-fiction works, mostly on espionage; he had worked in Britain's Special Operations Executive (SOE) during World War II. Seth subsequently wrote two other biographies in Cassell's 'Red Lion Lives' series – on British field marshal 'Montgomery of Alamein' (1961) and the pioneering plastic surgeon Archibald McIndoe (1962). Written simply, around 120 pages long, they were most likely easy earners for a professional writer like Seth – described by British publisher Anthony Blond, who occasionally used him, as 'a brilliant hack who never slept'.[12] Seth subsequently published two more books with Cassell in the 1960s: *Forty Years of Soviet Spying* (1965) and *The Executioners: The Story of Smersh* (1967), altogether five books for Cassell in a decade.

In 'How This Story was Written', the final chapter of his Menzies biography, Seth notes, 'This is the first time that the story of Robert Gordon Menzies's life has been written at any length'. He describes his 'relief and delight' when Menzies' private secretary, Helen Craig, telephoned to say the prime minister would see him one Saturday morning before he went to watch England play South Africa at Lord's; since 'play was timed to begin at 11.30 am, I did not expect I should be able to spend more than an hour with him'.

> He seemed to sense exactly what I wanted to know, and this helped considerably. At the end of an hour, we had reached about half-way. He glanced at his watch. 'I shall have to be going soon', he said. 'What else do you want to know?' And he talked for another hour, forgoing his cricket at Lord's to do so.

Pattie Menzies also agreed to meet Seth and 'for her kindness in answering another long list of questions frankly, I express my sincere thanks', he writes. 'By great good fortune, the Prime Minister's elder brother, Mr Frank Menzies, was also in London' and was 'another very important source of information'. Eric Harrison, a former political colleague and friend of Menzies of twenty-five years standing, and at that time high commissioner to London, also spoke to him as did Victoria's then agent-general in London, William Leggett, a law school and bar colleague of Menzies in Melbourne. Seth cites two magazine articles and two books, including Menzies' own *Speech is of Time* (1958), as his other sources.[13] Seth's *RG Menzies* is perhaps the ultimate 'friendly'.

Menzies biography mystery

We know somewhat more about Menzies' attitude to biography than we do in relation to other Australian prime ministers. Hazlehurst notes that as early as 1934, Menzies himself 'wrote approvingly of what he called a "new historical method" which would "bring the great men and women of earlier days so near to us that, while their heroic proportions may be occasionally diminished, their actual existence becomes credible and significant"'.[14] In a modest way, he tried his hand at it in 1949 with a biographical sketch on Winston Churchill, himself a biographer (of the Duke of Marlborough) and, like Menzies at the time, Leader of the Opposition, though in a different polity. 'Churchill at Seventy-five' appeared in the *New York Times Magazine* and was later included in Menzies' collection of speeches and articles, *Speech is of Time*. In it he takes a novel tack, casting the profile in response to the question, 'What was his secret?'[15] This may have been the peg supplied by the commissioning editor at the *New York Times Magazine* but, irrespective of the inspiration, it prompted interesting insights and anecdotes.

Six years later Menzies returned to the theme in 'Churchill and his Contemporaries', an oration to a medical audience at the University of Melbourne.[16] Menzies, who by then had two decades representing Australia overseas, talks of his personal acquaintance, and in some cases close personal friendship, with some of 'the great men of the era'. He recommends to the psychologists and psychiatrists in the audience contemplation of a 'strange quirk' in human nature.

> When we are very young and we read our history, we visualize the great men of the past as giants. Their very shadows appear to be enormous as they pass across the dim and distant landscapes of history. I have lived long enough and had sufficient experience to find that historic giants are quite human, that for the most part they are quite intelligible, that in many ways they think and

behave just as we do, and that one must discern their greatness, not by standing with dumb amazement before them, but by trying to discover what special quality each of them has which marks him out for fame ... The idea of an incomprehensible genius which once obsessed my mind in contemplating the noble figures of the past has long since deserted me ...[17]

This idea of a 'special quality' leads Menzies to a defence of three interwar British prime ministers – Ramsay MacDonald, Stanley Baldwin and Neville Chamberlain. All three historically suffer to varying degrees the stigma of their catastrophic complacency about the threat posed by Nazi Germany in the 1930s, and are contrasted sharply with Churchill, the prime minister credited with saving Britain in World War II. Menzies says he has 'what some of my friends regard as the eccentric belief' that Churchill 'could not have done quite so much as he did, but for their work'. Each had been 'at one time, no doubt, over-praised' but 'has subsequently been over-condemned'. To Menzies:

> It does little credit to our good sense that we should swing about so wildly in our judgments, treating today as mere folly our wild enthusiasms of yesterday. After all, if our superficial emotions are our only guide, we have no more assurance that we are right today than that we were wrong yesterday.[18]

Of course, Menzies' own experience as a failed wartime prime minister must have given him a personal empathy, perhaps even identification, with the three that made his defence of them latently – emotionally – a defence of his own earlier prime ministership. Like them he had been an appeaser and a critic of Churchill during the 1930s.

Menzies also gave some thought to the practical difficulties and implications of writing biography. Many books would be written about Churchill he commented, for example, looking back on his own attempts to write biographical sketches of him, but most would be 'dogmatic and superficial'. This was not solely due to their authors' limitations but also the subject's challenging character: 'the great problem for his ultimate biographer will be to discover at what point the great actor, the showman, ended, and the great and dedicated leader took over'.[19] The interesting implications of being a source for the writer of a contemporary biography also emerge in a letter Menzies wrote to his daughter Heather Henderson about a biography published two years after his retirement by a 'journalistic scribbler called Perkins'.[20]

> ... it is clear from reading his book, which I have done with some reluctance, that his source of material has been the press gallery, the gossip columns and the observations of my political enemies ... The interesting thing about the book is that I have no difficulty whatever in knowing who told him this or who told him that. Yet the next time I see one or other of them, he will assure me with tears in his voice that he thinks the book quite unfair![21]

According to Menzies, Kevin Perkins' biography of him contained 150 errors of fact. He told Henderson he intended dictating a note correcting them for the benefit of a future biographer.

Given Menzies' need to remake himself and revive his political fortunes after resigning the prime ministership in 1941, and in light of his reflectiveness about biography, the reasons for the lack of a contemporary biography during his active career, other than Seth's for young readers, requires explanation. One possible reason is Menzies' privileging of speeches and speechmaking over text in what he explicitly considered the 'art' of politics. '[A]s we look back over the panorama of history and select ... the political giants, we find ourselves identifying them as above all great artists', he wrote. 'For the artist is the man who knows how to use his materials; who has a sensitiveness to his environment and an understanding of humanity, and a great skill in execution'.[22]

Menzies was very much concerned with politics as *performance*. 'Skill at public speaking was one of Menzies' most valuable political assets, and had been crucial to his rapid rise in Australian public life', in Judith Brett's estimation.[23] Clem Lloyd puts Menzies' 'life-long espousal of the modulation and timbre of the human voice as the most powerful of political instruments' at the centre of his analysis of Menzies' media relations. Lloyd argues that rather than politics being the art of the possible, for Menzies it was the 'art of the adequate ... In short, do not do more than you have to do!'[24] It is possible that Menzies saw speech as a more potent way than text of remaking himself politically, or as a sufficient way in the sense of the 'art of the adequate'.

Another possible reason was Menzies' scorn for many, if not all, of those writers of the first draft of history, who also tended to be the writers of contemporary political biographies: journalists. As he told Heather Henderson, 'the Australian journalist has created a legend about me, my arrogance, my unapproachability, my wicked tongue ... Journalists cannibalise each other. If one starts a legend, the others borrow it and after a few years the legend becomes accepted history'.[25] Lloyd points to the unflattering references to journalists in Menzies' diaries. 'One was a "noodle", another "oleaginous", others were ill-mannered and illiterate', Lloyd writes. 'Even Menzies' occasional professions of respect were qualified by merciless physical delineation'.[26] Menzies' press secretary, Stewart Cockburn, says that while there were exceptions, his prime minister 'disliked journalists in the main' and had poor press relations. 'Basically he didn't conceal his dislike and/or contempt for most journalists and most newspaper proprietors – that's a reliable generalization', Cockburn says. 'And they sensed it or recognized it and returned it in kind'.[27]

Menzies also imputed intellectual laziness to the trend he perceived in political journalism towards 'criticism of persons, and less and less to the examination and criticism of ideas'. Criticising people is easy and 'can no doubt be great fun', he wrote. 'It can, indeed, be quite useful if the reasons for it are spelled out. But to criticise an idea, one must first understand it, and such an understanding involves study and serious thought'.[28] Menzies was prescient in his observation of the trend away from ideas and towards people, a shift that became more pronounced as the twentieth century drew to a close.

One would think the most likely explanation for no biography being published as part of Menzies' postwar re-imaging project is his dim view of contemporary biographies. 'The muse of history is an uncertain wench', Menzies, then opposition leader, wrote in 1947 in the foreword to John Reynolds' *Edmund Barton*, published in 1948. '[T]he course and character of the work and personality of a public man must be studied closely and carefully delineated if the truth is to emerge'. Such close and careful delineation was unlikely in a contemporary biography, he said, and his argument is worth quoting at length.

> It is the fashion, and no doubt always was, to over-praise or over-blame statesmen while they are alive, and to forget them or forgive them when they are dead. Biographies of living men are therefore usually extravagant and largely worthless. They are written, as a rule, by ardent admirers, and rarely possess any critical quality. They are, in short, propaganda documents to be discounted by the objective student.
>
> In spite of my disillusioned beliefs on this matter, the extravagances of contemporary writing, both gay and grave, never cease to astonish me. A new cricketer arises; he is before long 'the greatest in the history of the game' according to some writer whose memory embraces less than a small fraction of one per cent. of those good cricketers who have lived and played. 'The greatest speaker', 'the greatest debater', 'the most brilliant mind', 'the greatest scoundrel'; such phrases come trippingly from the mouths or pens of current recorders. Fortunately these flashy judgments do not live. All too frequently, in the reaction which follows the death of some noted man, his memory appears to

wither and the contemptuous indifference with which his name is recalled becomes as absurd, and in its own way as extravagant, as the superlatives which attached to him when living.

And then, in due course, there comes along the detached historian to read about him, to study him in the round, to see his lights and shades, to assess his work and influence, to tear away the distortions of propaganda and reveal the true man.

Such a task must be fascinating, but almost incredibly difficult. What material is of value? Nowadays most of us don't write letters except of a commercial kind, and the art of conversation is decaying. What contemporary records, then, are we to search? How can we get at the real inwardness of the statesman? By reading his speeches? I have heard hundreds of speeches in Parliament laboriously read by Ministers of the Crown, of which in most cases not one word was their own. By reading the contemporary press? Heaven forbid, since partisan writers always aim to create a popular picture, and so produce in the receptive mind a series of legends which are basically false. The contest in politics always seems – to the partisan – to be one between the *All* Whites and the *All* Blacks. But in truth it never is. At the best, the greatest statesman is a Grey Eminence.[29]

This is probably as good a summation of the case against contemporary biography as one will find directly from a politician's lips or pen. This makes it all the more intriguing that within a few years Menzies was cooperating on a contemporary biography of him by journalist Allan Dawes.

Dawes' unfinished and unpublished biography of Menzies is not well known. Brett refers to him briefly as 'Menzies' first biographer' and draws on his manuscript, along with the biography for young readers by Seth and the post–prime ministerial biography by Perkins, in her psychobiographical work, *Robert Menzies' Forgotten People*. She comments in a footnote that Dawes' 'draft has been read and corrected by Menzies, so I am assuming that, even if he was not the actual source of all of its material, and he clearly was of much of it, he was happy to regard it as an accurate account of his experience of his childhood and youth'. Perkins, whose post–prime ministerial biography Menzies opposed but who nevertheless gained interviews with Menzies' siblings Frank and Isabel, gave Brett access to his interview tapes, including that of his interview with Frank Menzies.

On Brett's account, Frank Menzies says the Dawes manuscript 'was written in 1950 and 1951 and that Menzies gave Dawes access to all his diaries and records' but that Dawes 'only completed a small part of what had been anticipated … and the work was never published'.[30] This is restated in the *Australian Dictionary of Biography* entry on Dawes by ANU academic HN 'Hank' Nelson, which in addition claims that Dawes 'was drinking heavily and unable to meet deadlines'.[31] However, the normally impeccable *ADB* fact-checking process failed in this instance: there is no source, no corroboration and therefore no crucial fact-checking 'tick' against the claim that excessive drinking stopped Dawes finishing the Menzies biography in the file underlying Dawes' *ADB* entry.[32]

The Dawes manuscript gets a second flickering moment of historical attention, a generation after Brett's *Robert Menzies' Forgotten People*, in Anne Henderson's *Menzies at War* published in 2014. Henderson posits the 'possibility' that Brett's analysis is 'not sustainable' because it partly relies on the Dawes manuscript and the Perkins biography. She in turn relies on private notes that Menzies' former colleague Paul Hasluck made preparing to review the Perkins book, in which he damns

Dawes in passing as a 'notorious' and 'bloated, and frequently sozzled journalist'.[33] Menzies' swingeing criticism of the Perkins book is cited earlier in this chapter, and Hasluck agreed with Menzies' assessment. However, Dawes and his manuscript biography are at risk of becoming collateral damage in fights to which he was not party, firstly by Hasluck lumping him and his work in with Perkins' biography; and latterly by Henderson as part of the conservative intelligentsia's push against historiography like that of Brett, perceived to be of the left.

Despite an extensive search, no private or public reference or any other evidence has been found to substantiate the claim which appears in the *ADB* that excessive alcohol consumption stopped Dawes finishing his Menzies biography. Nor does Hasluck make this claim in his comments on Dawes in the private notes cited by Anne Henderson.[34] Hasluck's slur arises rather from his disbelief that Menzies would in 1940 use a colourful journalist like Dawes as his messenger to Harold Holt, then undergoing AIF training at Puckapunyal, to recall him to the ministry after the Canberra air disaster killed three of Menzies' cabinet and the army chief of the general staff.

Because Hasluck could not imagine Menzies asking Dawes to be his messenger to Holt does not mean it did not happen. Tom Frame repeats the account of Dawes as Menzies' messenger to Holt in his biography of Holt, and refers to Dawes as 'a distinguished journalist who had been press secretary to Geoffrey Street', the Minister for the Army who was killed in the Canberra air disaster; indeed, it is in this capacity that Menzies may have used Dawes as his messenger.[35] Whitington acknowledges Hasluck as an 'outstanding historian' but argues he was jaundiced about journalists despite also being one himself. Hasluck 'vilified journalists' and newspapers in general, says Whitington: 'He had neither comprehension nor knowledge of the intricacies of newspaper work in the fifties, his association with the industry having been confined to one conservative newspaper with a monopoly in Perth twenty years earlier'.[36] Hasluck's comments on Dawes, in the absence of corroborating evidence, require extreme caution.

Menzies biography mystery

Reporting Dawes' death in 1969, in a story headlined 'Menzies Biography Mystery', the *Daily Telegraph* portrays the manuscript as unfinished but, notably, not due to any alcoholic incapacitation on Dawes' part.

> The death in Melbourne this week of journalist Allan Dawes brings to mind a secret which has mystified politicians and writers for almost 20 years.
>
> Mr Dawes, a distinguished newspaperman, poet and author, was commissioned in the early 1950s to write an official biography of the then Prime Minister, Mr Menzies.
>
> The PM co-operated to the full, answering questions into a tape recorder and much valuable material was gathered.
>
> The manuscript was written, but never published and over the years various stories have gone the rounds as to what happened to it. The most popular theory is that the material unfortunately was lost ...
>
> It can be revealed here that the material is in the Menzies' family archives.
>
> The manuscript consists of at least 13 chapters, setting out the details as Sir Robert saw them of events leading up to his resignation as Prime Minister in 1941, about which so little has been written.
>
> In his own book, *Afternoon Light,* Sir Robert passed lightly over this episode, saying merely that his colleagues had found him wanting and admitting how hurt he had been by their attitude.

> The material written by Mr Dawes is a valuable contribution to our political history – let's hope that one day we may see it in print.[37]

Dawes' manuscript biography of Menzies – at least part of it – was indeed in the Menzies archive, and ended up in the Menzies Papers at the National Library of Australia. It was this surviving manuscript material that Brett partly drew on in *Robert Menzies' Forgotten People*, and her bibliography locates it at 'series 10, box 354' of the Menzies Papers.[38] Allan Dawes' papers are also at the National Library (MS 8792).[39] They include another part of the surviving manuscript along with papers which raise another possible explanation for, as the *Telegraph* put it, the 'Menzies Biography Mystery'.

Dawes was certainly a drinker but during his active reporting years apparently a high functioning one, and his journalism was highly regarded. Whitington, for example, in his memoir *Strive To Be Fair*, describes Dawes as 'outstanding', and includes him in his list of Australian journalists who 'would have held their own, and excelled, anywhere in the world'.[40] Dawes enjoyed an excellent reputation as a war correspondent. Appointing him to a travelling party inspecting Canada's war effort in 1944, Prime Minister John Curtin referred to his 'high reputation as a writer' and 'wide experience in operational areas'.[41] Whitington, also selected for the Canada visit, said it was a 'pronounced success' and that Dawes, 'a born thespian and an enthusiastic drinker, was an enormous attraction in the faded correspondent's uniform he wore throughout the tour'.[42]

Other journalists shared Whitington's opinion, including Cecil Edwards who, as Stanley Bruce's press officer in the 1925 election, observed him on the campaign trail. Edwards writes of the 'restless genius' that was 'slender, bubbling Allan W Dawes, who could charm information from the grumpiest, scariest politician, and write like an angel'.[43] By mid-life Dawes developed 'a Chestertonian figure which, somehow, he managed to haul up and down the mountains of New

Guinea, when he was a war correspondent'.[44] At 40 the 'witty and weighty' journalist weighed around 108 kilograms.[45]

Late in the war, writes Edwards, when the AIF 9th Division was to march through Melbourne, the Melbourne *Herald* planned to run matching pieces by its two war correspondents who had been with the 9th: Dawes who covered it in New Guinea, and Jack Hetherington who covered it in the Middle East.

> Hetherington lodged an excellent piece in good time, tailored for the allotted space. No copy from Dawes. No Dawes either, or word of him. Edition time approached. Someone found Dawes fast asleep somewhere in the office after a heavy night. They woke him and sat him at a typewriter. Copy came in slip by slip. 'Just cut it off when you've got enough', he said. It just caught the edition. Dawes's piece written against time out of a none-too-clear head, was the better.[46]

So when the war ended, Dawes was middle-aged, overweight and a keen drinker but, this anecdote suggests, still writing very well.

Dawes left the *Herald* and freelanced for, among others, the 'Liberal Party ... to reorganise its public relations office'.[47] This was not his first contact with conservative politics. From 1938 to 1941 Dawes did press work as a public servant for the Lyons and Menzies governments.[48] Initially he was employed to help launch the ill-fated 'National Insurance' scheme. When it foundered, Dawes became public relations officer for the Army under Minister for the Army, Geoffrey Street, effectively becoming Street's press secretary. In March 1941, some months after Street died in the Canberra Air Disaster, Dawes moved to the newly formed Department of Labour and National Service. Reporting the appointment, the Melbourne *Herald* described Dawes as 'one of Australia's most brilliant journalists'.[49]

Thus Dawes' work was regarded highly by his peers. It was highly regarded by both sides of politics, as attested to by his repeated appointments as a press aide in the Lyons and first Menzies governments, by Curtin's comments when appointing him to the Canadian tour, and by his reorganisation of the Liberal Party public relations office in 1948. What is more, his good reputation continued right up to his death. Dawes had the 'flamboyancy and rough humour of copybook war correspondents', the *Sydney Morning Herald* reported when he died in 1969. 'But he also had a strict regard for the truth'.[50]

Cameron Hazlehurst has analysed Morgan Gallup data during Menzies' career from 1941, and concludes that 'the level of approval and support for Menzies as party leader and Prime Minister fluctuated significantly'. Hazlehurst cites Menzies' press secretary at the 1946 election, Charles Meeking, saying that Menzies was astonished by his loss to Chifley, and notes the Melbourne *Herald* report two days after the election attributing to Menzies a significant role in Labor's success.

> There is a wide feeling that this can only be explained by the fact that in its personalities, the Liberal Party still lacks electoral appeal.
>
> Most members of the Labor Party claim that for election-winning purposes, Mr Menzies is their greatest individual asset.
>
> Throughout his campaign, for instance, Mr Chifley played heavily on Mr Menzies, and usually concluded his addresses with a declaration that 'the alternative to a vote for Labor was a vote for a Menzies Government'.
>
> There has been evidence lately that Mr Menzies's public standing has increased; but the election result hardly suggests that it has increased to the point where he is again a popular leader.[51]

The *Herald* report continued that the Liberals were likely to retain Menzies as leader out of gratitude for his strenuous efforts – and because the 'Parliamentary Liberal Party remains so bankrupt of outstanding personnel that no big figure is available to succeed' him.

Chifley's announcement in August 1947 that he intended to nationalise Australia's banks proved deeply unpopular. In late October the Morgan Gallup organisation reported that Chifley 'would be fortunate to escape defeat if an election were held now'. Hazlehurst points out that while the Liberal Party's polling improved during this period, Menzies' popularity actually slipped, and that by November 1947 he was the first choice as Liberal leader among only 41 per cent of Liberal and Country Party voters, ahead of Liberal Party federal president Richard Casey on 40 per cent by the slimmest of margins. Luckily for Menzies, Casey did not have a seat in parliament at that time. Thus Hazlehurst argues that the polling evidence suggests, in the short term at least, that 'Menzies did not personally benefit from the overwhelming surge of anti-Labor sentiment' and that it took a 'renewed development of anti-communist attitudes ... to give Menzies a boost'.[52]

When anti-communism swelled as a domestic political issue, so the man wielding the anti-communist cudgel grew in stature, a symbiotic process. By January 1949, Menzies was the preferred Liberal leader among 53 per cent of Liberal and Country Party voters with Casey's support ebbing to 27 per cent. That same month, however, as Ian Hancock notes, the Hansen-Rubensohn Company, in a public relations campaign proposal to the Liberal Party organisation, said Menzies was 'known' to few electors and that the party's prospects at the next election 'will largely depend (on) the public conception of the possible Prime Minister'. Voters had to be acquainted with 'the real Mr Menzies', interested in things other men were interested in, the Hansen-Rubensohn pitch continued: 'The illusion that he is the champion of the "moneybags", the aloof somewhat enigmatic cynic could, we think, be dispelled by a discreet, well-conceived public relations campaign of a personal character'.[53]

Hancock describes in detail the 'subtle offensive' subsequently conducted by Sydney journalist and public relations operative Stewart Howard during 1949 to give Menzies a 'human face'.

> Menzies was variously depicted chatting to miners with a beer in his hand, ironing a dress at a Bathurst factory, and smiling benignly in Kurri Kurri at the few who jeered and called him 'Pig Iron Bob'. Meanwhile the organisation was busy constructing its own version of 'Bob Menzies' as the homely father figure and the people's friend to match 'RG Menzies', the statesman and the gifted speaker and intellect.[54]

The Liberal Party campaign included the publication that year of 330 000 copies of the booklet described earlier in this chapter, *How Well Do You Know This Man?*[55] At the year's conclusion, on 10 December 1949, Menzies returned to the prime ministership with a massive 27 seat anti-Labor majority in an election dominated by the Liberal and Country Party's trenchant anti-communist rhetoric.

In office, Menzies' popularity among conservative voters rose. Whitington points out, however, that despite the continuing potency of the 'communist bogey', the Menzies Government lost three seats of its own as well as a conservative independent at the next federal election on 28 April 1951. In Whitington's estimation, it 'was obvious something drastic was required if the Government was to retain office' at the next election, likely to be held three years later in 1954, since the ALP had not yet split, Labor leader Bert Evatt had not yet been discredited, and economic conditions 'pointed strongly to an electoral rebuff'.[56] While hard to credit in retrospect, the view of Menzies in 1951 as a prime minister with a limited future was widely held among senior Canberra Press Gallery journalists according to Menzies' press secretary from 1951 to 1954, Stewart Cockburn.

> Charlie Meeking was his first press secretary, then Jack Hewitt of the Information Bureau, who died of a ruptured duodenal ulcer,

filled in, as did Mick Byrne on loan from Artie Fadden for a time. Then I came in. Menzies didn't want a press secretary. Menzies reckoned he could handle his own public relations best and in my view he probably could. But the cabinet stood over him and said, You must have a press secretary. Reg Leonard, who was reorganising his public relations on loan from the *Herald*, as I understand it, probably said to him, well, try Irvine Douglas or try Alan Reid, and they of course wouldn't have a bar of it.

So that all the more obvious choices were canvassed and most of them, I believe, thought Menzies would be down the drain at the 1951 double dissolution election – or if not then, very soon afterwards. They had no faith in him, at that stage, having a long and successful career in federal politics. Well, they were wrong and eventually it came down to me because Menzies evidently said to Leonard, 'Well, what about that young bloke I met in London in 1948?'[57]

Cockburn had been the Melbourne *Herald*'s London correspondent in 1948 when Menzies, then opposition leader, visited England on a trip that was 'partly holiday, partly work'. Cockburn saw Menzies daily, got some good stories out of him and grew to like him. 'He evidently remembered me and picked my name out of the hat' when the press secretary appointment was reluctantly embraced, Cockburn said.[58]

It is easy to see how an image-burnishing contemporary biography of Menzies could have been an element of the conservatives' political strategy for re-election in 1954. The Liberal Party organisation's campaign to give Menzies a human face with its *How Well Do You Know This Man?* pamphlet may well have provided encouragement.[59] In this light it is unsurprising that in the early 1950s Menzies entertained the thought of a friendly biography – not despite his perception of such works as 'propaganda' but rather because of it.[60] Alternatively, like the idea of a press secretary foisted upon him by cabinet, or perhaps even as part of Leonard's advice in his public relations revamp of the Menzies operation, it may have been something Menzies accepted with grudging reluctance. Either way, by 1951 a contemporary biography of Prime Minister Robert Menzies was underway.

Nor is it surprising that Dawes should be the person to undertake such a project for – or should one say, with – Menzies. He had done biography-based image work for conservative politicians before. Working as Geoff Street's press secretary in the first Menzies Government, for example, Dawes 'made sure that editors were served with lively biographical material on his chief'.[61] He had done the same as a war correspondent. In New Guinea for the *Herald*, Dawes 'propagated digger characteristics that Australians wanted to read about – shop-assistants and stockmen transformed into tough, independent soldiers, "lean and hard and muscular" (and) fostered the Australians' belief in themselves as jungle fighters, men in loose, "faded, sweaty, mud-stained green", with Owen guns slung'.[62] Dawes' AN Smith Lecture in 1946, 'Caesar's Ghost: the journalist, the statesman, the spokesman', showed he had thought long and reflectively about the power and techniques of image-making.[63] In 1948 he was sufficiently trusted by the Liberal Party to reorganise its press operations – something hardly credible if he was not known to and trusted by Menzies. Two years later he would have been a logical choice to write a sympathetic contemporary political biography of Menzies, and Menzies was intimately involved in helping him do so.

Dawes' biography of Menzies was developed partly through direct interviews and partly through dictated lists of questions tape-recorded by Dawes, transcribed by Menzies' staff and relayed to Menzies for response. 'Mr Prime Minister – you were good enough, when last I spoke to you to tell me the inside running of the case of Mrs Freer ...' begins one, seven foolscap-page transcript which has survived in the

Dawes Papers.[64] Appended to its front is a typed note from Cockburn, on 'Prime Minister, Canberra' letterhead: 'MR MENZIES: I have roughly corrected a very rough transcript of this reel'.

There is no sign of a sozzled journalist at work. Rather the Dawes memorandum shows an experienced journalist diligently pursuing the story. At times, for example, he pushes Menzies: 'I feel there is more to that story than meets the eye. I wonder if you would tell me that?' Dawes is asking about Menzies' departure from the McPherson Ministry in Victoria in 1929 ostensibly over a policy disagreement – an old and possibly uncomfortable memory for Menzies who subsequently did the same in his federal career, in a move considered by some a stunt to destabilise his then leader, UAP prime minister Joe Lyons. Here Dawes shows he carefully checked facts, even trivial ones: 'Would you tell me again your story about your Aunt and the South Street competitions, which you once told to a photographer and myself when we were travelling in a car from Kew to the City, I think, but my memory of it is imperfect and I would like to hear it again'.

There is no doubt the biography is a collaboration, one in which the author allowed the subject's hand to move invisibly, as the subject considered necessary, over the text. 'No book of this character would be complete without a few "Billy" stories', Dawes says of Hughes, still a member of parliament. 'Have you any printable such? They need not necessarily be attributed to you, though it would be much better if they were'. A little later in this memorandum, Dawes explicitly reveals his acceptance of Menzies' veto. Asking about another controversial incident in Menzies' Victorian political career, Dawes says: 'If this proves embarrassing or a betrayal of confidence, don't bother with it'.

Yet the memorandum is full of reminders that while Menzies has a veto, Dawes is not supine. Here he disagrees with Menzies and asks him to reflect again on an issue:

> The press, you say, must bear a heavy responsibility for the
> decline in the standards of Parliamentary conduct and practice

over the last fifty years; but don't you think that the press was pretty corrupt in the days when Federal Parliament operated from Melbourne and was pretty corrupt in its association – in the Victorian governments, to say the least – before Federation?[65]

The memorandum shows that Dawes did not rely on Menzies alone as a source: 'White, Parliamentary Librarian, told me of your encounter with Somerset Maugham, hitchhiking in Europe. He also told me you succeeded in getting manuscripts for the National Library from Maugham. I wonder if you could tell me this story? Did Maugham have anything to say on Australia and Australians? I believe he once described Melba as "a superb monster"'.

Dawes encourages Menzies to tell more, not less, even when the matter is sensitive. This example relates to the interwar scandal concerning Thomas Blamey whose police badge was found in the hands of a man caught in a Fitzroy brothel raid in 1925.

> In the Victorian era in your political life – did you have any association with the appointment or the subsequent removal of Blamey as Commissioner of Police, and if so, were you thereby embarrassed in selecting Sir Thomas Blamey as the Leader of the AIF? I seem to recall some conferences [sic, confidences] on the part of Brigadier Street, when I was working for him in the Department of the Army. You may be assured that I do not intend any muck-raking in this matter; but history is history, and the facts might be set down without any loss of taste, I think. Of course, there is no need to quote you in the matter and I will be guided by you as to whether we go into the question at all.[66]

Dawes establishes a pattern recognisable to journalists, pushing for more, then reassuring lest the subject be scared off, sometimes adding domestic touches which by association de-escalate any rising tension. After the Blamey parry, Dawes asks Menzies whether he had experienced any 'period of honest doubt' on the matter of religion: 'Once again, if some of these questions touch too closely, do not hesitate to wipe the ribbon clean; in fact to say "What business is it of yours at all". In playing these questions back I am impressed with their general grim solemnity – I trust you won't answer them in the spirit in which they are asked! (That, by the way, was a kookaburra under my window – apparently he feels the same way about it as it [sic, I] do'.)[67]

The memorandum – the transcript of one of Dawes' tape-recorded questions for Menzies – is the only one that survives, and part of it is missing. The seventh page ends mid-sentence, as Dawes compares 'parliamentary morality' and 'parliamentary usage' in the Australian parliament's earlier decades with that of the mid-twentieth century.

> I remember ... the general attitude of disregard for private morals and public interests which characterised the lower grades of politician at the time. Parliament House itself was the scene of many unpleasant scenes which could not but inspire a certain contempt for the men who were the tribunes of the people; but to use Parliament House as they might the Tower of London Night Club! There were even people who used it as a means of escaping the bailiffs – they rushed in when they saw the 'bluey' coming up the steps and they stayed there!

> I don't see that going on in Parliament today – in Parliament House, I mean. You can say of some of the lesser politicians of today that they are dull fellows but they mean well enough, I suppose. Of course, you have your Ed Wards but we had our equivalents, I think, in those days [who] used their parliamentary position for purposes which were not entirely ethical.[68]

At the point the missing pages begin, Dawes has moved on to 'parliamentary usage' and is canvassing the difference between 'Miss 1900 and Miss 1950' in a way which is unfortunately inexplicable without reference to the missing page or pages.

Another document in the Dawes Papers – what looks like a roneoed transcription from another Dawes tape recording sent to Menzies via his office – includes a detailed plan for a work of 27 chapters, including chapter titles and chapter contents, and contains extensive notes by him on his approach to the project. Dawes refers to 'a visit to The Lodge' at which he gathered materials, and also to his use of Menzies' diaries: 'I will have to submit the material at some stage for his careful perusal as there may be much of this so personal that he would not be inclined to expose it outside of his family circle'. That Menzies trusted Dawes with his diaries speaks for itself.

In this document Dawes also mentions interviews with Menzies' cousin, Douglas Menzies QC, and High Court judge Owen Dixon, and foreshadows forthcoming interviews with two more judges, all for the chapter on Menzies' legal career tentatively titled 'The Rustle of Silk'. After that, Dawes continues, 'I contemplate visiting a number of other people in the field of law including Sir John Latham, who has also agreed to help me, and a number of colleagues and adversaries at the Bar, who will doubtless be able to give me a better picture of such cases as the Engineers' Paper Sacks, and other cases which seem to tell a story'.[69] Thus the picture further builds of a serious research enterprise which, while in the service of effectively an authorised biography with all its attendant veto rights, is not trivial in its intentions.

The crucial thing about this second document in the Dawes Papers is how far down the track it reveals Dawes was in writing the biography, how long he had been working on it, and how at least one credible reader – Justice Sir Owen Dixon – had reacted positively, on Dawes' account anyway, to reading excerpts of it. 'Something has been written of practically every chapter but the new material I have recently obtained induces me to rewrite pretty well everything I have written already in the light of what has now been disclosed to me', he writes. 'Some of this material I doubtless should have had to begin with, but I was unaware precisely where to find it'.

By the final page of this document, notes, most likely written by Cockburn, begin to appear interspersed with the transcription of Dawes comments. 'Dawes next proposes', one reads, 'to ask the Prime Minister to confide to him those records of crises in his career which he discussed with Dawes just before his recent departure for abroad'. Another reads, 'Dawes has shown some of his material to Sir Owen Dixon and is obviously very pleased by what he terms "Sir Owen's heartening reactions"'.

A crucial comment transcribed on the last page suggests the date of this memorandum was most likely 1952 since the transcription has Dawes saying, 'The last chapter will deal with the recent tour abroad and the prospect for 1953'.[70] Menzies' brother Frank estimated Dawes worked on the book in 1950–51.[71] Dawes' comment in this memorandum suggests the time frame was more likely at least as long as 1950–52, if not longer. This is confirmed in the draft chapter by Dawes titled 'The Sampson Line – Menzies in Parliament', contained in the Menzies Papers and personally annotated by Menzies himself, which refers to the death of his former cabinet colleague Sir George Pearce in 1952.[72]

So what is there of this manuscript, this mystery biography of Menzies? The Dawes Papers contain a chapter with pages numbered 1 to 48 titled 'In the Middle East' covering Menzies' visit to the Second AIF in 1941, en route for Britain.[73] There are pages 55 and 56 from the same typewriter and on the same paper stock, which appear to be the final two pages of a chapter on Menzies' school education. There are five unnumbered pages, four of which concern Menzies' attitudes to literature while the other canvasses his views on rhetoric. There is a 12-page chapter on Menzies' 'Jubilee Pilgrimage' in 1935. There are also several pages which are heavily marked up earlier drafts of the foregoing material, all of which is on quarto paper. The rest of the Dawes Papers are on foolscap paper. There are five pages from the 'Beleaguered

Britain' chapter concerning Menzies' long visit to Britain in 1941; nine more pages, numbered 6 to 14, which also appear to be from the same chapter; and seven pages covering the same period, numbered 123 to 129. This last section, given its page numbering, appears to be from a later draft in which Dawes had begun numbering pages cumulatively. It leaves us on page 129 with Menzies still in London, and still prime minister – first time round.

How does this compare to the surviving Dawes manuscript in the Menzies Papers? There are three copies of the opening six chapters of the Dawes manuscript, including one personally marked up by Menzies himself. There is also a typewritten memo from Menzies' confidential personal secretary, Eileen 'Lennie' Lenihan, and another typewritten note likely to also be by Lenihan. The memo is addressed to 'Mr Frank' – almost certainly Menzies' brother, Frank. Writes Lenihan:

> The copy I've taped up, and with the note attached, is for the PM – because I have marked in ink on the various pages the special bits I've brought to his attention.
>
>   Copy herewith for you;
>
>   Also a copy for Stewart Cockburn if he wants.
>
>   I've taken 3 copies down to Melb. and all the rest of the papers are in the office here – except that I'm also including herewith the actual manuscript from which I've worked – on the basis that I don't expect Mr Dawes will be chasing it this weekend.
>
>   Lennie[74]

The other typewritten note, which is adjacent in the papers and likely accompanied the memo, reads:

> This is the whole of the manuscript sent to me by Mr Dawes (barring one chapter which Stewart C. is doing)[75]

Interesting points emerge from these two notes. The first is that the Dawes biography was treated by Menzies and those closest to him as effectively a group project. Lenihan herself marked up a copy before passing it to the prime minister for his mark up and comments. Frank Menzies and press secretary Stewart Cockburn are also intimately involved. So no fewer than the prime minister, his confidential personal secretary, his brother and his press secretary all devote serious time to it.

The second is the way Lenihan respectfully refers to the author as 'Mr Dawes'. While perhaps a standard form of politeness at the time from a secretary to someone having significant dealings with her employer, the absence of any tone of doubt or condescension one might have for a writer of the kind alluded to by Hasluck in one of his private working notes and by *ADB* contributor Hank Nelson without any attribution – namely, a drunkard – is telling. Menzies and his office clearly took Dawes and his manuscript seriously; there is no evidence that the project fizzled out for the reason Nelson alleges.

That leaves the question of how to square the conflicting evidence of the mere six chapters in the Menzies Papers, and the far lesser and different material in the Dawes Papers, with the report in the *Telegraph* obituary of Dawes in 1969 that Dawes wrote 'at least 13 chapters' including a chapter 'setting out the details as Sir Robert saw them of events leading up to his resignation as Prime Minister in 1941'.[76]

The obvious suspicion arising is that up to seven other chapters the Dawes obituary suggests were written may have been disposed of before the Menzies Papers went to the National Library. A prima facie, and apparently powerful, defence against this charge is that the

Dawes Papers themselves do not contain these chapters. However, the provenance of the Dawes Papers is not what it seems: they did not come from Dawes or his family. Rather they came to the National Library courtesy of Cockburn, Menzies' press secretary at the time the manuscript was being written, according to correspondence between National Library staff member Cathy Santamaria and Cockburn in which she thanks him for the material.[77]

There are three matters that do not prove, but do lend weight to the possibility, that Menzies cooled off, and ultimately ran dead, on the project after reading the six chapters that are in the Menzies Papers, whether Dawes went on to write another seven chapters himself or not.

The first is the fact that none of the manuscript material in either the Dawes Papers or the Menzies Papers covers Menzies' controversial rise to the prime ministership which some saw as over the dead body of Joe Lyons, whom he was perceived to have systematically undermined. Even cast in a benign light in a friendly biography, it might ultimately have been judged unwise to remind voters. Menzies' period as attorney-general in the Lyons Government is the last point reached before there is a break in Dawes' chronological narrative, which suddenly resumes in a chapter called 'The Living Present' which has Menzies as prime minister during World War II, touring the Middle East. If Dawes wrote anything about the ugly mechanics of Menzies' rise to the prime ministership first time round, it does not remain in the Menzies Papers. It is possible that parts of the Dawes manuscript which cover controversial incidents too candidly or cast Menzies in too unattractive a light – even whole chapters of such material – have been deleted from the Menzies archive. It is impossible to know.

The second reason Menzies may have cooled on the biography is a changing political climate, from the backdrop of a 1951 election in which the government's majority declined, to a 1954 election in prospect with Menzies' popularity still rising and the Liberal Party buoyed by his use of the Petrov Affair to make the Cold War central to Australian political debate. Hazlehurst points out that support for Menzies as leader among

Liberal and Country Party voters was 87 per cent in October 1954, on its way to peaking at 90 per cent in April 1955.[78] Against the backdrop of these extraordinary levels of support, Menzies may have calculated he had potentially more to lose from a biography – even a friendly one – than he had to gain.

The third possibility is Menzies' attitude to the Dawes manuscript, as indicated by Menzies' own annotations on the six chapters which survive in his papers. To begin with, these are matter of fact. On page 4 of the first chapter, 'Eureka's Shattered Lantern', Menzies queries whether a footnote defining 'mate' might be helpful and, similarly, on page 7, whether the word 'squatter' should be defined; this suggests he may have had a British edition of the biography in mind as well as an Australian one. In the next chapter, 'A Young Man From The Provinces', Menzies begins copyediting. On page 22, for example, in one of a plethora of minor edits, Menzies strikes 'at no time doubted' and inserts 'beyond doubt'. When Dawes writes of 'Menzies' sister Belle, a few months his senior' on page 26 of this chapter, Menzies strikes 'few months' and inserts 'year'. To assist Dawes, he occasionally amplifies one of his points, as in this note penned at the top of page 27 of this chapter.

AWD

> At this time, the railway was at Jeparit.
> The new question was whether it should be
> Extended West.

RGM

The first sign of exasperation appears shortly afterwards. 'You have repeated this ... ! RGM', appears on the bottom of page 32 in relation to his reading of Dickens. In the next chapter, 'Judkins Junior's Schooldays', on page 41, Menzies exclaims again: 'AWD (James) Ainslie was not at school with me!' Many edits are innocuous, often directed at references to Menzies' family. Menzies strikes 'Syd', for example, and replaces it with the more formal 'his brother Sydney' on page 33. He softens Dawes' depiction of Menzies' grandmother on page 42. Dawes has, 'She was not very well educated'; Menzies added, 'but she had the root of the matter in her'. Menzies changes it to, 'She was not a scholar, but she had strong views, and a strong faith'. Menzies changes 'peppery parent' to 'disappointed father' on page 52.

Sensitivity to the question of his non-service in World War I emerges on page 68 where Menzies strikes, 'When he was asked, the story goes, why he remained safe in Melbourne while so many of his University associates were in the firing line, he replied: "Oh, it's all right for them to go to the war, but a future Prime Minister of the Commonwealth has to be protected"'. Menzies' standard explanation that follows the struck passage – as Dawes puts it, 'What really happened ...' – is naturally allowed to stand, namely that 'a Menzies family conference decided that Robert should be the one to stay home and look after his ageing parents and younger brother while his elder brothers ... served in the forces'.

On page 78, in the chapter 'The Rustle of Silk', Menzies strikes 'diffident' from Dawes' characterisation of him during his early years at the Melbourne bar as 'a slight, tall, diffident young man, a little condescending but never stiff'. The 'Menzies myth of arrogance' is canvassed in this chapter on page 90. Menzies strikes, 'He is said to have borne the surreptitious sobriquet of 'God' at Wesley College'. Menzies also sets in parentheses, 'even to his latest political days he has found it hard to unbend to intellectual inferiors', and annotates it somewhat ambiguously, 'I cannot admit this, but printing it will fix it! RGM'. He also strikes out an entire anecdote on this page concerning his alleged comment as a young counsel in conference, responding to the other side's citing of the then High Court Chief Justice, Sir Isaac Isaacs, that 'Isaacs is an old fool'. On page 94 Menzies strikes, '"I'm a poor judge of character", he says, "but my wife is never wrong"'.

While Dawes does not seem to have got himself into trouble with his subject too much to this point, Menzies was clearly exercised about the fifth chapter concerning his segue from the Victorian bar into state politics, titled 'The Sampson Line – Menzies in Parliament', on the front of which he writes: 'SC See me about this!' His press aide, Cockburn, was the likely addressee. Menzies puts into the third person some of Dawes' direct quotations of him concerning his success at the bar, yet lets stand the very next sentence incorporating a very particular direct quote, 'Menzies was, in fact, in his own phrase, "working like a nigger"'.[79] On the next page, in a Dawes footnote describing the wide range of techniques Menzies used to win legal cases, Menzies strikes the words 'everything from white lies to black magic'.[80]

A few pages later Dawes describes Menzies' attitude to the Country Party, apparently too candidly for political comfort. The first sentence is, 'Menzies is said to have shown a healthy respect for the Australian Labour [sic] Party but seemingly to have seen no justification whatever for the Country Party'. Menzies strikes 'no justification whatever for' and inserts 'little virtue in' and adds, at the end of the sentence, 'which had, some years before, unseated his own father in the division of Lowan'. Menzies goes on to strike the rest of the paragraph in its entirety, which read:

> 'Whenever we met about this time', said Sir George Pearce a few days before his death in 1952, 'we discussed our ailments, or rather, our ailment. It was the Country Party in both of us, a sort of political appendix'. Again, 'nothing could exceed the political cowardice of the Country Party', Menzies said to (Sir) Harold Clapp, discussing that party's 'torpedoeing' of transport legislation in Victoria just as it showed some sign of becoming effective.[81]

On the next page Menzies strikes a reference to his 'contempt for' Victorian state Country Party MP Albert Dunstan, and replaces it with 'distrust of'. However strongly Menzies was motivated to camouflage his dislike of the Country Party for reasons of political diplomacy, he could not resist letting stand his witty reference while a member of the Victorian Legislative Council to Dunstan as 'one of the Four Horsemen of the Eucalypts'.[82]

Later in the chapter, moving to the topic of economic policy in the 1930s, Dawes quotes Menzies that in New York, Paris and London 'I found myself talking to people with immeasurably greater authority than I will ever have on these financial matters'; Menzies puts this into the third person and eliminates the modesty, writing, 'Menzies found himself talking to people of authority on these financial matters'.[83]

The conversions to the third person become systematic by this point in the manuscript. Menzies writes at the top of page 33 of this fifth chapter, 'This stuff must be taken out of quotes RGM'. It is impossible to tell whether this is for reasons of readability, or whether Menzies sought to eliminate signs that he was cooperating with the author or otherwise in league with him.

The chapter ends with Dawes perhaps, from Menzies' point of view, itemising rather too many missteps in the Victorian state politics phase of Menzies' career. These included the 'popular sneer' that Menzies was considered a '"nonagenarian's delight" but without contacts among his contemporaries', a charge against which Dawes goes on to defend him; that at times Menzies 'had rather more enemies than most'; quoting *Argus* leader writer WA Brennan that Menzies 'now and then ... got off on the wrong foot'; that his resignation from the Victorian ministry over a policy issue 'fell flat as a demonstration'; and that while minister for railways he 'was forced to withdraw an unpopular transport measure'. 'Not so', Menzies writes at the top of the page, after striking the clause. 'I put it through!'[84]

As with the previous one, on the front of Chapter 6, 'A Citizen of Two Cities: Menzies Goes to Canberra' covering his election to federal parliament and years as attorney-general in the Lyons Government, Menzies writes, 'SC See me about this! RGM'. Again, from Menzies' point of view, Dawes is possibly too candid about Menzies' position in the Lyons Government and his colleagues' attitudes to him. Dawes writes that Lyons did not greet Menzies with 'entire approval'. Doubts about him were raised in Lyons' mind by Menzies' near defeat in the seat of Kooyong by an independent at the 1937 election, leading him to 'regard Menzies as an electoral risk, maybe too serious for the Party to carry' despite Lyons' 'own personal affection and regard, which induced him to overlook irritating incidents in Cabinet and in the Parliament in which the young Victorian's personality was the anvil from which sparks flew right and left'.[85]

Dawes' pattern is now well established: write rather than hide the attack on Menzies, then knock it over. A typical example is Dawes' juxtaposition of Latham and Menzies as attorneys-general: 'In Cabinet, though old hands sometimes tended to contrast his inexperience with the soundness of Latham, it was refreshing, it was remarked with respect, to hear a Constitutional point explained in minutes rather than hours'.[86] Menzies inserted 'a few' before minutes and struck 'rather than hours', perhaps out of respect for Latham who had been chief justice of the High Court for nearly a generation and retired in 1952, the year Dawes likely wrote and Menzies likely annotated, this chapter.

Dawes' 'declare then demolish' technique must have made uncomfortable reading for Menzies who might well have preferred difficult episodes simply not to appear at all. Towards the end of this chapter Dawes outlines three 'picturesque highlights' of Menzies' attorney-generalship. The first involved the Immigration Restriction Act's notorious 'language test' arbitrarily used to deny certain people entry into Australia, usually but, as these cases showed, not always, people of colour. Immigration officials proposed a Gaelic test for Egon Kisch, an anti-fascist activist and alleged communist fluent in a number of European languages. When he refused the test, he was arrested, bailed and, after protracted legal proceedings, eventually offered a deal by the Lyons Government which stopped litigation in exchange for an agreed departure day. The second of Dawes' examples was the 'celebrated case of Mrs Freer, a lady from India tangled in the affairs of a young Australian officer on service there [who] attempted to land in Sydney' following his return home – a passage Menzies described in a margin note on the Dawes manuscript as 'defamatory'. Mabel Freer was a white, Indian-born British subject denied entry on nebulous grounds thought to relate to her relationship with the married, but soon to be divorced, officer. Her failure to pass a language test in Italian saw her controversially excluded, with exhaustive legal proceedings delaying her arrival so long that the relationship had expired before she was admitted. The third of Dawes' examples was the sale of scrap-iron to Japan, on Menzies' watch, in the run up to World War II which earned him the nickname 'Pig Iron Bob'.[87]

The chapter closes with Dawes saying that when Menzies entered federal politics he decided to cancel the 'general retainers which he then held from a number of important organisations in the commercial world (including) Shell and Vacuum Oil'. In doing so, Dawes says 'a measure of mischief had already been done to him politically' over them, and defends Menzies against critics who:

> faulted on ethical grounds his action in representing the Shell Company before a Royal Commission which had been appointed by the Commonwealth on April 7, 1933, to investigate the importation and distribution and sale of petrol in Australia. Politically, however, some of his friends doubted whether the step was well advised. He was at the time Attorney-General of Victoria. He had not, however, up to this time thought it necessary to resign his long-held retainer from the Shell Company.[88]

Dawes continues that 'from time to time afterwards the Shell Company's retainer has raised its voice, like the Ghost of Hamlet's father, to distract if not to embarrass Menzies, in and out of Parliament'.[89] While Dawes' defence of him is trenchant, the content is undoubtedly embarrassing to Menzies and, in the hands of political enemies, damaging. It is little wonder that Menzies annotated this chapter and the preceding one with a sharp message to his press secretary, 'See me about this!'

The *Daily Telegraph*'s source on there being 'at least 13 chapters' of the Dawes manuscript is most likely to have been other journalists, or possibly Dawes' widow or sons, or perhaps parliamentary or press gallery hearsay. The reliability of the statement, absent of other evidence, is impossible to evaluate. Should the half dozen manuscript chapters in the Menzies Papers and the lesser amount in the Dawes papers therefore be accepted as all that Dawes in fact wrote? Possibly. A typewritten note included with the six chapters in the Menzies Papers says, 'This is the whole of the manuscript sent to me by Mr Dawes ...' However, the chapters are not enumerated. Even if they were it would not preclude the possibility of others later being written, and even sent, that were eliminated from or otherwise not included in the Menzies Papers.

The documents that *do* survive show Dawes not as the unreliable drunkard portrayed by Nelson in the *Australian Dictionary of Biography* but rather as a diligent professional working methodically at his task – perhaps too diligently, in the sense of too independently, for Menzies' liking. There is no evidence that this changed, nor that the biography was not completed and published because of Dawes rather than Menzies, whose exigencies and calculations of risk and return from such a project may well have changed both because of his strengthening political position as well as Dawes' perhaps unexpected 'disclose all' style. Crucially, the sense of an author disintegrating under the influence of alcohol is not conveyed by the chapters which survive in the Menzies Papers and the somewhat dubiously named Dawes Papers, which this research shows came to the National Library via Stewart Cockburn, who may well have weeded them with his former employer's notations in mind. The surviving chapters are uniformly strong, without the trailing off quality one would expect from a professional writer succumbing to disabling alcoholism.

Correspondence in 1961 between political scientist LF Crisp and Longmans, publisher of Crisp's *Ben Chifley: A Biography,* confirms that Menzies' office propagated the story that Dawes' drinking derailed the Menzies biography.[90] Longmans had asked whether Crisp might follow up his Chifley biography with one of Menzies, who was still in office. 'Now about your question on the life of Menzies', Crisp began.

> I ran into one of his Press Secretaries on Saturday morning and asked him straight out what the position was. He confirmed what I already knew, that some eight or nine years ago a well-known Melbourne journalist called Alan Dawes ... had undertaken such a work, but was beaten by the bottle which had been his enemy for some time previously and had had the job withdrawn from him. According to this local source there is no biography in progress at the moment though he tells me that Menzies carefully files away papers of biographical significance and he believes that Menzies has in mind to write memoirs himself.[91]

Canberra's population at this time was 52 000 with the bulk of residents in, or connected to, the business of government. If this version of the biography's demise was being retailed by Menzies' office, it is unsurprising it would have permeated in the intervening period as far as the office of an ANU academic. That Crisp also heard it directly from a Menzies staffer, who added that the job had been 'withdrawn' from Dawes with Menzies himself planning a memoir, intensifies caution – in the absence of any corroboration and in the face of considerable circumstantial evidence contradicting it – about the story that alcoholic incapacitation stopped Dawes finishing the book.

Thus Australia's longest serving prime minister governed without a contemporary biography during his combined eighteen years in office, other than the biography for young readers written by Seth in 1960 for Cassell. Menzies had a long association with Cassell who published his *Speech is of Time* (1958), *Central Power in the Australian Commonwealth*

(1967) and, after his retirement, *Afternoon Light* (1967) – '[it] has made the Cassell directors most excited'[92] – and *The Measure of the Years* (1970). The 'cloak of urbanity', as Whitington describes Menzies' public face, was not lifted during his active political lifetime.

Menzies' deep hostility to contemporary political biography, his nevertheless active co-operation in beginning the production of one, the growing alarm which emerges in his personal notations on draft chapters, and the project's lack of completion point to some of the ambivalences inherent in it. The reason the biography was not finished and published remains moot. There is no evidence to support the claim it was due to Dawes' incapacitation by alcohol. There is, on the other hand, circumstantial evidence of Menzies' concern about Dawes' disclose-and-rebut style rather than diplomatic silence about contentious aspects of Menzies' career. There is the possibility, too, that Menzies' changed standing between the 1951 election, when it was not strong, and the 1954 election by which time his personal polling was extraordinarily high, eliminated the perceived need for it, leading him to run dead on the project. A political biography's potential as a political intervention is contextual. If the context changes, the abandoned Menzies biography suggests, so might the risk and reward calculus attending it.

So it was that Menzies' novel engagement with what would have been Australia's first example of political biography as domestic political intervention lapsed. In retirement, Menzies chose British expatriate Lady (Frances) McNicoll as his official biographer.[93] A personal friend, McNicoll was a long-time *Economist* correspondent who had never written a book. Given Menzies' bleak view of the genre, she was perhaps the perfect choice: the biographer who did not write a biography. McNicoll was engaged for the project in 1969. When Menzies died in 1978 the biography was not finished and never would be.

Chapter 4
World War II to the end of the Menzies line

It is a pity that an author who writes a sex novel is provided with a mansion, while the author who writes history goes unrewarded.

John Curtin

Country Party leader Arthur 'Artie' Fadden was a conservative coalition prime minister in his own right for forty days from August to October 1941, between Menzies' fall and John Curtin's ascension. Fadden was also frequently acting prime minister during Menzies' long absences overseas, through both his prime ministerships, in line with the coalition convention that the Country Party leader rather than the deputy Liberal leader fulfil that role. On Fadden's own reckoning he acted as prime minister for 692 days which, adding the forty days as prime minister in his own right, put him at the helm for just over two years – longer than the prime ministerships of Harold Holt, George Reid, Chris Watson and several others. No biography was written during his active political career.

The fact that he became prime minister at all, though, has a slight biographical angle: Fadden was boosted personally over a sustained period at Menzies' expense in the *Sydney Morning Herald* by its political correspondent, Ross Gollan. In his company history of the *Herald*, Gavin Souter describes Gollan's systematic disparagement of Menzies during his first prime ministership 'by the implications in his praise of Fadden'. Souter relies in part on gallery journalist Alan Reid's account of 'the quite major influence that Gollan exercised upon other members of the gallery', suggesting he 'probably quite subtly influenced other fellows in the gallery into looking upon [Fadden] as a ... successor for Menzies'.[1]

Reid puts it bluntly: Gollan 'set out to make Fadden Prime Minister. He succeeded'. This put Gollan in a unique position as a journalist according to Reid, becoming the prime minister's 'Grey Eminence, privy to decisions, consulted on tactics, kept posted on developments, and with constant and seemingly unlimited access to the Fadden presence'. This lasted only as long as Fadden's short-lived prime ministership – 'for 40 days and 40 nights [as] Ben Chifley, with a chuckle, described the duration of the Fadden regime'.[2]

The Fadden Government fell on 3 October 1941, when two independents sided with Labor to vote the government down.[3] Arthur Coles, of the retailing family, and Mallee wheat farmer Alec Wilson administered 'the death blow', as Whitington put it.[4] Labor's John Curtin became prime minister and died in office in July 1945. In this time he became only the second Australian prime minister to be the subject of a published contemporary political biography.

Curtin was a sometime journalist and former editor of the labour weekly, *Westralian Worker*, for a decade from 1917. As prime minister Curtin wore his Australian Journalists' Association membership badge on his coat.[5] Lloyd Ross notes Curtin was a financial member of the AJA until 30 June 1945, five days before his death.[6] Curtin's view of history and biography can be gleaned from an article in the *West Australian* in 1933 written while out of parliament for a term, having lost his seat at the 1931 election. It was unfortunate, Curtin argued, that history was not held in higher esteem.

> It is a pity that an author who writes a sex novel is provided with a mansion, while the author who writes history goes unrewarded. Were real histories available public opinion today would probably be very different from what it is. It would be better informed as to economic effects and realities ... [and] it would not be beguiled and misled as it is now by the glittering personalities of its Neros, its Cleopatras, its Alexanders, its Napoleons; the tinsel lives of the egotistical and selfish-great would be in the background of the world's consciousness instead of in the foreground.[7]

Curtin believed it did a nation good to remember its sufferings, because memory of them and their origins could help prevent their recurrence. Otherwise, 'A Napoleon appears in Europe and suddenly kicks throne after throne over with his foot; a Hitler appears in Germany and suddenly the trade unions – their press, their political representatives, and their leaders – are stricken dumb'.[8]

Curtin was the subject of the contemporary political biography *John Curtin* by Alan Chester, a novelist and, as one reviewer described him, 'Curtinite'.[9] Published by Angus & Robertson in 1943, mid-way through Curtin's wartime prime ministership, Chester's stated aim was to 'present an accurate picture of an important part of John Curtin's life' – namely, his career as an editor, as a member of parliament, opposition leader and prime minister. To Chester, Curtin had 'pulled the Labour [sic] Party up by its hair and forced it to stand on its feet', and in the process 'revolutionized Australia's world status'.[10] In 1935, when Scullin retired from the opposition leadership due to ill health, the press considered Frank Forde's success over the low-profile Curtin, the only other nominee, a foregone conclusion. Curtin's victory created a 'knotty problem' for journalists:

> Who – what – was John Curtin? There was only a handful of Labour [sic] men in Sydney who knew him even by sight. Their information about him was meagre – very little more than they

had gleaned from the articles already written. The reporters ferreted and searched and worried, until at last they were able to summarize their discoveries.[11]

By the time Chester's biography was published two-thirds of the way through World War II, and a few weeks before the 1943 election, Curtin was widely known and secure in his reputation as a gifted leader. The book was designed to convey and explain Curtin's achievements in a way that energised and inspired the reader. Chester described, for example, how Curtin, 'engendered confidence' as he did the national rounds of the party, despite being little known outside Victoria where he was born and spent his early decades, or his home base of Western Australia:

> His tour was marked by a distinct glandular revival of the turgid channels. After listening to him, State executives of the party no longer felt that they were fighting a hopeless battle. He injected into them the sense of urgency that he himself was feeling so strongly.[12]

This might well be a description of Chester's intended impact with the biography, boosting readers' confidence that Australia was in safe hands at a time of exceptional peril. Chester's Curtin is an ordinary man who before the war enjoyed a plunge into the Cottesloe surf, a game of billiards and copious reading – 'everything from Edgar Wallace ... to novels, biographies, history, economics, exploration'. Yet Chester's Curtin is also a man whose integrity and superb wartime leadership explained 'why the nations listen when Australia speaks ... why world newspapers suddenly want to know what is going on in Australia'.[13] The back cover was a full size display advertisement urging people to keep buying war bonds because, 'It is better to "shell out" for Australia than to be "shelled out" by Japan', along with a plea to pass the book on after finishing to 'some man in the services who needs good reading'.

The narrative benefited from Chester's novelistic skills. Instead of drily setting out Curtin's conviction about the likelihood of Japanese aggression in 1937, and the reasoning behind it, for example, Chester conveys it through a domestic scene where Curtin returns for a rare visit home to Perth before the 1937 election. Curtin's home is by the sea and the hardworking opposition leader gets to enjoy the company of his children, Jack junior and Elsie – 'now a tall, cool, pretty girl, and a daughter of whom Curtin was openly proud'.

> He sat with her on the back lawn that overlooked the rolling blue of the Indian Ocean. Skirting the horizon to westward was the low-lying, elongated coast of Rottnest Island, where Vlamingh the Dutch explorer had landed so long ago. The white sand of the beach was clearly visible in the crystal air. Curtin considered it lazily for a long time.
>
> 'Thinking of the election, dad?' Elsie asked.
>
> Curtin looked up at her quickly. 'No, not the election', he answered, unsmiling.
>
> 'Then what?'
>
> He hesitated a moment. 'I was just thinking', he said quietly, 'what we would do, what our reactions would be, if we saw the Jap fleet coming in past the island now'.
>
> 'Do you think they ever will?'
>
> 'I've stopped wondering *if* they ever will', said her father. 'The only question to be answered now is, when?'

World War II to the end of the Menzies line

Elsie's mind flashes back to a speech her father had given two months earlier, a device which allows Chester to insert a few paragraphs of it into the text, finishing with Curtin's sentence: 'Yet above all, we must have preparedness against foreign aggression'.

'Was it Japan you meant when you spoke of foreign aggression?' she asked.

He smiled as he got up from the grass. 'Well, I don't imagine the United States or the Eskimos have designs against us', he said, gently.[14]

In a handwritten notation dated July 1943, in the copy of *John Curtin* sent to literary collector Philip Whelan upon publication, Chester explained his approach. While a comprehensive biography of Curtin would later be written, 'for the needs of today ... a concise and easily readable book' was necessary.[15] Emotional appeal and a wide readership was imperative.

The Curtin Government had been in office for nearly two years when *John Curtin* was published. The narrative culminates in Curtin's historic appeal to the United States over the Pacific War, against the backdrop of the Japanese military 'entrenched firmly in a semi-circle right across the north coast of Australia'. Under Curtin, 'Australia stands up, stronger than ever', Chester wrote.[16] The book simultaneously highlights immediate dangers, heightens the urgency of the war effort, and reinforces confidence in Curtin's leadership without sacrificing the facts.

Chester's inscription in the copy of *John Curtin* sent to Whelan also makes clear he saw it as something of a postcard to the future, 'to underline the work of an Australian leader under whose wise guidance we have seen the birth of a new Australian consciousness' – something he felt was unlikely to be properly appreciated at the time.

> One day it will be. Our nation today is a greater nation than it was two years ago; it stands inviolate and strong. In the council halls of the great countries it is regarded with respect and admiration. John Curtin achieved this, but in the emotional stress of modern war the human memory, engulfed and overwhelmed by the word machines of our age, has great difficulty in following the bright thread of progress which is so often blurred by extraneous matters of no real or lasting importance. That is why I wrote this book.[17]

It was Chester's only non-fiction work. While Curtin's reputation shone in succeeding decades, as Chester hoped, the biography's contribution to that is difficult to assess – except to say it was the sole book-length biography of Curtin until Lloyd Ross' *John Curtin: A Biography* was published in 1977, some thirty-four years later.[18] As such it would have been a logical starting point for those interested in, and themselves researching, Curtin's life. Ross was aware of the Chester biography, noting, for example, Chester's excoriation of Sir Keith Murdoch's attacks on Curtin as part of his (unsuccessful) campaign for Labor's defeat at the 1943 election. Ross cites Chester's assessment of Murdoch: 'Such men are the white ants of democracy. They harbour their happy illusion that it is possible to play their golf, make their profits, take their holidays and beat the Japanese too'.[19] However, Ross goes on to point out that Chester's defence of Curtin and excoriation of Murdoch was 'printed in a biography of the Prime Minister which few people would have read, whereas Murdoch's attack appeared in his own newspaper which ... about a million people read each evening'.[20]

After Curtin's death his deputy, Frank Forde, was caretaker prime minister for a week in the interregnum before caucus met to elect

Treasurer Ben Chifley to succeed him. Chifley was prime minister from July 1945 to December 1949. There was no contemporary political biography of him – perhaps surprising given his stature as a much-loved Labor icon. Or perhaps not. The Melbourne *Advocate* noted during his prime ministership that Chifley 'lacks the professional politician's sense of personal publicity'.[21]

Biography played a not insignificant role in Chifley's self-education, helping to make up for the scant schooling he received in rural Bathurst as a child. The teenage Chifley subscribed to Dymock's Library in Sydney and would receive parcels of eight books at a time on loan. The 'staple was historical biographies and general historical works', according to political scientist and author of the first posthumous biography of Chifley, LF 'Fin' Crisp, with Plutarch's *Lives* remained a Chifley favourite. 'For a keenly ruminative lad,' Crisp wrote, 'the way of endless historical biographies may well have offered a more rewarding approach than the classics of socialist theory to the realities of politics – and especially Australian Labor politics'.[22]

For Chifley the human dimension was important. Treasury official Sir William Dunk recalls that Chifley 'loved stories which shed light on human foibles, human failings, or for that matter human strengths', including his own.[23] The journalist Jack Fingleton recalls Chifley recounting the story, for example, of a meeting at which Chifley and his labour movement foe, former NSW premier Jack Lang, both spoke.

> Jack Lang was blaring away on the opposite corner, and it was the early days of the loud speaker. Well, Chif had no loud speaker – in fact, he had very little audience. There were just a few chaps there, including a most miserable-looking character down in the front who never took his eyes off Chif. And Chif told us how he got down from the platform at the finish, and this chap looked up at him and said, 'By gawd, you're hated, aren't you?' Well, Chif told this story with great relish.[24]

At least one person encouraged Chifley to agree to a biography while in office and, failing that, offered assistance should he wish to write an autobiography. Fin Crisp knew Chifley personally and twice 'discussed with him the possibility of his having his life written and I did in fact offer to help in any way if he chose at any stage to write an autobiography', he told Chifley's friend, solicitor Bill Taylor, after Chifley's death.[25] 'He was, I think, mildly interested but always rather shrugged off a definite decision on the subject'.

Chifley was probably humouring Crisp. Politely entertaining the idea, then doing nothing, was more likely part of what political scientist AF Davies describes as 'life-long self-effacingness, a determination, as it were, not to have a private life, or emotions that others could seize one by, but to be the free-standing, unruffled, impossibly conscientious one, asking nothing for himself, immolated in saving work'.[26] Davies, in fact, used the adjective 'ruthless' at the beginning of this observation, which seems at odds with Chifley's famously quiet confidence and easy-going demeanour.

Changes affecting the Canberra Press Gallery after Curtin's death suggest, however, that distance may have been a deliberate element of Chifley's political method, at least compared to Curtin. In a *Sunday Telegraph* piece headlined 'Canberra has lost all its old zest for living' published a year after Curtin's death and Chifley's ascension, Whitington details a drastic curtailment of media privileges under Chifley, ranging from far less prime ministerial access to restrictions on the amount of alcohol and cigarettes journalists were able to purchase at Parliament House.[27] In contrast to the 'Curtin Circus' of a dozen senior journalists who were 'almost a part of his official entourage' and travelled with Curtin constantly, under Chifley, 'When the PM travels, he travels alone, except on election tours'.

An unsourced note in Crisp's research files provides a detailed account of Chifley's attitude to his attire, saying that while he disliked ostentation he was 'very particular as to quality, fit etc'. His shirts were made to order by Myer, his shoes were by 'Johns' of King Street, Sydney, and his tailor was 'Day & Co.' at Bull's Chambers in Martin Place.[28] Attached to the note, and lending credence to it, are carbon copies of two letters Chifley wrote in the last year of his prime ministership to Myer concerning his shirt purchases. One says that shirts recently supplied were 'rather wide in the opening', and requests an invoice since the one accompanying the shirts showed no charge.[29] The other has Chifley informing Myer that he has sent by separate mail a shirt and collar of the correct material and fit, asking them to produce '3 shirts with 4 collars for each shirt to the same measurements and from similar material, but without stripes'. The previous shirts supplied 'were a shade on the tight side, and the collar opening was not quite right'.[30]

Why is this important? Public perceptions of Chifley were apparently well established but in a way that contends with this picture of the careful dresser. As journalist Victor Courtney wrote in a Perth *Sunday Times Magazine* profile a few weeks after Chifley became prime minister, 'He was an engine-driver, as you know', as though this was his very essence.[31] Chifley told caucus in the run up to the 1946 election that he knew his limitations and was under no illusions about them. 'Within myself I am nothing', he said. 'We cannot win ... unless from the ranks come strength, warmth and friendliness'.[32]

Academic Leicester Webb suggested in observations made soon after Chifley's death that there was more of a consciously thespian side to his political persona than generally understood. 'No estimate of him can ignore the fact that he was a superb actor and that the popular conception of him was the one which he assiduously played for'.[33] In Webb's view, this did not imply insincerity. 'Chifley, one suspects, knew that he was required to set an example, and he set it with real artistry', Webb wrote. 'Integrity is the quality which emerges most clearly ... the quality which made him a transcendent political leader'.

Chifley's comment to Labor MP Fred Daly suggests there is something to Webb's insight. '"You know Daly," he said, "you want to be scrupulously honest, but there's nothing to stop you being a bit bloody foxy." And I thought it was pretty sound advice'.[34] The unsourced note in Crisp's research files which details Chifley's care concerning clothes includes anecdotes perhaps illustrating Chifley's advice.

> I told Mr Chifley on one occasion when he returned from a trip to London that there had been a par in the Sydney papers to the effect that 'Mr Chifley arrived in London yesterday, looking very fit, in what appeared to be the same suit he had worn two years ago' which pleased him very much, as he did not like any article of clothing to look 'new'. He was very pleased with a camel hair overcoat which Dr Evatt brought back from overseas. He had owned something similar previously, which he referred to as his 'dead man's coat' as some old chap whom he knew only slightly bequeathed it to him. He wore that one till the new one appeared on the scene.[35]

That care over his clothes was confined to his public presentation is underlined when the source of the note goes on to say that Chifley did not begin wearing a dressing gown until a couple of years before he died, and prior to that at the Hotel Kurrajong, where he lived when in Canberra, used to 'stroll round the corridors ... in his pyjamas' and 'if the weather was cold, he would add his cardigan'.[36]

Chifley believed public opinion was 'fickle' and was unlikely to have considered contemporary political biography a political tool of lasting impact. '[T]hough they may be praising you today they can very easily turn round and condemn you tomorrow', he told Labor MP Gil Duthie.[37] 'Still ... it is good to have them on your side at least sometimes'.

Chifley's defeat at the 1949 election by Robert Menzies was one such fickle turn of events. The failure of Menzies' first prime ministership, during a time of utmost national peril, had seemed final. Yet he got a second chance, which resulted this time in a record sixteen years in power. How Menzies handled lingering doubts about him the second time round is described in the previous chapter. His coalition successors who saw out the 1960s, Harold Holt and John Gorton, heralded a nascent turn from the old to a new kind of Australia.

Harold Holt succeeded Menzies to the Liberal leadership and prime ministership in January 1966 and died in office in December 1967. Beyond the characterisation of him as 'Fair, firm, forthright, friendly' in a mid-term eight-page Liberal Party pamphlet, he was not the subject of a contemporary biography written during his political career.[38] The first, Tom Frame's posthumous biography *The Life and Death of Harold Holt*, was published nearly forty years after the end of his prime ministership through death by drowning at Cheviot Beach in Victoria. Frame says Holt was 'not a great reader and showed little interest in history', and that there is no evidence Holt ever considered writing an autobiography or was interested in a biography being written of him.[39]

Frame makes this judgment partly on the basis of an exchange between Holt and former prime minister Stanley Bruce. After Holt succeeded Menzies, Bruce suggested how he might handle intending biographers. Bruce's main point was that in cooperating with Cecil Edwards' biography of him, he had maintained the right of veto over anything from his personal papers. 'Any vetoing I have done has been very limited and mainly confined to not including any of my private notes regarding people who are still alive', Bruce wrote, implying this might be a position useful for Holt to adopt in similar circumstances.[40] 'Holt's reply bordered on indifference', according to Frame; beyond maintaining a scrapbook of clippings concerning his political career from 1934 onwards, Holt, he says, 'appeared largely unconcerned with how history would view him or his government'.[41]

However, Frame does not support his claim concerning Holt's alleged indifference. There is no letter from Holt in reply to Bruce's on file to back it; rather, Bruce's letter has a note that 'PM thanked Lord Bruce when he was in England in July' pencilled onto its bottom left-hand corner, likely by a Holt staffer.[42] Moreover, that Holt maintained a scrapbook for his entire political career suggests that he was at least somewhat concerned with how history would view him rather than, as Frame suggests, the reverse. It is a practice which at least one other modern prime minister with no particular accord for the written word, but with a passionate interest in how history would view him, maintained: Paul Keating.[43]

Holt did, in fact, have an image problem. Frame cites the parallel Geoffrey Bolton later drew between Menzies and Holt with Winston Churchill and Anthony Eden, that Holt was 'too long the crown prince'; journalist Craig McGregor's view of Holt as a 'smiling, dapper, plasticine man'; and psychologist and social commentator Ronald Conway's assessment of him as an 'intelligent, decent man (but) ... also a garrulous public bore – yet another bookkeeper thrust upon high'.[44] Journalist David McNicoll judged Holt 'too long in the shade of the Menzies oak'.[45]

The most compelling description of Holt's image problem, however, comes from the memoir of Holt's brief army, and long-time parliamentary, colleague and Liberal whip, Henry 'Jo' Gullett. Gullett describes meeting the then thirty-something Holt in a Seymour hotel early in World War II, when Holt had joined the AIF and been posted to the same artillery regiment. Holt liked army life and was looking forward to overseas service, according to Gullett, but soon made what was in Gullett's view the mistake of accepting Menzies' call in 1941 to rejoin the government frontbench after three key ministers including Gullett's father, Sir Henry Gullett, were killed in the Canberra Air Disaster.[46]

> In the years after the war I came to know him well and he was a very good politician. But he lacked authority and public reputation. A very nice man, an experienced fair-minded man, yes. But to the mass of his fellow Australians what was he? What label could they put on him? He was not an engine driver like

Ben Chifley. He did not have Menzies' brilliance. He was just another professional politician. And he could so easily have been 'Digger Holt'.[47]

Nevertheless, as Frame notes, Holt was acknowledged by both sides of politics as Menzies' obvious successor, and the media, many of whose members reciprocated Menzies' dislike of them, initially treated him well. Frame quotes from a *Current Affairs Bulletin* commentary at the time of the succession in 1966, that Holt's personality was more in keeping with 'contemporary Australia' than that of Menzies.[48] 'His physical appearance is that of an active rather than a spectator sportsman', the commentary continues. 'Privately a hard, methodical, cautious worker, Holt takes care to project a gay, debonair, vaguely reckless public image'.

This public image was created through photographs of Holt spearfishing, tackling vigorous surf and, notoriously, being photographed with young, beautiful women, as in the famous Portsea picture with his three bikini-clad daughters-in-law taken shortly after becoming prime minister. If a picture is worth a thousand words, such photographs saved Holt the hundred thousand or so words which a contemporary political biography designed to bolster his image would have required. It suggests the schoolboy talent for sport and theatre noted by Ian Hancock, combined with strong entertainment industry connections – his father and brother worked in the film and radio industries, and Harold himself in 1935 was secretary of the Cinematographic Exhibitors' Association. Holt had his own method of moulding and projecting his image independently of biography.[49]

There is another possible explanation, beyond text not having much resonance for Holt, and the comparative efficacy of photographic images in projecting a more attractive image: irregular aspects to his family history and his apparently chronic infidelity. After Holt's death, in response to the claim of his last lover Marjorie Gillespie that he had planned to leave his wife Zara for her, Zara Holt claimed there 'were dozens of women in the woodwork ... it was going on all the time'.[50] This added a new complexion to Menzies' private view that politically, Holt's 'besetting sin (was that) he wanted everybody to love him'.[51]

There were several additional factors from earlier in his life which could also have made a contemporary biography risky for Holt. His parents divorced while he was a boy, for example; and his own early love life had not gone smoothly. At 27 years old, despite a long relationship with Zara Dickens with whom he planned marriage, Harold formed a relationship with 24-year-old Viola 'Lola' Thring. Frame argues this may have prompted Zara Dickens' decision to travel overseas where, in Britain, she met the India-based British army officer James Fell, whom she soon married. Harold's continued pursuit of Lola Thring was complicated by the fact that his father Tom, 25 years her senior, was also wooing her. The next year, in 1936, Harold's father won Thring's hand and to Harold's chagrin, Lola became his stepmother.[52]

In 1937, the now Zara Fell returned to Melbourne for the birth of her first son. By the time she returned to India, she was pregnant with twins, conceived in Australia in 1938. Her marriage to Fell ended shortly afterwards, and she returned to Melbourne. When Zara married Holt in 1946, Holt adopted her sons as his own. Frame surmises the several years between the end of Zara's marriage to Fell and her marriage to Holt was to protect Holt from any implication he caused the break-up. Further, there was a 'long-standing Holt family "secret"' that Holt, not Fell, was the twins' father, confirmed by the strong likeness between Holt and the twins.[53] These were not the kind of personal complications a serving politician could afford to have aired without, given the times, considerable scandal and political damage.

John McEwen was caretaker prime minister during the 23-day interregnum between Holt's death in December 1967 and John Gorton's election as Liberal leader and Holt's successor in January 1968. Like

Fadden before him, McEwen was the long-serving leader of the Country Party, the junior member of the Liberal-led governing coalition of the day. In line with coalition convention, McEwen acted as prime minister ten times during Menzies' tenure, often for long periods.[54] Peter Golding, author of a posthumous biography, reckons McEwen's acting prime ministership at a cumulative 550 days over the Menzies, Holt and Gorton governments combined – longer than the prime ministerships of Watson, Reid, Cook and Page, and almost as long as Holt and McMahon.[55] This paralleled the experience of Fadden who at a cumulative 692 days as acting prime minister, and prime minister in his own right for 40 days after Menzies' leadership imploded in 1941, slightly outdid McEwen in terms of days served at the top.

In terms of policy influence, however, there is no contest. McEwen – nicknamed 'Black Jack' by Menzies, who varied it on occasion to 'Le Noir'[56] – was one of twentieth century Australia's most influential politicians. Through his generation-long tenure in the commerce and trade portfolio, McEwen acted as the sheet-anchor for the protectionist economic policies which defined postwar conservative politics for decades, and was Australia's advocate in the more sophisticated approach to international trade negotiations which developed in the postwar period. In the early 1950s, Menzies repeatedly hinted to McEwen that he should switch parties and 'get in line behind him' for the prime ministership. 'Menzies came back to this point again and again over a period of about five years, but I could not contemplate leaving the Country Party for my own preferment', McEwen wrote in a privately published memoir after his retirement.[57] There was no contemporary political biography of him.

McEwen's personal and policy distaste for the free-trader William 'Billy' McMahon saw him veto a possible McMahon succession after Holt's death, telling McMahon, 'Bill, I will not serve under you because I don't trust you'.[58] Liberal Party reliance on Country Party MPs for a majority in the House of Representatives made McMahon's candidacy impossible and he withdrew, opening the way for Senator John Gorton to stand for and win the Liberal leadership – the first and only time a prime minister–elect has come from the other place. Gorton resigned from the Senate, stood for the late Holt's seat of Higgins and entered the House of Representatives as prime minister thanks to McEwen's veto of McMahon.[59]

———

Gorton was prime minister from January 1968 to March 1971, and the subject of one contemporary biography: Alan Trengove's *John Grey Gorton: An informal biography* published in December 1969, just after Gorton successfully fought the 1969 federal election. Seven decades after Federation, Gorton was only the third Australian prime minister to be the subject of a published contemporary political biography, after Hughes and Curtin, or the fourth if one includes Seth's biography of Menzies for young readers. He seems to be the first Australian prime minister to use a biography pre-emptively to introduce sensitive personal matters into the public domain, before his political enemies exploited them.

The biography's genesis lay in an interview Gorton gave Trengove in the lounge of his Narrabundah home the morning after he became prime minister, among evidence of the previous night's celebrations. Trengove was a feature writer with the Herald & Weekly Times group, attached to its mass-selling Melbourne morning daily, the *Sun News-Pictorial*, at the time the book was written. It was neither a definitive biography nor a 'profusely annotated political work', Trengove says at the outset, but rather 'is journalism'.[60] The book 'attempts to tell as simply as possible the story of a complex man who, through an extraordinary series of circumstances, found himself Prime Minister of Australia on 9 January, 1968'.

The circumstances were extraordinary indeed. The then opposition leader Gough Whitlam, in Tokyo when Gorton became prime minister–elect, sent him a message: 'Your party's given me a formidable opponent. I'm looking forward with zest to our contest'.⁶¹ Whitlam's press secretary Graham Freudenberg later commented that 'more than zest, he was looking forward to it with great curiosity as to what the bloke was like'.⁶² Trengove himself was something of an admirer.

> Indeed I would not otherwise have embarked on the inherently difficult exercise of trying to write an honest book about a living person. While it may be that in the upshot what I have written is generally of a favourable tenor, there are several facets of Mr Gorton's story which few practising politicians, let alone a Prime Minister, would relish having published about themselves. That Mr Gorton, who read the final manuscript, did not try to effect any suppression or make any major changes, reveals in itself something about the man.⁶³

In this sense, Gorton was a precursor to the knockabout, tell-all confidence later manifested by Labor prime minister Bob Hawke.

Indeed, Gorton's life was one of knockabout confidence, Hemingwayesque in tenor. Trengove reveals that as a student at Brasenose College, Oxford, Hemingway was Gorton's literary hero and Gorton had a 'vague ambition' himself of becoming a writer. Hemingway started off writing short stories, and while at Oxford so did Gorton. With other Oxford friends he holidayed regularly in Spain, of which Hemingway was a noted habitué. Gorton took in fiestas and bullfights, went on long ocean swims and met his future wife Bettina 'Betty' Brown, a Sorbonne languages student and sister of his Rhodes Scholar mathematician friend Henry Brown. He befriended the son of *39 Steps* author John Buchan, and spent a vacation with him roughing it as a deckhand on a fishing trawler working between Britain and Iceland. The Buchan connection helped Gorton place a novel by his father's friend, Jean Campbell, with the London publisher Hutchison, for which Gorton – 'nearly always broke at Oxford' – sought expenses and something in lieu of the then standard 10 per cent agent's fee.⁶⁴

On his return to Australia, with the now Betty Gorton, he intended becoming a journalist and was to join the Melbourne *Herald* staff; Betty, just 20 years old, was to resume her interrupted romance languages study by enrolling as an undergraduate at the University of Melbourne. These plans derailed when in January 1936 Gorton's father fell ill and died, leaving Gorton responsible for the family's debt-ridden 350–acre orchard near the northern Victorian town of Mystic Park. 'This unhappy development compelled his son to give up ideas of journalism or any other occupation, and to concentrate upon saving the orchards', Trengove writes. It also dashed Betty's study plans.[65] They moved north and undertook the heavy grind of making an orchard on a 'harsh piece of inland Victoria, flat, dusty and extremely hot' work.[66]

At that time Mystic Park was not on the main power grid. The Gortons, writes Trengove, ordered books regularly from a Melbourne library and often read them under the 'soft light of Aladdin lamps' because their own 32-volt generator frequently broke down. They shared a common interest in the American Civil War. Betty, originally from the northern state of Maine, argued the Union case while Gorton, favouring the underdog, defended the Confederacy while ultimately conceding that a Union victory was necessary for the United States to emerge as a strong, cohesive nation.

Abraham Lincoln's life was a crucial influence on the young Gorton, according to Trengove: 'Gorton read every important biography of Lincoln, whom he came to admire more than any other man in history'. While others had left their marks on him, 'the trials and triumphs of the sixteenth President of the United States, recorded in countless books, deeply impressed him'.[67] Trengove even detected a touch of Gettysburg Address in a 'polished, emotional and evocative speech' Gorton gave at the 500 person–strong Mystic Park dinner in April 1946 welcoming returning soldiers from the area home. Gorton had had a dramatic World War II experience, in which he suffered two near-death plane crashes. A few months after the Mystic Park dinner he took up his first representative role as councillor for the North-West

Riding of the Kerang Shire Council.[68] Twenty-one years later Gorton was leading the nation.

Trengove observed that no Australian prime minister had created such enormous controversy in such a short space of time as Gorton, and that his personality had consequently been subject to unprecedented and often unfavourable scrutiny by commentators and rivals.[69] The matters of personality and character were paramount at this particular moment within both the Liberal Party, whose leader in government was by convention prime minister, as well as within the wider coalition, as the last of the Menzies 'line' exhausted itself competing for leadership without policy differences between them really being an issue.

Upon Holt's death, Gorton and Paul Hasluck 'were either supported or rejected on grounds largely of personality and character' in the contest to succeed him, Hancock notes.[70] McEwen and McMahon were bitter adversaries over trade and economic policy, but it was personality and character – 'I will not serve under you because I don't trust you'[71] – that drove the McEwen veto of a McMahon candidature at that point, not policy differences. In these circumstances, Trengove's biography of Gorton, early in an already controversial premiership, could be of major tactical importance, especially against the backdrop of attacks by a lacerating Whitlam. 'The Augustan simplifications of Sir Robert Menzies and the cheery simplicities of Mr Holt have been replaced by the confused superficialities of Mr Gorton', Whitlam opined upon Gorton's succession.[72]

For an admitted admirer, Trengove maintains a fair equilibrium in the biography. Not until his final chapter, 'The Gorton Style', does a hint of open advocacy emerge, but by then it is unmistakable. 'I believe criticism is all part of politics', he quotes Gorton in this chapter:

> But I don't like criticism when it becomes very personal. And then again some criticism in this country is repeatedly wrong because it is based on wrong premises. The critics appear to operate on the assumption that by continually using a wrong 'fact' such as so-

and-so is a crony or that there has been a radical change of policy they eventually make it right.

If Gorton succeeded, Trengove concludes, Australia will become an 'industrially and spiritually strong nation with a new sense of national identity', leaving behind 'her piffling and costly inter-state rivalries' and denying none the 'chance to fulfil himself in his chosen field or stake a claim in national development'. Australia would 'care for those who are beyond adequately caring for themselves', Trengove continued, and externally 'pose a threat to no-one'.[73] Journalist Allan Barnes in his review of the biography wrote that while Trengove is 'strongly prejudiced' towards Gorton, he also 'exposes honestly many of his weaknesses as well as his strengths'.[74] In this sense, just as Gorton presaged something of the Hawke style, so did his biographer, who in revealing Gorton's illegitimacy anticipated the revelatory approach Hawke biographer Blanche d'Alpuget would later employ.

Gerard Henderson argues that Gorton's problem was not that his behaviour was 'dramatically unusual or untoward' but rather that he failed to conceal his 'unorthdoxy' while prime minister.[75] This made Trengove's book more than usually important; it disappointed neither Gorton's admirers nor his critics. The former were rewarded with, at 251 pages, a surprisingly good biographical story, concisely and well told, covering Gorton's irregular childhood, his Oxford years, World War II fighter pilot exploits, hard grafting as an irrigation block orchardist at Mystic Park, and surprise ascension to power.

Gorton's critics could seize on the fact that the man whom they considered, as the Australian argot had it, such a bastard, literally was one. Gorton's father separated from his first wife Kathleen and fell in love with Alice Sinn, with whom he fathered a daughter, Ruth, then a son, John. Kathleen would not give John's father the divorce necessary for him to marry Alice, hence Gorton's illegitimacy. Upon Alice's death from tuberculosis when John was 7 years old, his father sent him to be brought up by his childless wife, Kathleen, who had already taken in Ruth as Alice's health declined.[76] While merely a sad personal story now, it was somewhat scandalous in the social mores of late 1960s Australia; comments Henderson, 'it was a big story'.[77] This was compounded by the fact that even had John's father and Alice Sinn been married, it would have been 'mixed' since Gorton was Anglican and Alice, child of an immigrant German father and Irish mother, was Catholic – still a matter of comment to some in late 1960s Australia despite the precedent of the Catholic Ben Chifley's marriage to Protestant Elizabeth McKenzie.[78]

Henderson surmises that Gorton 'briefed his biographer' about his illegitimacy.[79] Hancock, author of a second, late life biography of Gorton, suggests the reverse, that when Trengove 'came upon the story of illegitimacy, Gorton confirmed it'.[80] Either way, as Trengove points out in his author note, Gorton read his final manuscript and declined to make any 'major changes'; he had the opportunity to conceal his illegitimacy and did not take it.[81]

This was something of a risk given the times and it was typical of Gorton to run it. It marked a distinct break in the culture of both Australian politics and contemporary political biography in Australia. Publication of Trengove's book was the moment when disclosing, rather than concealing, sensitive personal information not only became an option for leaders, but also a potential inoculant against political rivals, internal or external, using it in a more devasting manner. Trengove was also the first Australian journalist–biographer subsequently thanked by a later historian–biographer for his efforts. 'In the process, he collected priceless material covering John Gorton's life before politics, and he was most generous in passing on copies of important letters', Hancock wrote in the acknowledgments of *John Gorton: He Did It His Way*, written when Gorton was in his early nineties.[82]

William 'Bill' McMahon became prime minister after Gorton's maverick style combined with internal Liberal Party division saw Gorton fail to carry a confidence motion in his own party room, casting the deciding vote against himself and forfeiting office. This time the Country Party, now led by Doug Anthony who succeeded McEwen just a month before, dropped the veto which blocked McMahon from becoming prime minister after Holt's death. McMahon's term of office lasted from March 1971 until December 1972. 'He was determined, like other little Caesars, to destroy Mr Gorton', Gough Whitlam declared of him. 'He sat there on the Isle of Capri [in Surfers Paradise] plotting his destruction – Tiberius with a telephone'.[83]

McMahon was extremely mindful of the historical record. The guide to the McMahon Papers deposited at the National Library of Australia runs to 171 single-spaced pages.[84] Yet there was no biography of McMahon until 2018, although it is Canberra lore that McMahon was always on the hunt for a biographer. His drive to be storied is perhaps comparable to that of Hughes who at one point had three different writers working on contemporary biographies of him in ignorance of each other. McMahon was acutely aware of both sides of the political biography equation: its potential to either lift up or drag down a subject's standing. The McMahon Papers include a file, for example, containing all five excerpts of the serialisation in Herald & Weekly Times group newspapers around Australia of Trengove's biography of Gorton upon its publication in December 1969. Each excerpt has negative and therefore potentially exploitable material concerning Gorton – useful to a rival like McMahon – marked in pen. Whether this is by McMahon's own hand or that of one of his staff is somewhat academic since the file has been expressly retained in McMahon's own papers.[85]

Peter Sekuless notes that McMahon's reputation 'has been defined by his enemies' but this, he says, was McMahon's own fault since, 'He frustrated attempts to publish his memoirs and closed access to his personal papers'.[86] Parts of the McMahon Papers remained closed for decades after his death. In the early 1980s, Whitlam employed Mark Latham to work on his political memoirs.[87] Latham's office was adjacent to McMahon's and he recalls it was cluttered with filing cabinets of documents containing the 'full archival history of the Menzies, Holt, Gorton and McMahon governments'.

> His abiding frustration was in getting his memoirs published ... Billy employed a succession of researchers and ghost writers, but none of them could satisfy his demand for an immaculate memoir: the prime minister who never made a mistake.[88]

According to Latham, McMahon even asked him to undertake a biography, apparently unperturbed by the political divide; Latham declined the invitation. Patrick Mullins' biography, *Tiberius with a Telephone: The Life and Stories of William McMahon* was published in 2018.[89] Running to nearly 600 pages, McMahon would likely have approved.

Two months before the December 1972 election, political scientist Henry Mayer reviewed the relative positions of McMahon and Whitlam. Whitlam had 'low approval figures', Mayer noted, while McMahon seemed to be a case of 'the Peter Principle – people are promoted until they reach their level of incompetence – at work'. Mayer cast back to early 1971, when McMahon's image was positive and contrasted favourably with that of Gorton who by then had 'a reputation for being a brumby – wild, unpredictable, unreliable'. Poor touch in office quickly turned McMahon's perceived positive qualities in 1971 into negatives by 1972, a 'series of new clichés', as Mayer puts it, taking hold.

> McMahon is fatally indecisive. (1971: he is properly cautious.) He dithers endlessly over the phone. (1971: he consults widely.) He has no guts, otherwise he would have chopped off the heads of Gorton and his pals and shut them up. (1971: he cannot afford to split the party further; he must seek consensus.) He lacks even an ounce

of charisma. (1971: charisma means risk – see Gorton. Let's have safety.) He looks bad on TV; has the wrong voice; his ears are too big; how can one respect little Billy Boy? (1971: what a fighting Bantam cock, not handsome, but game. Remember how tall Napoleon was?)[90]

McMahon lost the 1972 election and the 23 year run of conservative federal governments ended, and with it the Menzies line. Something more changed too: the culture of contemporary political biography. With Whitlam's advent it would become a presence in Australian politics as it had never been before.

Chapter 5
The modern era begins

Is it possible that Australians so easily allowed the destruction of the Whitlam Government, and then endorsed those who had procured its destruction, because they saw a government so palpably reflecting themselves – and, after the shock of self-recognition, were rather relieved to see the image smashed?

Graham Freudenberg,
A Certain Grandeur: Gough Whitlam in Politics

No Prime Minister worth their weight in superphosphate should be without an autobiography.

'Beckett Green', Great Frasers of Our Time

Gough Whitlam won office in December 1972, Labor's first prime minister in twenty-three years and the first Labor prime minister elected from opposition since Jim Scullin in 1929. It was an ecstatic moment for those who longed to shake off the old imperial yoke to which conservative coalition governments had kept the country tethered. The government's legislative agenda dramatically modernised Australian life and ushered in the first great social justice push since the Chifley Government lost power in 1949. Whitlam governed until 'The Dismissal' in November 1975 when Governor-General Sir John Kerr sacked him and appointed opposition leader Malcolm Fraser caretaker prime minister in a still controversial 'constitutional coup'.

Whitlam's election also heralded a new era in contemporary political biography in Australia. His personal standing with voters was not high according to market research in the two years leading up to Labor's 1972 election win, yet he would go on to become an iconic prime minister. Whitlam would also become the most written about Australian prime minister, rivalled only by Bob Hawke.

An intriguing, dramatic and historically significant subject, Whitlam was the focus of two substantial biographies during his active political career, the first by Canberra Press Gallery journalist Laurie Oakes, and the second by his own speechwriter, Graham Freudenberg.[1] The Oakes biography was one of his quartet of books covering Whitlam and his government, two of them co-written with *Canberra Times* political correspondent David Solomon, an old friend from Sydney University student days. Together Oakes and Solomon wrote *The Making of an Australian Prime Minister* charting Whitlam's ascension to office, and *Grab For Power: Election 74*.[2] In between Oakes, as sole author, wrote *Whitlam PM: A biography*, published in 1973. The fourth work, Oakes' *Crash Through or Crash: The Unmaking of a Prime Minister* was published after Whitlam was sacked as prime minister and was once again opposition leader.[3] While only one of these is strictly a biography, Whitlam is the protagonist in them all and together the books form a prime ministerial quartet unmatched in scope and depth in Australian political biography, with a classic 'rise and fall' narrative arc. Graham Freudenberg's *A Certain Grandeur: Gough Whitlam in Politics* was published in late 1977 during Whitlam's second period of opposition leadership, and was launched just before Fraser called an early election.

The lives of exceptional leaders – Alexander the Great, Julius Caesar and especially Napoleon, of whom he made a particular study – were a childhood preoccupation for Whitlam. Significantly it was the civic and legal, rather than the martial, achievements of Napoleon which appealed to young Gough.[4] The interest in biography continued into adulthood. Whitington noted that the bookshelves at Whitlam's home in Cabramatta when opposition leader were 'loaded with biographies'.[5]

Something of the mature Whitlam's attitude to biography emerges in his foreword to Irwin Young's 1971 biography of EG 'Ted' Theodore, the treasurer in Scullin's Depression-era government. Theodore's political career was ruined by the so-called 'Mungana Affair' in which he was accused of secretly profiting from the sale of mining leases around Mungana in North Queensland. A royal commission called by a politically hostile Queensland state government found against him. Theodore arranged to have criminal charges brought against himself in a bid to clear his name but despite his acquittal, gross damage to his reputation had already been done.

Whitlam comments on the potentially devastating consequences of a reputation besmirched: 'The Labor story of the next two years is of the total eclipse of Theodore, the twilight of Scullin', and, with the emergence of Curtin and Chifley, 'the slow dawn of Labor recovery', he wrote. This was significant for both Labor, and Australian, history. Labor's Depression-era treasurer was arguably 'the first Keynesian with power', albeit one frustrated by internal Labor (in the person of Jack Lang) and external political foes including a hostile Senate, a conservative banking establishment and continuing constraints imposed by the imperial relationship with Britain. This made Australia's experience of the Depression that much worse than it needed to be, Whitlam argued. While the United States had the morale-boosting 'New Deal', Australians had to 'make do with the divisive, discriminatory and demoralizing Premiers' Plan'.[6]

In the foreword Whitlam also reflected on Churchill's reluctance to write the biography of his forebear, the Duke of Marlborough, fearing he might find Macaulay's charges of corruption and treason against Marlborough correct. He recounted how Churchill delayed for twenty years, only to find that fear ill-founded. With Theodore, a 'similar inhibition may have discouraged Australian writers and historians from dealing in depth with the career of one of Australia's few authentic statesmen', Whitlam wrote. 'Even our noblest historian, Manning Clark, with all his poet's compassion and philosopher's comprehension for the human weakness within all human greatness, dismisses Theodore in an unusually harsh and untypically shallow paragraph'.[7] The misfortune dogging Theodore's political career dogged Young's biography of him too, Whitlam noted. Young amassed facts and laid the foundation for a definitive work but died before finishing it, with the result that the book 'remains the scaffolding of the definitive life' of Theodore, considered by Chifley Australia's greatest treasurer and by Whitlam as one of Australia's best parliamentarians.[8]

This ill luck and neglect was characteristic of the thread of failure and frustration that seemed to stalk Australian leaders, and which led Manning Clark to see our history in 'essentially tragic terms', according to Whitlam.

> There is indeed a deep poignancy in the fate of a remarkably long list of our chief figures from the very beginning: Phillip embittered and exhausted; Bligh disgraced; Macquarie despised here and discredited at home; Macarthur mad; Wentworth rejecting the meaning of his own achievements; Parkes bankrupt; Deakin outliving his superb faculties in a long twilight of senility; Fisher forgotten; Bruce living in self-chosen exile; Scullin heart-broken; Lyons dying in the midst of relentless intrigue against him; Curtin driven to desperation and to the point of resignation by some of his own colleagues at the worst period of the war.[9]

Most poignant of all is that four years after writing this, Whitlam himself became an addition to the list.

Whitlam had faith, or at least hope, in the power of biography. Despite the perceived shortcomings in Young's Theodore biography, he hoped it would 'explode' the myths surrounding Theodore, including the 'myth of Mungana'.[10] He was not, however, completely convinced of the virtues of biography in relation to himself. He did not reply to an interview request from James Walter, for example, who began research on a psychobiography of him in 1976 when Whitlam was in his second stint as opposition leader.[11] Walter found accounts of Whitlam's reluctance even to have profiles written. 'When in conversation the editor of a literary journal broached the subject, Whitlam simply pretended not to hear', Walter notes. 'But when a well-known journalist and novelist, who had been doing an esoteric series on Labor notables for a national weekly, approached him, Whitlam is reported to have responded: "A man would have to be a nymphomaniac for publicity to talk to you!"'[12]

Laurie Oakes was a young, emerging force on the national journalism scene when in 1970 he decided to wrestle with the mystery that was Whitlam. Oakes was Canberra bureau chief of the Melbourne *Sun News Pictorial*, Australia's biggest selling metropolitan daily newspaper, when he began researching *Whitlam PM*. Like Trengove's biography of Gorton, it would be published about a year into his subject's prime ministership.

Voters neither understood nor particularly liked Whitlam as opposition leader, and this remained the case in the run up to the 1972 election – the first at which Labor used market research at a national level as part of its campaign planning.[13] Mick Young was Labor's national secretary at the time and later revealed the dire perceptions of Whitlam as opposition leader underscored in polling conducted after a 'mini-campaign' in 1971. Direct quotes about Whitlam from voters in qualitative research groups at the time included:

> Ignores questions, and is evasive; justifies too much; cold, distant, not human; gives impotent answers to potent questions;

never seen with women; oily, irritating voice (but better than McMahon's); intelligent, intellectual loner; talks and qualifies too much; always knocking the government; not what he says, but the way he says it; does not hold attention; bends over backward *not* to offend; not rugged or manly; sorry for him ... seems to be in the wrong party; don't trust him; does not come across as strong.[14]

The findings contrasted with Oakes' own positive experiences with and perceptions of Whitlam, whom he found consistent in his attitudes and policies over the years, as well as displaying the utmost personal propriety; rather than insincere, he noted Whitlam was often criticised for being too frank.[15] Young commented later on Whitlam's 'healthy personal friendship' with many senior press gallery journalists, including 'the very young Laurie Oakes', but noted this 'was not helping to get rid of negative feelings the electorate at large had for the leader'.[16]

Oakes was part of the new generation of journalists, some like him with university educations, which in the 1960s began to displace the reigning one personified by Alan 'The Red Fox' Reid.[17] Oakes would later say, 'No other Australian political journalist has exercised such influence' as Reid, who was reporting on the Curtin Government when Oakes was born in the NSW steelworks city of Newcastle in 1943.[18] Oakes' mother, a department store retail assistant, resigned her position upon marriage and became a full-time homemaker. His father was an accountant in the resource sector and job moves during Laurie's childhood took the family from the east coast to the far north-west of Western Australia, then to central New South Wales. Oakes was educated at Lithgow High School, then the University of Sydney; Germaine Greer, Robert Hughes, Clive James and John Bell were varsity peers. Oakes edited the Sydney University student newspaper *Honi Soit* and graduated with a Bachelor of Arts in 1964. His journalistic rise was meteoric; he became the *Sun News Pictorial*'s Canberra bureau chief at the age of 25 in January 1969 and quickly became a press gallery titan in both print and broadcast media. Nearly a half-century later, in 2017,

Oakes retired from his final post as the Nine Network's longstanding national political editor, just eclipsing Reid's 48-year Canberra press gallery tenure.

Speaking to a journalism summer school in Canberra in 1965, Reid underlined the relative powerlessness of journalists to influence news coverage relative to their proprietors. Journalists are bricklayers, Reid said, and 'management has the right to reject any or all of the bricks he supplies or to lay them as it chooses'. In a more extended metaphor, Reid said that in the 'everyday, market place journalism of newspapers and periodicals which provide the great majority of Australian journalists with employment', the journalist is merely 'a private soldier'.

> A private soldier does not determine how any army is run. Nor does he decide where, when, how or why battles are fought. He can do what he conceives to be his duty to the best of his ability. He can fight courageously. He can live up to his concept of what should be the standards of his profession. He can ask – and keep on asking even at the risk of being charged with insubordination – that his officers give him a wider discretion. He can point out to his officers why the conferring of such discretion upon the individual – or at least the individual of tested ability – would be in the officers' and overall command's longterm interests.
>
> But it is the officers and the high command who make the ultimate decision on whether he is to be accorded that discretion. In fact, the journalist's role when described in realistic and not romantic terms has a resemblance to that attributed by Tennyson to those British horse soldiers who on October 25, 1854, galloped towards the Russian guns. 'Theirs not to reason why, Theirs but to do or die'.[19]

Reid was no private soldier. When Oakes arrived in Canberra in 1969, the extent to which Reid was a participant in political events rather than simply a journalist recording, reporting and explaining them was both obvious to him and the subject of considerable discussion among press gallery journalists. 'It is very difficult to report politics without getting involved to a degree', says Oakes, 'but to some of his peers Reid seemed almost as much of a political player as a journalist'.[20]

Oakes' talent lay in achieving Reid's degree of influence without himself becoming a political player. Journalist Sydney Deamer draws a crucial distinction between journalistic objectivity and fairness:

> There is no such thing as a good objective journalist. If you are not sensitive enough to feel for your subject, to have a point of view, to suffer joy or agony or sympathy about a story you are covering, you will never be a good journalist. Don't strive to be objective. Strive to be fair.[21]

Few would dispute that Oakes embodies Deamer's journalistic ideal.

Oakes began researching Whitlam in 1970, puzzling 'over what manner of man Whitlam really was'. By mid-1972, with the election only months away, 'misconceptions and confusion' about Whitlam's character were still reflected in adverse market research findings about him.[22] Whitlam's psychology was an object of inquiry in which Oakes employed, along with the standard journalistic ones, a novel approach. He wrote to artist Clifton Pugh, who he knew was painting Whitlam's portrait over the course of multiple sittings. 'When Pugh paints a portrait he draws his subject out, carefully studies the person's character, and tries to gain an understanding which he can project on to canvas', Oakes later wrote. 'He is quite a psychologist.'[23] Pugh, however, was struggling, telling Oakes he was on this fifth 'go' at a portrait and yet to find 'the man inside'.[24]

There were others also trying to work Whitlam out. Around the same time, only months before the 1972 election, David Frost asked Whitlam about Don Whitington's book *Twelfth Man?*, comprising profiles of the prime ministers he considered Australia's 'first eleven'.

Whitington approached the task with a psychological bent, informed partly by the work of University of Melbourne political scientist AF 'Foo' Davies, a key influence on the small but significant body of psychobiographical work on Australian politicians written in the postwar period.[25] In a chapter titled 'The Enigma', Whitington explores Whitlam as a potential twelfth man in his 'first eleven' of Australian prime ministers – with a question mark, since Whitlam was still opposition leader and, as the chapter title suggested, something of a mystery.

> FROST: Did you like the chapter about yourself?
>
> WHITLAM: Well I liked some of it, I didn't like other bits. But there again I don't mind. Don Whitington is a very perceptive writer. There were some things which he said which I hadn't fully realised.
>
> FROST: What revelation was there in the book ...
>
> WHITLAM: (I) think it would appear that I'm the first Prime Minister, or candidate for Prime Minister, since Robert Menzies, who's had an orthodox family background. You know, parents of his own ...
>
> FROST: They've all had parents, haven't they?
>
> WHITLAM: I don't want to pursue that ... it's a bit of an 'in' one in Australia. I think he makes this point which I hadn't so fully realised was an advantage to me. That is I was serene at home and I've had the usual chronology of married life since.[26]

Oakes found that Whitlam admired Menzies and was flattered by comparisons with him which were made as early as 1962, when he was acting opposition leader while Arthur Calwell was on medical leave. Whitlam saw a parallel between Menzies' reconstruction of the non-Labor parties over two parliamentary terms, leading to electoral victory in 1949, and his own internal reforms of the ALP over two terms of opposition, designed to result in a Labor victory in 1972.[27] Like Menzies, Whitlam tended to diffidence with colleagues and had a low tolerance for fools which, given the nature of politics and the typical makeup of the parliamentary ranks, made them relatively isolated figures within their own parties during their active political careers.

In choosing that aspect of Whitington's chapter, 'The Enigma', to comment upon, Whitlam avoided addressing its main thrust: Whitlam's lack of public definition as a leader and as a person in the run up to the 1972 election. 'Many voters regard him as inconclusive and indecisive, vacillating and hesitant, unconvincing because he lacks conviction himself', Whitington writes.

> Whitlam is the riddle of Australian politics in 1972 ... He is extremely ambitious, yet gives an impression of diffidence. He has vanity, but appears to be modest and unassuming. He is aggressive but apologetic, positive yet uncertain, strong and determined yet deceptively gentle. He can be defiant, even arrogant, yet gives an impression of humility.[28]

The Whitlam riddle, Whitington said, would be solved only when the electorate went to the polls.

In retrospect, Whitlam's lack of definition in the electorate while opposition leader, and the mystery he posed even to accomplished political journalists like Oakes and Whitington, seems incredible given how quickly he came to personify a most distinctive government. In 1974, while Whitlam was still prime minister, journalist Mungo MacCallum attributed this to the 'cynicism (which) has taken over Australian politics'. He noted the outrage some felt when Whitlam in power systematically did the things he had said he would in the decade leading up to office. 'Wasn't Whitlam meant to be just a pretty face, another well spoken private school product, a sheep in wolf's clothing who, when it came to the point, wanted to change very little?' MacCallum posed. '[V]ery few people had understood what Whitlam was about, and many of those who did couldn't believe it. He just didn't *look* like the traditional Australian idea of a socialist, democratic or otherwise, so no one believed he would act like one'.[29]

The dissonance in that early 1970s environment between Whitlam's background and party allegiance probably explains some of the puzzlement over the pre–prime ministerial Whitlam. Not all of it, though; he was indeed 'complex', as Oakes observed, adding, 'it is not surprising that there were misconceptions and confusion about his character'.[30] Oakes himself was something of an enigma: powerful, a persistent newsbreaker and somehow, in personality terms, unreadable. He and Whitlam were both in the vanguard of a new type of person in their respective fields: in Oakes' case, as a university educated journalist succeeding the previous generation of craft-trained reporters, and in Whitlam's, a federal Labor politician who was flagrantly middle class, not working class. Oakes would later point out in the biography that Whitlam was not the first university-educated federal Labor politician. HV 'Doc' Evatt was a University of Sydney medallist and Doctor of Laws (LLD). But unlike Evatt, the working-class son of a widowed mother, Whitlam grew up in solid middle-class circumstances, the son of Australia's crown solicitor.[31] Oakes quotes Whitlam's fondness for declaring, 'I was the first of the middle-class radicals'.[32]

Oakes began his research by interviewing Whitlam's wife Margaret, his sister, Presbyterian Ladies' College principal Freda Whitlam, and others who knew him from childhood. 'Most of them were still alive then', Oakes notes. 'They're not now'.

> I was fascinated by Whitlam. No-one knew anything about him. No-one knew anything much about his early life and it was fascinating ... I got a fair bit of material together first and made

sure that I had a book. And before I did any interviews with Gough, I made sure I had a publisher.[33]

The response of publishers was problematic. Oakes wrote to 'three or four' who expressed interest but wanted to see a completed manuscript, which 'wasn't any bloody use to me'. Richard Walsh at Angus & Robertson was the exception. Walsh signed the book after reading some chapters and wanted to publish it quickly but it did not appear until late 1973.

Earlier that year Cheshire had published *The Making of an Australian Prime Minister* concerning Whitlam's election to office, co-written by Oakes and Solomon. In the opening lines they place readers in the 500-strong crowd chanting 'We want Gough!' in the prime minister–elect's Cabramatta backyard on election night, 1972. It takes them then into the middle of the jostling press pack, scuffling for position outside Whitlam's sunroom door; blood spurts from a radio journalist's nose after a photographer punches him; Whitlam staffer Richard Hall places a cautionary hand on Whitlam's imposing son Tony who, trying to subdue the roiling press pack, is 'patient at first, then ... flushes angrily and clenches a fist'. Hall counsels, 'Easy, Tony'. In Bellevue Hill, across the other side of Sydney – at 'a far grander residence in a far grander suburb' – Bill McMahon watches Whitlam's victory speech on television and makes his own melancholy statement to the media: 'Then he turns away and ... plunges into the crowd clustering around the wrought-iron double gates and across the gravel driveway ... [his] diminutive figure ... lost from sight as he moves among the well-wishers ... accepting condolences'.[34]

Oakes and Solomon sum up the 1972 election with the observation that Labor won 'comfortably enough' but that the victory 'was a patchy one, and nothing like a landslide' – a fact which has since been lost from view. Labor actually lost seats in South Australia (Sturt), Western Australia (Forrest, Stirling) and Victoria (Bendigo), but picked up six in New South Wales, four in Victoria, and one each in Queensland

and Tasmania, leading to a net gain of eight seats. Liberal voters who switched to Labor in 1972 overwhelmingly attributed their decision to 'It's time for a change' according to exit polls cited by Oakes and Solomon. However, they went on to argue there was nothing 'magical' about the coalition's twenty-three years in office, and that the same voters could easily have, but did not, reach that conclusion six or nine years earlier. Interrogating the 'It's time' proposition, Oakes and Solomon conclude that Whitlam was 'an essential ingredient' in Labor's victory, and that it was the Menzies-like 'style and presence and intellectual depth' expected by voters which Whitlam possessed but McMahon, and before him Gorton, lacked, that made a difference. 'Whitlam is very much in the Menzies mould, and in many respects has been influenced by the former Liberal Prime Minister', they wrote. 'He acknowledged as much in a letter to Menzies nine days after the election'.[35]

Yet Whitlam's personal standing was not especially positive in the run up to the 1972 election and he suffered from nebulous, and in some respects negative, perceptions in the eyes of voters.[36] Nor does Whitlam's leadership emerge as a factor in the exit polls cited by Oakes and Solomon in *The Making of an Australian Prime Minister*. The book closes on a cautionary note: that the Liberals' experience from 1966 to 1972 showed that unity and discipline were needed as well as the advantage of incumbency to keep a party in power. 'The question for the Labor Party is whether the parallel between Menzies and Whitlam can be carried a stage further', Oakes and Solomon conclude. 'If Whitlam is able to exercise the authority over his party which Menzies exercised over the Liberals, Labor could be in office for a long time'.[37]

Whitlam PM appeared a year into his prime ministership. 'Gough was the sort of bloke you had to think about in psychological terms', Oakes recalls. 'He was different, and he was hard to work out'.[38] Oakes did so through a detailed and hitherto unknown account of Whitlam's forebears, childhood and life before politics as well as his animosity-marred rise through Labor's ranks to Australia's highest office.

The book opens with a playful take on Old Testament patriarchal lineages, beginning with Gough's great-grandfather.

> Frederick Whitlam, a former British army officer fresh from service in the Sikh wars in India, arrived in Victoria in the mid-nineteenth century, driven to the colony by grief over the death of his fiancée in England. He wandered around the Victorian gold diggings for a time, and then settled down to design and manage the Castlemaine botanic gardens. Frederick Whitlam begat Henry Hugh Gough Whitlam who begat Harry Frederick Ernest Whitlam who begat Edward Gough Whitlam who was destined to become the 22nd Prime Minister of Australia.[39]

In details large and small, the biography was a revelation. Gough's privileged Canberra childhood as the crown solicitor's son, for example; attribution of an otherwise inexplicable vocal style (directly and emphatically addressing people in conversation) to growing up the child of a near-deaf mother; coming to the notice of keen radio quiz listener Ben Chifley through his successes in ABC Radio's Treasury-sponsored 'Security Loan Quiz Championship' in the late 1940s – *Whitlam PM* revealed much about a person voters, and other press gallery journalists for that matter, knew so little about.[40]

While Oakes was fascinated by Whitlam, the biography was no panegyric; among the positive remarks, Oakes scatters hard truths. One concerned Whitlam's tendency 'to bore an audience with too little fire and too much detail, to act like a schoolmaster rather than a politician'. Oakes commented it was something 'he has never really overcome; in fact, something he has shown little desire to overcome'.[41] He wrote that Whitlam would 'lower his own standing by impetuous comments and outbursts of temper' in parliament in the 1960s, making hubristic statements which irritated some opposition colleagues as much as government MPs.[42]

Nevertheless, the overwhelming impression left by *Whitlam PM* is that of a rather brilliant and somewhat difficult person of immense potential impact on the nation. 'It is not without surprise that I have reached the conclusion, after reading the book, that Gough Whitlam, despite the warts, is a great Prime Minister, and a great man', Liberal MP Edward St John, friendly with Whitlam as fellow students at the University of Sydney but from the other side of politics, wrote in a review upon the book's publication. 'Time was when I repeated with approval the quip that "Gough Whitlam is a good performer, but not a leader" ... The book has helped me to see Gough in a truer perspective. I was wrong'.[43]

In the 'golden summer of 1972–73', as Freudenberg later described the immediate post-election period, Whitlam thought he would be prime minister for eight years and that Labor would govern for at least three terms.[44] By the time Oakes finished writing *Whitlam PM* just months later, in October 1973, Whitlam briefly, privately, resigned himself to only three years in office, before snapping out of his gloom after comprehensively besting opposition leader Billy Snedden in a parliamentary censure motion. Labor's stocks slumped for several reasons, important among which was party ill-discipline. The importance of Whitlam personally to his government's survival emerged strongly in Labor's own polling and caucus sensed that mood in the electorate. A 'despondent party had decided that he was its one real electoral asset, and expected him single-handedly to lift it out of the trough', Oakes wrote on the last page of *Whitlam PM*.

> This was put to him in depressingly blunt terms ... [H]is press secretary, Eric Walsh, and [ALP national secretary] David Combe, went to his office for a discussion on what could be done, and told him: 'You're the one thing the Government has going for it'. Whitlam, who had sprawled on a couch while he listened, told them wearily: 'As you say, the Government has one thing going for it – and if I were you, I wouldn't waste his time'.[45]

Six months later, in April 1974, Whitlam called a double dissolution election for 18 May in response to persistent opposition obstruction in the Senate. The government was returned with a barely decreased majority and, in the historic joint sitting of parliament afterwards, passed key legislative reforms, including the main bill creating Medibank (now Medicare), and the bill entrenching 'one vote, one value' electoral distributions. Oakes' and Solomon's account *Grab for Power: Election '74* remains the most detailed campaign book ever written in Australian politics. Labor's 'greatest assets' in the election were Whitlam's image, education policy and perceptions the government had not been given a 'fair go'. Oakes and Solomon conclude: 'Swing voters clearly perceived Whitlam as superior to Snedden, and this made a far greater impact on them than policies, issues or slogans'.[46]

The final book in Oakes' quartet on Whitlam and his government, *Crash Through or Crash*, details the downfall in what was described then, and probably still remains, the most dramatic year in Australia's peacetime political history. The opposition-controlled Senate blocked the government's budget bills, and on 11 November 1975 Kerr – an unelected vice-regal official – sacked the government and, for the first time, appointed as prime minister a person without a working majority in the House of Representatives, pending a December general election. Fraser had won the Liberal leadership on 21 March 1975 after sustained intrigue against the incumbent Snedden; now he was the architect of Whitlam's demise. Fraser's enemies said he was 'born with a silver spoon in his mouth – and a silver dagger in his hand', wrote Oakes.[47] His victim was hailed as a 'fallen hero' by Labor's own. Yes, 'Whitlam had crashed', but he got credit for 'almost single-handedly 'bringing Labor to power in 1972 and achieving major reform in office. '[T]he ALP was not prepared to send him into retirement in disgrace', Oakes observed. 'It refused to deprive him of his place in history. When Whitlam left politics it would be with honour'.[48]

Thus ended Oakes' 1409-page account of Gough Whitlam's rise and fall, 541 pages of which were sole authored and another 868 pages co-authored with Solomon. Even Boswell's *Life of Johnson* only took 1104 pages in the telling.⁴⁹ Many books were written by others on Whitlam's rise to power, as well as on his fall in the Dismissal; none, however, were part of an overall construction with a standalone biography as its central pillar like the Oakes quartet. No other Australian prime minister has received so much biographical attention, in such detail and with such a high standard of writing, post-career, let alone contemporary with their active political career.⁵⁰

This sustained account of Whitlam, with its fidelity to events and a top journalist's knack for dramatic narrative and the telling moment, is a peerless achievement in Australian political biography. Yet Oakes did not consider himself Whitlam's Boswell. He saw long-time Whitlam staffer Graham Freudenberg in that role. Oakes' *Whitlam PM: A Biography*, in fact, begins with a dedication, 'For Graham Freudenberg, the real Boswell'. Oakes recalls that he had 'always assumed [Freudenberg would] write the definitive biography, which he did'.⁵¹

Freudenberg undertook his biography of Whitlam in dramatically different circumstances to those when Oakes began his research in 1970 for *Whitlam PM*. Oakes set out with a human puzzle in his hands – Whitlam and his enigmatic persona – in an atmosphere of hope and nascent political excitement given the potential for major change flowing from a possible Labor win in 1972. By the mid-1970s when Freudenberg began work on *A Certain Grandeur: Gough Whitlam in Politics*, Whitlam's career already manifested a tragic symmetry. The book would inevitably be a factor shaping Whitlam's reputation in the run up to what would likely be his last election and, therefore, last chance to win back the prime ministership torn from his hands. Further, Freudenberg would do it from the vantage point of someone more Boswellian than Boswell in terms of closeness to his subject –

so close, in fact, that the characterisation does not really hold. Freudenberg was beyond being a Boswell; he had become Whitlam's alter ego.

The Dismissal was traumatic for Australia, especially for Labor loyalists who felt government had been wrenched illegitimately from Whitlam's grasp. Less well documented, and easily forgotten, is the personal trauma endured by figures at the centre of the crisis and their intimates – 'still a raw wound on the spirit of those whose lives have been irreversibly changed by them', Freudenberg would write – from the Dismissal and subsequent events.[52] In the aftermath, for example, vicious rumours were spread about Whitlam and his marriage. Since Whitlam remained opposition leader and would lead Labor to the next election, a low political motive for the rumour-mongering is probable. For so long Labor's signal strength, it was likely designed to further damage Whitlam's standing, undermine morale, and head off any political resurrection. Susan Mitchell wrote that at the beginning of 1976, Margaret Whitlam, immensely distressed at the vicious disinformation campaign, 'toyed with the idea of writing a book about her husband' as he really was. Mitchell quotes from handwritten pages torn from Margaret Whitlam's journal dated 26 March 1976, where Margaret explores the idea.

> I'm sick of hearing how he beats me – how we're divorcing, how much money we've stashed away in foreign countries, how many ruins we've visited or caused. Oh, what rot it all is, but at the same time how offensive and how hurtful that people should believe it.
>
> Wasn't it enough for the G-G to ruin our lives? Is there to be no end to speculation and jubilation?
>
> The man that I married is, as he was, a gentle man. Two words or one, take your pick. Both apply ... Next week the old man and I will have been married thirty-four years. We shudder at the

headlines commissioned by enemies. We thought we'd never have to but glow in the knowledge of our steadfastness.[53]

Margaret Whitlam did not write a book. Freudenberg did. Manning Clark launched *A Certain Grandeur* at John Curtin House in Canberra on 24 October 1977, declaring it would 'play a major role in the battle for human hearts' in Australia. The book had 'everything going for it', added Whitlam, including an author whose name was both 'cerebral and sinister'.[54] It was 'oddly fascinating to close one's eyes whilst Freudenberg followed his subject in addressing the company', Fin Crisp said, 'and feel at moments that it was still Whitlam speaking'.[55] Within days, Fraser called an early election for 10 December 1977. If Freudenberg's book was to be a weapon in the 'battle for human hearts', as Clark said, Fraser ensured the political battlefield would be as contained as possible. Calling an early election meant there would be just 45 days between the book's launch and election day. No-one expected Whitlam to stay on as opposition leader if he lost.

Freudenberg was born in Brisbane in 1934 to a middle-class family strongly aligned with the UAP and its successor, the Liberal Party. His father, a stretcher bearer at Gallipoli of Prussian heritage, was a commercial traveller in Queensland for Colgate in the 1930s and 1940s; his mother was a third generation Australian of Scottish heritage who still referred to Britain as 'home'.[56] Freudenberg was educated at Brisbane's Church of England Grammar School and sources his lifelong 'political virus' to reading a Pelican paperback edition of André Maurois' biography of Disraeli while home from school with chicken pox, aged ten, in 1944.[57] 'I was so rapt, so inspired by this, that from that time on I was determined to be a politician', he says. 'As Disraeli had found the path to politics as a writer and as a journalist of sorts, that's really why I hit on the idea of being a journalist rather than, say, a lawyer. But reading that book was quite a decisive thing'.[58]

A teenage encounter with the works of Edmund Burke began a lifelong engagement with them, deeply imprinting on Freudenberg 'the richness of the English language as oratory and ... the importance of party allegiance'. All his life, from cycling through Europe in 1956 through to travelling with Whitlam and, later, as Prime Minister Bob Hawke's speechwriter, Freudenberg always carried one of his books to reflect on 'Burke the writer, Burke the orator, Burke the user of this marvellous thing called the English language, but Burke also the man of party'.[59]

Freudenberg became a cadet reporter in 1952 for the now defunct *Brisbane Telegraph,* whose training program included undertaking arts subjects at night at the University of Queensland. While not taking out a degree, he studied Australian history with Gordon Greenwood, and political science with Tom Truman. Freudenberg describes the *Brisbane Telegraph* as one of the worst metropolitan daily newspapers in Australia but one of the best at which to do a cadetship, dominated, as it was, by 'a lively group from interstate, Labor to a man', who were devotees of 'Pentonese' – journalistic tenets practised by crusading 1940s Sydney *Daily Telegraph* editor Brian Penton. The elements were 'an arresting introduction, the shorter the better; every sentence a separate paragraph, preferably 10 to 14 words long; every sentence in the active voice; all quotes in direct speech with quotation marks', aiming for 'clarity, brevity and accuracy'.[60] Freudenberg moved to the *Daily Mirror* as a fourth-year cadet, then, as a graded journalist, to the Mildura *Sunraysia Daily* and later the Melbourne *Sun News Pictorial*. By 1958, he was deputy news editor at GTV9 in Melbourne.

Freudenberg worked for nine years as a journalist in all, squeezing in a trip to London in early 1956, by which time 'I realised that I wasn't a very good reporter' and did not like reporting anyway: 'I realised that, in fact, my ambition to be a writer was not really being fulfilled, or likely to be fulfilled, by being a newspaperman'.[61] In contrast to Oakes, who was nine years younger, and would join the *Sun News Pictorial* a decade later and be dubbed 'scoop artist' by a gallery colleague,[62] Freudenberg perceived that:

I didn't have a competitive urge, so I ... always ran the risk of being scooped. [I] had vague ideas that when I returned from the grand tour I might take up law. Still, you see, with politics in view.[63]

The Suez Crisis, which Freudenberg followed in London while working at the Maida Vale branch of the Paddington Borough Library, transformed his politics: 'It was an eye opener to me about the real meaning of Toryism and, you know, the sheer stupidity of it'. At the same time he followed the intense debates going on within the British Labour Party, in which Anthony Crosland, Richard Crossman and Labour opposition leader Hugh Gaitskell were central, about the 'application of democratic socialism or social democracy in a Cold War world'. By 1956 'I was ... ripe for conversion (and) Suez was the catalyst'.[64]

Philosopher Bertrand Russell, British Shadow Foreign Secretary Aneurin Bevan and Gaitskell addressed a political rally in Trafalgar Square in October 1956 which Freudenberg attended, so loud it could be heard from Downing Street. Two Africans standing in front of Freudenberg 'were just jumping up and down with joy at the brilliance of Bevan's speech and his wit'. But the Cambridge philosopher turned activist Russell, rather than the Welsh firebrand Bevan, was the bigger influence: 'Like most of that generation of Australians who became part of the left, we were really permeated by English liberalism ... really of a late Victorian, Edwardian kind, which Bertrand Russell really represented, you know. He epitomized that English liberalism, which embraced a kind of non-Marxian socialism'.[65]

Freudenberg not only became a political progressive in London but also 'became an Australian', he says: 'One realised ... that one wasn't British and that Australia was different, and one felt better. I became very anxious to get home'. On his return in early 1957, Freudenberg joined the ALP's East Melbourne branch in Calwell's seat of Melbourne.[66] Four years later, in August 1961, Freudenberg joined Calwell's staff as the opposition leader's press secretary, where he served until February 1966.⁶⁷ '[I]t became pretty plain to me quite quickly that I didn't have the particular qualities that would have made me either an effective member of parliament, much less a minister', Freudenberg says. Since his job seemed to have all the benefits of being a politician – 'not least being able to make speeches, even if someone else was delivering them' – without the downsides of pursuing preselection, being in parliament and having to make the requisite 'lifestyle and habits' adjustment, this did not come as a blow.⁶⁸

Calwell very nearly won the December 1961 election – Freudenberg's first – against the backdrop of a credit squeeze. Labor picked fifteen seats up from the conservative coalition parties, won a majority of the two-party preferred vote (50.5%), and cut Menzies' majority to just two seats. The previous year Whitlam had become deputy opposition leader, beating Eddie Ward 38 votes to 34.⁶⁹ Freudenberg points out that Whitlam 'bore the main burden of the Queensland campaign' in the 1961 election where eight of the fifteen seats Labor picked up were won. Conversely, Labor did not win any additional seats in Calwell's home state of Victoria, where the swing to Labor was less than half the national average. 'It took a few days for even the best-informed politicians in the Labor Party to realize the full extent of the great gains Labor had made', Freudenberg wrote in *A Certain Grandeur*:

> But the shrewder men within the Party cut through the euphoria to the essence; that was that Whitlam was the first deputy or leader in living memory, not excluding Chifley or Curtin, to appear positively and demonstrably to have changed votes where votes were needed or could be changed.⁷⁰

Freudenberg worked as Calwell's press secretary – and speech writer – until 1966 when he resigned in disgust after Calwell knowingly handled the Labor policy relating to state aid for schools in a way that involved collateral damage for Whitlam. The state aid tussle coincided with the February 1966 by-election for the federal Queensland seat of Dawson, which Labor had a serious possibility of winning from the Country Party.[71] In the ALP federal executive brawls which occurred in ensuing weeks, national president Joe Chamberlain moved for Whitlam's expulsion from the party, leading Whitlam to declare in a television interview, 'I can only say we've just got rid of the 36 faceless men stigma to be faced with the 12 witless men'.[72] Freudenberg recounts Labor MP and later Whitlam Government minister Lance Barnard, who attended as a Tasmanian delegate, noticing Calwell reading a book during one of these 'interminable [federal executive] brawls'. At one point Calwell 'dropped off' and Barnard looked to see what he was reading: 'It was *Lives of the Popes* by von Ranke'.[73]

Freudenberg was 'totally disaffected' with Calwell by this point: 'I thought it was just outrageous that he was determined to hang on as leader, despite the fact that he was unfit'.[74] There was an unspoken understanding, but no guarantee, that Whitlam, when he succeeded Calwell, would employ Freudenberg. In between, Freudenberg returned to the *Sun News Pictorial*. On 8 February 1967, about an hour after becoming leader, Whitlam rang and asked: 'When are you coming to Canberra?' Freudenberg replied, 'Will next Monday be OK?'[75]

Freudenberg was one of an opposition leadership staff which had been expanded from four to six people.[76] Whitlam's senior adviser, John Menadue, preferred John Stubbs or Eric Walsh to Freudenberg for the job.[77] However, 'Gough felt, I think, that I had other ... qualities that would serve him'.[78] Whitlam's office as opposition leader worked so that each staff member was de facto press secretary depending on the political correspondent concerned: whomever the particular reporter was closest to in the office became their main point of contact.[79] Nevertheless, Freudenberg was the one who 'actually was entitled to speak in the leader's name', Oakes recalls, a reflection of the total trust between them.[80]

> Freudenberg was undoubtedly the backbone of the staff …
> [and] after his years with Calwell, had a natural 'feel' for the
> Labor party, an understanding of its moods and habits which
> Whitlam lacked. He also had a somewhat aggressive personality
> which compelled Whitlam to take notice of him when he
> thumped the table and offered advice. He and Whitlam had a
> common interest in history and a common feeling for words,
> and they built up such a rapport that Freudenberg even began
> to sound like Whitlam when he spoke and to adopt the same
> mannerisms.[81]

Oakes recounts how often Whitlam would not know 'he' had made a statement until he read it in the papers the next day, the quotes being Freudenberg's issued under Whitlam's standing authority for him to speak on his behalf.

When it came to speeches, Freudenberg 'quickly adapted to Whitlam's alliterative style of oratory'.[82] Deploying a term coined by American political scientist AL George, James Walter points out that 'the "operational code" remains Whitlam's alone'.[83] Freudenberg could dictate eloquent speeches to a secretary with little or no consultation given his understanding of that 'operational code', how Whitlam's mind worked, and absorption of his rhetorical style. Relationships this close were rare in Whitlam's life; he was a man with few intimate friends and marked difficulty expressing affection, according to Oakes. 'One Labor colleague with a smattering of Freudian psychology theorises', Oakes wrote, 'that "it's as if he was never cuddled or fondled as a child"'.[84] The observation makes this Freudenberg recollection at Whitlam's memorial service in November 2014 all the more significant.

> We had developed a little ritual between us. Before an important
> speech, he would touch me on the shoulder for luck. He didn't
> forget, even amid the tumult of Blacktown. 'It's been a long road,
> comrade. But I think we're there'. He knew how much the words,

and the touch, would mean to me at such a moment. You would go to the barricades with such a man.[85]

While Whitlam was prime minister, Freudenberg was his 'special adviser'. After the Dismissal he took a year off to work on what would become *A Certain Grandeur*.[86] Freudenberg then worked part-time for New South Wales Labor premier Neville Wran, 'which enabled me to eat as well as write'.[87] *A Certain Grandeur* was completed in July 1977, at which point he rejoined Whitlam's staff as special adviser again in time for the Budget session of parliament. Canberra was not what it had been:

> Caucus was sullen and despondent ... Mutual animosities separated the parties and the staffs. Fraser had imposed new-fangled security measures in Parliament House. The non-members' bar was now a gloomy place ... Whitlam himself remained indomitable, resilient as ever, but tense and touchy, the old blazing passions fanning a smouldering rage.[88]

Whatever his precise job title at any given time, history sees Freudenberg – or 'Freudie' as he was known – as Whitlam's legendary speechwriter who, after 'the other Member for Werriwa' as he dubbed Margaret in his speech at Whitlam's memorial service, was closest to 'the great man'. There is significance in the preposition in his statement on the same occasion that, 'You would go to the barricades with such a man' – the 'with' rather than 'for' implying an equal rather than hierarchical relationship.

In fact, they *had* gone to the barricades together, as much as a politician and their staff alter ego could. Whitlam repeatedly clashed with the Labor machine during opposition in his drive to increase the federal parliamentary Labor Party's influence relative to party officials. To illustrate their mode of working, Freudenberg uses the example of Whitlam's 'great onslaught' against the Victorian ALP executive which began at the annual Victorian state conference on the Queen's Birthday Weekend in June 1967. Freudenberg accompanied Whitlam on a swing through northern and north-western Australia and, in between stops, they would work on speeches together. They included one for the Victorian state conference known to history as the 'Impotent are Pure' speech because of Whitlam's famous line, 'only the impotent are pure' – a reference to the Victorian branch's predilection for policy purity over electability. Whitlam's counterpoint was that power was the necessary precondition for being able to implement policy of any kind at all. The speech, a denunciation of the Victorian ALP executive, was 'a declaration of war', Freudenberg says, delivered in a 'great scene, [a] great tableau' of a packed hall full of delegates jeering, booing, laughing and catcalling. Knowing exactly what he was doing, Whitlam 'ploughed on'. Of 'only the impotent are pure', Freudenberg comments:

> Now, that phrase, of course, is pure Gough. But taking the line I expanded it with a lot of rhetoric – some would say bullshit – which gave a context to an otherwise vulgar assertion. So anybody who reads that speech now can see how we did effectively collaborate in how I could take a thought or an idea or a phrase and develop it ... Sometimes to give them more point, sometimes to blunt the point if I thought that it was a bit over the top.[89]

With Whitlam, 'I was so much on his wavelength – or had become so through this intimate relationship – that I had no difficulty at all' writing speeches like this for him, spurred by a key phrase or thought.[90] Freudenberg was the yeast to Whitlam's dough; the Labor leader's rhetorical bread would have been far less appetising had not Freudenberg lifted it beyond Whitlam's tendency to pedagogic point making. Freudenberg told Walter there was 'give and take – I adopted his style and he adopted mine'.

> It would be very difficult to say where one began and the other ended. He always accused me of being too dithyrambic – I had to look it up in the dictionary, of course. It means a Bacchanalian dance. He meant, you know, I go a bit heavy on the rhetoric. He admits his own style is too desiccated, too dry, too spare and sparse. The combination wasn't bad, I think.[91]

Whitlam was no pliant tool; he did not always accept Freudenberg's advice. Oakes recounts how in 1971, for example, Whitlam was invited to visit the People's Republic of China, then closed to the west, and phoned Freudenberg at home to ask whether he thought he should go. The answer was 'no'. Freudenberg subsequently changed his mind but, by the time he got to the office to say so, he found that Whitlam had accepted the invitation anyway.[92]

Craig McGregor's retrospective account of his experience as a journalist in the week running up to the Dismissal on 11 November 1975 also underlines the practical limits of Freudenberg's ability to shape Whitlam's actions.[93] On 4 November, McGregor went to Parliament House, Canberra, which seemed 'in perpetual crisis: divisions, censure motions, exhausted politicians filing into the House, voting obediently and then filing out again' as the theatre of the opposition's long-running denial of supply ground on. He visited Fraser's press secretary, David Barnett; they had been cadet reporters together on the *Sydney Morning Herald* years earlier.[94] 'Our position now ... is exactly as it has been for some time', Barnett told McGregor. 'The Governor-General must intervene to dismiss the government. There is no other possible solution'.

An incredulous McGregor visited Freudenberg, 'one of the inner circle of Whitlam's apparatchiks', the next day, 5 November, thinking, 'I hope to Christ Gough's got Kerr in his pocket; he appointed him, he must know what he's doing'. Freudenberg, 'a man who says nothing without measuring it first, frowned and lit a delicate cigarette', recalls McGregor.

'The advice of Byers, the Solicitor-General, to us is that the Governor-General must follow the advice of the Prime Minister'. Freudenberg seemed harried, nervous.

'What's the government's strategy?' I asked.

'We've got no plan of campaign. It's ridiculous', Freudenberg admitted suddenly. True, he said, every so often Labor's top strategists would meet, discuss tactics, decide on what should be done. 'The difficulty', said Freudenberg pensively, 'is to communicate it to Gough'.[95]

The next day, Thursday, 6 November, McGregor watched Whitlam say his patience was unlimited and that 'parliament will sit until the senators call off their strike'.

On Friday 7 November McGregor again visited Barnett, pressing him about his previous statement that the governor-general had to sack the government. Barnett's equivocal reaction convinced McGregor it would occur. 'In all likelihood, Fraser knew what was going to happen', he writes. 'Barnett probably knew. Otherwise, why would Barnett have backtracked so fiercely?' McGregor now went to see Freudenberg.

'Graham, what will the Labor government do if Kerr attempts to dismiss it?'

There was a long pause. 'He won't'.

'Look', I said. 'David Barnett has told me, formally, that Kerr must intervene ...'

'Gough's position', said Freudenberg, 'is that the Governor-General must heed the advice of his Prime Minister'.

'But what is your contingency plan if Kerr does exactly what Barnett says, and moves to dismiss the government?'

I realised that Freudenberg might not be willing to reveal the government's hand, but he answered, 'We haven't got one'.[96]

Freudenberg had thought Whitlam's lack of a plan to deal with a dismissal by vice-regal fiat was 'ridiculous' and that the 'difficulty is to communicate it to Gough'. The fact that there still wasn't a plan two days later etches the limits of Whitlam's special adviser's influence.[97]

Looking back on that period in *A Certain Grandeur*, Freudenberg says the 'two essential elements of Whitlam's strategy were to keep up the pressure and to buy time', to which end emergency finance was arranged so that from 30 November public servants and essential contractors could be paid after the money ran out by government-guaranteed vouchers, redeemable at banks: 'They were part of the political effort to force a political solution to a political problem'.[98] On 9 November, two days after McGregor's second conversation with him, Whitlam 'at last' decided to call a half-Senate election, says Freudenberg, 'the last turn of the screw in the battle of tactics which he was waging and which he and most observers believed he was winning'.[99] There was still no plan to deal with a potential dismissal by vice-regal fiat. As a result, when it came, Kerr's ambush of his prime minister was a fait accompli.

The publisher Macmillan approached Freudenberg and signed a contract with him for the book after seeing a press snippet that he had a Whitlam biography in mind.[100] Macmillan made the most of the special relationship between the two men in its publicity for it. 'No man knows Gough Whitlam better than Graham Freudenberg', reads the flyleaf, 'his confidant and speechwriter throughout most of his political career; and no man is better equipped by association, close political insight and recognized brilliance as a writer and political historian to write the ultimate chronicle ...' Nor did the author pretend objectivity but rather disclosed that he was 'privileged to be a close observer and occasionally a participant' in the events described. Little worthwhile would ever be written if holding strong views disqualified one from writing 'contributions to history', Freudenberg argued in the preface, going on to quote Churchill's characterisation of his book on World War I, *The World Crisis*, in support: 'It is a contribution to history strung upon a fairly strong thread of personal reminiscences ... Throughout I have set myself to explain faithfully and to the best of my ability what happened and why'. Freudenberg quips at the end of the preface that 'EG Whitlam offered his services as a research assistant and proved quite satisfactory on the few occasions I thought it proper to avail myself of them'.[101]

The book's title, *A Certain Grandeur*, was taken from *Out of the Wilderness* (1974) by Clem Lloyd and Gordon Reid, which covered Labor's return to the Treasury benches after more than two decades in opposition. 'In the generally undistinguished, and often tawdry, atmosphere of Australian national politics', Lloyd and Reid write, 'it is impossible to deny the Whitlam Government a certain grandeur'.[102] Freudenberg's book itself turned out to be worthy of its title, in 1977 winning *The Age* Book of the Year Award. '[O]f all the millions of words I might have written, the book was the first thing in my own name', Freudenberg recalls.[103]

Billed as the 'insider's view', those unfamiliar with the period and its personnel might expect Freudenberg's book to be merely an apologia for the fallen hero.[104] In fact, *A Certain Grandeur* contains a serious argument about the economic factors contributing to the Whitlam Government's fall; it makes explicit an ideological and institutional argument about whether Australia's organs of government could be harnessed for social democratic change; and it flags a sociological argument about Australians' attitude to themselves and how that played into the domestic politics of the period. Crucially – and this is the denouement of a continuous seam in commentary and analysis during Whitlam's active political career, in contrast to the period after his retirement – Freudenberg frames the story from the prime ministership of Menzies to that of Whitlam. *A Certain Grandeur* covers the decade from Menzies' retirement in 1966 to Whitlam's fall in 1975.

Freudenberg sets out to explain why, despite Whitlam taking Labor 'from disaster to power' in six years as Menzies did in a comparable time with his own party in the latter part of the 1940s, he failed to govern for as long as Menzies – or at least had failed to do so to that point.[105] Freudenberg uses the Vietnam War as the foundation for this Menzies-to-Whitlam frame. These were, above all, the Vietnam years, Freudenberg argues; Vietnam was not just the name of a country or a war but the name of an epoch, and that epoch began with Menzies.

> Vietnam and its consequences – its economic consequences even more than its shattering political consequences – dominated the societies, the economies and the politics of the United States and Australia. The world economic disruption of the seventies springs from Vietnam. Every Australian Prime Minister involved with Vietnam was damaged by it. All save one – the Prime Minister who first locked Australia into the war – Robert Gordon Menzies. In a profound sense, the Whitlam Government was one of the last casualties of the war in Vietnam.[106]

This is a largely ignored but intuitively persuasive element of enormous significance to both the narrative arc of Whitlam's own story as well as that of the government overall. One can immediately point to the obvious factors often cited to explain Whitlam's demise, notably the lack of discipline and basic political craft of MPs from the top of the ministry all the way through to the lowliest parts of the government's backbench, at times not excluding Whitlam himself. However, the extent to which long-term external economic factors impacted on, and beleaguered, the Whitlam Government, as well as what constitutes its actual as opposed to its perceived economic record was and remains one of the great unwritten histories of the latter twentieth century.

To answer the, by then, reflex criticism of Whitlam's lack of economic expertise, Freudenberg sets out to explain 'why Whitlam's thinking turned on programmes of social reform rather than economic theory'. From 1953, he writes, to 1970 when the economic cost of Vietnam began to register, western economies had enjoyed sustained growth; they were years of 'fine tuning' when small trade-offs 'between a little more inflation or a little less employment', and strong economic growth overall, solved the tension between the need for profits and demand for welfare in the 'mixed economy'. In the 1950s and 1960s, in short, 'it was quite possible for politicians to believe that the days of the primacy of economics were past'. Whitlam responded at the time to critics of his lack of economic expertise by pointing to the successful prime ministerships of Curtin and Menzies, who lacked any particular background in economics too; it was not regarded in the 1950s and 1960s as being a necessary requisite even for treasurers.[107]

Freudenberg contrasts this with the period from the early 1970s on when the western world, including Australia, began to 'pay the price for Vietnam'. Throughout the industrialised world inflation rose somewhat, then sharply; growth slumped, unemployment grew. He quotes ANU economist Fred Gruen at length on the inflationary consequences of successive US governments financing the Vietnam War by printing money instead of pursuing prudent fiscal policy.[108] The related 1973–74 oil shock intensified the destructive Vietnam-driven economic forces already at work, creating the conditions for the stagflation which plagued the west for the rest of the 1970s and early 1980s.[109]

Freudenberg was right to draw attention to this. Writing in 1977, he could not have foreseen how drastically neglect of this factor in the historiography of the Whitlam Government would influence its long run reputation.[110] General government sector receipts – a rough proxy for the tax take – were equal to or lower during all three years of the Whitlam Government as a proportion of gross domestic product (GDP) than they were in any year of the Fraser Government, and lower than in any year of the Howard Government.[111] General government sector payments – a rough proxy for government spending – was lower as a proportion of GDP in all three years of the Whitlam Government than in any year of any other government, Liberal or Labor, since.[112] Freudenberg himself points out that the third Whitlam Government budget, delivered by Bill Hayden who became treasurer on 6 June 1975, was its most restrained and fiscally responsible – yet it was blocked by the Fraser-led opposition supposedly concerned with sound economic management.[113] Freudenberg's argument concerning the broad role of the economy in the demise of Whitlam and his government, including its Vietnam War–related dimension, awaits serious attention from political and economic historians, as do the facts of its economic management record.

Freudenberg's second argument in *A Certain Grandeur* concerns 'ten years of struggle for the idea of the Australian parliament as the principal instrument of change and reform in Australia; how that struggle was briefly crowned with success; and how the parliamentary system itself was used to destroy a government led by the Australian who ... fought hardest and longest for the meaningful survival of the system' – namely, Whitlam.[114] It contextualised the Dismissal in the Australian labour movement's long-running debate about the practical scope for progressive change by parliamentary means. Freudenberg juxtaposed those who believed parliament to be 'a sham and social democracy a sell-out' with Whitlam who went to the 'edge of expulsion and political destruction' to persuade Labor that parliament could be an 'instrument for social change'.

The Dismissal temporarily seemed to vindicate 'those on the Australian "left" who despise the system and detest Whitlam as its champion ... (and) who argued ... that even if Labor secured a majority in the House of Representatives and formed a government, it would never be allowed to govern and would be destroyed by any means'. Freudenberg concedes that Kerr's actions exposed the shortcomings in Whitlam's philosophy but points to that philosophy's continuing hold as manifest, for example, in the election of state Labor governments like that of the Wran Government in New South Wales.[115] There have been many Labor governments elected since, state and federal, suggesting that Whitlam's electoral philosophy became entrenched within the ALP despite the rending experience of the Dismissal.

Another argument flagged but not pursued in *A Certain Grandeur* is a sociological one about Australians' attitude to themselves and how it plays into domestic politics. Freudenberg asks: 'Why then was the Government so easily destroyed?' His tentative answer is that perhaps, in the form of larger-than-life Australians like not only Whitlam but also Rex Connor, Clyde Cameron, Lionel Murphy, Jim Cairns, Bill Hayden, Fred Daly and Tom Uren, we saw ourselves and did not like it.

> Their strengths and faults were very visible and very visibly Australian – their independence, their turbulence, their touchiness, their irreverence, their impatience with 'proper channels' ... and, after the shock of self-recognition, were rather relieved to see the image smashed?[116]

Freudenberg quotes Manning Clark's comment in the 1976 Boyer Lectures that, after observing 'men in high places closely in Canberra', he agrees with the author of Ecclesiastes, the Greek tragedians, Shakespeare and others that 'men suffered from a fatal flaw in their being which stood between them and what they wanted to achieve'. Rescuing Whitlam from blame, Freudenberg follows the Clark quote by asking rather, whether the 'fatal flaw lies not just in those we put to lead us, but in our dislike of ourselves as Australians?' It was something, he went on, with which Australians would have to come to terms sooner rather than later.[117]

Freudenberg closes *A Certain Grandeur* contrasting the 'metaphysic pessimist' Fraser with the 'rational optimist' Whitlam, and, in a last jab at Kerr who resigned in July 1977 as the manuscript was being finalised, quotes his leader: 'How fitting that the last Bourbon should bow out on Bastille Day'.[118] His analysis of how Fraser undid Whitlam provides a reminder of the roots of recent Liberal political tactics in opposition. Fraser's performance, Freudenberg wrote, 'was one of the most concentrated, single-minded and effective exercises in political destruction ever undertaken' in Australian history.

> His great success was that, in the end, he had the majority of Australians believing not merely what he believed but believing that there *must* be much more in it all than he was willing to say. In the end, for every one who would dare say it, there were ten who believed the Labor Government was corrupt. The constant repetition of the word 'scandal' and its indiscriminate application to any controversial action of the government worked.[119]

Freudenberg's biography of Whitlam is more than a political operator's close analysis of noble failure: it contains an historical argument through which readers can contextualise events in a bigger framework, revealing the powerful political and economic forces that buffeted an idealistic administration. Published as Whitlam geared up for the 1977 election, his last chance to overcome the stunning blow of the Dismissal, *A Certain Grandeur* gave voters who read it the opportunity to get up and out of the trench warfare view of the Whitlam Government and gain a bigger perspective. Was it in itself a political intervention? Certainly. 'I mean, I regard myself as a politician', Freudenberg would say at the end of his career, looking back.[120] 'I am the last to quibble at the Whitlam legend ... I have been pretty active in fostering and defending it myself'.[121] Readers open to *A Certain Grandeur*'s content would have been more, not less, likely to vote for Whitlam at the 1977 election.

The choice of Clark to launch *A Certain Grandeur* is significant. Mark McKenna argues that Freudenberg, Whitlam and Clark 'believed they were on the same mission', intellectual and political leaders being obliged to 'provide the country with an ambitious, even epic, political vision'. McKenna quotes from a Freudenberg letter to Clark: 'Your unique insights are needed, now as never before, to explain to us the grand themes of our history ... we need an understanding of the whole story ... [otherwise] we shall all fail in the search for the true meaning of existence in Australia'.[122]

A Certain Grandeur was Freudenberg's attempt to himself live up to his exhortation to Clark. To an extent greater than any other contemporary biographer of an Australian prime minister, Freudenberg achieved that goal. First published in 1977, republished in 1978 with an afterword taking in Whitlam's 1977 election defeat, republished as a tenth anniversary edition in 1987, and republished again in 2009 with an epilogue, *A Certain Grandeur* became an evergreen of Australian political biography. 'In his rich and mellow autumn, he worried occasionally lest he be, like King Charles, remembered mainly for losing his head', Freudenberg said at Whitlam's memorial service in 2014.[123] *A Certain Grandeur* gave the bigger story a continuing life.

―――

Malcolm Fraser came to office in more controversial circumstances than any other postwar prime minister. The exercise of conservative political muscle to a degree unprecedented in Australia, through the exploitation of uncodified vice-regal power, created a persistent air of illegitimacy around Fraser's prime ministership. It began in a caretaker capacity in November 1975, was confirmed by a general election win over Whitlam the following month, and lasted until March 1983.

This atmospheric was barely mitigated by Fraser's landslide 1975 and 1977 election wins, or his third win from behind courtesy of Labor ill-discipline in the final week of the 1980 election campaign.[124] In his later years Fraser was critical of the Liberal Party and espoused policy positions more in line in some respects with those of the Greens. Reviewing Fraser's years in office, however, Patrick Weller accurately sums up Fraser's overwhelming public image during his parliamentary career, and for decades afterwards, as the 'picture of a dominant and determined leader with his mind made up and intolerant of other views, with a history of leaving those who dared to disagree defeated and trampled in his path'.¹²⁵ This held true until Fraser shifted to become a persistent critic of the Liberals, which won him something of a following as a moderate on particular social policy issues.

Fraser was the subject of one modest but interesting biographical effort: John Edwards' *Life wasn't meant to be easy: a political profile of Malcolm Fraser*.¹²⁶ Russell Schneider's *War Without Blood: Malcolm Fraser in Power* also appeared during Fraser's prime ministership, published just before the 1980 election. *War Without Blood* does not purport to be a profile as Edwards positions his book, but rather a portrait of Fraser during his five years in the prime ministership to that point, focussed on his 'habit of command'.¹²⁷

Edwards' *Life wasn't meant to be easy*, at 123 pages long, appears slight; its subtitle, *a political profile of Malcolm Fraser*, realistically structured reader expectations that the book would be long-form journalism in style rather than a comprehensive biography. Oakes points out that while chances to write long-form journalism abound now, they were few then: political journalists were 'frustrated at the lack of opportunities'.¹²⁸ A book like *Life wasn't meant to be easy* would more likely now appear as an edition of, say, Black Inc.'s *Quarterly Essay* rather than a stand-alone book.

Edwards was born in Sydney in 1947, and grew up mainly in Strathfield. His father owned a small timber business which failed during the 1961 credit squeeze; his mother was engaged in home duties. Edwards attended Trinity Grammar where he enjoyed the teaching of 'good though eccentric' English teachers and a good economics teacher who laid some foundations for his later interest and postgraduate study in economics.¹²⁹ Opposition to the Vietnam War and support for Whitlam's rise in the ALP were defining positions for Edwards during his student years at the University of Sydney, from which he graduated with a Bachelor of Arts in Government and English.

In 1969, aged 22, Edwards joined the *Australian Financial Review* in Sydney. *AFR* editor Vic Carroll, with 'both a fine intelligence and a wonderful way of encouraging people in journalism', was a major influence. Edwards read much fiction, mainly novels, at school; now he immersed himself in the work of leading practitioners in his new profession. 'I read a vast amount of journalism ... in the first years in the game – [David] Halberstam, [James] Cameron, [Tom] Wolfe, [Oriana] Fallaci who did wonderful interviews, contemporaries like Evan Williams, Gavin Souter and Craig McGregor', Edwards recalls. 'And magazines – *Listener, The New Statesman, New Yorker, New York Review [of Books], Rolling Stone*. I wanted to write profiles and narratives'.[130]

After three years at the *AFR*, Edwards joined the staff of Clyde Cameron, a Whitlam Government minister, as press secretary – in retrospect, 'a dopey decision', he says. Edwards resigned four months later, winning a certain renown among colleagues for being the only press secretary in memory to resign during an overseas trip.[131] He then joined the *Sunday Telegraph* in Canberra as a political reporter and, less than a year later, moved to *The Australian* after Alan Ramsay fell out with head office over differences in political interpretation. Edwards, in turn, was sacked after the 1974 election 'which I had hugely enjoyed'.[132] Eventually he moved back to Sydney to take up a position on the *National Times* at the invitation of influential Fairfax executive Max Suich. 'The book was published in 1977 just before my thirtieth birthday, when I was about to leave for the *National Times* posting in Washington', Edwards says.

> There were, in fact, only about five copies actually available at the launch, due to a timing miscalculation. Bob Hawke launched the book. Everybody got noisy and drunk. The book sold quite well – I got enough out of it ... to put a deposit on a house in Washington, which I wish I had kept.[133]

Life wasn't meant to be easy began as a series of articles for the *National Times*. While in Canberra in 1973, Edwards shared a house with John Iremonger from ANU Press and Whitlam Government press secretary Megan Stoyles. Like Edwards, Iremonger was now in Sydney, in the process of founding publishing firm Hale & Iremonger with Sylvia Hale and Roger Barnes. He encouraged Edwards to turn his *National Times* Fraser articles into a book. Initially Iremonger suggested Richard Walsh at Angus & Robertson as his best publishing prospect but Walsh thought the manuscript needed more work. By the time Edwards had done this, Iremonger was in a position to publish it himself under Hale & Iremonger's 'Mayhem' imprint.

Fraser had given Edwards an interview upon becoming prime minister for the *National Times* articles and expressed no opposition to the project being developed into a larger work. 'I spoke to his sister in Rome – again, no problem', he says. 'I interviewed many of his colleagues without any difficulty that I recall'. In an indication of how deep the Liberal leadership fault lines ran at the time, Edwards says that pinning down Fraser's role in bringing Gorton down as prime minister was the only real challenge in writing the book. 'People who knew were reluctant to talk, and those who didn't told the most fantastic lies', he says. 'Part of the work in a book of that kind is winnowing out the lies, or as many as possible. In that respect it was helpful to talk to Fraser'.[134]

Fraser's post-retirement biographer, Philip Ayres, recounts an occasion in 1974 when Fraser, then the opposition frontbencher shadowing Cameron, went to talk to him and insisted on Edwards leaving before he would speak. 'He wasn't embarrassed in doing this, he was quite comfortable about telling Edwards to get out of the room', recalled Cameron. 'He didn't want to discuss things in the presence of underlings'.[135] This would not necessarily have struck Edwards as surprising since, as Weller later noted, Fraser was renowned for uneasy dealings with outsiders and a 'formal, stilted' demeanour. In turn, this affected voter sentiment. 'Respected he may have been', writes Weller, 'but the electorate did not warm to his public image'. Nor did journalists warm to Fraser. 'Relations between Fraser and the press gallery started out icily and they never really improved', according to Weller. 'One press officer commented that, as a consequence of 1975, "whatever Fraser did was assumed to be wrong and evil"'. But if, as

Weller argues, Fraser's means of attaining power 'soured' relations with Canberra Press Gallery journalists, it was an intensification of an existing problem, not a new one.[136] Nor was it Fraser's only problem.

Fraser's identity was contested territory well before the Dismissal; his enemies beat him to it, forcing him into rearguard action to redefine it. Fraser in opposition stalked Liberal leader Billy Snedden, unsuccessfully challenging him before dislodging him on a second attempt. Ayres recounts how Fraser's 'political enemies in the Liberal Party', in a bid to destroy him as a leadership alternative to Snedden, circulated rumours his marriage was in trouble and that he was seeing a psychiatrist. These enemies had t-shirts printed 'bearing slogans like "Relieve Mafeking. VOTE MALCOLM FRASER", "Put Value Back in the Pound. VOTE MALCOLM FRASER", "Support Our Boys in Korea. VOTE MALCOLM FRASER"', implying he was a 'political troglodyte'.[137]

Fraser's allies counselled a softening of his image to counter these damaging characterisations. He approached International Public Relations (IPR) in Melbourne with a view to remaking his image; however, the firm declined to take Fraser on because two other federal Liberal politicians were already on its books. IPR recommended Royce PR instead, which accepted the account and assigned Alister Drysdale to manage it. Ayres notes Fraser was 'now playing in a game he could not afford to be left out of, unless he wanted to see his image further reduced by the public relations activities of others'.[138]

The writing of a friendly biography seems not to have been considered, perhaps because of the degree of difficulty this would involve given Fraser's nature and record of repeated Liberal leader assassination. Even writing a simple profile of Fraser was a challenge. Ayres describes journalist Trevor Hawkins' weekend at the Fraser property 'Nareen' in the Western District, organised by Drysdale, which led to a *National Times* story headlined 'WATCH OUT BILL! WATCH OUT GOUGH! *Malcolm still wants your jobs*'.

[Fraser] had talked to Hawkins for a while in an apparently relaxed way until he was asked 'Who would you have in your Cabinet?' Fraser told him to wait a minute while he thought about whether he should go into that. He got up, walked out of the room and asked Drysdale what he thought – would that be going too far? Drysdale told him he was being too cautious: he should answer the question but say the details were off the record. Fraser wanted to get Tamie's opinion. He was very uneasy about it all ... There was a series of breaks during the interviewing sessions when Fraser would take Drysdale aside for a concerned chat. Should he talk about the qualities needed in a leader? – Hawkins was asking him about that. 'He was raw, totally raw on the matter of press politics' Drysdale claims. 'It was worry, worry, worry'.[139]

What Fraser lacked in press finesse, he more than made up for in an instinct for the ruthless exercise of power against his own party leaders, Gorton and Snedden, as well as against external political opponents like Whitlam. Further, he had the personality necessary to sustain long, uncomfortable tactical positions while executing audacious power plays. Fraser was yet another Australian political leader who on the way to power, and, in his case, while in power, was a mystery to those around him. Cartoonists during his prime ministership personified him as a 'grim Easter Island statue'.[140] When Fraser teared up in his concession speech on the night of the 1983 election when the Hawke Government was elected, *Canberra Times* cartoonist Geoff Pryor drew him as an Easter Island statue shedding a single tear, his visage otherwise as stony and unreadable as ever.[141]

Perhaps because Fraser was such a polarising prime minister, he seemed to stimulate more than the usual number of satirical treatments, in at least one case cast in mock biographical form. Beckett Green Publishing produced an eponymous book *Great Frasers of Our Time*. The introduction noted:

> An apology is due to the person who should have been Mr Fraser's official biographer, his favourite author, the last of the great materialist writers, the last of the just, Ayn Rand. Not having her compassion or picturesque language, we have settled for a more pictorial presentation and let Mr Fraser speak for himself. More or less.[142]

The body of *Great Frasers of Our Time* is made up of photographs of Fraser, variously depicted, accompanied by humorous speech bubbles, often ostensibly in his own voice.

Steve Crabb's book *The Prefect*, attributed to 'Nick Machiavelli with Steve Crabb', mimics Machiavelli's *The Prince*.[143] Quotes from *The Prince*, with 'Prince' replaced by 'Prefect' – a Fraser nickname used by his critics – begin each chapter. Short quotes follow from the press and Fraser's political opponents inside and outside his party, attesting to his political perfidy. Since Fraser was directly implicated in the demise of two Liberal leaders by this point – Gorton when prime minister, and Snedden when opposition leader – as well as pulling off what many considered a constitutional coup against Whitlam, such quotes were plentiful and would have been easy to compile. Chapter by chapter, the book makes the identification of Fraser with the calculating and devious Renaissance political figure Machiavelli quite plausible.

A third type of satire on the unpopular Fraser played on his given name, Malcolm. Perth *Daily News* cartoonist, Allan Langoulant, produced *A Mal for all seasons: The Book of Mal*, for example: 'Grand Mal', 'Petit Mal', 'Primal', 'Malicious' and so on, each accompanied by a drawing expressing the play on his name. Kevin Pappas and Dennis Welsh took a similar approach in *The Mal Book* – 'malady', 'abysmal', 'animal', et cetera. Other cartoonists produced compilations of cartoons published over the several years of Fraser prime ministership, such as *Fraser Country* by Patrick Cook, cartoonist for the *National Times* and the *Australian Financial Review*.[144] Even Edwards'

Life wasn't meant to be easy, the first dedicated attempt at any length to analyse and contextualise him, included drawings by Patrick Cook.

No Australian prime minister had come to power 'in such extraordinary circumstances, after such a perilous career, with so few friends, so many enemies, or so large a majority' as Fraser, Edwards wrote in his preface to *Life Wasn't Meant to Be Easy*. Australians 'had only the vaguest idea of who their new Prime Minister was, where he had come from, what he believed in, or where he wanted to take them'. The book was designed, Edwards said, to 'discover' his likely influence on Australia by examining Fraser's twenty years in politics to date.

> Throughout those twenty years of his political career Fraser had been developing a conservative political philosophy as sharply opposed to the middle ground of liberalism of his colleagues as to the social democracy of his opponents. It was a philosophy as much about what leaders should be as what they should do; it emphasised the perils of inflation at home and communism abroad; it held that Australia was becoming too soft a society to deal with either, and that only far sighted and firm leadership could restore the vigour and enterprise that could make Australia great.[145]

The family history with which Edwards begins the book is a significant feature. Oakes broached Fraser's family history in *Crash Through or Crash* but Edwards chased down and described more fully the 'three generations of wealth and conservatism' that made Fraser. This included more detail than hitherto known outside academic circles on his grandfather Simon Fraser, the Canadian-born son of Scottish immigrants who arrived in Victoria in the 1850s gold rushes and inside twenty years 'accumulated a fortune in land and capital, moving from gold digging to retail trading, to government contracting and finally to land and finance'.

The zenith of Edwards' account of Simon Fraser's rise and rise concerns his directorship of the City of Melbourne Bank and its fate in

Victoria's 1890s economic crash. In April 1893, Fraser told shareholders to disregard rumours concerning the bank's problems and not to sell their shares. 'Three months later the bank crashed', writes Edwards. 'An enquiry revealed that the directors had lent themselves more than £2.5m of the bank's funds, including £9000 to Fraser and Company. Simon Fraser was not prosecuted'. While the rest of Melbourne suffered in the economic slump, Simon Fraser survived it 'comfortably', according to Edwards, going on to commission a portrait of himself by English painter Sir John Millais for 3000 guineas. Edwards cites historian Michael Cannon's comment that Simon Fraser's 'land boom manipulations do not stand up to close scrutiny'.[146]

Contemporary readers of Edwards' book would likely have drawn a parallel between Simon Fraser's 'manipulations' and those of his grandson Malcolm in the Dismissal. The Patrick Cook drawing accompanying this section shows a teddy bear–toting toddler Malcolm Fraser gazing up at a statue of his grandfather who wears top hat and tails, one hand holding a lapel and the other a sign, 'Land For Sale'; the inscription on the plinth reads, 'Sir Simon Fraser 1832–1919 "Never Give a Sucker An Even Break"'.[147]

Edwards characterises Malcolm Fraser's childhood with doting parents on a large Riverina property as a time of 'freedom and loneliness', and 'indulgence and loneliness', which prepared him for long periods of political isolation in his adult life that 'would have rattled others'. He argues these same conditions also led to a 'failure to learn at an early age the techniques of relationships with equals', underpinning the 'series of struggles for dominance' which typified Fraser's backbench and ministerial career to that point. Edwards lists General Daly from Army, Sir Hugh Ennor and Sir Arthur Tange from the public service, and from politics Gorton, Snedden, Andrew Peacock and Whitlam as prominent examples of Fraser equals with whom he could not deal with the equilibrium others managed. 'All politicians have to struggle with competitors on the way to the top', writes Edwards, 'but Fraser's struggles have been singularly savage'.[148]

He contrasts this with Fraser's willingness to engage unproblematically with clear hierarchical superiors like his father's friend Richard 'Dick' Casey, something of a mentor to him. Edwards anticipates and deflects criticism of these modest psychological insights in a way perhaps typical of journalists defensive about going beyond the empirical, or at least concerned about the likely sceptical responses of their colleagues.

> This speculation owes nothing to Freud or to more modern theories of psychology. It is plainly apparent that a child of nine has already developed the outlines of the character he or she will have through life, and the roots of a person's characteristics were commonly sought in childhood long before Freud. It is not psychoanalysis but simply commonsense to think that a lonely child, encouraged to consider himself as in some way superior, could grow up to be an aloof, ambitious and uncommunicative politician.[149]

Edwards' book mostly eschews the psychological in favour of recounting Fraser's political career from winning the Victorian seat of Wannon in 1955 through to the early years of his prime ministership, and from that gleaning Fraser's thinking and its sources. Fraser blended 'despotism and quixotry' in office, Edwards argues, proving 'less illiberal' than his rhetoric suggested. What is more, Edwards wrote presciently, 'Fraser ... is giving every sign of being a Prime Minister who intends to last'.[150]

The motif of class privilege appears repeatedly throughout the book. There is a story of Fraser's sister Lori visiting parks in Depression-era Melbourne with their grandmother Lady Fraser, in the family's chauffeur-driven car, to distribute 'arrowroot biscuits to the unemployed'. There is Fraser's nickname 'Freezer' at Melbourne Grammar School, which 'said as much about his manner as it did about his pronunciation'. There's an interview exchange with Mike Willesee discussing the social composition of the Melbourne Club, of which Fraser was a member. 'Fraser claimed its membership was drawn from a wide section of the community', Edwards writes. 'Willesee asked him if he would be likely to meet someone there who worked with his hands. Fraser replied that he often did; pressed, Fraser instanced doctors'.[151]

Fraser's narrowness comes through strongly. Edwards notes that Fraser was not forthcoming in the media about 'his private life or interests', but this is not put down to obfuscation. 'The truth, I think', writes Edwards, 'is that he has very few interests and scarcely any life outside politics, the family and his farm'.[152] One gets a sense of two dimensionality about Fraser from Edwards' account that does not apparently derive from any lack of insight or skill on the author's part. The memoir of former federal Liberal politician and party whip Henry 'Jo' Gullett, published nearly a decade after Fraser lost office, includes an anecdote corroborating this narrowness. Gullett was a friend of Fraser's father Neville, and a fellow Melbourne Club member. After Malcolm returned from Oxford with his third-class honours degree, Neville Fraser asked Gullett to lunch with him and Malcolm to discuss Malcolm's political ambitions. Gullett found Malcolm '[f]ormidable ... rather than intelligent'. Seats were becoming available 'where the Frasers had their sheep station' and Neville and Malcolm wanted to know, 'What did I think of that?'

> Well for a start he was very young.
>
> Not substantially younger than Kim Beazley and Bill Falkinder had been when first elected, or myself when I first stood, they pointed out.
>
> No, but Beazley had been a recognised academic and one of known political views. Falkinder was a famous flying man and a first rate cricketer. I had been a soldier of repute and it was wartime when I first stood. But what was he, a jackaroo? So assuming he won the seat, what was his base of particular

knowledge? In what subject could he claim to speak from experience and with authority?[153]

Gullett's story highlights a problem political biographers might strike more often than those working on other kinds of subjects, and Edwards seemed to with Fraser: that there turns out to be less to a subject than meets the eye. If Fraser's inner life was hard to locate, and if the character depth that comes from a good education, serious life experiences and deep reflection proved elusive, the possibility that they barely exist in the first place cannot be discounted. In such a case it is the biographer's problem rather than the biographer's fault, and one often not considered in the first flush of enthusiasm when committing to write one.

―――

Russell Schneider's *War Without Blood* is a portrait of Fraser's prime ministership from 1975 to 1980, the year the book was published. Schneider was a Canberra Press Gallery journalist who in March 1975 became press secretary to Reg 'The Toecutter' Withers, a Liberal from Western Australia, then Leader of the Opposition in the Senate. In Withers' office Schneider thus became a staffer at the centre of the Liberal political offensive which culminated in the Dismissal. He served as a Fraser Government staffer until mid-1979, at which point he wrote *War Without Blood*. The experience 'fascinated me, but also left me asking a basic question: why do people like Malcolm Fraser and Reg Withers thrive in a business which is so time-consuming, frustrating and sometimes infuriating?' Schneider discussed it with Fraser's then chief political adviser and speechwriter, former La Trobe University political science tutor (and later the Member for Kooyong), Petro Georgiou. There was only one answer, Georgiou told him: 'the adrenalin effect of politics – or as he put it, war without blood'.[154]

Schneider's book is a valuable guide to Fraser's style of governing. Rather than a work of biography, *War Without Blood* throws a powerful and often harsh light onto aspects of Fraser revealed in action. Schneider dates the effective beginning of Fraser's political career from the death of Harold Holt who first made him a minister. Fraser had 'hounded Holt in his last days', Schneider writes. Fraser 'thinks ... in incredibly short time spans', was 'not dishonest, but ... given to rescinding his resolutions within a few minutes', and these 'rapid changes ultimately put his credibility in doubt'. Behind the scenes 'Fraser's four years have spelt more chaos than many realise', Schneider says.[155]

This is the main burden of *War Without Blood* which, unusually among such works, weaves the bureaucratic thread of the story into the politics. For Schneider wanted to correct a picture of the Fraser Government which 'is altogether too orderly'; in showing Fraser at work in cabinet, interacting with ministers and public servants 'sometimes in small groups, at others one by one', Schneider began to 'unravel this enigma' without writing a biography as such.[156]

The fact that a former Liberal staffer could be so critical of a serving Liberal prime minister may seem surprising. However, the party was heavily factionalised and jockeying was already underway to succeed Fraser as Liberal leader. Senator Withers, for whom Schneider had worked, had been a Fraser Government minister sacked by the prime minister for the improper exercise of ministerial influence. Withers had a runner in the race to displace the unloved Fraser: Peacock, the Member for Kooyong, Menzies' old seat. While Schneider does not spare Peacock in *War Without Blood,* he went on to write a sympathetic political biography of him, published the following year, by which time he was Fraser's main rival. This was *The Colt From Kooyong: Andrew Peacock, a political biography*; Withers was widely considered the colt's 'trainer'.[157] But another devotee of the track in the person of Bob Hawke would shortly end Fraser's grip on power and stop Peacock from ever winning it.

Chapter 6
Bob Hawke, writ large

Only when they'd read the book did they realise he was actually a great man. Because all they'd seen before was a drunken lout, a drunken larrikin.

Blanche d'Alpuget, interview with the author

No-one has ever been as lucky in their biographer as Bob Hawke.

Bob Hawke, interview with the author

Can a contemporary political biography influence the course of history? The career of Australia's twenty-third prime minister, Robert James Lee 'Bob' Hawke, suggests both the extent and limits to which this can be so. Hawke won office in March 1983 and lost it in December 1991 after being defeated 56 votes to 51 on the second challenge from his former treasurer, Paul Keating. Hawke is Australia's most successful federal Labor leader, winning four elections and serving a total eight years and 284 days as prime minister, exceeding the previous record for a Labor prime minister set by Andrew Fisher. Fisher won two elections and formed three governments in the early twentieth century, serving four years and 297 days as prime minister. Hawke is the third longest serving Australian prime minister overall, his time in office exceeded only by the Liberal Party's John Howard who won the same number of elections but served for a total of eleven years and 267 days as prime minister; and by Robert Menzies who won as many elections as Hawke and Howard combined, serving as prime minister for eighteen years and 160 days. The Hawke and Keating governments are remembered as drivers of major economic reform, managers of a collaborative wages policy, a concern with social justice and positive engagement with the world, especially Asia.

Hawke's career can be divided into three long phases: eleven years as a university student at the University of Western Australia, the University of Oxford and the Australian National University; twenty-two years in the peak body of the labour movement's industrial wing, the Australian Council of Trade Unions (ACTU); and eleven years as a politician, nearly nine of which he was prime minister. During the first two phases, covering some thirty-three years, Hawke was a hard but high functioning drinker, sports lover and philanderer who, in spite of an unusually high level of education for both his times and milieu, came to personify both the industrial wing of the labour movement and a certain kind of Australian man.

In the third phase, during which he forsook alcohol, Hawke emerged as a disciplined politician leading a quality government along traditional Westminster lines – the last twentieth century Australian government of which this can be said. Hawke was the best educated and one of the most economically literate of prime ministers. His ability to match the right talent with the right portfolio and give his ministers scope to act and initiate policy within the government's broad economic policy framework – largely set during the Labor leadership of Bill Hayden in the two terms of opposition leading up to Hawke's 1983 election win – was critical to the government's success. It was complemented by a golden era in Australian foreign policy of creative problem-solving diplomacy, warm regional relations, and a distinct assertion of Australian priorities within the continuing Australia–US alliance.

Bob Hawke, writ large

But Hawke had his demons; they came in bottles. 'When it came to the point of seriously making the decision and going into parliament, I knew I'd have to give up drinking, because I'd done some silly things in drink and I wasn't prepared to offer myself for the highest office in the land in a situation where I could disgrace myself or the country', Hawke recalls.[1] Hawke's drinking was very much part of his public persona. His charisma and obvious lust for life made his 'womanising' implicitly sensed if not explicitly known beyond those in the interlocking circles of industrial relations, politics, business and media who encountered Hawke directly through work or socialising before he entered parliamentary politics. 'I think it's ... fair to say that voters probably like me because they think I'm natural', he says. 'I didn't consciously go about saying: How should I look if I'm going to be prime minister?'[2]

Hawke's life presented rich potential for biographers. 'His life was an open book – in fact, three open books, with biographies by John Hurst, Robert Pullan and, best of all, Blanche d'Alpuget, before he reached the Lodge', Hawke speechwriter, Stephen Mills, later commented.[3] There was a fourth while Hawke was in power: a psychobiography by Stan Anson appearing late in his prime ministership, published between Keating's two leadership challenges in 1991.[4]

With two exceptions, every prime minister in postwar twentieth century Australia served at least two decades in parliament before reaching the prime ministership. The common understanding was that voters – and parliamentary colleagues – liked to have a long, hard look at someone before trusting them with the big job.[5] The first exception was Menzies who served six years in the Victorian parliament, then just five years in federal parliament, before becoming prime minister – eleven years parliamentary experience in all. Hawke is the other exception having served less than three years in parliament before becoming prime minister.

However, Hawke had been a public figure since 1959 when he argued his first wage case for the ACTU. After decades as ACTU advocate and then president, Hawke was already one of the best known and most popular identities in Australian public life when he arrived in Canberra in 1980 as the Member for Wills, the larrikin Mr Fixit of Australia's then stormy industrial relations scene. Augmented by a period as ALP national president in the 1970s, Hawke was seen as the workers' friend and major extra-parliamentary ALP presence – and, as he drew closer to a parliamentary career, seemingly on an unstoppable trajectory to the top. Combined with a complex, volatile personality and alcohol-drenched lifestyle, it made him a compelling biographical subject. This was the context in which Hawke's first two biographers, John Hurst and Robert Pullan, wrote their books.

Hurst's *Hawke: the definitive biography* was published by Angus & Robertson in 1979. Born in 1934, Hurst was a British born, Melbourne University–educated journalist, and a veteran of the Brisbane *Courier Mail*, the ABC, *Nation Review* and *The Australian*, where he was the industrial relations correspondent, when the book – his first – was published. He spent eighteen months on research during which he 'had the confidences and reminiscences of leading Labor politicians, talked to Hawke's family and intimate friends and extracted hitherto well-guarded information from the man himself'.[6] Hurst styled himself as a 'leading writer on industrial affairs' and 'close Hawke watcher since the 1960s'. The reader is invited to see him as, if not on a par with Hawke, then not far below – for example, in the flyleaf boast that extensive travel in and reporting from the Middle East makes him 'able to match his understanding of the problem against Bob Hawke's commitment to Israel', a well-known feature of his politics.

In the foreword's very first sentence, Hurst identifies himself as a Hawke drinking companion, along with federal Labor frontbencher Mick Young: 'Not so long ago, Bob Hawke, Mick Young and I were drinking at the Southern Cross Hotel when an attractive young woman approached us'.[7] In the second sentence he establishes Hawke's sexual magnetism: 'She had eyes for only one of us – Bob Hawke'. In the third sentence he establishes Hawke's credentials for conquest: 'She was quite overcome at the sight: here he was in person'. In the fourth he establishes this as a routine occurrence: 'Hawke is used to such situations'. In the fifth he points to the media's role: 'They tell him they've seen him on the telly'. In the sixth he signals Hawke can see off antagonists: 'There are others who want to abuse him and Hawke can cope with such situations, too'. In the seventh sentence Hurst hints at Hawke's work hard, play hard life, his pleasure in attention and his good upbringing: 'he looked a little low and jaded after a heavy week' but 'enjoyed being recognized' and was 'polite'. In the eighth he hints at Hawke as a free-floating object of antipodean female desire: 'The lady said that she often wondered what he was like', comparing 'his fame to that of a pop-star'. In the ninth he explains that Hawke did not contradict her and 'invited her to sit down'. He and Young 'did not want to come between a pop-star and his fan', Hurst comments in the tenth sentence, establishing their male solidarity before, in the eleventh, establishing Hawke's inchoate attractiveness to men too: 'We moved to another part of the lounge and there we talked about – what else but Bob Hawke?'

These eleven sentences, forming the first two paragraphs of the Hurst biography, concisely outline the perceived wisdom on the pre-parliamentary Hawke. The author locates himself firmly as a Hawke familiar, and the reader's likely preconceptions about Hawke are confirmed. Hurst then establishes Mick Young's authority as the unabashedly masculinist, quintessential Australian man's man – 'a tough, hard-drinking, hard-swearing ex-shearer' – and quotes him making the popular case for Hawke's leadership credentials.

> Hawke's a good performer. He's a great crowd pleaser and can fill the halls. I had doubts on some occasions about how the middle class were copping him. But there was no doubt what the working people thought. They liked him. He's a good chairman of meetings. That's very much a part of his make-up. More than anyone else in politics he reflects the Australian lifestyle. He's raucous, if need be, but intelligent. He likes all the things

Australians like and commands respect by what he has to say. He's very adaptable. Even those who are politically hostile listen to him. He has built up his leadership, his popularity, on what makes the Australian character, combined with his own brand of obvious intelligence. Australians like his style. He expresses himself the way they like, directly. They like their leader to have a few beers with them. And he can talk to them about the things they are interested in – footy and horses and unions and things that are happening in other states that they've never heard about.[8]

In one page, Hawke as he was then publicly understood is presented. The rest of the book details the conventional narrative of his life in the most detailed form it had appeared to that date. This was Hawke as the child of a small town Congregationalist clergyman father and strong-willed mother, both teetotal; Perth Modern School, then Law and Arts degrees at the University of Western Australia; a Rhodes Scholarship to Oxford for a BLitt, writing a thesis on the Australian arbitration system; doctoral studies at the ANU dropped to become the ACTU research officer; success and notice as the ACTU national wage case advocate in 1959; ascension to ACTU presidency and for a while, presidency of the ALP, culminating on the book's final page with Hawke's decision in 1979 to run for parliament.

The personal dimension is related along the way including the influence of his politician uncle, Bert Hawke; the early death of his older brother Neil from meningitis, and his own near death in a motorcycle accident in Perth; marriage and children with Hazel (nee Masterson); and life as ever more public property going from one high profile industrial dispute to another, dousing workplace conflagrations and moving slowly but inexorably towards parliamentary politics. In the one dedicated personal chapter, 'The semi-private man', Hurst asks at the outset, 'Is there another Bob Hawke?'[9] It makes poignant reading, putting the best complexion on – effectively concealing – family difficulties flowing from Hawke being a hard-working, hard-drinking, often absent father and philandering husband. Hawke comes across in the book as equal parts professionalism, popularity, potency and plonk. Ominously, it is in this chapter that Hawke mate Col Cunningham candidly identified Hawke's affliction.

> The one fault Cunningham found in Hawke was his bouts of heavy drinking. He eventually decided to offer him a bit of frank advice: 'It's your worst enemy. You can't let yourself go on this way when there are so many people depending on you to do things for them'. Cunningham said there was little point beating about the bush. 'People are desperate for a leader and here you are trying to destroy yourself'.[10]

Hawke's chronic drinking contributed to damaging scenes like that at the Rotunda Bar of Adelaide's Gateway Hotel during the 1979 federal ALP conference, when Hawke abused the then Labor leader Hayden in foul terms to journalists, then turned on the journalists themselves.

> He cooled down after a time, but erupted when media people crowded him while he tried to make a phone call ... 'For Christ's sake, piss off. I'm making a private call'. Later, he ... told journalists that if they believed that voters would be influenced by what some particular candidate had done on a particular day, they were 'wanking' themselves.[11]

The media was 'almost unanimous in writing off Hawke after the events of the conference and his outbursts after it', Hurst writes.[12] This was followed soon after by the 1979 ACTU Congress at which Hawke suffered high profile defeats over uranium mining and elections for the ACTU executive.

Despite otherwise being a relatively unqualified encomium, Hurst's book closes at this point in a downbeat and fairly abrupt manner. Deadline pressures no doubt figured in the conclusion's brevity but there is also a sense that Hurst is hedging himself against the chance that the Hawke train, which for a couple of hundred pages seemed to be heading straight for The Lodge, might career off the rails before reaching it.

The book's third last paragraph details Hawke's sudden health problems. 'He looked haggard after the congress', Hurst writes, noting partial hearing loss and a suspected tumour, a suspicion happily unfounded. Medication and 'a change of diet' was recommended by a medical specialist, though Hurst does not mention whether the proposed dietary changes included changed drinking habits.

The penultimate paragraph records that Hawke's 'private agony' over whether to run for parliament ended on 23 September 1979 when he announced he would run for the Victorian seat of Wills at the 1980 election. 'One question remained in the minds of the journalists who crowded the room: would he become Labor's parliamentary leader?'[3]

The final paragraph recounts a bet – a $100 wager between jockey Roy Higgins and Hawke about whether Hawke would become prime minister before Andrew Peacock, the likely successor of Malcolm Fraser as Liberal leader: 'It still looked like an each-way bet, but Higgins, though a Liberal sympathizer, now reckoned that the odds were shortening a bit in Hawke's favour'. Hurst himself makes no call. The positive glow of the rest of the book is absent at its end.

Pullan's *Bob Hawke: A Portrait* was published by Methuen in 1980 and, like Hurst's book, closes with Hawke's announcement that he will run for Wills.[14] Like his subject, Pullan is a law graduate of the University of Western Australia, but of a later generation. Born in 1944, he was a university contemporary of Bob McMullan, then of the Labor Left faction and, by the time Pullan wrote *Bob Hawke*, Labor's WA state secretary.[15] Pullan was from a politically conservative family but of progressive inclination himself. His father was an accountant who became chief executive of Swan Cement and his mother, a dental nurse before her marriage, did volunteer community work. Pullan went to the Perth Anglican boys school Guildford Grammar which, while not noted for its academics, had some good teachers, Pullan recalls, including an English teacher who 'uttered a thing which still resonates' with him decades later. 'He said that every sentence that is spoken or written down in English has three levels of meaning', Pullan recalls.[16] 'The speaker's attitude to the speaker, the speaker's attitude to the audience, and the speaker's attitude to the subject in terms of the content, and then we have the content'.

Pullan became a journalist with the Perth metropolitan daily newspaper, the *West Australian*, and did a stint in its Canberra bureau. The *West Australian*'s conservatism occasionally discomfited Pullen who nevertheless, in the way journalists and barristers do, learned to separate personal sentiment from the professional task at hand.[17] In 1972 he was posted to New York for the Herald & Weekly Times group of newspapers and, after four years, moved to Washington where he freelanced for two years, contributing mostly to *The Australian* and the *Bulletin*.

Pullan returned to Australia in 1978 and became a *Reader's Digest* contributor. Colleagues praised his occasional biographical sketches, including one of novelist George Johnston commissioned by *The Australian*, and others of Papua New Guinea's prime minister Michael Somare and Australian prime minister Malcolm Fraser for the *Reader's Digest*. '[T]hose exercises intrigued and fascinated me', he says, and indirectly led to his first book length work.[18]

> I drifted into the Hawke biography via a friend who had contributed to the *Digest* and was looking for work, like we all were, and mentioned it to a character called Peter Taylor [who was] a book packager. I had lunch with Peter for the purpose of deciding on a book, and I said, 'Well, I enjoy writing biographical sketches. Perhaps a biography could be interesting'. I knew that

biographies tend to sell okay, and he said, 'Yes, it's a good idea. Of whom?' And I said, 'Bob Hawke'. And his eyes lit up.

I thought, 'Why was I interested in Hawke?' Well, a Labor Party person, an interesting character, then on the news all the time, and the fact that there wasn't a fully fleshed out account of this character who even the Liberals thought would be prime minister. I thought, well, that's an obvious opportunity to get myself published in book form.[19]

Peter Taylor placed the book with Methuen and got Pullan a $2000 advance, the equivalent of around $11 000 now.

Pullan identified with Labor. His friends in Perth included several Labor identities and, 'because my father was a reactionary, I was looking for ways of connecting to the other side'. There was no question of choosing a conservative politician as a subject: 'I thought of myself as progressive and ... nothing could have interested me less than writing a biography of a Liberal politician. I would have equated Liberal with boring'. A 'very disappointed' Pullan subsequently found that neither Hawke nor his family would cooperate with the project. He remembers thinking, 'It's up to the writer to make the decision about whether the biography happens, not the subject'.[20]

Pullan then proceeded in the standard journalistic manner, identifying potential interviewees and approaching them to talk, getting cooperation from Hawke classmates from Perth Modern School and people in the labour movement. There was no archival research: 'I looked through the clips'. Bob Carr and Malcolm Turnbull were two rising journalists at the *Bulletin* when Pullan was a *Bulletin* contributor working simultaneously on the book. Hearing of the project, Carr pulled out a clip on Hawke to draw his attention to a specific quote, a kindness Pullan recalls fondly. The editor of *The Australian*, Les Hollings, was another who heard about the biography and commissioned a Hawke profile from Pullan for the paper: 'I called Bob and he naturally agreed to cooperate on the piece for *The Australian*, (so) I got something', Pullan says.[21]

The description of his two-hour interview with Hawke provides insight into the 'making do' aspect of journalism which regularly requires reporters to wring a lot out of little. Two hours worth of questions and answers may seem impossibly short to scholarly biographers, and such limited (or non-existent) access may even lead to a project being dropped; Hazel Rowley, for example, gave up on a proposed biography of Germaine Greer after failing to secure the cooperation of her subject. For a journalist, however, if two hours access is all that is on offer, the professional challenge is to make that work. It can be enough, at least, with skill and luck, to get something different and important from the standard lines on high rotation in the clippings files, as well as the chance to sense and assess the subject directly. That approach is demonstrated in Pullan's account of the interview, which took place one afternoon in 1979 at Hawke's then favoured Sydney hotel, the Boulevard, on William Street.

At the hotel Hawke, then still married to Hazel, had a young woman with him 'whose name and phone number', Pullan recalls, 'I regrettably failed to get'.[22] Hawke introduced them. 'He wasn't in the least embarrassed and she ... wasn't overtly embarrassed'. She appeared in neither Pullan's profile for *The Australian* nor in his biography of Hawke – one of the legion of instances where potentially relevant but damaging facts are kept from the public record by journalists for reasons rarely articulated.[23] The interview began. Pullan's impression was that 'the Hawke you see on television [is] the private Hawke' as well.

> I didn't see any distance between the public and the private. I'm not saying there wasn't any. I'm saying that it wasn't [obvious]. You know how, when you are evaluating people, you meet them and think, 'Okay, how close is this to what they appear to be on the screen?' And quite often there's a fair distance, but not

> with Bob. And what surprised me about him was that he was talking about his motorbike accident ... He's talked about it, you know, twenty, thirty, fifty, hundreds of times. But he's reliving it – the pain. He is re-enacting his own past. I thought there was something lovably authentic about this ...
>
> And so I'm evaluating him and the way he looks, but I'm also conscious that it's an interview and there are only so many sentences in it. And you can't get a life story out of a couple of hours.[24]

Pullan remained surprised that Hawke declined to cooperate with his book since 'he had no reason to think I was out to bag him', and that McMullan and other Labor insiders would have vouched for him had Hawke asked.

> But I expect all politicians to act solely out of self-interest when they are dealing with journalists and especially pesky biographers who might find [certain things] out. For example, somebody told me that Hazel had aborted twins to preserve Bob's Rhodes Scholarship, and this was a secondary source. I went to the source and he said, 'If you report that, I'll deny it'. And I thought, 'Well, so it's true, but how on earth can I report it?' And I didn't.[25]

Had Pullan confirmed and published this story, the impact on Hawke's nascent political career would have been incalculable. It would also have transformed *Bob Hawke: A Portrait* from a thoughtful book designed to 'give an account of the sort of person Hawke is' into a media sensation.

The traditional craft training of journalists (degraded since the decline of the apprentice-style system of cadet training), and the potential impact of defamation law, combined to prevent that happening.

Traditionally, journalists require a second source to confirm a piece of information to make it publishable. Pullan could not find a second source to confirm the story, without which defending it in court would have been difficult. It is significant that the professional scruples of a journalist trained in the craft's traditional mores saved Hawke from a public revelation potentially far more damaging than any drunken or philandering escapade. An action which could have been represented as Hawke being so ambitious he was prepared to sacrifice his unborn children to get ahead was a potentially career-ending problem, at least in terms of his immediate political prospects, had it emerged publicly then.

Not long afterwards, Hazel Hawke told Blanche d'Alpuget the same story but insisted she not publish it. D'Alpuget checked Hazel's account with another primary source who confirmed it, but she stuck by her agreement not to publish.[26] 'Hazel had a well-developed narrative about Bob at this stage in their marriage: he was a ruthless bastard, a cad even, and she was his victim, staunchly putting up with what no woman should be asked to', d'Alpuget says.

> Already the Saint Hazel, Sinner Bob story was held by a group of people, especially women, who knew them as a couple. Concerning the abortions, Hawke was so emotionally traumatised that even thirty years later he would make strange references to it that, if one did not know his psychology, would be meaningless. After Hazel had told me I wormed a curt account of it from him. He looked shame-faced but refused to elaborate. But he did elaborate, unconsciously, in dozens of guilty asides right up to the 1980s.[27]

Pullan's book is notable for its inherent modesty. In the introduction he denies it is even a biography, describing it rather as 'an attempt to sketch a portrait of Bob Hawke through descriptions of the major events in his life, the ideas that move him and the passions of his heart'.[28] Compare and contrast fellow journalist Hurst's claim in the title of his book, that it is *the definitive biography*.

Unlike Hurst who had the inside running with his subject, Pullan had to make insight his comparative advantage. 'I came to think that the intriguing process of trying to think your way – our way – into other people's heads is practically universal', he says.[29] 'We all do it, all the time. We just see people playing tennis and there's a character reading coming down the line ... We see people walking down the street and we start to form an opinion'. Pullan's desire for professional challenge and development was central to his writing of the book.

> I wasn't doing it for the money. I was doing it for the fame [laughter]. I sort of thought of publishing a book as a step to another level from journalism. Partly because it lasts a bit longer, and partly because it's testing you in a way which daily journalism isn't.[30]

Unlike Hurst, who flashes a couple of warning signals at the end of his de facto authorised biography without exploring their implications, on the eve of Hawke's arrival in Canberra, Pullan made clear the risk and reward binary of a parliamentary Bob Hawke. He frames it in Hawke's evocation of Labor icon John Curtin during the press conference announcing his run for Wills. In talking about Curtin, Pullan writes, Hawke is 'drawing a portrait of himself; the five strands of Curtin's character which Hawke most admires are strands Hawke has woven into public perceptions of himself'.[31] The fifth strand was Curtin's struggle with the drink, and Hawke notes that Curtin 'accepted ... responsibility' when the party wanted him as leader in the 1930s.

> Though he had presented it by talking about Curtin and not about himself, it was an honest portrait, revealing of what he could do – split and ruin the Labor Party, or take it back into power; help Australians to cope with an economy carried on the backs

of the children of the poor, or pour the wine of Australia down his throat in rage and misery while men who did not have his gifts ran the government and the country. Though he was utterly untested in parliament and government, he could subliminally compare himself to the most revered of all Australian Labor leaders without the unstated ambition seeming grotesque. He was about to test himself on an entirely new stage, where the pressures on his stamina would be merciless, the analyses of his psyche endless and the questions about his weakness relentless, because he was the first Australian leader to make his character the issue which enveloped all others. He stood in the doorway of the ACTU board room, his arm around Hazel's waist, smiling for the photographers, grumbling about their demands, looking oddly vulnerable. Looking into the eighties.[32]

With some reflectiveness, insight and historical perspective, Pullan produced an account of Hawke that could fairly claim to begin taking us *into* Bob Hawke in a way Hurst's comprehensive but essentially surface account did not. Pullan pointed to the questions, even if he did not provide answers, about what lay within.

That task was taken up in the third and fourth Hawke biographies, d'Alpuget's *Robert J Hawke: A Biography*, published in 1982, the year before Hawke became prime minister, and Stan Anson's *Hawke: An Emotional Life*, published in 1991, the last year of his prime ministership.[33] Both were psychological biographies, though in profoundly different ways, and both authors were members of the Labor Party.[34] The Anson psychobiography used d'Alpuget's biography as its primary source. So dependent was Anson on d'Alpuget's book that he acknowledges at its outset – in the first edition, at least – that without it, 'the present study could not have been written'.[35]

Historian Joy Damousi has traced the diffusion of psychoanalytic ideas in Australia after World War I along with resistance to them.[36] She points to Stephen Garton's argument that the character of the Australian medical fraternity is a factor in that resistance, dominated as it was by Scottish Presbyterians and English Anglicans whose empiricist heritage gave them more sympathy to 'facts ... than speculation'.[37] But Damousi goes on to argue that the story of the impact of psychoanalysis in Australia was still transformative in changing the doctor–patient relationship from one where doctors analysed the body of a patient alone to that where 'a patient would speak freely, not only of their illnesses but other aspects of their lives'.[38] Popularised through the media, those same ideas contributed to a 'collapsing of public and private life' into the confessional culture now pervasive throughout the western world.[39]

> In Australia, it should be added that its method was one which was part of an evolving cultural emphasis on confession, communication and intimate conversation, where the private was increasingly being made public, especially through new technologies. It signalled too, a search for the meaning of inner life, which Australians have generally not been associated with, as they have not replicated European models in this pursuit. In Australia, psychoanalytic ideas were discussed in a climate of intellectual eclecticism, drawing from developments in Europe, Britain and the USA.[40]

One manifestation of the reception of psychoanalysis in this antipodean climate of intellectual eclecticism was the psychobiography arising from particular developments in the University of Melbourne's Political Science program. This was an influence on the d'Alpuget and Anson biographies of Hawke.

Both d'Alpuget and Anson thank Graham Little in their acknowledgments. Little had a PhD in sociology from ANU. During a Yale fellowship from 1969 to 1971, he engaged with social scientists Harold

Lasswell, David Riesman and, in Yale's 'Psychology and Politics' program, Robert Lane.[41] Lane styled himself, as Little himself would later, a 'political psychologist'. On returning to Australia, Little joined Melbourne University's political science department where he became a close friend and ally of AE ('Foo') Davies, already known for his work on psychoanalysis and the political self.[42] Davies had been a lecturer in politics at Melbourne since 1946 and was appointed to the chair in 1968.[43] While at London's Tavistock Institute in the late 1950s, Davies underwent psychoanalysis with Hedwig Hoffer, who had moved from Vienna to London with the father of psychoanalysis, Sigmund Freud, in 1938. So Davies' contact with psychoanalytic ideas came from close to their source.

On his return to Melbourne, Davies melded dream interpretation and the application of psychoanalytic concepts with political research in his teaching program. Davies' books *Private Politics* and *Images of Class* were written during this period.[44] Around the time Little arrived, Davies published a collection of essays which included 'The Tasks of Biography', extolling the approach Yale psychologist John Dollard laid out in *Criteria for the Life History*.[45] 'Davies' influence can ... be traced in the texts and footnotes of biographies and histories written by his contemporaries', James Walter notes, 'including the work of his closest successor, Graham Little, who, not only as an academic but as a journalist and broadcaster, kept Davies' legacy in the public eye'.[46]

This psychologically, and usually specifically psychoanalytically, informed 'Melbourne School' approach was exemplified in works like Little's *The Public Emotions* which, as colleague Michael Crozier noted in his obituary of Little, 'dares us to think about the role of feelings in public life'.[47] Crozier described Little's forte as 'mapping complex connections between the political and the psychological' and sharing his insights 'without obfuscation'.[48] Against the backdrop of a political culture suspicious of, and generally hostile to, reflection on the self, the Melbourne School 'psychosocial' approach informed and inspired those interested in the inner life of politics and politicians.

Little observed, 'A psychosocial education is not easy to obtain (and a) psychosocial education is not easy to give, either'.[49] Philosopher Douglas Kirsner traces a line from Davies' 'itinerant seminars over a number of years for a loosely named "Biography group"'; to the 'Freud Conference' instigated by Kirsner from his vantage point at Deakin University, and held annually in Lorne from 1977 and, from 1992, in Melbourne; to the Melbourne Psychosocial Group, based at Melbourne University's department of political science. These brought academics and clinical psychoanalysts together in discussion.

In Kirsner's account, the desire of some Freud Conference participants like Judith Brett for more frequent discussions between academics and clinical psychoanalysts helped establish the Melbourne Psychosocial Group.[50] Davies and Little were central members; others like Walter, Brett and Angus McIntyre, in turn, became prominent exponents of psychobiography in Australia. Brett and McIntyre carried the torch forward at La Trobe University. Walter did likewise at Griffith University and later Monash University. Davies' and Little's shaping of the next generation can be seen, for example, in the detailed notations each made on Walter's draft doctoral thesis.[51] In his preface to the thesis, Walter says discussion arising from his presentation of seminar papers at the 'Melbourne Psycho-Social Study Group' contributed to its development.[52]

D'Alpuget and Anson were both influenced by this approach. D'Alpuget had met Little through McIntyre, whom she knew from Indonesia – in 1966 he was an Australian student in Jakarta. She consulted Little during the research for *Robert J Hawke: A Biography*, along with others of psychoanalytic bent like Melbourne psychiatrist Michael Epstein.[53] Little supervised Anson's MA thesis at the University of Melbourne, 'Representing RJ Hawke', submitted in 1988, five years into Hawke's prime ministership, from which *Hawke: An Emotional Life* grew.[54]

Psychologically, let alone psychoanalytically, informed political analysis was and remains controversial. 'To admit to using psychoanalytic ideas in biographical work is immediately to find oneself on the defensive, facing a salvo of arguments ranging from "Freud is bunk" to "You cannot psychoanalyse the dead"', Brett has commented, for example. 'And as one argument is rebutted, a new one is produced, and then another, until the first one reappears in a slightly altered form: the language is so ugly, psychoanalysis is reductionist, literature is a better guide to the inner life and, in these post-universalist days, Freud is only of historic interest'.[55]

This scorn extends to political journalism in Australia which eschews the psychological in favour of football-style reporting where opinion polls provide the ongoing match score. This makes the Hawke biographies by d'Alpuget and Anson all the more remarkable. Coming from different specific positions, with differing expertise and motivations, completely different in tenor and, ultimately, antagonistically contending, d'Alpuget and Anson nevertheless share the distinction of being the most psychologically driven in the corpus of contemporary Australian political biography. Melbourne Psychosocial Group members would bring psychological tools to the biographical table in work on politicians who were dead or whose active careers were over – Walter on Whitlam, for example, Brett on Menzies and McIntyre on Indonesia's President Suharto – and in the Australian scene, that was itself bold enough.[56] D'Alpuget and Anson went further and applied them contemporaneously during the active career of a very much alive Bob Hawke.

D'Alpuget was born in 1944, the daughter of Lou d'Alpuget and Josie Stephenson, and grew up in Sydney's eastern suburbs. She attended Sydney Church of England Girls' Grammar School (SCEGGS) and, briefly, the University of Sydney before becoming a journalist with the *Daily Mirror*, rival newspaper of the *Sun* where her father worked. A hyper-masculine yachtsman, champion boxer, wrestler, water polo player and, in youth, Bondi lifesaver, Lou d'Alpuget in the newsroom once shouted at cadet journalist John Pilger so ferociously for getting his facts wrong that Pilger fainted. He taught Blanche to box, surf, sail, fish, fire a rifle and execute basic unarmed combat moves, the last because he thought girls should be able to defend themselves against assault.[57] The journalistic gene was not fully transmitted though. 'I was always aware of the fact that I was not a good journalist', d'Alpuget says.[58] 'I had no news sense. It *is* a sense, and I haven't got it. I still haven't got it'. Unusually, Lou recommended the works of Cambridge English literature don Arthur Quiller-Couch to *Sun* cadets, not an obvious choice as an influence on Australian journalistic prose. While Lou's news sense was not transmitted to Blanche, the literary bent this suggests in him was.

D'Alpuget was on the *Mirror*'s full-time payroll in Sydney for just three years: life as a novelist lay ahead. First, though, there was a spell in London followed by nine years living in South-East Asia, including two periods living in Indonesia with her husband, journalist turned diplomat Tony Pratt. In 1970, the year d'Alpuget first met Hawke, Pratt was second secretary at the Australian Embassy in Jakarta. 'I showed visiting "firemen" around Jakarta', she recalls.[59] 'I was very good at that. It was one of the things expected of the wives'. Hawke, recently anointed ACTU president, remembers seeing 'this vision' for the first time, en route to the annual meeting of the International Labour Organisation (ILO) in Switzerland. 'I met her first in Jakarta on my way through to Geneva when Rawdon Dalrymple was the counsellor in the embassy there', he recalls. 'I was sitting on the verandah of his house having a beer and this vision in white appeared from around the corner and I thought, my god!'[60] For her part, d'Alpuget formed an immediately positive impression of Hawke.

> I thought he was a good person for a particular reason. It goes back to Jakarta, and to showing around visiting firemen. All of them, without exception, would want to visit the Jakarta slums. And I

> used to take people there and ... they'd get this warm inner glow
> of the superiority of our culture while looking at the poor slum
> dwellers as if they were animals in a zoo, which I really hated.
>
> Bob was the only person, when I asked, 'Do you want to see
> the *kampongs*?' who said, 'No, I don't want to see poverty'. And
> I thought, ah, a good guy. And really my respect for him was
> based just on that.

She would see Hawke once more in Indonesia – the following year, in 1971, when he was again en route for the ILO. As well as squiring visitors around Jakarta, d'Alpuget worked variously at the Australian Embassy, including the press office, during her time in Indonesia. She wrote human interest pieces 'with the blessing of the Australian embassy' and tacit approval of the Indonesian intelligence service, to be placed in the Australian media, smoothing the way for the first visit to Australia by an Indonesian head of state: President Suharto in 1972, in the still sensitive post-*Konfrontasi* period.[61] It was a life of 'pleasure and ease ... friends and parties, horse riding in the early mornings, swimming in the afternoons', married to Tony: 'We ... were boon companions'.[62]

D'Alpuget returned to Australia in 1973 and lived in Canberra where Pratt worked for the Department of Defence 'with consequences he had not foreseen, and he was miserable'.[63] She felt socially restricted and stood out in a national capital then only 200 000 strong, the vast majority of whom were in the paid workforce as public servants. 'I don't much like bureaucrats and they don't much like me', she adds.[64] Her friend, feminist activist Susan Ryan, who became a Labor senator for the ACT in 1975, recalls d'Alpuget then as a 'vivacious, unconventional woman in her thirties'.

> Dazzlingly pretty and petite, she looked like a Thai beauty with
> blond curls ... Blanche was full of fun. She liked to make loud,

outrageous observations about people, particularly about their sexual demeanour ... In an era of dull and careless feminist dress codes she was a welcome sight at [Women's Electoral Lobby] meetings, a little bird of paradise in gold high-heeled sandals, tight black slacks and a mink jacket to keep out the Canberra cold, topped by perfectly ordered blond curls, her face luminous with detailed make-up.[65]

Pratt, in turn, was an 'Adonis' in Ryan's recollection. 'I loved my husband, whom I'd met when I was seventeen, and felt fiercely loyal to him', d'Alpuget has written. 'In the decade we had journeyed together we had both taken side trips, but we were mindful of each other's feelings, and discreet'.[66] They divorced in 1986.

It was during this period that d'Alpuget established herself as a writer. 'I was not keen on taking a job, because of our young son'; instead she wrote a novel set in Jakarta. Twenty rejection slips later, including one from publisher Richard Walsh who described it as 'just a straggle of events' – he 'was right, but I felt like pulling out his tongue and feeding it to the cat' – she set the novel aside.[67] 'But I had discovered the pleasures of writing and wanted to do it again'. D'Alpuget did, winning Fellowship of Australian Writers' prizes for two short stories in 1975. Then came an unexpected, perhaps fated, opportunity to write a biography of Sir Richard Kirby, a long-serving judge and former Conciliation and Arbitration Commission president. D'Alpuget knew Kirby's daughter Sue from school. At the time Sue lived in Canberra and her parents occasionally visited. When Kirby and d'Alpuget met in Canberra through Sue, they found a common interest in Indonesia, especially the late Indonesian president Sukarno. 'Kirby had known him personally when he was at the height of his power', d'Alpuget later wrote, 'I as an observer in the last days of his shattered dream'.[68]

During a conversation about Sukarno's Indonesia of the 1940s, d'Alpuget asked to see Kirby's photographs of the period; Kirby instead sent the transcript of his NLA oral history interview. Shortly afterwards, at her father's request, Sue sounded out d'Alpuget about whether she would be willing to help him with his memoirs. D'Alpuget was interested but the logistics were unworkable: she had a young son and the Kirbys divided their time between Melbourne and the NSW South Coast. D'Alpuget suggested she write his biography instead. Kirby agreed.[69] It would be published in 1977 as *Mediator: A Biography of Sir Richard Kirby*. During the process they became friends; Kirby nicknamed d'Alpuget 'Blanco'.

D'Alpuget began work on the book without a publishing contract in hand. Getting a publisher for a serious biography was easier than for a first-time novel, however, and at Max Suich's suggestion d'Alpuget proposed it to Melbourne University Press publisher, Peter Ryan.

> It's very fashionable to say, oh, he's a terrible old right-wing tyrant and so forth. And indeed, he was a martinet. But he was marvellous. He took it on on what he'd seen – the couple of chapters I wrote plus an outline.
>
> And he really taught me how to be an author. He hand wrote me a letter every single week. First of all he gave me the style manual for the house ... When I'd do something wrong, I remember once he sent me a drawing of me having my head chopped off with a guillotine. He drew it falling into a basket with a ZUT! three times after it. But he was very, very good for a young author. They don't do that these days.[70]

Before d'Alpuget sent a chapter to Ryan she would send it first to her stepmother, journalist and editor Tess van Sommers. It was a production line that forged her as an author. D'Alpuget credited both Ryan and van Sommers for turning her 'into a writer'.[71] Applying the lessons learned from writing the Kirby book, d'Alpuget did a six-week rewrite of the rejected novel and immediately found a publisher; it became the prize-winning *Monkeys in the Dark*.[72]

Research on the Kirby biography included long walks along Berrara Beach, near Jervis Bay, during which Kirby gave d'Alpuget a crash course in Australian industrial law – unique in the world at that time in consisting of court-based arbitrated rulings on cases triggered by disputes between unions and employers, and the creation of court-sanctioned 'awards' that embodied agreements on wages and conditions between them. To that point, d'Alpuget's only experience with the law had been as a teenage runaway when at her parents' instigation police nabbed her and her much older boyfriend interstate.[73] D'Alpuget had also done some court reporting at the *Mirror*.[74] D'Alpuget was no student of biography either. 'At that stage, I'm ashamed to admit, I had never read a biography', she recalls. 'I was much too busy ... going to parties!'[75]

As the long-standing Arbitration Commission president, Kirby knew Hawke and had come to like him very much. When he first observed him, Hawke was an impatient ANU research student assisting ACTU advocate Richard Eggleston QC in the 1958 national wage case hearings. 'He couldn't sit still', Kirby told d'Alpuget. 'You could see he was practically going mad with frustration at not being able to have a say ... From the bench we used to watch him with some curiosity and amusement'. Hawke, 28 years old at the time but looking to the bench 'only twenty-two or three', asked for an interview with Kirby in his chambers.

> He came in and explained he was a research student at the ANU. He began asking me a series of questions which I found quite objectionable in tone; how did we judges make our decisions? Did we believe we had the economic training necessary for the job we were trying to do? He more or less suggested we were a lot of economic ignoramuses, and things would be better off without us. I got pretty annoyed and indicated I thought him offensive.[76]

In the next few pages of the Kirby biography, d'Alpuget recounts the unexpectedly riveting story of Hawke's arrival on the public stage and his role in transforming the conceptual basis of Australian wage-fixing at that time from 'capacity' to 'productivity'. Hawke dropped out of his ANU doctoral studies, became the ACTU's first university-educated employee and, not yet 30 years old, was appointed ACTU advocate for the 1959 basic wage case. The presiding judge, Alf Foster, sent word via back channels to ACTU president Albert Monk 'that he thought senior counsel and not some unknown student' should present the union case. Monk stuck with Hawke whose 'assault on the concepts of wage fixation was immediate, savage and effective', d'Alpuget records.[77]

Kirby was galvanised by Hawke's arguments. 'In the off-season I later sought discussions with economists like Nugget Coombs, Joe Isaac and Dick Downing to help me understand in some depth what Hawke was talking about', he told d'Alpuget.[78] D'Alpuget herself was galvanised by Hawke the man. In March 1976 she went to Melbourne to interview him for the Kirby book.

> I did not initially recognize him as the man-passing-through-town with whom, six years earlier, I'd spent an hour *tete-a-tete* at a party (to which I'd worn, I remembered, a new white dress my mother had made). Nor did I realise what he would do in my life: I did not know when I encountered him again that the Muse had arrived. I did not know that, old, young, black, white, as himself or masked, I would draw him or some characteristic or saying of his, in book after book.
>
> With mutual, wordless consent it was agreed we would become lovers as soon as possible – which happened to be in a different city, the following night.[79]

The city was Canberra.[80] Hawke was late and wearing pancake make-up. They would meet every few weeks; in between there were 'no phone conversations, no notes, messages, nothing'. Hawke was rarely out of d'Alpuget's mind. She tried never to mention his name but everything seemed to evoke his image, and all of it 'shimmered with life'. D'Alpuget's interior world was alight: 'Researching was a joy; writing was a joy; everything was a joy'.[81] She carefully diarised their meetings.[82] But 'slowly, dreadfully, I came to realise he was having affairs with women all over the country, that his love life was a kind of freewheeling, decentralised harem, with four or five favourites and a shoe-sale queue of one-night stands'.[83]

The relationship continued nevertheless and in November 1978 Hawke told d'Alpuget about a dream in which she and 'Paradiso', his long-standing lover in Geneva, were standing on a roulette wheel. 'The wheel spun, and came to rest at me', d'Alpuget writes in *On Longing*. 'It meant, [he] said, he must choose me: *to marry*'. She was, she writes, 'slain with delight' but told him she would think about it and respond in the New Year. Practical considerations arose in her mind but did not seem decisive. Some were especially telling, including the fact that he mispronounced her surname, did not know whether she had siblings and, essentially, 'knew little about who I was'. She asked a psychiatrist friend to interpret Hawke's dream: 'He laughed aloud at my obtuseness. "It means throwing in his lot with you is a gamble"'.[84]

More than the roulette wheel was turning, however, by the time 1979 arrived. Hawke rang daily: 'I felt safe', she says. But d'Alpuget had an emerging realisation that she knew him as little as he knew her: 'We were enigmas, peeping at each other through keyholes'.[85] D'Alpuget began to research her second novel, *Turtle Beach*.[86] It became an exercise in 'unconscious autobiography', d'Alpuget wrote later, as had the rewrite of her first novel after the Kirby biography was finished; the writing of both stories reduced the pressure of her clandestine relationship with Hawke to bearable levels, partly by channelling her and Hawke's personae into those novels' fictional characters.[87]

Hawke's attention, meanwhile, had turned to the increasingly tense question of whether he should enter parliament – this against the backdrop of disasters at the 1979 ALP conference and ACTU Congress, the death of his mother Ellie, and trouble at home in Royal Avenue, Sandringham. His life was now awash with 'out-of-control drinking'. At the back of his mind, too, was a calculation that divorce could cost Labor a few percentage points at the ballot box should he become leader. Hawke stopped calling d'Alpuget. After some weeks, in a phone conversation lasting half a minute, Hawke told her he was not getting divorced.[88] 'Each of us asked the other to leave', Hazel Hawke wrote later in her memoirs. 'We both stayed'.[89]

From being 'slain with delight' at the marriage proposal nearly a year before, d'Alpuget now first thought of killing herself, and then of killing Hawke. Each proposition was considered in practical detail over a number of days before a 'shard of vanity' and the realisation that 'giving my son a murderess for a mother was hardly better than a suicide, and that if I were in jail I would not see him often' terminated that line of thought. 'Without revealing too many details, and certainly none of my murder plans, I told (Kirby) the story. He listened, and after a silence said, "Thank God, Blanco, that it's over. You would have ended up sticking a knife in him"'.[90]

Is it possible that d'Alpuget really did know Hawke as little as she claims in *On Longing*?

> No, I didn't get to know him well at all. I really didn't, because it was a completely sexual relationship. Brief encounters that had to be fitted in between him doing a thousand other things ... I only ever saw him behind a closed door.[91]

D'Alpuget disavows even an appreciation of Hawke's powerful public projection at the time 'because I never saw him in public', and in any case, 'I'd been writing novels ... I wasn't all that interested'.[92] Rather, rivals were on d'Alpuget's mind. In *On Longing* she recounts looking at a 'luscious minx' on page three of the *Mirror*, for example, and wondering if she was another of Hawke's *'petites amies'* – this while rewriting *Monkeys in the Dark* whose heroine's fascination with her lover 'was mixed and corrupted with anger and tension'. She continued: 'We write out our sicknesses in books, Hemingway said. Well, yes and no: Hemingway shot himself'.[93]

At this point, in 1979, d'Alpuget was author of the critically well-received Kirby biography, had two novels in the pipeline that would be published in the next two years to acclaim, several literary prizes and foreign translations of her works but little in the way of financial reward. She wanted to write another biography and initially chose Hawke's mentor and predecessor Albert Monk, the ACTU's first full-time president whose tenure overlapped substantially with Kirby's at the Arbitration Commission. This idea fell victim to the resistance of Monk's widow who was disinclined to give d'Alpuget access to his papers.[94]

D'Alpuget has said that 'the Hawke book came about because of the Kirby book', and there is a symbiotic feel to the projects, even down to their respective book launches. Nearly five years to the day after Hawke launched d'Alpuget's Kirby biography at Canberra's Lakeside Hotel, Kirby launched d'Alpuget's Hawke biography at the same venue.[95] Melbourne Psychosocial Group members Graham Little and Angus McIntyre, and psychiatrist Michael Epstein, all attended the latter. The Kirby book required mastering the intricacies of Australia's unique industrial relations system and d'Alpuget did so convincingly. The language and concepts she acquired enabled her to understand Hawke's long engagement with labour market theory and practice which dated from his research at Oxford in the mid-1950s on wage fixing under the Australian arbitration system. Interviewing Hawke for the Kirby biography brought about the fateful re-meeting of biographer and subject.

What were d'Alpuget's conscious motives for the Hawke biography? In 2014 she presented it as a simple instrumental decision after she unsuccessfully 'tried and tried' to get Monk's widow to give her access to his papers: 'She turned me down ... So I thought, okay, I'll try the second president'.[96] Earlier, in *On Longing* in 2008, d'Alpuget 'noted that the news media presentation of [Hawke] was mostly so simplified as to be not much more than a cartoon'.[97] D'Alpuget 'was offended that public debate relied on such spindly legs, and wanted to do something about it; I wanted to make my own presentation of [Hawke] in a biography'. Earlier again, in 1986, d'Alpuget told Jennifer Ellison that 'with the Hawke biography – I just had to make some money. I mean, that wasn't the only reason, but I had that practical reason. Nobody can expect to make money out of writing fiction, so I wanted to write a book which I thought would finance me for a couple of novels, which it has'.[98] The interrelated fiction and financial factors behind the book were related earlier still, in 1985, to Candida Baker, 'because I knew it would help make me so well-known in Australia that all future fiction writing would be easy to sell'.[99]

D'Alpuget told Ellison another factor was that Hawke 'wasn't entirely happy' about another biography being written at the time, though she does not specify whether that concern related to the Hurst or Pullan book. D'Alpuget also evinced genuine interest in Australia's arbitration system; Hawke had wanted to do a doctoral thesis on it, and had spent half a lifetime working in it, while she had written a 'part-history of that system' in the Kirby biography.[100] 'And there was a genuinely shared curiosity: you know, if you've once dreamed of going to Krakatoa and then you meet someone who has travelled there, you want to talk to him or her'. D'Alpuget told Baker that Hawke had rung her in 1978 to say that Hurst was thinking of doing a biography of him, wanting to know how much demand on his time a biographer was likely to make: 'So we had a talk about it, and I said as a joke, "Well if somebody's going to do a biography of you, why don't you let me do it?"'[101] This has been d'Alpuget's most frequent response to questions about the book's genesis. A more expansive account was given at a *Canberra Times* Literary Luncheon in 1982, shortly after its launch.

> [I]n 1978 he got in touch with me and he said that somebody wanted to do his biography and I was the only biographer he knew and how much time was he going to have to devote to it.
>
> So we had this conversation, you see, and it was going on and I didn't know at that stage really but I perceived it intuitively that he's a man who leaves a great deal unspoken and that you have to understand what he's saying intuitively. And I thought while he was talking, that he was thinking that if you were going to be the subject of a life, he would quite like me to do it. That's what I thought in any case.
>
> So I said jokingly – as any shrink will tell you, there are no jokes, especially in these circumstances – I said jokingly, 'Well if you're going to have a biography done, why don't you let me do it?'. And he laughed and so I laughed and that was the end of it. It was officially a joke.[102]

In the same speech, d'Alpuget says that as early as February 1976 she had a sense of how interesting Hawke could be as a subject when a woman sitting next to her at a Canberra dinner party one Saturday night, who knew Hazel Hawke, raised Bob's intriguing mother. The woman told d'Alpuget:

> 'I've already complained to Hazel about how aggressive Bob is', because Hawke in those days was extraordinarily aggressive, he was like a blast of a furnace fire.
>
> I said, 'Oh yes'.
>
> And she said, 'And Hazel said, "if you think Bob is aggressive, you ought to meet his mother"'.

> Anyway when I heard that, I thought, there's a story in that man, because it seemed to me that there was in that remark – that Hazel has repeated to me – an effect or, if you like, the tension between free will and determinism which I think is the tension or the dynamic of all narrative.[103]

D'Alpuget refers to this 1976 dinner party conversation as the 'seed' of the Hawke book, and the 1978 conversation with Hawke, triggered by their discussion of Hurst's planned biography, as its 'germination'. In between, in 1977, growth was driven by 'that marvellous human need – that is, the need to eat'. Little income had accrued from the Kirby book despite its critical success; *Monkeys in the Dark* had been rewritten and found a publisher but had not yet come out; and d'Alpuget wanted to apply for a Literature Board grant to enable her to continue writing. When her original plan to write a biography of Monk fell over, 'I started thinking again about Hawke'.

> So I approached him ... in late 1978, because by then it was obvious that he would have to make his move to parliament either soon or not at all. I was very conscious [of] my effrontery ... and I expected, I think, that he'd either laugh about it again or just turn me down flat, as Mrs Monk had done.
>
> Anyway I was surprised by his reaction, which was positive and interested and, I think, despite my work with Kirby, I hadn't realised at that stage just how flattering it is to be made the subject of a book, nor I think had Hawke realised just how traumatic it can be. We made this agreement in principle [that] assuming I could get a grant, I would start work on him in 1980.[104]

In the interim d'Alpuget completed her second novel, *Turtle Beach*, which would be another critical success upon publication in 1981. From the vantage point of late 1979, however, when after four years' full-time writing d'Alpuget still did not have 'even enough to pay the telephone bill', she decided she would either have to make some money or return to journalism, 'a fate worse than death'. She hoped and expected that a Hawke biography would be financially rewarding. It was one of the things that kept her going.[105]

D'Alpuget got the Literature Board grant. On 3 January 1980 – her 36th birthday and just a few months after Hawke's reneged marriage proposal drove her to suicidal, then homicidal, thoughts – the first interview for *Robert J Hawke: A Biography* was conducted. 'We set up a meeting ... in Sandringham just around the corner from his house, in the house of a friend of mine', d'Alpuget recalls.[106] Says Hawke: 'It developed rather intimately ... but it didn't affect what I had to say'.[107] Hawke's agreement was conditional on it being a 'warts and all' portrait, a judgment based on his belief that voters understood he was human like them. 'I just reckon I know the Australian people', he says, conflating them with Australian men. 'A hell of a lot of them could recognise themselves in both my drinking and my womanising. I think they make a judgment on the full person'.[108]

Unlike the Kirby biography, the book did not immediately find a publisher. Peter Ryan at Melbourne University Press 'knocked it back straight off – said, "Oh no, he's alive!"'[109] In a letter to d'Alpuget later, Ryan reiterated his 'old-hat preference for "Life" which is dead, career complete, personality finished and the surrounding events reduced to proportion by the perspective of the years'.[110] Penguin Books also rejected the proposal.

D'Alpuget's literary agent, Rose Creswell, suggested Morry Schwartz whose innovative Melbourne publishing house Outback Press had recently folded but not before releasing contemporary Australian classics like Kate Jennings' *Come to Me, My Melancholy Baby* and *A Book about Australian Women* by Carol Jerrems and Virginia Fraser.[111] Outback Press also had some unlikely commercial successes including the Kate Jennings–edited *Mother, I'm Rooted: An anthology of Australian women poets*, which sold 10 000 copies in an Australia whose then population was less than fourteen million people.¹¹² Schwartz had a colourful reputation – 'the kindest thing said about him was that he was "a cowboy"', says d'Alpuget – and was a long shot as a publishing bet. But the book was a long shot for Schwartz, too. There were two biographies in the marketplace already. More serious still was Hawke's extreme behaviour when drunk, and political embarrassments which made some conclude his ascent was over. 'It was thought that he'd absolutely shot himself in the foot', d'Alpuget recalls. Max Suich told her, for example, upon hearing about the planned biography, 'Well you'd better be quick, dear, because he'll be "Bob Who?" in six months'.¹¹³

She and Creswell flew to Melbourne to talk to Schwartz. The meeting took place in the street. 'Morry, who was around thirty and drop-dead good looking, conducted the interview leaning against a low, fast, navy blue–coloured car that he owned, or hired, or had borrowed', says d'Alpuget.¹¹⁴ 'One was never quite sure. He rested an elbow on the car roof and from time to time turned his Hollywood profile to snatch another black grape from the bunch he held by its stem between thumb and first finger'. Schwartz backed the book with zest, offering an advance big enough to research the book properly. In d'Alpuget's view he did this for two reasons: '[F]irst, he was a businessman, and sensed the book could become a best-seller if Hawke's career flourished. Second, as a Jew, he deeply appreciated Hawke's support for Israel at a time when doing so was literally dangerous and potentially disastrous for Hawke's career. Of these two, I think the second reason was paramount'.¹¹⁵ In d'Alpuget's estimation, Schwartz was also capable of publishing the book with unusual speed. 'I have attacks of being politically canny', she said later of her conviction that Malcolm Fraser would call the federal election early and that the book therefore must, to avoid irrelevancy, be out before the end of 1982.¹¹⁶

D'Alpuget had the Literature Board grant, the agreement of her subject, a publishing contract, a healthy advance on royalties, had begun conducting interviews and was on her way to producing the book. Hawke's memory of the process is 'a hell of a lot of interviews'.¹¹⁷

In a letter written late in the manuscript's preparation, d'Alpuget told Peter Ryan that, 'To say ... working with him is a nightmare is the blandest understatement: once, in a 2-hour taping session, there were 27 telephone calls'.[118]

Four things were happening simultaneously, in fact, in the nearly three years between the first interview in January 1980 and the book's publication in October 1982. Firstly, Hawke was on the road to seizing the Labor leadership, the necessary prelude to becoming prime minister. Secondly, d'Alpuget was making a political intervention to help Hawke achieve his goal. Thirdly, d'Alpuget was symbolically reclaiming Hawke as a man before, after publication, putting him aside. And fourthly, through the biographical process conducted by d'Alpuget, Hawke was settling and projecting an identity which formed the personal plank of the platform from which he pursued and conducted his prime ministership.

The first of these elements, that Hawke was bent on seizing the Labor leadership, was widely known and understood at the time, though the story behind-the-scenes – that Hawke 'had more blood on him than the entire stage at the end of *Hamlet*' – still remains largely submerged.[119] Hawke had been vaunted as a potential prime minister for years. His leadership credentials were the focus even at the press conference when he announced his candidature for the seat of Wills, as Hurst and Pullan both pointed out in their biographies. 'Newspaper files had grown fat on reports of his deeds and on speculation about where he was headed', Mills notes, '[and] he was in demand by TV interviewers'.[120]

D'Alpuget argued in her biography of Hawke that his success in using the media, at least that outside Canberra, 'was so great largely because publicity – being the centre of attention – corresponded perfectly with a major element in his personality, laid in infancy and childhood'. Beginning with his parents, Hawke 'relished and had the knack of mesmerizing' his audience. D'Alpuget quotes Hawke's personal assistant, Jean Sinclair, on the extrapolation of this to his later career. 'It was cruel to watch Bob with journalists', Sinclair told her. 'They were lambs to be slaughtered'.[121]

Canberra Press Gallery journalists proved a tougher audience than those outside the national capital, however, and parliament itself was the prism through which gallery journalists rated politicians. As a parliamentarian and as shadow minister for industrial relations, Hawke failed to enchant gallery journalists, impress Labor colleagues, or cow conservative prime minister Malcolm Fraser. In *The Hawke Ascendancy,* Paul Kelly quotes from a 1981 report by Laurie Oakes, then Canberra bureau chief for the Ten Network, after Hawke guest-compered a popular daytime television program, *The Mike Walsh Show.*

> Since Mr Hawke entered Parliament he has not done himself justice. He does not perform nearly as well in Parliament – or in Caucus by all accounts – as he did yesterday as a television compere. His media skills are unquestioned. But a politician requires other skills as well …
>
> Mr Fraser so far has not found Mr Hawke much more difficult to deal with than a number of other Opposition frontbenchers … There is more to politics, especially in the big league at the national level, than making like a television star.[122]

In private, including among members of the Labor caucus, comments were frequently much the same. Labor frontbencher Senator Susan Ryan shared Oakes' assessment of Hawke rather than that of her friend d'Alpuget.

> Blanche, characteristically, had formed an instant and immovable view: her subject should become prime minister of Australia as soon as possible. I was very far from that view. Often on a Canberra Sunday evening, a regular night off for us both, we would debate and argue Bob's leadership potential. She made

some memorable observations about him; memorable because they turned out later to be true. When I pointed out that his contribution in the parliament and shadow Cabinet was, although perfectly workmanlike, not spectacular, she said that Bob would only flourish fully in the number one position: only leadership could provide the optimal psychological environment for him.[123]

Some other Labor frontbenchers like Tom Uren thought Hawke 'brought a charisma, a folksy, friendly, "good bloke" relationship with the Australian people he had built up over the years' as ACTU president – the same point Labor frontbencher Mick Young made at greater length to biographer John Hurst, quoted by him on the opening page of *Hawke, the definitive biography*.[124] But at the time d'Alpuget was writing her book, that sentiment was still a minority one and did not deliver Hawke the numbers to displace Bill Hayden. Was d'Alpuget's biography part of some Hawke master plan to seize The Lodge? Not according to d'Alpuget in March 1985, two and a half years after the book's publication.

> People ever afterwards said, 'Oh isn't Hawke clever!' It's faintly irritating. I had to consider all these bloody things, all the time. Bob had no idea of the timing, in fact for ages it was unreal to him, and it was only right towards the end of the process, when I started showing him the manuscript to read, that it started to become real. Up until then he'd been interviewed by at least five million people, and it was just something that he did. Part of the day's work.[125]

Hawke himself says he had not considered writing an autobiography or organising for someone else to write his biography. 'No, I hadn't thought about it at all', he says. 'I was extraordinarily busy, couldn't do it myself. I was just doing my job. This came along. I knew she could write'. Hawke didn't want a hagiography.

> I wasn't regarded as a lilywhite kind of person (and) I was more than happy to stand on my record of achievement ... I don't think it did me any damage. I think on balance it probably helped. I think people made a judgment about me. On the whole they knew the foibles but they knew the pretty substantial record of achievement I had under my belt.[126]

The second thing happening in this period was a political intervention by d'Alpuget to help Hawke achieve his goal. D'Alpuget did not declare this as her intention. Nevertheless, the Hawke biography was authorised and d'Alpuget had her subject's cooperation. D'Alpuget was not going to write a book that would *hurt* Hawke's chance of winning the Labor leadership and thereafter the prime ministership, though upon first reading some did not grasp the sophistication of her approach. It was a sign of Hawke's self-confidence as well as, he would say, his confidence in the Australian people, that it had to be a 'warts and all' portrayal, and d'Alpuget largely provided it. 'I'd become convinced that despite all evidence to the contrary, he would somehow make it to prime minister', d'Alpuget says.[127]

Another aspect of her role in this was not publicly known. Hawke asked d'Alpuget to try and turn a Hayden vote for him. 'Bob had told me how he was going to unseat Hayden', d'Alpuget says. 'And he'd asked my help with a particular Hayden supporter in the caucus. He'd asked my help in trying to turn this person, to vote for him'. There was a 'unique angle' according to d'Alpuget: 'I was good friends with this person'.[128] It was Susan Ryan. In the second edition of her Hawke biography, d'Alpuget would describe herself openly as a 'Hawke camp insider' in the notes at the front; but not in the first edition.[129] It was concealed even from her publisher, Morry Schwartz, at the time.

> It was incredibly frustrating. Because the book came out in October, and all of this was going on October, November, December, January, February – all of this plotting and so forth.

So maybe it was sort of November, December, January. And I knew what was happening. [A]nd and I couldn't say a word – I couldn't say to Morry, 'Morry, print some more copies!' I didn't tell anybody.[130]

This underlines the dual nature of the author as both biographer and political player. While those roles were congruent, d'Alpuget's verve and high estimation of her subject underpinned artistic risks from which a lesser, more instrumentally focused, biographer in this situation would shrink.

The choice of cover photograph for *Robert J Hawke* is an example. 'Morry Schwartz and I sat on the floor in his office in Melbourne and we went through gazillions of photographs', d'Alpuget recalls. 'And we picked that one. If you know Bob, you know he's drunk'.[131] The picture, by American photographer Rick Smolan, shows Hawke, eyes heavy-lidded, head leaning sideways on a hand with a cigar clenched between two fingers, his expression poised between bored bemusement and impending explosion. Hawke's crisp, stylish business attire is juxtaposed against his intense, glowering gaze. The cover's drama is heightened by its stark black and white palette and the containment of Hawke's face in a tight square at its centre.

The third thing happening during this period was d'Alpuget symbolically reclaiming Hawke as a man and then putting him aside. The background was Hawke's years of hard drinking, philandering and fighting with wife Hazel, from whom he had only a few months earlier tried to separate in order to marry d'Alpuget, but failing since neither would agree to be the one to walk out of the marriage.[132] 'It was a very difficult situation for him because Hazel hated me', d'Alpuget says, and Hazel knew about their previous relationship and assumed, correctly, that it had resumed.[133] Moreover, Hazel Hawke was not the only hostile rival d'Alpuget had to contend with in the writing of the book. There was also Jean Sinclair and others.

[Hazel] said to me a marvellous thing once, much later. She said, 'Blanche, you know what Bob's like. When he's drunk he'd fuck a goat'. ... But she talked to me, while hating me. So he had the difficulty of Hazel being against me, and also of course he was in a very long term relationship with Jean Sinclair, his private secretary. And Jean was aware of our relationship. So he had this great difficulty – trapped – three women. Jean and I managed to get on well, well enough – we were professional about it. But it was difficult for him. So he took minimal interest in the book for those personal reasons.[134]

D'Alpuget thanks Sinclair in the foreword to *Robert J Hawke: A Biography* for 'spending so much time in passing messages to him from me, and in finding research material'. She describes Sinclair in the body of the book as 'Hawke's right arm' and spends a few pages sketching out her story as, like Hawke, an 'exotic' ACTU employee.[135] Sinclair was schooled at Melbourne Girls' Grammar School, had an economics degree from the University of Melbourne, had worked for the management consulting firm McKinsey and was a director of her family company.

Sinclair's description to d'Alpuget of the state of the ACTU administration upon taking up her job in 1973 is vivid, and familiar to anyone familiar with the labour movement at that time: variations of this kind of administrative chaos were replicated at busy union head offices around the country.[136] D'Alpuget describes how Sinclair bore the workplace brunt of Hawke's belief that 'every day contained forty-eight hours and that he should be awake and occupied for all of them', and remarks that 'a good week for her was one in which she dissuaded him from committing himself to a major scheme: agreeing to write a book, for example'.[137] Sinclair was Hawke's personal assistant and companion for more than twenty years, and she and d'Alpuget 'disliked each other'.[138] The extra demands on Hawke's time would have been only one of the reasons Sinclair opposed the book given her own ongoing relationship with him.

Hazel Hawke's cooperation did not come without a fight. Hazel wrote a letter to the editor of *The Age* in November 1979 registering her 'utter revulsion' at press coverage of a court case involving a prominent politician's son. 'My main argument is that any politician or public figure must be assessed on his job performance, and that whether his wife and family are glamorous and interesting or have two heads and are naughty should be irrelevant', she wrote. She continued that 'no public figure who is good enough' needs the ego-boosting or public image softening that 'nice little stories' involving their families entail, and further, that, 'The electorate which makes this demand avoids its responsibility of properly assessing the worth and performance of that figure on the contribution he makes, or does not adequately make, in his particular area of public affairs'.[139]

In the foreword to *Robert J Hawke*, d'Alpuget says the only area she avoided, at Hazel's request, was the Hawke children 'whose privacy has already been invaded over many years'. It was, she wrote, 'a price worth paying for her help and unflinching frankness, both in giving information and in reading the manuscript for accuracy of detail'. D'Alpuget wrote that she had been 'guided by her perceptions a great deal, while exercising the responsibility to reach my own conclusions'.[140]

Hazel in turn, in her own memoirs published after Hawke's prime ministership was over, characterised herself as an opponent of the biography, then a reluctant starter and, ultimately, a supporter. She felt Hawke's flaws being brought into the open ahead of his run for the prime ministership had a kind of inoculation effect, as well as relieving the pressure she personally felt over public perceptions of their marriage.

> [I]n May 1980, Blanche d'Alpuget, who was writing a biography of Bob, came to our house to talk with me about the book. This was not easy for me ... I was not in favour of the biography.

Although Bob had authorised the book, it had been embarked upon without my approval even though it would clearly need to refer to myself, the children and Bob's personal life. But now it was happening and I would cooperate. I must say that I have since been glad the book was written. It broached areas of Bob's life, drunkenness and marital problems, which could have been used against him later by the sensationalist press. When he entered parliamentary politics, voters had an understanding of the man they were considering for election. The biography also released me from feeling I needed to protect the marriage totally from public scrutiny.[141]

Sue Pieters-Hawke has written that her mother was 'distressed and angry' about her father's relationship with d'Alpuget, and that wider knowledge of their relationship affected the interviews Blanche obtained from Hazel loyalists amongst the Hawke family's closest friends. 'Intimates who knew of Blanche's relationship with Bob closed ranks in support of Hazel', Pieters-Hawke says. 'As Marj White put it, "I said, 'Well, my mouth's closed. Anything that appears in that book will be absolutely mundane. I will not relate anything personal'".[142]

D'Alpuget had, in fact, pulled off a coup in terms of her power vis-à-vis the two other women closest to Hawke at that time. Within only a few months of Hawke ceasing contact and then breaking his offer to leave Hazel and marry d'Alpuget, she was spending hours interviewing him at a house a couple of minutes from his own in Royal Avenue, Sandringham, had his intimate amanuensis Sinclair passing messages and doing minor research for her, and had Hawke's wife corralled into an interview against her will. This was an act of triumphant repossession, all in the name of a greater good the other two women were hard pressed to obstruct: Hawke's advancement.

Hawke would foreswear alcohol in the interests of his political career, while Hazel fell more deeply into its clutches. 'The monster drink had gone from Bob's life but infidelity had not', Hazel wrote later in her memoir. 'I felt extremely unsure about our future and was lonely. Now I would often drink alone, at home, with my solitary dinner, a very unwise practice'.[143] Sue Pieters-Hawke says her mother was 'distressed and angry' about Bob and Blanche's ongoing relationship, and 'was by now capable of striking back when she, too, had been drinking'.[144] Hazel made a number of phone calls to Morry Schwartz's office demanding information about the book, making it clear that Hawke and d'Alpuget were lovers. Once, after newspapers in Sydney, Melbourne and Canberra published a photograph of subject and biographer on the steps of Parliament House, Hazel phoned the Schwartz office and told the person who answered the phone, 'Get that fucking bitch off the front page or I'll blow the whistle. I'll blow the whistle and he'll never be prime minister'.[145]

The intensity of Hazel Hawke's battle against the biography is revealed in letters at the time from d'Alpuget to Peter Ryan, her old publisher and mentor at Melbourne University Press, to whom she sent 'the Bird Tome' for critique prior to finalising the manuscript.[146]

> Hazel Hawke, who is a hill-billy termagant, is doing hand-springs in her efforts to prevent publication of the book. I have left out that her children are drug addicts, that she is a lush and a bully and have presented her as quite the Cecil Brunner rose. For that I get an hour & a half of telephone abuse. At this very moment she is, no doubt, giving the Bird the rounds of the kitchen about it all. What she wants, I think, is a hagiography of herself, and pillorying of him. She hates him, & her greatest pleasure in life is to make him suffer. Were her portrait ever to be painted it would be with a log, a banjo and a vat of moonshine.[147]

In the acknowledgements of *Robert J Hawke*, d'Alpuget thanks Ryan for reading the manuscript when she had reached 'exhaustion and despondency' under pressure of meeting the tight publication deadline.[148] This perhaps explains the closing paragraph of the letter from d'Alpuget to Ryan containing her unvarnished comment on Hazel that, 'She would make great copy in the Lodge. But I don't think we can look forward to that'.[149] It was a brief down beat in d'Alpuget's usually unrelenting belief that Hawke would indeed make The Lodge. She subsequently revised her view of Hazel's capacity to perform as a prime ministerial spouse, based on actual performance. 'I was wrong', d'Alpuget says now. 'I had seen only her worst self. Once in The Lodge she rose to the challenge'. Hazel had hypnotherapy to stop smoking, moderated her drinking and conquered her shyness to become a good public speaker. Says d'Alpuget, 'Hazel changed into the model prime ministerial wife'.[150]

In her speech at the book's launch at Canberra's Lakeside Hotel in October 1982, d'Alpuget describes Hawke as a 'fighter' by nature who had fought with many, including her, and had fought for the book.

> We had an argument at our first interview for this book
> and almost three years later, when he was reading the final
> manuscript before it went for typesetting, we were still arguing.
> We were arguing over adjectives and nouns and verbs and
> my interpretations. While the book was being written and
> particularly in the last few weeks, Bob has had to argue with
> those who thought that a mid-term career biography should not
> be published.
>
> Indeed, he has fought for this book and he's done so because he
> shares, I believe, my view that people should be able to make
> judgments not guesses about their political leaders, and that
> therefore the more we know about them the better. He has
> maintained this principle despite the fact that from the outset
> of my work on his biography, he knew it would be treated as a
> curiosity, misused, trivialised and distorted. And I must say that
> events have borne out that weary foreknowledge grossly.[151]

D'Alpuget told the audience she had tried to write a frank account and that the biography was intended as 'an early step in a movement for more penetrating analyses of people in Australian public life'.

It was a significant break from the usual mould of contemporary political biography, and initial reactions and calculations about it were wider of the mark the closer one got to Parliament House, Canberra. Many Canberra Press Gallery journalists assumed it would seriously damage Hawke's standing. So did some of Hawke's rivals on the opposition frontbench, like fellow leadership aspirant Paul Keating. Hawke recalls a member of Labor's NSW Right faction telling him at the time, in relation to the book, 'Keating's very, very happy, reckons that's the end of you. With all that stuff in it, all your drinking and womanizing – that that'll be the end of you'. Hawke replied, 'Well, I think that shows how little Paul understands the electorate'.[152]

It did prove the end of the d'Alpuget relationship, though. 'I'd been burnt, when we'd broken up', she says, recalling the breach over Hawke's failure to honour his promise to leave Hazel and marry d'Alpuget in 1979.

> Although we resumed sexual relations while I was doing the book I wasn't going to fall in love with him. And also when you study somebody to that degree, it's like having too much chocolate. You never want to see another chocolate again! So by the end of the research, and certainly by the end of the book, I really didn't want to see him again. I was so sick of him. You can't give so much energy to another human being, unless it's your own baby.[153]

This repossession and then relinquishing of Hawke had a satisfying symmetry.

They next met three years into Hawke's prime ministership for a newspaper profile d'Alpuget undertook for the *Sydney Morning Herald*. 'The room was quiet and felt empty', d'Alpuget reported, and Hawke was distant. 'Hawke has defined his Prime Ministership as super-respectable', she wrote. 'He said repeatedly that physically he was on top of the world. Indeed, his skin tone and colour looked excellent. But ... my overwhelming impression was of a lack of vitality, that he was vanishing'.[154] Two years after that Hawke rang d'Alpuget and their relationship resumed; covert meetings were organised during the latter years of his prime ministership.[155] In December 1991 he was ousted as prime minister by Paul Keating and he resigned from parliament shortly afterwards. The Hawke marriage ended in 1994 and Bob married d'Alpuget in 1995. They spent 24 years together until his death in 2019.

Three of the four things happening simultaneously between January 1980 when d'Alpuget conducted her first interview for *Robert J Hawke*, and October 1982 when it was published, have so far been canvassed. Hawke was on the road to seizing the Labor leadership, the necessary prelude to him becoming prime minister. D'Alpuget was making a political intervention to help Hawke achieve that goal. D'Alpuget was symbolically reclaiming Hawke as a man before relinquishing him post-publication.

The fourth thing happening was that, through the biographical process conducted by d'Alpuget, Hawke settled and projected an identity which formed the personal plank of the platform from which he pursued and conducted his prime ministership. D'Alpuget describes *Robert J Hawke* as 'a well-built book' with a good structure. 'It's internally strong', she said later.[156] 'I was actually thinking of the architecture of a Congregationalist church I'd seen in South Australia when I was writing it: well-proportioned stone, four-square'. In the process of construction, it could be argued that d'Alpuget did some rewiring of her subject, or at least enabled him to do some rewiring of himself through the biographical process, that helped stabilise his behaviour and settle his life generally, junking the self-destructive behaviour which jeopardised the achievement of his political goals.

It is not a claim that should be overstated; Hawke's personality is highly distinctive and of robust continuity. Nor is it a proposition that can be dismissed. Some of d'Alpuget's impact on Hawke was straightforward and attitudinal – for example, concerning the position of women. In *Robert J Hawke* d'Alpuget describes his unreconstructedly sexist attitudes about, and behaviour towards, women, noting it did not change until Hawke in his fifties read Simone de Beauvoir's *The Second Sex*.[157] D'Alpuget omits to mention that she was the one who lent Beauvoir's book to him.[158] The Hawke Government went on to pass landmark sex discrimination and affirmative action legislation for women through the auspices of the Minister for the Status of Women, Senator Susan Ryan. In other respects, though, the change in Hawke's behaviour between 1979 when he was largely written off by political insiders because of his reckless, drunken and abusive behaviour, and the early 1980s when he gave up alcohol and (at least publicly) curtailed his obvious philandering, was dramatic. Even if one ascribes the change entirely to his May 1980 decision to give up alcohol, the question remains, how was he able to give up drinking this time when he had failed on all previous attempts?

Upon the book's publication, d'Alpuget described it as 'an attempt on my part to wrap a narrative around an analysis of personality'.[159] 'I spend the first 76 pages of the Hawke biography on his infancy, childhood and youth. That's really an unusually long time to devote to that sort of early conditioning but I thought it was essential to give it so much time to adequately be able to explain what comes later, and that is Hawke, the folk hero of the 1970s'. D'Alpuget went on to describe the unusual family dynamic before concluding that for Hawke, 'In psychological terms, which I don't use at all in the book, I think it was a hypercathexis of his intellect'. This was a rare intrusion of psychological jargon which d'Alpuget kept from the biography itself. While jargon free, however, there is no mistaking the bent with which she approached the project.

In *The Interpretation of Dreams* Freud wrote of 'the royal road to the unconscious'. In the therapeutic setting, patients undergoing psychoanalysis lie on a couch and are questioned about their earliest memories and their dreams, and encouraged to reflect and expand upon them. For Hawke it was a trip from his home on Royal Avenue, Sandringham, to the nearby home of d'Alpuget's psychiatrist friend Michael Epstein, where she would question him about his earliest memories and encourage him to reflect and expand upon them.

In these interviews d'Alpuget stirred up memories, unconscious and otherwise, and foreclosed resistance to them on his part when he could not or would not remember, by bringing to the biographical couch stories told to her by surviving family members. The most important was d'Alpuget's revelation that the all-powerful Ellie Hawke had committed Bob, when he was a small child, to the teetotal path ascribed to Nazarites in the Hebrew bible, the word 'nazir' having the spiritually highly charged meaning 'consecrated'.

> My research turned up all of this stuff that he would never have told me about, [like] his mother enrolling him as a little Nazarite. They were sworn never to drink in their lives. She was a … teetotaller. Obviously in her background there'd been drunks. At the age of 8 he was sworn that alcohol would never touch his lips.
>
> And when I started research I went straight to the family in South Australia and turned all of this up, and I came to him and asked him about it. I started in January. He gave up grog four months after I told him [in] February …
>
> I tell you it was a high moment when the family in South Australia told me all this background about the drinking, because no way was Bob going to tell me that, let alone Hazel. And really they were the only two people whom I'd met up until that point who knew.[160]

Hawke was 'tremendously uncomfortable' when d'Alpuget raised it with him. Whether causal or coincidental, the fact that he successfully swore off alcohol within proximate range of d'Alpuget drawing key scenes like this from his childhood inescapably into his view is highly suggestive. Nor was it the only uncomfortable truth d'Alpuget brought to the surface.

> We shared this other strange thing. My mother had wanted me to be a boy, and his mother had wanted him to be a girl. And unless you've had that experience of actual maternal rejection, which is completely denied – completely denied – at a very young age, you don't really know what it's like. But it gives a certain sympathy. There's a certain symmetry to your lives.
>
> He didn't know that about me, but I knew that about him. And I'd discovered that in South Australia too – that his mother wanted him to be a girl. So, all the tension around masculinity. What do you get? Hypermasculinity. All the tension about, well, the disappointment about, not being a girl – well, therefore you've got to be prime minister. Over-compensation. And he must be a teetotaller. So for someone who wrote fiction, this was just all magic material, if you had any psychological insight. The rejection, the disappointment. It's there, imprinted forever, like a dagger.[161]

Empathy over shared problems like this, the novelist's expert handling of rich source material, and a classic narrative arc emerging during research – the hero nailing himself to the cross of alcohol and then getting himself off in time to pursue the prize – all contributed to the satisfactions of the book from the readers' standpoint. 'I did believe his virtues far outweighed his vices, and that he had succeeded in this enormously difficult task which was overcoming his drinking', d'Alpuget says.[162] 'So to that extent I thought it was a book about a personal triumph. But I didn't set out to do that. He did that. I just described what happened'.

Labor MPs whose knowledge of Hawke extended only to his sodden and aggressive union folk hero years got from *Robert J Hawke* a whole new perspective: one of long and innovative service to the industrial wing of the labour movement, laced with the magic of a family mythology that ordained he was the chosen one. All leaders need a quest story by which they and others can make sense of their path and be motivated to join it. D'Alpuget divined and drafted Hawke's when he would not, or could not, do it himself.

The resumption of sexual relations between biographer and subject did not influence the book, d'Alpuget says, not least because, unbeknownst to Hawke, she was in another relationship with someone of greater importance to her at the time: 'Actually I was having an affair with someone else.'[163] Thus d'Alpuget was no Hawke cipher – or, as d'Alpuget's friend Graham Little, the Melbourne University political psychologist, might have put it, she was no 'Echo'. Little made the following observation in a completely different context but it uncannily explains the likely outcome had that been the case.

> Narcissus drowned in himself not because he was vain but because in Echo he had a friend who didn't dare to judge for herself, or didn't know how to, and did not respond to what she heard and saw. Friends are sometimes mirrors for our hopes, cheering us on, but they must also be witnesses to who we really are. The dying Hamlet enjoined Horatio:
>
> > *If thou didst ever hold me in thy heart*
> > *Absent thee from felicity awhile*
> > *And in this harsh world draw thy breath in pain*
> > *To tell my story.*[164]

Hawke may have literally drowned – in alcohol – had d'Alpuget played 'Echo' rather than being witness to who Hawke really was and reflecting it critically back to him through the biographical process.

For d'Alpuget, while the book was motivated by the reasons outlined earlier – because Monk's widow said 'no', because of a shared interest in Australia's industrial relations system, because it would make money and cross-subsidise fiction writing, and because she wanted to correct what she saw as unfair media representations of Hawke – perhaps subconsciously it was also about working through and overcoming the trauma caused by Hawke's dashing of their marriage plans in 1979.

After the biography's publication d'Alpuget went to Jerusalem to research her next novel and, within months, Hawke moved into The Lodge with Hazel to begin governing. It was a resolved if not ebulliently happy Blanche d'Alpuget that one encounters during this period in, for example, extended interviews conducted by Jennifer Ellison and Candida Baker for their books on Australian novelists.[165]

D'Alpuget is unique in Australian political biography – possibly unique in the history of modern political biography – in the degree and sheer longevity of her engagement with her subject and the impact of her work on his career and life, and vice versa. D'Alpuget dug, divined and finally drafted a Hawke narrative that made coherent an otherwise hard to credit tale of early and sustained achievement nearly undone by personal demons. It underpinned his ascension to the highest office of the land. There is no precedent in Australia, nor is there an obvious one elsewhere. The only biographer and subject as deeply entwined for such an extended period, though in a profoundly different way, are perhaps Boswell and Johnson.

D'Alpuget's relationship with her subject ranged from, in order, 'vision'; interviewer; lover; estranged lover; biographer and lover; ex-lover; interviewer; clandestine lover; spouse, business partner and, once again, biographer when she wrote *Hawke: The Prime Minister* in 2010. From its inception in 1970, and over the nearly half century since, this may well qualify as the ultimate case of Macaulay's '*Lues Boswelliana*' – unqualified admiration – since d'Alpuget has been among the staunchest of public and private Hawke backers. If so, one would have to add the qualification Leslie Stephen made in relation to Boswell, that d'Alpuget's genius is that 'adoration never hindered accuracy of the portraiture'.[166] As she said to this writer later, 'If he'd remained a hopeless drunk I don't think we'd be sitting here'.[167]

Four months after the publication of *Robert J Hawke* he was opposition leader, and a month later, prime minister. Political journalists Robert Haupt and Michelle Grattan wrote after he won office that Hawke was 'the most thoroughly psychoanalysed man in Australian political history'.[168] D'Alpuget's biography was not exactly nurtured in the bosom of the Melbourne Psychosocial Group but there was an overlap between key members and her circle of friends, including Little. 'We talked a lot about psychosocial issues and, no doubt, Bob', d'Alpuget recalls of their friendship.[169] Little pointed d'Alpuget to Davies' work including his *Skills, outlooks and passions: a psychoanalytic contribution to the study of politics*, which had just been published.[170] He travelled the 670 kilometres from Melbourne to Canberra for the launch of *Robert J Hawke* and d'Alpuget quoted from his work at some length towards the end of her speech, saying he was 'starting to set the balance straight in studies of Australian political leaders'.[171] Another Melbourne Psychosocial Group member, Angus McIntyre, also travelled from Melbourne for the launch. The book constituted the peak of psychoanalytically informed contemporary political biography in Australia, a fact disguised by d'Alpuget's elimination of psychoanalytic terms from her prose. Nine years later, in 1991, Little protégé Stan Anson would launch an assault on that peak with his book, *Hawke: An Emotional Life*.[172]

Anson, like d'Alpuget, was an ALP member but unlike her was not enamoured of the direction Hawke led Labor. Little had supervised Anson's 1988 MA thesis at Melbourne University, 'Representing RJ Hawke', in which literary criticism was the dominant mode. In it Anson explored how Hawke represented himself ideologically in his

1979 Boyer Lectures, *The Resolution of Conflict*; how he represented himself autobiographically in relation to John Curtin; and how he was represented biographically in d'Alpuget's *Robert J Hawke*. Anson offered his own 'psychological representation of Hawke informed by these explorations' in the thesis: 'The assumption is that political actors (and ordinary people) have a symbolic existence which, although it is subject to determination in the last instance by their real existence, is susceptible to analysis on its own – symbolic – terms'.[173]

Anson's *Hawke: An Emotional Life* grew out of the third chapter of the thesis, 'L'Ecriture Blanche? Narrative and Rhetoric in *Robert J Hawke: A Biography*'. It was written as the leadership struggle between Hawke and Treasurer Paul Keating peaked, and was published after the leadership ballot in which Hawke prevailed over Keating in June 1991. An updated edition was published after the second leadership ballot in December 1991, which Keating won, taking into account Keating's ascension to the prime ministership.

Anson's book created a storm – a small localised storm within the interlocking worlds of politics and publishing, but a storm nevertheless. It ended d'Alpuget's friendship with Little who was caught between the two authors, and required the writing of a substantial cheque by its publisher to d'Alpuget. Anson's acknowledgments in the original edition begin with the comment that while the book 'draws on a wide range of scholarship ... in the interests of clarity and brevity, chapter and verse aren't always given'. Special mention needed to be made of Hawke's biographers, he said, and, 'Of these d'Alpuget is obviously the most important: without her *Robert J Hawke: A Biography* the present study could not have been written'.[174]

Together these two statements put publisher McPhee Gribble, then recently acquired by Penguin, in a weak position when d'Alpuget threatened legal action under the Trade Practices Act for 'passing off' – that is, Anson passing off her work as his own. Outrage about some of the content partly drove d'Alpuget's action but one does not have to spend much time reading *Hawke: An Emotional Life* to be struck by the jaundice permeating it without even going to questions of accuracy. As Anson mocks and derides Hawke, so he mocks and derides d'Alpuget's biography of Hawke.

> The fruit of their symbiosis, *Robert J Hawke, A Biography*, is a stylish melodrama which wholeheartedly endorses Hawke's fantasies of splendid isolation, predestination and rebirth. Like King Arthur, its hero gives amazing proofs of unsuspected majesty, sits at Round Tables and pursues Holy Grails; like Odysseus, he outwits, outbraves and out endures every obstacle to his homeward progress; like Christ, he is restored to grace after being relieved of the impediments of the flesh. The book explained and verified the metamorphosis that saw the Hawke of the 1970s, maverick and fixer, reinvent himself as the Hawke of the 1980s, healer and visionary, Phar Lap and Francis of Assisi rolled into one.[175]

It made wonderfully enjoyable reading if one were a conservative-voting Hawke-hater, or a Keating spear carrier hopeful a bit more undermining might see Hawke yield at a second attempt; and it encapsulated a certain view of the prime minister and his biographer held by some. A front cover endorsement by James Walter that it was 'the best explanation we have of Bob Hawke' would be echoed by others in the broader Melbourne group. To d'Alpuget, however, Anson's book was 'a prejudiced, paranoid, lefty Freudian bitch about Bob'.[176] Later Judith Brett, in *Political Lives,* condemned d'Alpuget's 'passing off' accusation because it challenged 'the legitimacy of any work which draws on and reinterprets already published research'.[177]

Those traditions derive from the scholarly world, and Anson's book, had it been confined to the academy, would probably have been a roistering in-house success enjoyed by the politically attuned who could also distinguish their id from their ego. Coming out of the academy into the world of parliamentary politics, however, *Hawke: An Emotional Life* looked more like psychoanalytically-driven political polemic. From a subject's standpoint, it was like an enemy appropriating the clinical notes from their therapy sessions and being beaten with them in public. The *Sunday Age* reported Anson's denials that the book's publication was timed to help Keating's leadership challenge but claimed there was 'strong evidence to suggest that others used his findings for that purpose'. Anson 'has strong links with the ALP's Victorian socialist left, the faction whose senior Victorian – although not federal – members campaigned so strongly to bring about Mr Hawke's downfall', Caroline Wilson reported. 'A psychobiography examining the narcissism of Mr Hawke, his oedipal exaltation and castration anxiety proved an ideal weapon'.[178]

When the updated edition of *Hawke: An Emotional Life* was published, Anson's acknowledgments had been adjusted in light of experience. The previous opening – 'This book draws on a wide range of scholarship' – was replaced with, 'This book is mainly based on original research from primary sources'. The declaration that without d'Alpuget's biography his own would not have been possible was struck from the text. Instead we learn that, 'Blanche d'Alpuget's data form the indispensable basis for the analysis in Chapter Two of this book'.[179] Anson was cheerful in his public statements and pleased about the updated edition of his book.

With historical perspective it seems that the embryonic body of psychoanalytically informed biography building up from its academic base in Melbourne, which enjoyed a mainstream success in d'Alpuget's *Robert J Hawke*, was struck dead by Anson's *Hawke: An Emotional Life* – certainly as far as contemporary political biography is concerned. The tragedy is that this is where it is of greatest potential use. What aspiring leader would risk their inner life and tensions being exposed now, though, having seen what Anson did with the disclosures obtained and published by d'Alpuget on Hawke? The fact that sensitive revelations of the self could be turned into political bullets for one's enemies – gallingly in this case, to the potential advantage of one's internal political rival, not even an external one – made contemporary political biography in Australia revert to the old business-as-usual basis. It had come full circle, back to the 'political journalism–plus' model typified by Hurst's *Hawke, the definitive biography*. Voters know just that much less about their potential and serving prime ministers as a result.

Chapter 7
Polaroids of a busy life

In the long run, snapshots in time are useful.

Paul Keating, interview with the author

I have a bit of a theory that it's not a good idea to have a book written about you.

John Howard, interview with the author

Australia's final two twentieth century prime ministers, Paul Keating and John Howard, were both well read in biography and wary of contemporary political biography, yet possessed diametrically opposed views of its value. For Keating, contemporary political biography was provisional and often flawed but valuable in its potential to inform substantive biographies written later with historical perspective. Howard considered them at best superfluous, and at worst politically risky for the subject.

Paul Keating, Labor prime minister from December 1991 to March 1996, was the subject of contemporary biographies by two authors, Edna Carew and Michael Gordon, both journalists but coming from significantly different professional perspectives.[1] Carew was a pioneering, Sydney-based financial markets journalist who was based in Sydney when she wrote her biography of Keating during his treasurership. Gordon was a senior second-generation metropolitan daily newspaper journalist from Melbourne posted in the Canberra Press Gallery when he wrote his biography, during Keating's prime ministership.

For Keating, contemporary political biographies are imperfect objects which nevertheless possess their own virtue. On the one hand, he says, 'while informative ... they can only trace you, they can't really paint you three dimensionally or in full colour'.[2] On the other, they are 'like Polaroids of a busy life' that, whatever their strengths and weaknesses, help inform works written later with historical perspective. 'In the long run, snapshots in time are useful', he says.

> It's like an old picture, you never quite know who's in it. When you get it early, a picture, a snapshot of your career or life at a certain point, there's a whole lot of issues and people who get interviewed that won't ever get interviewed again. So it's like a kind of a plateau – they're plateaus in the life story. Now, they may be indifferently written, poorly researched, they may even be prejudicial, but what they will pick up is contemporary feeling, contemporary issues.

Thus Keating was prepared to 'moderately cooperate' with Carew and Gordon 'to effect the Polaroid phenomenon', with an eye to their usefulness for a future biographer writing with sufficient distance to contextualise the 'plateau' stories properly. 'One hopes that one's life is such that you never have to write your own biography', he says, '[that] there's a Richard Ellman somewhere waiting to do the real one. And that person will always need the early ones'.[3]

One could draw a second conclusion about Keating and contemporary political biography from the remarks of his speechwriter, Don Watson, on what is arguably its most potent form. Watson linked English essayist and critic William Hazlitt's observation that a 'nickname is the heaviest stone the devil can throw at a man', to the custom, in the political argot common in Parliament House during the 1980s, of attempting to 'nail' a political rival. Or as Watson said Keating used to say, 'nail it to his forehead'.

> It is done in the hope that one's enemy thereafter will be branded and the public will interpret his every word and action in this light: he cannot be trusted, he is weak, he is a loser, and so on. The same effort is made to destroy his policies and his beliefs. It is a form of caricature or satire. This means it can be the distilled truth or an outrageous lie. It doesn't matter so long as the public believe it.[4]

Keating – who in his time dubbed John Hewson a 'feral abacus', declared that Alexander Downer had a 'face like a knee', destroyed the standing of Jim Carlton by calling him 'Old Rosie', and called Ian Sinclair 'a political carcass with a coat and tie on' – had a high aptitude for quick, short, lethal biographical epithets. However, there was no intrinsic pleasure for Keating in the parliamentary combat that the pursuit of public policy via democratic political means entails. 'If I could have done the job privately and not publicly I would have taken the private option', he says, 'but you can't do that in public life'.[5]

An aptitude for devastating epithets was one aspect of a much broader use of biography by Keating in politics. Just how fundamental an element it was in his political toolkit emerges in *Mates: Five Champions of the Labor Right*, by journalist Fia Cumming, published in 1991, the year Keating succeeded Hawke. *Mates* is 'an unusually intimate examination of a network of friends': Keating, Laurie Brereton, Graham Richardson, Bob Carr and Leo McLeay, all of whom began their political lives in the NSW Labor Right faction and all of whom were at some time ministers in federal Labor governments, with the exception of McLeay who became Speaker of the House of Representatives.[6] While Cumming expressly states that *Mates* is not a biography of the five men concerned, it contains a rich lode of contemporary biographical material gathered with real curiosity about, and insight into, the politicians concerned.

Cumming reports Keating's account of his arrival as a young MP in Canberra, where he shared an office with the older and more experienced NSW Labor MP, Lionel Bowen. Bowen 'applied very hard tests' to people, Keating told her, 'all these little behavioural give-aways, about the personality'. Examples were how people treated the parliamentary dining room staff, whether they were careful with money, whether they stuck to agreements and so on. Bowen, said Keating, was a great observer who had 'worked up a model in his head of what to think about a person on the basis of all these behavioural give-aways ... (and) it was very highly developed'. Keating continued:

> And I think what happened over the years is, I developed my own. Because in politics every personality is a problem. Everyone who's in front of you, you've got to assess them quickly. And mostly be right, otherwise they may give you a problem. But no-one's going to help you assess them, you've got to do it yourself. So you've got to develop a framework for how you relate to people and how you assess them. Well, a lot of people never get the framework right, right through their entire life. They just don't know how to assess other people.[7]

Keating married this to what Watson describes as a powerful sense of history's 'machinery and direction – the energy in it', and a special sense of the 'calamitous price of failure in policy and leadership'. Thus it was that historian Barbara Tuchman on the outbreak of World War I, and William Manchester's biography of Winston Churchill, were Keating favourites.[8]

An example of Keating as a serving politician drawing strength from the life story of another politician is recounted in a post–prime ministerial biography written by John Edwards. In the period between the Carew and Gordon books, Keating readied to challenge Hawke for the prime ministership. Keating had decided to relinquish the treasurership after the challenge, whatever the result; the ballot would either send him to The Lodge or the backbench.

In a reflective frame of mind, unsure whether he would win or lose the as yet undeclared challenge, Keating was reading the second volume of Manchester's Churchill biography, *The Caged Lion,* and one day discussed it with Edwards, then on his staff. Manchester's book covered Churchill's long exile on the Conservative Party backbench in the 1930s. 'I don't have any heroes', Keating told Edwards during the discussion on Churchill's period of political exile, 'because when you get to my age you realise they all have flaws, but if anything Churchill was a hero'.

> The way he fought against his party for seven years. When he walked into the chamber in the 1930s young Tory members jeered at him. Chamberlain, the foreign secretary ... Halifax, Dawson at *The Times*, the ambassador in Berlin ... they all admired Hitler, were convinced by him. It was a tragedy. Czechoslovakia had a big army. It could have fought, but it didn't.[9]

Keating took comfort from Churchill's example of fighting courageously against the odds, and of being right even though temporarily defeated, says Edwards, as personified in Churchill's determination to convince England of the Nazi threat despite his colleagues' derision. There was, too, the fact that Churchill ultimately triumphed; he may have been politically marginalised during the 1930s but by 1940 he was prime minister, leading Britain to victory in World War II. These were companionable thoughts, sustaining thoughts, as Keating risked rejection by his own party and, like Churchill in the 1930s, the prospect of exile on the backbench.[10]

The Hawke challenge was still some years off when Edna Carew began work on her biography of Keating during his Treasury years. Carew was born in Scotland in 1949 to first-generation Scottish parents whose own parents had moved some fifty years earlier from Lithuania and Russia to Britain. As is common in migrant families, there was a strong emphasis on education. Many in her family pursued careers in medicine; 'dinner table chatter was about health and illnesses and psychology'.[11] Her much older brothers followed in their parents' footsteps, studying at the University of Glasgow where Carew's father had graduated in medicine and her mother in arts; Edna bucked it, studying Modern Languages at the University of Edinburgh. After a few years in London, where she was a translator, Carew moved to Sydney in 1974 and worked as a money market dealer. Five years later, in 1979, the Campbell Committee of Inquiry into the Australian Financial System was established. Its influential 1981 report made the case for overhauling Australia's tightly regulated financial markets.

A contraceptive disaster while at her desk in the merchant bank trading room where she worked was the serendipitous beginning of Carew's writing career. Her intrauterine device (IUD) had spontaneously moved into a painful position, and she quickly sought out a nearby Macquarie Street gynaecologist who 'whipped the offending beast out'.[12] Carew wrote a story about the experience called 'Giving Birth to a Crab' and sent it to Bettina Arndt, then editing the sex advice magazine *Forum*, who published it. While still working as a money market dealer Carew wrote several more articles for *Forum*, building a sufficient reputation for Sydney publisher John Iremonger, now with Allen & Unwin, to seek a lunch meeting to canvas a possible book on sex therapists.

By this time Carew, who wanted to write rather than trade, had swapped a career in merchant banking for a position with the *Australian Financial Review* (*AFR*). As Iremonger was leaving the office, Allen & Unwin chief Patrick Gallagher, learning the identity of his luncheon companion, said, 'Oh, see if she's interested in writing a book about financial markets'.[13]

The idea of a book on sex therapists was quickly forgotten and Carew instead wrote the groundbreaking *Fast Money: The Money Market in Australia*, which went through multiple editions and was the precursor of a slew of authoritative books by Carew throughout the 1980s and 1990s demystifying the strange, new world of flexible financial markets. *Fast Money* was technically uncompromising yet written in a clear and accessible style which gave market players and determined general readers alike – not least puzzled journalists and policy makers – an understanding of the new financial market arrangements reshaping the Australian economy.

Carew was an unabashed advocate of these developments. In her acknowledgements at the front of *Fast Money*'s first edition, Carew explains how she updated the manuscript continually right up to publication, to ensure the book was current. 'If, on publication, this volume has been overtaken by further innovations, then I can only applaud the speed with which progress has been made', she wrote.[14]

In retrospect, the reforms made to that point were modest compared with what was to come. The Fraser Government was tentative about opening up the Australian economy to the world, implementing only a few uncontroversial recommendations of the Campbell Report. Australia still had a controlled exchange rate when *Fast Money* was first published in 1983. Chapter 6 includes a section titled, 'How the $A is set each day', describing arrangements which already seemed anachronistic to Australian financial markets players dealing with liberally regulated financial market regimes internationally. Carew was committed to market deregulation and criticised the fixed currency regime in *Fast Money*, declaring 'Australia's controlled foreign exchange environment has spawned markets whose sole aim is to find ways around these controls'.[15]

By March 1983, when Labor won office and Keating became treasurer, Carew was the *AFR*'s financial markets editor in Sydney.

'The conventional thinking – the fear – in financial markets was that Labor would reverse, or at least stall, the momentum that had built up, not just in Australia but worldwide, favouring fewer government controls on capital markets', Carew recalls.[16] This fear proved unfounded and the Hawke Government with Keating as treasurer not only continued the reform process but dramatically intensified it, ending exchange rate controls and floating the Australian dollar in December 1983. 'So here was a Labor treasurer, a son of the NSW right-wing faction of the ALP, implementing financial reforms to a degree that had eluded the previous Liberal Coalition government which ... had initiated the process'.[17]

In 1985 Allen & Unwin published Carew's book-length financial markets glossary *The Language of Money*, and *Fast Money 2*, which updated the first edition to take the floating of the Australian dollar into account, followed in 1987 by Carew's *New Zealand's money revolution* which covered financial market liberalisation in Australia's near neighbour.[18] Keating was the champion, political face and public policy pedagogue of the profound changes in Australian policy Carew followed and fervently supported. Carew in turn, through her books and journalism, was its principal expert interpreter.

Iremonger suggested a Keating biography when discussing future book ideas with Carew. He had been a Whitlam Government staffer and retained a keen interest in politics, especially Labor politics. 'John recalled Paul's admiration for Labor legends such as Jack Lang and Rex Connor', Carew says. 'Now Keating was showing his talent for making friends with Labor's enemies, remaining a passionate supporter of the self-made, working man while rubbing shoulders with the Big End of Town'.[19]

By the time Iremonger's idea morphed from a suggestion to a contract, Carew had left the *AFR* and become founding editor of a new capital markets magazine, *Triple A*. She was keen to interview Keating for the magazine and secured a meeting, which was useful as well for the book. Generally, however, 'getting time with Keating was no easy matter', she says. 'His staff were upfront that they were interested in the following day's headlines, not books on shelves. I began interviewing people who could shed light on elements of Paul's life while hoping to secure another formal interview with him'.[20]

Carew had a couple of 'sessions' with Keating in 1987 and then, in September, attended a lunchtime talk he gave in Sydney. Afterwards she approached him and he asked how the book was progressing.

'Slowly', I said, 'as I need more time with you'.

'Well, let's sit down', he said.

So we sat at an empty table, in a large Sydney hotel dining room deserted by all except staff who were clearing up and vacuuming, and launched into our discussions. Eventually he had to leave to catch a plane back to Canberra.

'But get in touch', he said. 'We'll make time'.[21]

More interviews took place, Carew driving to Canberra and seeing Keating in his Parliament House office. Many more interviews were done with those who had known or worked with Keating – family members, former classmates, associates from the music industry and business worlds, political friends and foes, friends from the antique trade, many of whom would not to talk to Carew until they cleared it with Keating.

She spent a day with Paul and his wife Annita at their Red Hill home. Keating's mother Min and sister Anne helped out supplying photographs of the young Paul for the book.[22] To this point, Keating had deterred potential biographers.

There were others I refused – there's quite a few. I can't say there's anyone who came along whose name you would recognise as a sort of professional biographer who made a proposal that I refused, but there were over the years various people who have said, 'Look, I'd like to sort of write about you. Could I come in and conduct a series of interviews?' And I'd say, 'No'. I'd always turn them away. [However] there's also a cost in being a nark and saying, 'No, look, I won't cooperate with you at all, go away blow fly, go away', that cost coming in terms of relations with the spurned writer.[23]

Carew's reputation, expertise and quiet persistence transformed the usual rebuff into acceptance and, ultimately, cooperation. 'Edna was a serious person with real standing', says Keating. 'I knew she would know what I was saying'.

The sources Carew pursued for the biography were significantly different from those she was used to talking to on the banking and finance rounds. 'I hadn't before dealt with the Irish Catholic tribal/family loyalty I encountered, among not just the immediate Keating family but among a wider group of their friends', she recalls.[24] Strong, at times inexplicable, sentiments in the other direction were also evident. 'I think I was — and even now still can be — struck by the venom that Keating can arouse in some people, people who have never met him, know nothing about him but have formed a hostile view nonetheless', Carew says. 'People invariably have an opinion on Keating, love him or hate him. And now ... many admit they wish he were back'.

Keating put no 'overt constraint' on the research; he 'didn't tell anyone they could *not* talk to me'. Some sources 'chose to duck and weave for their own reasons but they were senior government ministers with their own agenda'. What Carew did not know, and Keating could not tell her, was that the Kirribilli Agreement, under which Hawke secretly agreed to stand aside for Keating to succeed him as Labor leader and prime minister after the 1990 election, was being negotiated as Carew finalised the manuscript. 'With the benefit of hindsight, those unwilling to speak were in the Hawke camp', she says. Keating did not, and did not ask to, read Carew's text prior to publication. 'He was, however, interested in the photographs', she recalls, 'especially the cover shot'.[25]

There was a certain meanness of spirit in some quarters in relation to the project. Several people commented, 'rather ungenerously' in Carew's view, that writing a biography of someone Keating's age – he had just turned 39 when he became treasurer and was 44 at the time of *Keating, a biography*'s publication – was 'rather a mid-term report'. Since then biographies have been published of people in their twenties, Carew points out; and in any case, 'Keating was clearly an agent for change, a boy and then a man in a hurry, with an agenda and a narrative'.

> One or two who reviewed the book commented that I had been 'beguiled' by Keating's acquired veneer of sophistication – that underneath the Ermenegildo Zegna suits he was still the rough-edged Bankstown boy they had known (sub-text: 'I know Paul better and for longer than Edna Carew).
>
> So what? Keating had changed over the years. He is a contradictory individual not a cardboard cutout. We all change, develop, mature in ways that arguably those who knew us in earlier years might not like, understand or accept. Who is the real you? The one at 20? 40? 60? To me those comments came across as sour grapes – Keating had made it to the big stage when many who had aspired to similar had not.[26]

Keating recognised the value of Carew's biography in terms of giving key constituencies new insights into him. 'I think Edna's book was interesting for a lot of people that didn't know me', he says, 'like the investment banking community, the stockbroker community, the trade union community, a whole lot of people who needed to know me better than they could ever have known me'. This was not just in terms of his treasurership, or even his broader political career, but also in terms of Keating's deeper identity. He feels Carew 'broadly got it right' and 'had me better than John Edwards had me in the same period in his book, a better understanding of who I was'. This 'better feel' for him came, Keating thinks, partly from the way Carew 'threaded' all the family interviews together. 'I think she came to a better understanding of what my early life meant and was about', he says, 'than maybe John did who worked with me'.[27]

While not designed to contribute to the rising leadership tensions between Hawke and Keating, the Carew biography inevitably stoked them insofar as she reported the realities on the ground as she wrote. Keating's star rose as his relentless and persuasive reform advocacy against the backdrop of undeniable economic crisis made him central not only to the government's policy agenda but to its very survival. The government's 1988 May Economic Statement, Carew wrote, for example, 'brought a high point in the mounting speculation about Keating's claim to The Lodge'.

She goes on to describe the *Bulletin* magazine cover at the time proclaiming 'Prime Minister Paul Keating', quotes former Whitlam Government minister Jim McClelland's comment that 'Keating already is for all practical purposes the leader of the government', and cites polling that while Hawke was seen as more 'friendly and likeable', Keating was seen as 'more positive, less prone to changing his mind and less influenced by big business and the trade unions'. And what kind of prime minister would Keating be? 'He'll be the same kind of prime minister he is now', was a backbencher's comment.[28]

Three years and a broken Kirribilli Agreement later, on 19 December 1991, Keating became prime minister in fact and was sworn in the following day. Within months Carew published a second edition of the biography, titled *Paul Keating, Prime Minister*. Towards the end she mounts a strong defence of the man who 'cultivated a tough exterior, as politicians must ... to be a winner in the bare-knuckle arena of parliament'. Family and close friends did not recognise the 'cold and arrogant figure' portrayed in the media, Carew writes: 'The likeable Paul Keating is the private one … a passionate man for whom family and children are of first importance'. Keating had refused 'to "sell" himself, to soften his image and promote himself and his family to the public' as treasurer, according to Carew, but now, as prime minister, carried responsibility for the popularity of the government overall. She quotes the then ACTU secretary Bill Kelty that it would not be difficult to 'package' Keating, a tough, visionary, family-oriented politician: 'That's not a hard act to sell – it's just that it hasn't been sold'.[29]

Keating is, essentially, a private person, an introvert who made forays into the public arena to do what was necessary to achieve his goal, retreating then, each time, to the hearth to enjoy his family, listen to music and pursue his deep interest in objets d'art. In contrast to Hawke, who recharged his batteries by being among people, Keating recharged his by withdrawing. 'I don't like the interviews about these sorts of personal, close-in matters, I don't really like it', Keating says. 'I'm doing the job, that's all I really need to do, that's the feeling I have all the time'.

> The other thing is that I'm fundamentally shy. I'm the antithesis of Bob, the narcissist – I'm the other end of that scale. I get embarrassed about it all, to be honest, so I don't want to sit there talking about myself. It's different talking about issues or having your way on issues or fighting, that's different. But 'you' is different … The more intimate characteristics of one's personality and the rest, common sense tells you to keep it to yourself.[30]

So it was that when in 1992 Michael Gordon, then the *Sunday Age*'s Canberra correspondent, approached the Prime Minister's office with the idea of writing a biography for publication in the run up to the 1993 election, Keating was not enthusiastic. 'I was always inclined not to do that', he says.[31]

Gordon was born in Melbourne in 1955 to a journalist father and artist mother. He grew up in Hawthorn, attended Auburn Primary School and Carey Baptist Grammar, then joined the *The Age* as a cadet journalist. Gordon completed a Bachelor of Commerce at the University of Melbourne part-time while doing his cadetship, but otherwise fitted the traditional model of the career journalist undergoing craft-based training, working his way up the journalistic hierarchy via assignment to increasingly important news rounds and positions. Gordon was on his third tour of duty in the Canberra Press Gallery when he pitched the biography proposal to Keating staffers Tom Mockridge, a former journalistic colleague, and Mark Ryan, then Keating's press secretary. Gordon knew them both well. They liked the idea. 'Clearly I think they felt Keating was an unpopular figure, and they saw value in a broader portrait of him emerging without it being authorised', Gordon later said.[32]

'I was encouraged to do it by my staff who were all Michael Gordon fans', according to Keating who felt Gordon did not have Carew's economic standing. But he did have 'a serious place in national journalism, and he wanted to do it, so I thought well okay, but I wouldn't ... put a massive amount of time into it'.[33] For Gordon, the Keating biography was a chance to fulfil the 'ambition of any journalist to do something more enduring than newspaper clippings' during a 'really enthralling period'.[34] Keating was 'such a powerful figure ... a towering figure' for him.

Gordon identified with his subject's advocacy of an Australian republic and Indigenous recognition, among other things; he was a supporter but not in a 'partisan' way. Gordon also 'loved the eccentricity, the way the passion asserted itself, the unorthodox approaches to work and the interplay of the other interests with the job' that he saw in Keating. During the half dozen interviews he got for the book, Gordon shared the experience of a small number of favoured colleagues, staff and public servants on the rare occasions they were invited into Keating's private domain, of sitting 'equally distant between the speakers while Mahler or Rachmaninoff, I think it was, played'.[35] This was a privileged position, sharing a favourite Keating method of escaping the obligatory grind to a place of peace and inspiration. Keating's attitude to the book was that 'I didn't need it, didn't ask for it', any more than he had needed or wanted the Carew biography. Key staff advisors, however, felt differently. The resulting biography, *A Question of Leadership: Paul Keating, Political Fighter*, although not authorised by Keating was facilitated by the prime minister's office.

Keating viewed his office as a 'sort of co-promoter' of the book. 'That's partly why I did it, because Mark Ryan was very friendly with Michael, and so was (senior adviser) Don Russell, and so were a couple of other people in the office', he says. 'So as much to please him, or as much about amplifying my life outside the place, there was sort of a common cause in it, you see, and I just sort of went along with them'.[36]

The office indirectly had other biographical irons in the fire, too. Keating speechwriter Don Watson was married to Pan Macmillan publisher Hilary McPhee. Around the time Gordon signed a contract for his Keating biography with University of Queensland Press (UQP), McPhee signed my own biography of opposition leader John Hewson.[37] Hewson held a commanding opinion poll lead at the time with his *Fightback!* political manifesto yet to be politically dismembered by Keating.[38] The biography had a public interest motive. The polling suggested Hewson would coast into the prime ministership at the 1993 election, yet little was known of him among press gallery journalists reporting his ascent beyond him being a champagne-drinking, Ferrari-driving economist. The Hewson biography was designed to find out who he was for the benefit of journalistic colleagues as well as voters, in the interests of better-informed reporting and voting. In his biographical portrait of Keating, *Recollections of a Bleeding Heart*, Watson writes that the prime minister 'wondered if the coming task would be made easier' by the Hewson biography: 'We all strenuously hoped it would reveal some scandal' about him.[39]

UQP publisher Laurie Muller signed the Gordon book after seeing a draft first chapter and proposed structure; Muller had published books by Michael's father, journalist Harry Gordon, so his writing pedigree was understood. Gordon was advised to give each chapter more dramatic focus than evident in the initial sample. He set out to write the 60 000 words of his first edition in six months, simultaneously with doing his day job at the *Sunday Age*, so it could be published in time for the 1993 election.

Gordon came from a sports-mad family. Harry Gordon was a war correspondent, editor and sportswriter who, along the way, managed to cover ten Olympic Games. It rubbed off on Michael who conceptualised the task of writing the Keating biography as akin to playing limited overs cricket. He stuck a broad piece of white paper on the wall of his Canberra home 'with a run rate, (listing) how many words and whether I was ahead of the run rate or behind the run rate'. It would vary. 'But that was quite clinical. It might have been six months, 60 000 words – so clearly 10 000 words a month – and it might have even been ten chapters, so 6000 words a chapter'. There were 'a lot of ... voices', mostly documented through taped-recorded interviews, but no research assistant to help him with the time-critical project. 'So I did the interviews, I transcribed the interviews and tried to stay in tune with the required run rate'.[40]

There was some symbiosis between Gordon's day job at the *Sunday Age* and the 'limited overs' writing sprint he conducted at night and on weekends, mostly positive but on one notable occasion, negative. Independently of the Canberra bureau, a report on Keating's private assets was compiled by reporters at the *Sunday Age* head office in Melbourne, published along with an extensive graphic. 'Paul was very unimpressed', Gordon recalls, and telephoned the paper's editor, Bruce Guthrie, to tell him so with some force.[41] Keating told Guthrie he would 'cut Michael Gordon dead' because of the piece, even though he had no hand in it, to punish the paper for its invasion of his privacy. Guthrie promptly published Keating's phone comments in the paper. 'So (there was) this slightly bizarre situation where for a period the *Sunday Age* was barred from cooperation with his office, but he was still cooperating with the (biography) project', recalls Gordon. 'So I was still having access to members of his office, members of his staff, for researching the book' but banned in terms of the day-to-day *Sunday Age* reporting.[42]

The assistance Keating's office provided sometimes related to difficult to obtain material, such as access to the 'Placido Domingo' speech Keating made on 7 December 1990 at the Canberra Press Gallery's end of year dinner at the National Press Club. These speeches were traditionally made under 'Chatham House' rules in which journalists agree neither to record nor report them. The rule does not apply to the speaker or their staff, however, and Ryan recorded it as a precaution. Keating's comment that, in contrast to America, Australia had never had the great leaders it needed and deserved, was interpreted as a deliberate provocation of Hawke and perceived as the beginning of Keating's active campaign to wrest the Labor leadership from him. Contrary to the Chatham House convention, news of the speech was quickly reported, but getting a transcript of the full text for the biography was a coup for Gordon. 'I was able to obtain that, and [it] was a nice springboard into the book', he says.[43]

Hawke did not agree to an interview for Gordon's book. There would have been little to gain contributing to the biography of one's chief rival, especially one likely to be a 'friendly'. However, Gordon was able to draw on 'strong, trusting relationships' with Hawke associates to make up for it, as well as deep contacts in the broader labour movement, some of which dated back to his days as an industrial relations reporter for the Melbourne *Age*.

Gordon showed Keating the completed manuscript at the end for fact-checking purposes. 'The basis of it was, "I'll check this for accuracy, mate"', Gordon says, leading to some of 'his lovely handwriting annotations on my manuscript' but no deletions.[44] 'Keating clearly was happy with what I'd written. I think in one conversation he compared it to *Caucus Crisis*', Warren Denning's classic account of the Scullin Government, written while Denning was a press gallery member in the 1930s, and held in high esteem by Keating.[45] The Gordon book conveys well 'what makes me tick and how I think and why I think particular ways', says Keating.[46] Gordon himself felt it 'stands up as a pretty objective inside account of an extraordinary period'.[47] He would go on to get two more editions from the book, one after Keating's surprise 1993 election win and another after he lost the 1996 election to John Howard.

In 1993, for only the second time in Australian federal election campaigns, biographies of both the prime minister and opposition leader were published in the run up to the poll.[48] In parallel with Gordon's biography of Keating, the Hewson biography was being readied. Keating's speechwriter Watson 'got to read the (Hewson) book in manuscript over Christmas' 1992 and found the impression 'of a hungry fellow; and perhaps a rather hollow one'.[49] Pre-publication excerpts in the *Sydney Morning Herald* described, as Watson puts it, 'how the Baptist proto-missionary for Christ became a full-blown missionary of the markets and how, in the course of becoming moderately rich in the previous decade, the leader of the Opposition managed to consistently pay tax at only 15 cents in the dollar'.

While done using legal tax minimisation techniques, Watson notes that Hewson himself had condemned such practices as reflecting a 'tax cheat mentality' and Keating could not let it pass. Keating publicly accused Hewson of 'dubious and slick practices', and within a fortnight called an election for 13 March.[50] The Liberals blunted the impact of Keating's attack by retaliating with claims concerning Keating's business interests. However, the tax revelation took the shine off Hewson's hitherto impeccable reputation; he went from being perceived as someone above, and better than, most people in politics to being just another politician.

So it was that *Daily Telegraph* political correspondent Amanda Buckley could write, reviewing Gordon's biography, that, 'Luckily for him, this warm and readable biography contains no embarrassing revelations about personal finances – he has escaped the fate of Opposition Leader John Hewson, whose tax minimisation schemes, as set down by biographer Chris Wallace in a book published last week, are still causing him angst'.[51] Keating pressed his psychological advantage and over the course of a gruelling campaign unravelled Hewson's candidacy through the application of massive pressure on him to explain new tax proposals so complex Hewson visibly struggled to cope. The 1993 poll became the so-called 'unloseable election' that Hewson lost: Keating won, increasing Labor's majority by six seats.

John Howard was the third of three Liberal opposition leaders Keating faced as prime minister after winning the 1993 election. Contrary to undertakings that he would depart the opposition leadership should he lose the 1993 election, Hewson stayed on. His principal patron in the parliamentary Liberal Party was Andrew Peacock. Peacock had helped install Hewson as leader in the first place and persuaded him to continue after losing the election, partly from a desire to block Howard, his long-time rival, from regaining the leadership. Peacock and Howard had alternated as opposition leader throughout the 1980s in a poisonous competition of semi-permanent leadership destabilisation. When Hewson's leadership ultimately became untenable, Peacock was influential in ensuring Alexander Downer succeeded him, again blocking a Howard resurrection. By early 1995 Downer's lack of leadership maturity translated into dire opinion poll results. The parliamentary Liberal Party finally turned to Howard whose stocks were not high but was seen as a safe if unglamorous choice after the two younger prospects burnt out.

Howard succeeded where they failed, winning four elections

and serving as prime minister from March 1996 to December 2007. Howard had been in parliament more than twenty-one years when he won office. As treasurer in the Fraser Government, as an exponent of market liberalisation in the 1980s, and given that he was opposition leader from 1985 to 1989, it is perhaps surprising that no biography of him had been written up to this point. 'I certainly didn't encourage it', Howard says.

> I think some people, perhaps more so now than before, try to whip up interest in writing a book about them. I have a bit of a theory that it's not a good idea to have a book written about you in anticipation that you're going to become prime minister because, in most cases, you won't end up becoming prime minister.[52]

The example of Hawke, the subject of three pre–prime ministerial biographies who nevertheless went on to win office, is 'atypical' Howard says, pointing instead to the two biographies written of his own treasurer, Peter Costello, who wanted the top job but never got it, as more typical. Contemporary political biography can actually be damaging to a politician, in Howard's view.

'Unless the book has a degree of spontaneity and third-party endorsements about it', he says, 'it can look fairly much like a patent piece of promotion and will therefore work against you'. In any case, Howard argues, 'people … don't need them, because they've got the actual behaviour of the politician on which to base their judgment of that behaviour'. Thus Howard sees contemporary political biography as dangerous territory for the subject. In contrast to Keating who looks at biography with an eye to posterity, Howard's reasoning operates on a purely current political calculus.

Howard is nevertheless on his own account 'a big reader of biographies'. In addition to books on subjects one would expect like Churchill and Menzies, he lauds biographies of people to whom one might think him antipathetic. He describes Robert Skidelsky's multivolume biography of John Maynard Keynes as 'magnificent', for example, and praises David Marr's biography of Patrick White. Less surprisingly, he cites John Lewis Gaddis' biography of George Kennan, Andrew Roberts' biography of Halifax, and James MacGregor Burns' book on the three Roosevelts as memorable, as well as Charles Moore's biography of Thatcher – 'outstanding' – and biographies of AJP Taylor and Lord Denning.

He recounts having a drink with presidential biographer Doris Kearns Goodwin after taking part in a conference in Boston in 2011. When Howard was prime minister, Tom Schieffer, then US ambassador to Canberra, had given him Goodwin's *Team of Rivals: The Political Genius of Abraham Lincoln* to read, and later read her dual biography *The Bully Pulpit: Theodore Roosevelt, William Howard Taft, and the Golden Age of Journalism*. He cites Fin Crisp's biography of Ben Chifley as well as David Day's biographies of Chifley and Curtin in significance. It is the 'persistence stuff that comes through', he says. 'It's pretty clear, the more you read (biographies) of political figures, you find that persistence is not a rare commodity. It's a fairly common commodity'.[53] Persistence was a defining feature of Howard's political career and its repeated reinforcement via political biographies as a crucial quality for success can only have lent heart to a politician who knew long years in the political wilderness.

Two biographies of Howard were written during his prime ministership: *John Howard, Prime Minister* by David Barnett with Pru Goward, published a year into Howard's first term, and *John Winston Howard* by Wayne Errington and Peter van Onselen, published in his final year in office.[54]

Barnett and Goward were Canberra Press Gallery journalists at the time work began on *John Howard, Prime Minister*. However, Howard appointed Goward director of the Office of the Status of Women soon after taking office, so Barnett wrote the book alone, drawing material on Howard's early years from interviews Goward did for her ABC-TV series *The Liberals* broadcast a few years earlier. Barnett and Goward, husband and wife, had been close to Howard for decades. Howard entered parliament in 1974, when Whitlam was prime minister and Barnett was poised to become Fraser's press secretary; their friendship dated from then. Goward was a long-serving ABC journalist and knew Howard professionally and socially in that capacity. She later became a minister in the Liberal state governments of Barry O'Farrell and Mike Baird in New South Wales.

The authors of the second biography, Wayne Errington and Peter van Onselen, are academics. Van Onselen later pivoted to journalism, working for News Corporation and the Ten Network. Earlier in his career he had been a staffer for Liberal politicians Tony Abbott, Julie Bishop and Malcolm Turnbull. He was a friend of Howard's son Richard too, with whom he had been a university debater. Given the personal connections involved, both books might be expected to be 'friendlies', and the Barnett book certainly was. However, the Errington and van Onselen book turned out somewhat differently in practice, its independence reinforced by the authors' academic scruples and, given van Onselen's second life as a journalist, nose for a story.

Barnett was born in 1931. 'I grew up in the Depression and the Second World War – these are events that make you think, and make you think at a very early age', he told James Walter. A biography of Stalin read in the fifth grade – 'one of those things in yellow covers that that fellow Nicholson put out' – made an impression. Not that Barnett started out on the conservative end of the political spectrum. 'I think that thing of, not a socialist at twenty, no heart, still a socialist at forty, no head – I think that fits me', he said.[55]

Barnett began his journalistic career as a copy boy on Sydney's *Sun* newspaper in 1949, going on to a cadetship at the *Sydney Morning Herald* the following year. In 1955 he went to London and began thirteen years in Europe and Asia working for various news agencies including Reuters. In 1971 he established the Australian Associated Press (AAP) Canberra bureau. Barnett saw himself very much as 'a professional journalist', not a political activist. However, the trajectory of the Whitlam Government, for which he had voted in 1972, had him worried by 1974. 'I just felt that the country wasn't being run properly, that the Government really had no grasp of the difficulties of making the system work and was concerned with changing and reforming the system instead of making it function'. Interestingly, he saw opposition leader Billy Snedden as a factor likely to keep Whitlam in office.

> [We] were heading towards economic disaster and you looked at Billy Snedden and you thought, 'well, he'll never tip Gough out because faced with the choice between [the] rather attractive, flamboyant personality that was Gough and the way that Billy Snedden was approaching the role ... Gough was going to go on forever. And while he went on forever the economy would continue to slide. And you looked around and you saw Fraser standing there on the floor of the House, and he looked to me to have the qualities of character and personality and temperament that were required to take over the leadership of the Opposition and take it to government.[56]

In retrospect, Barnett realised he was 'part of the conspiracy' in which Fraser saw off Snedden as opposition leader. When Fraser's first tilt against Snedden failed Barnett stiffened the resolve of Fraser spear-carrier Tony Staley, telling him it was the right thing to do and, through Staley, encouraged Fraser to have another go. 'And when they did have another go, and it was successful, I went down to the office ... and offered my services'.

In the preface to *John Howard, Prime Minister*, David Barnett dates his long-held belief that Howard would one day be prime minister from the time Howard, after only four years in parliament, succeeded scandal-plagued Phillip Lynch as treasurer in the Fraser Government.

'Except for two interludes', Barnett continues, 'it was just as clear to me during the following years that he was the only Liberal Leader able to lead Australia from the morass into which it had sunk'. Barnett thus made explicit his personal investment of hope in Howard and belief in his ability to provide political deliverance; his point of view is declared and readers are forewarned an encomium is likely to follow. Howard is incorporated into the project suggestively in the preface with Barnett thanking him for his 'generous' time in 'establishing facts' in a life story 'he allowed me to take up'. At the same time, writes Barnett, Howard 'also accepted that I would be telling his story as I saw it, and not as he might find convenient'. The assertion that all books are about their author as well as their subject is borne out in the preface with Barnett saying the biography would also reflect 'observations and conclusions reached' during his own twenty-six years in Parliament House which was, of course, the reader deduces by paragraph's end, three years longer than his subject.[57]

John Howard, Prime Minister starts off somewhat unexpectedly, with Barnett portraying a young, newly anointed Treasurer Howard 'swaying, just slightly', in the public bar of the Kirribilli Hotel in November 1977. He had been sworn in by Governor-General Sir John Kerr at Admiralty House in Sydney four hours earlier and, after champagne on the lawns there, Fraser had hauled him off to the pub up the road. 'There, Howard, 1.72 metres and 69 kilograms, had gone along with the Prime Minister, 1.93 metres and 108 kilograms, middy for middy, for three hours', writes Barnett, at which point Fraser cheerily announced he would send his economic and political advisors to brief Howard in the morning before his first press conference as treasurer.[58]

Barnett's serviceable account of Howard's career lacked much further colour. Laurie Oakes commented that the biography 'unfortunately portrays its subject as rather a grey, boring, one-dimensional figure'.[59] Howard himself saw it 'as very much just a recounting of what I'd done'.[60] There was no end of potential drama in Howard's career, including policy tensions with the prime minister late in the life of the

Fraser Government; internecine warfare with leadership rival Andrew Peacock in opposition during the 1980s; the seemingly terminal career low after losing the Liberal leadership in 1989; and the rhetorical and policy sleights of hand deployed through 1995 in the lead up to his 1996 election win, later reconciled through the device of the 'core' and 'non-core' promise.

However, Howard himself embodied, and never sought to embroider, the 'plain man' persona that had served his political interests well. Barnett had only so much to work with in the writing of the biography in terms of Howard the man. Further, since Howard had been in office for such a short time when the book was published, and given Barnett's loyalty to the Howard political project, the 795-page text almost inevitably was a 'biography of record' tallying his career to that point. 'I didn't spend an enormous amount of time with David', Howard says. 'He didn't seek an enormous amount of time, but I didn't spend an enormous amount of time with him'.[61] Reliance on the public record perhaps made more contact between author and subject superfluous.

The Errington and van Onselen biography *John Winston Howard*, published at the other end of Howard's prime ministership, is of a significantly different complexion. Howard's prime ministership straddled the twentieth and twenty-first centuries, and *John Winston Howard* showed the first hints of a less linear way of portraying its subject compared to earlier contemporary political biographies in Australia.

Errington was born in 1969 to an electrician father and teacher's aide mother in the Illawarra region of New South Wales. While Errington's mother was active in her union, there was little political debate at home. Errington was educated at Keira Boys High School in Wollongong and completed Year 12 before joining the Royal Australian Navy (RAN) as an executive branch officer. Upon discharge, he attended the University of Western Australia (UWA) as a mature age student. Errington completed a BA in history and politics, then did a doctorate in political science where he shared an office with fellow doctoral student van Onselen. He became an academic and was a lecturer in political science at ANU when *John Winston Howard* was published. Errington describes himself as a 'classical liberal' for whom no current Australian political party has resonance.

Van Onselen was born in 1976 and grew up in the wealthy Sydney suburb of Vaucluse, not a scion of the rich but rather the son of the resident matron of the Strickland House convalescent home. This could well have laid the foundation for van Onselen's insider/outsider persona in his dual careers as academic and journalist. Schooled at Scots College in Sydney, he went on to an honours degree in political science and a master's degree in public policy at the University of New South Wales (UNSW), then a doctorate in political science at UWA. When *John Winston Howard* was published, he was an associate professor of politics and government at Edith Cowan University in Perth.

Interestingly, van Onselen both partly identified with Howard and attributed to him a critical role in his own decision not to pursue a political career. 'I had always felt a sense of commonality with his economic views but I have very different social outlooks – perhaps a generational thing', he says.[62] Howard's ability to switch between public and private personas, observed by van Onselen first hand when John and Janette saw him and Richard Howard off on a trip to the world debating championships, made van Onselen reconsider a political career. Within minutes of leaving the public part of the airport and arriving at the private airline lounge, Howard visibly changed. 'He seems someone who enjoys the organizational and internal strategic politics of it all, accepting he only becomes his relaxed self around trusted family and friends', van Onselen concluded. 'I know my own limitations. I couldn't do that because I'd blurt out what I really think of people in a way Howard was too clever to ever do. I see that as a political strength he has that I realised my personality limits me from having'. While the private airline lounge encounter made an impact, it was not the only reason van Onselen ruled out a political career. 'I had already started to question if the Liberal Party was progressive enough for me', he says.

Errington and van Onselen mark a break in the pattern of contemporary prime ministerial political biography in Australia. Firstly, they are academics, albeit in van Onselen's case, an academic whose perspective is informed by experience as a parliamentary staffer and political journalist.

Secondly, though they wear it lightly in terms of their conceptual framework and prose, Errington and van Onselen are more consciously modern compared to their predecessors: 'There are many John Howards', is the first sentence of the book.[63] Flowing from this, the biography considers the self-fashioning stratagems, rhetorical gambits and ambiguities of Howard the politician as well as broadening the context to include, for example, the impact of Janette Howard on her husband's political evolution and operation.

Finally, *John Winston Howard* is distinguished from other contemporary prime ministerial biographies in Australia by its explicitly damaging, on-the-record comments on the subject from a senior colleague. In these three respects, Barnett's *John Howard, Prime Minister* and Errington and van Onselen's *John Winston Howard* represent divergent poles in the history of contemporary political biography in Australia, despite the fact they were written within a decade of each other.

Errington and van Onselen wrote the Howard biography, according to Errington, 'because nobody else did ... (and) I thought it was a bit of an indictment on Australia's intellectuals that three election wins did not flush out a host of bios'.[64] At one stage there were more biographies of Labor's former opposition leader Mark Latham than there were of Howard, he notes. 'I found the conflict surrounding Howard more interesting than the man himself. I suppose everyone's life is interesting the closer you look'.

From van Onselen's viewpoint, Howard was the most significant politician he observed through childhood and young adulthood. The fact that he was still serving by the time, post-doctorate, he could turn to thoughts of writing a book, was influential. Howard was a 'natural fit as a subject' for that and two other reasons. 'My Liberal connections, as opposed to Labor connections – at that time, anyway', he says, and 'the friendship with Richard made me think I might face lower barriers of entry to writing it'. However, van Onselen 'made a very conscious effort not to (push) the friendship to help the project'.

> The co-operation was a long time coming, which probably helped the book because we wrote our draft version long before getting inside stories and perspectives from serving pollies or personal friends, who only started cooperating *after* Howard did. This helped the narrative and ensured it was ours and not others'.[65]

Errington and van Onselen already had an established partnership for academic and opinion piece writing. 'We had an unusually close relationship as co-authors, with license to change anything in the text', Errington says.[66] 'Peter is a good networker, so he set up and conducted a lot of the interviews while I did a lot of the historical and policy analysis'. Van Onselen interviewed Janette Howard on his own, and John Howard gave 'several' interviews to van Onselen, one of which was conducted jointly with Errington. But the principal interviews, including two with Treasurer Peter Costello, were done together. Though Howard was restrained he was nevertheless 'interested in shaping his legacy', in Errington's view, and his cooperation 'opened up a lot of opportunities with other interview subjects ... most notably with his wife, which proved very fruitful'. Melbourne University Press chief executive Louise Adler approached the authors and signed the book after noticing references to the project in their newspaper opinion pieces.

The two interviews with Costello and the interview with Janette Howard generated most of the immediate political flak surrounding the book. Costello discussed his view, disputed by Howard, that

Howard had reneged on a deal to make way for him as prime minister. In her interview Janette Howard rubbed Costello's nose into the folly of believing a succession deal was in place. 'You talk about a whole lot of things when you're trying to convince people to do things', she told van Onselen, 'but you don't go back and honour every single one of those unless you have made a firm commitment about it and John wasn't into making firm commitments'.[67]

The authors posed, 'Does Costello feel betrayed by Howard?' Costello replied, 'What do you expect me to do? I don't cry myself to sleep ... I expected it to happen, it didn't happen, and that's the reality and I deal in realities, so life moves on. The dogs bark but the caravan moves on and here I am'. Errington and van Onselen write, 'No amount of quoting Costello's words can capture the disappointment in his voice'.[68]

Costello gave them at length his frank assessment of the prime minister, saying Howard had 'not been a great reformer' as treasurer in the Fraser Government; that the Howard treasurership 'was not a success in terms of interest rates and inflation'; that contrary to Howard's subsequent claims he 'certainly didn't' have major disagreements with Fraser over industrial relations policy; that there was no evidence Fraser blocked Howard's economic reform efforts but rather 'the truth of the matter is if he had really wanted to push it he could have pushed it'; and that Howard's commitment to the 'dry' economic policy agenda associated with the right-wing HR Nicholls Society was more a matter of him 'looking for a constituency in the Liberal Party'. According to Costello, Errington and van Onselen write, 'Howard was even "very dubious about going" to the famous Southern Cross dinner of the HR Nicholls Society when he was opposition leader. "He turned up in the end but he was very reluctant"'.

The most politically damaging allegation made by Costello was that Howard's fiscal profligacy had built structural problems into the federal budget. Errington and van Onselen document the fiscal indictment of Howard by Costello which has continuing resonance years hence: "'I have to foot the bill and that worries me ... and then I start thinking about not just footing the bill today but if we keep building on all these things, footing the bill in five, and ten, and fifteen years and you know I do worry about the sustainability of all these things'".[69]

John Winston Howard was published in July 2007, and the federal election was held just four months later on 24 November 2007. In a typical media reaction to the book, ABC-TV's Kerry O'Brien prefaced an interview with van Onselen with the comment that,

> after 11 years ... in office, who would have thought for a moment that Peter Costello would give two interviews over several months to the authors of a biography on the Prime Minister, offering some pungent and politically destructive criticisms of his boss, calling his economic credentials and personal integrity into question, knowing that the comments would hit the streets (in) a politically unpredictable election environment.[70]

That this move was a deliberate one by Costello was underlined in reply. 'In terms of the interview, Peter Costello seemed very interested in talking', van Onselen told O'Brien. 'He seemed very deliberate in most of what he had to say. Right from the very beginning of the interview, on tape, his tape as well as ours, Peter Costello made it very clear that he was giving this for the biography'.

The book made public what political insiders had long known about the internal workings of the Howard Government. For those who would not read the 403-page text, in media interviews van Onselen paraphrased the content. 'The impression we got was their relationship is a very strained one', he said of Howard and Costello. 'There's no doubt that both men are professional enough in cabinet as well as in their general dealings to be business-like and get the job done and they've done so for many, many years, longer than any other partnership like this. However, there's no love lost between them. There's no rapport between them. It is business as usual and that's really where it starts and ends'.⁷¹

The authors were candid that their then lack of journalistic experience worked perversely to their advantage in the Costello interviews. 'I think that, not having the journalistic experience, we were sort of naïve in the way we asked questions – Costello would answer, then pause and we would blurt out our next question and he would continue with the rest of his answer to the previous question – so he was more than willing to keep talking', van Onselen told *The Age*.

> If we had been trained interviewers we probably would have jumped in more, trying to pin him down, to get him to explain what he meant. That would probably have got his guard up ... So really it was just dumb luck on our part that we managed to get from him what we got.⁷²

The small, telling detail that John and Janette Howard, during the entire eleven years of the Howard Government, had not once invited Peter and Tanya Costello to their home for a personal dinner said so much. Reported Errington and van Onselen in the biography, '"It's a fucking disgrace", said one minister, who didn't want to be named'.⁷³ The Howard Government already trailed in the polls when the biography was released. 'It was a pretty unhelpful thing at that time', Howard says in retrospect, mildly. 'But anyway ...'⁷⁴

Van Onselen being personally known to Howard through his friendship with Richard may have provided a comfort factor that turned out not to be well founded from the Howard camp's perspective. Howard himself says that the personal connection was not the reason for cooperating with the biography. 'He was around a bit', Howard says.

> Richard and Peter were quite friendly, and I knew Peter and his wife Ainslie [but] that wasn't the reason why. He didn't sort of prevail on Richard to prevail on me to agree for him to do the

biography. He decided to do it and pursue the thing and I was not unfriendly towards him, but I didn't spend an enormous amount of time with him. But I did agree to talk to him and ... it was an okay book. It was good – gee, it was good in parts. Some bits of it were wrong but some other stuff that was quite good ... I don't carry any grudges about it'.[75]

Errington notes that the book would have been quite different had the subject not been in office at the time of the biography's research and writing. 'Talking to colleagues while the subject still has a lot of power made some interview subjects, including Howard, less than full and frank', he says.

As a political scientist Errington feels he 'wasn't ready for the inherent inter-disciplinary nature of the exercise', especially the religious aspect of Howard's life story, and 'had to do a lot of reading in that area'. He voices concern about the quality of political psychobiography in Australia, citing Stan Anson's *Hawke: An Emotional Life* as an 'unreadable' example. 'That made me nervous about drawing too many conclusions about mummy and daddy issues, even though they do seem important to Howard and many other political leaders', he says. Errington contrasts Anson's work with that of James Walter who is 'good on the strong leadership archetype', for example, pointing to the possibilities political psychobiography still holds. 'Part of the problem is trying to say anything definitive about what is going on inside the subject's head', Errington says.[76] 'It often sounds speculative to me but some closer analysis regarding Howard in this light would be useful'. Nearly a century after the first contemporary biographies of a serving Australian prime minister were published, the inner life continued to be shied away from, yet remained as important – arguably more important – than ever.

Chapter 8
Political biography as political intervention

So what can we conclude about the idea of political biography as political intervention after looking at Australian prime ministers of the twentieth century?

These biographies from the first century of Australian politics present a picture to us over and over again that prime ministers are white men. As Wittgenstein said, a picture can hold us captive, 'And we couldn't get outside it, for it lay in our language, and language seemed only to repeat it to us inexorably'.[1]

Little wonder the onslaught in the early twenty-first century against Prime Minister Julia Gillard had such purchase. A hundred years of biographies of aspirant and serving Australian prime ministers contained not one picture of anyone like her, nor the possibility of one. How conditioned the populace was to the idea of prime ministers necessarily having a penis, and a white one at that. Given the biographical vacuum of alternative models, how easy it was for many to presuppose the accuracy of claims that Gillard was monstrous and should be 'put into a chaff bag and thrown into the sea' as Alan Jones, the now extinct volcano of misogynist rage in Australian politics, said.[2] It speaks volumes that many in the media were party to the rhetorical assault on Gillard, and missed the significance of her 'Misogyny speech' until global applause caused Canberra Press Gallery journalists pause.

If you think this is academic, you might be surprised to know how strong the belief remains in federal political circles that in Australia a woman is less electable as prime minister than a man. It is commonplace in Canberra to hear political professionals and journalists – not all of them male – say privately that female party leaders are problematic, 'because Queensland'. That's code for the view that Australians in frontier states won't vote to make a woman prime minister.

This idea is so entrenched that when the 'because Queensland' rationale is challenged, it is as though one has not spoken. Queensland has had a woman premier for more than eleven of the last fifteen years, in fact, and the incumbent, Annastacia Palaszczuk, has won three elections in a row. The political dinosaurs' hides are impervious to this data. Their reaction is worryingly like that of Pauline Hanson who early in her career dismissed as 'just paper numbers' objective immigration data contradicting her racist claims.

The objection that you won't get more biographies of women prime ministers and prime ministerial aspirants until there are more women in those roles is circular thinking. Specific to Australia, in this respect, is the problem that Gillard *has* been only female prime minister so far; her time in office was fraught and relatively short; and that this has provided fertile ground for the false idea to flourish that women are problematic prime ministerial candidates. It combines with a convenient obliviousness to Britain, New Zealand, Norway and Iceland, each with three women prime ministers so far; and many others.

What of whiteness? If it is so hard for a woman to be considered a viable prime ministerial candidate in Australia, how much harder again for a First Nations Australian or a person of colour? Where are the biographies of Australia's potential prime ministerial equivalents to South Africa's Nelson Mandela waiting in the wings, or to the United States' Barack Obama, or Samoa's Afioga Fiamē Mataʻafa?

So far there is just one: Margaret Simons' biography of Penny Wong recently rated Australia's most trusted politician – including in Queensland where her net trust score bettered that of Premier Annastacia Palaszczuk.[3] As a senator, Wong is quarantined from leadership speculation, since prime ministers must have a seat in the House of Representatives. John Gorton is the only senator since Federation to win the leadership of their party and switch to the lower house to become prime minister. So it is possible but unusual, and typically not considered a realistic option. This protects Wong from behind-the-scenes the chipping away that potential future leaders face in the lower house – for example, Labor's Tanya Plibersek – as rivals secure their competitive positions. (Of course it's not just women who face this; Labor Treasurer Jim Chalmers, for example, has been subject to similar pressures).

Far-sighted publishers should push beyond Wong as a subject, however, given how influential political biography can be. Why not commission diverse authors on diverse potential future leaders as a contribution to widening Australia's perceived leadership pool? Publishing today is not confined to the traditional trade paperback that needs to sell 5000 copies at $35 to be commercially viable. Shorter biographies, say 30 000 words, by diverse (including younger and emerging) authors, could be downloadable ebooks sold far more cheaply. Free online publication with a paid print on demand option, as ANU Press offers, has been an option for some time.

It's not just the subjects who lack diversity. The contemporary biographers discussed in this book are white, overwhelmingly male and nearly all journalists or ex-journalists by profession.

A journalistic background *can* be helpful, as Cecil Edwards noted, because journalists tend to be grounded in their political analysis.

> They have seen enough of the political field to know that it is not black and white, but a rather grubby grey. They would not have thought Menzies an infallible angel or Chifley a secret Communist. They know that democracy is not perfect, because it is a projection of imperfect human nature, but most think it better than one-party dictatorship. In this healthy cynicism, they are probably mirroring the opinion of most citizens.[4]

Political biography as political intervention

Graham Freudenberg, too, saw something special for the annals of history in the workings of journalists.

> Whatever their merits and defects, they are all invaluable as a contemporary record of who did what and who said what in an age without letters or diaries ... The other virtue of the journalists' records is that most of the persons whose actions and words they attempt to report are still living, and still able to reply, refute or litigate.[5]

Paul Keating believes contemporary political biography has utility for journalists at the time of publication and also informs biographers and academics who come to the subject later, with historical perspective. 'The book can only trace you', Keating says of contemporary biography. 'They can't really paint you three dimensionally or in full colour. But the tracings would be interesting to a gallery journalist. They're all info'. Keating sees the initial impact as modest.

> When these books came out ... they rustle around through the party caucus and the conversation, and people notice that they're out there. So they say this guy's either, one, promoting himself, or he's being promoted, but then again he might be, too, because he's actually doing a few things. So they create a bit of a rustle in the leaves – nothing much else, I don't think.[6]

In Keating's view, such books also confer value by picking up 'contemporary feeling, contemporary issues', for those writing later with longer perspective. We should be grateful to journalists for filling the vacuum on contemporary political biography because so much, as Keating points out, would otherwise be lost to subsequent biographers.

Journalists alone should not alone fulfil this critical civic task though. Historians, among others, could usefully write more contemporary political biography, more often. Commissioning more academics who can align biographical authorship with their teaching and learning activities, and who are in paid employment which values and rewards publication, open up a rich source of alternative authors, including diverse ones.

Authors drawn from a narrow band may only be capable of producing limited insights. 'Credibility and significance are touchstones of biographical and historical research', according to Cameron Hazlehurst. 'What is credible to the writer and reader depends on how much they know of the variety of human existence. What seems significant is determined by values as well as experience'.[7]

A corpus of contemporary political biography *not* authored so overwhelmingly by white male journalists could change the values and experiences that determine the dominant prism through which we get to know our political leaders. To do otherwise reinforces a political monoculture drastically in need of diversification for the polity's own good. Publishers have begun to commission more diverse authors to explain what our leaders think, why they think it and *how* they think, to illuminate the forces which shape a leader's character and potentially influence their actions in office. These biographies are important, not least to better inform votes.

Hopeful signs here include Karen Middleton's biography of Anthony Albanese, Annika Smethurst's biography of Scott Morrison, Margaret Simon's biography of Penny Wong and Jacqueline Kent's biography of Julia Gillard.[8] But the diversity metrics of contemporary political biography in terms of both subjects *and* authors have to improve former and faster for genuine equity and inclusion at the top of Australian politics to be achieved.

Prime Ministers themselves have a wide range of different views on the role of contemporary biographies written in the lead up to, or during, their prime ministerial careers. At the one end, there is the naked self-fashioning and aggrandising support for it from Billy Hughes. In the centre is Paul Keating's cautiously positive, posterity-driven view with a nod to contemporary biography's utility for the colleagues and current press gallery crowd. Towards the antagonistic end of the scale is John Howard's pragmatic point-in-time concern that 'it can look fairly much like a patent piece of promotion and ... work against you'.[9] The fact that Howard cooperated with two biographies during his prime ministership, however, suggests his concern is perhaps restricted to aspirants rather than prime ministers themselves. At the far end from the enthusiasm of Hughes is the outright opposition of Bob Menzies.

Menzies was scathing about biographies published during a politician's career, seeing them as outright propaganda. This didn't stop him actively assisting in the production of one even though, for reasons which are contested, he failed to follow it through to its conclusion. The case of the 'Menzies Biography Mystery', as the press tagged Allan Dawes' abortive book, points to the likely role of shifting political fortunes in decisions about them: the atmospheric may change considerably as the project proceeds.

Menzies' opposition is echoed in Howard's scepticism about contemporary political biography as more likely to generate unnecessary risk than reward. At the other end of the spectrum, Hughes' open appetite for laudatory biography is hilariously refreshing in its way: no biographical treatment could have been sufficiently praiseworthy for his liking. McMahon's biographical ambitions for an encomium worthy of him were so implausibly high that there was no contemporary biography of him during his political career.

Contemporary political biography was rare in the first half century after Federation but exponentially increased to a position of significance in Australia's political and publishing landscape.

Just seventeen contemporary political biographies were written and published in the lead up to, or during, the terms of office of Australia's twentieth century prime ministers – a strikingly low number.[10] The first three were wartime publications. Hughes was the subject of the first two, both published in 1916 for a British audience.[11] Alan Chester's *John Curtin* was published in 1943.[12] The only other one published in the first half century after Federation was a third biography of Hughes, Frank Browne's *They Called Him Billy* in 1946.[13]

To 1950 there had been sixteen prime ministers in all, including those whose term was brief (Page, Fadden and Forde), but only two – Hughes and Curtin – were the subject of contemporary biographies. Even allowing for the nascent state of the Australian publishing industry and Australian studies during this period, it constitutes a striking neglect; an almost determined lack of interest in Australia's first prime ministers. The inordinate wait before most even became the subject of posthumous biographies reinforces this perception. The failure of collective biographies written by journalists like Alfred Buchanan, Herbert Campbell-Jones and Warren Denning to be published at all, made the problem even worse. Australia's first prime ministers are lost figures to the consciousness of the nation. As a result, the founding fathers are mostly absent from the psyche of the nation – part of Julianne Schultz's 'terra nullius of the mind'.

The 1970s were a turning point in terms of the number and candour of contemporary political biography. In the generation following the publication of Frank Browne's *They Called Him Billy* in 1946, only one contemporary prime ministerial biography was published: Ronald Seth's biography for young readers, *RG Menzies*.[14] Then in 1969 came the harbinger of the modern era, Alan Trengove's *John Grey Gorton: An informal biography*.[15] The distinctive Australianness of Gorton as a subject, in the context of a new sense of national identity as Australia emerged from its heavy British Commonwealth overlay, pointed to what would come, fuelled by a new excitement about politics and enabled by the growth of a real Australian publishing industry.

There were eleven contemporary biographies of the five Australian prime ministers who served from 1972 for the rest of the century. First was Laurie Oakes' *Whitlam PM: A biography* published in 1973 and Graham Freudenberg's *A Certain Grandeur: Gough Whitlam in Politics* in 1977; then John Edwards' short *Life wasn't meant to be easy: a political profile of Malcolm Fraser* in 1977.[16] They were followed by four on Bob

Hawke, two on Paul Keating, and another two on John Howard.[17] Several had updated editions. Contemporary prime ministerial biography eventually became the norm, sometimes with multiple biographies of the subject.

Trengove's *John Grey Gorton* heralded a new candour in contemporary political biography, reflecting the more relaxed social mores which flowed from social liberalisation in the 1960s. The revelation of Gorton's illegitimacy, with Gorton's blessing, manifested a new thinking: that planned disclosure of uncomfortable facts could anticipate and negate an ambush by one's political enemies. This approach reached its zenith in d'Alpuget's *Robert J Hawke* in which carefully contextualised disclosures of its subject's alcoholism and philandering inoculated him against their use as political weapons by rivals.

While the majority of the biographies examined here were designed to boost reputations, the motivations behind them varied. Of the seventeen biographies considered, thirteen lifted the reputations of their subjects, though for quite varying reasons, two were neutral and only one drags its subject down. Sprigg (Hughes) and Seth (Menzies), being 'guns for hire' were likely fulfilling others' agendas. Sladen (Hughes), Chester (Curtin), Browne (Hughes), Trengove (Gorton), Freudenberg (Whitlam), Hurst (Hawke), d'Alpuget (Hawke), Gordon (Keating) and Barnett (Howard) had their own personal or political agenda, and sometimes both. In the case of Oakes (Whitlam) and Carew (Keating) the biographies reflected their puzzling over, and fascination with their subject.

The biographies written by Pullan (Hawke), and by Errington and van Onselen (Howard), had a more neutral affect. Anson (Hawke) is the only biographer diminishing its prime ministerial subject – an unequivocally negative outlier. There is no obvious example of a third party seizing a biography and exploiting it for purposes at odds with the author's intentions, though d'Alpuget's *Robert J Hawke* had that potential. Rivals, both internal and external, who believed the biography's personal revelations would damage Hawke turned out to be wrong.

The unexpected asymmetry between the number of biographies lifting a subject up compared with the single one designed to drag its subject down suggests either that Australia does not have an 'attack' culture of contemporary political biography – or that biographies can, indeed, hurt aspirants' prospects for power. Did other contemporary political biographies of twentieth century Australian politicians who aspired to but did *not* become prime minister play a part in their failure? This warrants further exploration.

Three biographers stand out. The intensity of attention to a prime minister exemplified by Oakes' Whitlam quartet; the long life of Freudenberg's *A Certain Grandeur*; and the trenchant research, psychological insight and narrative satisfactions of d'Alpuget's influential *Robert J Hawke*, show what is possible in the genre. The closing off of a more psychological approach to subjects seeded by AF Davies and the Melbourne Psychosocial Group is a loss. The reception of and legal concerns around Stan Anson's book likely played a role in this, but also significant is the decline in the authority of psychoanalysis in recent decades, and the lack of a dominant approach in psychology as a discipline to replace it. This should be no barrier to drawing on psychology broadly, though, and nor should a more psychologically informed approach be considered a barrier to broad readership. As d'Alpuget's commercially successful, psychoanalytically informed but jargon free *Robert J Hawke* shows, in the hands of a skilful writer anything is possible. The psychology of prime ministers, and even more so aspirant ones, should be an urgent focus for our attention as citizens, as voters. Underlining this most recently is the revelation of Liberal prime minister Scott Morrison's evangelical church sermon shortly after losing office, where he declared, bizarrely, 'We trust in Him. We don't trust in governments'.[18] That journalists seem especially shy of the psychological is a further argument for more diversity in the ranks of contemporary political biographers.

Political biography as political intervention

It's not necessary to privilege agency over structure in history to concede the obvious, that leaders are important – or that knowing more about them and understanding better how they think as a predictive tool for how they could act in office can only be a good thing.

Reputation is political capital. Biographers are among those who coin it, and who can destroy it, as well providing the materiel for others to do the same for their own multifarious reasons. None of the biographers in Australia's first century of national politics faced the potential frenzy I faced with the Gillard project early in its second century. Pressing on would have constituted a political intervention of an unintended kind. Some will say *not* pressing on itself constituted a kind of political intervention, to which I would respond by asking whether contemporary political biography demands a variation on the Hippocratic oath. First do no harm – unless it's deserved and intentional.

Notes

ABC   Australian Broadcasting Commission / Corporation
ANU   Australian National University
MUP   Melbourne University Press / Publishing
NLA   National Library of Australia, Canberra
SMH   *Sydney Morning Herald*
UQP   University of Queensland Press

Preface: Wait. What?

1. Email to Sue Hines and Rebecca Kaiser, Allen & Unwin, 9 June 2011.

1   Absent fathers

1. Alfred Buchanan, *The Real Australia* (London: T Fisher Unwin, 1907), Colonial Edition, 252–276.
2. Susan Marsden & Roslyn Russell, *Our First Six: Guide to Archives of Australia's Prime Ministers* (Canberra: National Archives of Australia, 2002), 7–8.
3. John Reynolds, *Edmund Barton* (Sydney: Angus & Robertson, 1948); Walter Murdoch, *Alfred Deakin: A Sketch* (London: Constable, 1923); Al Grassby & Silvia Ordonez, *The Man Time Forgot: The life and times of John Christian Watson, Australia's first Labor Prime Minister* (Annandale: Pluto Press, 1999); WG McMinn, *George Reid* (MUP, 1989); David Day, *Andrew Fisher, Prime Minister of Australia* (Sydney: HarperCollins, 2008); Edward W Humphreys, *Andrew Fisher: The forgotten man* (Teesdale: Sports & Editorial Services, 2008); G Bebbington, *Pit boy to prime minister: the story of the Rt Hon. Sir Joseph Cook, PC, GCMG* (Keele: University of Keele, 1988).
4. JA La Nauze, *Alfred Deakin: A Biography* (MUP, 1965), 2 vols; Walter Murdoch, *Alfred Deakin*; Judith Brett, *The Enigmatic Mr Deakin* (Melbourne: Text Publishing, 2018).
5. Herbert Campbell-Jones, 'The Cabinet of Captains: the romances of Australia's first Federal Parliament', unpublished MS, circa 1935, Papers of Herbert Campbell-Jones, MS 8905, NLA, 5, 9–10.
6. Lyndall Ryan et al., 'Colonial Frontier Massacres, Australia, 1788–1930, <c21ch.newcastle.edu.au/colonialmassacres/map.php>, accessed 5 June 2022.
7. Julianne Schultz, *The Idea of Australia: A search for the soul of the nation* (Sydney: Allen & Unwin, 2022), 1, 2.
8. Colin Clark, *Australian Hopes and Fears* (London: Hollis & Carter, 1958), 163.
9. Henry Gyles Turner, *The First Decade of the Australian Commonwealth: A Chronicle of Contemporary Politics, 1901–1910* (Melbourne: Mason, Firth & McCutcheon, 1911), p. 3.
10. George Reid, *My Reminiscences* (London: Cassell, 1917).
11. Campbell-Jones, 'The Cabinet of Captains', 282.
12. Buchanan, *The Real Australia*, 252–3.
13. Alfred Buchanan, 'Edmund Barton', 'The Prime Ministers of Australia', unpublished MS, 1940, 1; Papers of Alfred Buchanan, MS 3034, NLA.

14 Geoffrey Bolton, *Edmund Barton* (Sydney: Allen & Unwin, 2000), xi–xii.
15 Edmund Barton, letter to Thomas Bavin, 20 October 1903, Papers of Sir Thomas Bavin, MS 560, NLA. For a time after Barton went to the High Court, Bavin continued as his private secretary.
16 Edmund Barton, letter to Thomas Bavin, 22 March 1915, Papers of Sir Thomas Bavin.
17 JA La Nauze, *Alfred Deakin: Two Lectures*, the John Murtagh Macrossan Memorial Lectures, 958 (Brisbane: UQP, 1960), 8.
18 Alfred Deakin, 'Books and a Boy' (1910?), 12, MS, Papers of Alfred Deakin, MS 1540, 1540/4/123, NLA; Elizabeth Penrose ['Mrs Markham'], *A history of England: from the first invasion by the Romans to the 14th year of the reign of Queen Victoria* (London: Murray, 1857).
19 Alfred Deakin, notebook with newspaper clippings, (c. 1883–4), Papers of Alfred Deakin, MS 1540, 1540/4/585, NLA.
20 Alfred Deakin, letter to Walter Murdoch, 7 November 1906, in JA La Nauze & Elizabeth Nurser (eds), *Walter Murdoch and Alfred Deakin on Books and Men: Letters and Comments 1900–1918* (MUP, 1974), 28.
21 'List of Deakin's Books, before distribution among his family after his death', Papers of Alfred Deakin, MS 1540, 1540/4/694–5, NLA.
22 La Nauze, *Alfred Deakin*, 641–2.
23 Buchanan, 'Alfred Deakin', 'The Prime Ministers of Australia', 16.
24 Stuart Macintyre, 'Introduction', Alfred Deakin, *'And Be One People': Alfred Deakin's Federal Story* (MUP, 1995), vii–viii.
25 Macintyre, 'Introduction', Deakin, *'And Be One People'*, viii.
26 Buchanan, *The Real Australia*, 260.
27 Grassby & Ordonez, *The Man Time Forgot*.
28 Grassby & Ordonez, *The Man Time Forgot*, 7–19.
29 Grassby & Ordonez, *The Man Time Forgot*, 17–18.
30 Buchanan, 'The Prime Ministers of Australia', chapter on 'Watson, John Christian', 1–2.
31 Reid, *My Reminiscences*, 28–29.
32 George Reid, *The Diplomacy of Victoria on the Postal Question, and the True Policy of New South Wales* (Sydney: W Maddock, 1873).
33 Reid, *My Reminiscences*, 24.
34 Reid, *My Reminiscences*, 23.
35 Reid, *The Diplomacy of Victoria on the Postal Question*, handwritten inscription by Reid to Lang, 2.
36 Reid, *My Reminiscences*, 132.
37 Reid, *My Reminiscences*, 24.
38 George Reid, *Five Free Trade Essays* (Melbourne: Gordon & Gotch, 1875).
39 WE Gladstone, letter to George Reid, 13 July 1875, Papers of George Reid, MS 7842/3/19, NLA.
40 Cobden Club, *A History of the Cobden Club by Members of the Club* (London: Cobden-Sanderson, 1939), 16.
41 McMinn, *George Reid*, 11.
42 George Reid, *An Essay on New South Wales, The Mother Colony of the Australias* (Sydney: Thomas Richards, Government Printer, 1876).
43 Lord Salisbury, letter to George Reid, 1 March 1877; Henry Ponsonby, letter to George Reid, 22 January 1877, Papers of George Reid, MS 7842/3/19, NLA.
44 'Opinions of the Press' [*An Essay on New South Wales, The Mother Colony of*

Notes to pages 14–19

      the *Australias* by GH Reid], (1877), pamphlet, 12pp. in Papers of George Reid, MS 7842/4, 'Sir George Reid, Publications', NLA.
45 'Biography of the Hon. George Houston Reid', MS, 241pp., Papers of Sir George Reid, MS 2242, NLA [Reid biography].
46 Reid biography, v.
47 Reid biography, 6.
48 Reid biography, 17. McCormick is likely to be PD McCormick, an elder of the Presbyterian Church, and composer of 'Advance, Australia Fair' and 'Flower of Scotland'.
49 Reid biography, 109.
50 Reid biography, 31.
51 Reid biography, 33.
52 WG McMinn, 'Reid, Sir George Houstoun (1845–1918)', *Australian Dictionary of Biography*, National Centre of Biography, Australian National University, <adb.anu.edu.au/biography/reid-sir-george-houstoun-8173/text14289>, published in hardcopy 1988, accessed online 22 April 2014.
53 Reid, *My Reminiscences*, 12.
54 Reid biography, 38.
55 Undated clipping with the handwritten word 'Vancouver', referring to 'the Colonist', most likely from the Vancouver newspaper, the *British Colonist*, attached to Reid biography, 41.
56 McMinn, *George Reid*, 1–2.
57 McMinn correctly cites it as '2242' in a footnote in WG McMinn, 'The Making of a Politician: The Early Career of GH Reid', *Journal of the Royal Australian Historical Society*, 67, 1 (June 1981), 1–17. Again, the anonymous biography is not discussed.
58 cf. John English, *'Reid the Wriggler' or the False Prophet of Freetrade Tried and Convicted on his Professions, Promises and Performances* (Sydney: TJ Houghton & Co, Printers, 1895).
59 Reid biography, 53.
60 Buchanan, 'George Houston [sic] Reid', 'The Prime Ministers of Australia', 2.
61 Buchanan, 'George Houston Reid', 2.
62 Campbell-Jones, 'The Cabinet of Captains', 132.
63 Campbell-Jones, 'The Cabinet of Captains', 138.
64 DJ Murphy, 'Fisher, Andrew (1862–1928)', *Australian Dictionary of Biography*, National Centre of Biography, Australian National University, <adb.anu.edu.au/biography/fisher-andrew-378/text10613>, published in hardcopy 1981, accessed online 1 August 2021.
65 While it numbers among its 60 volumes *Ayrshire: Its history and historic families* (1908), *How to Learn Welsh* (1900) and Australian novelist Marie Bjelke Petersen's *The Captive Singer* (1917), a romance whose protagonist was based on Petersen's life companion Sylvia Mills, it contains only one biography: *Life and letters of Norman Carey Lucas* (1920), a Rhodes scholar and British Army Gallipoli veteran who was killed at Salonika in World War I. Papers of Andrew Fisher, MS 2919, NLA.
66 Day, *Andrew Fisher*, x.
67 Day, *Andrew Fisher*, x; Peter Bastian, *Andrew Fisher: An underestimated man* (Sydney: UNSW Press, 2009). For a good summary of Fisher's biographical misfortunes, see Humphreys, *Andrew Fisher*, 1–7.
68 Day, *Andrew Fisher*, x.

Notes to pages 21–29

69 Campbell-Jones, 'The Cabinet of Captains', 1–2.
70 'Literary Australians. Mr Alfred Buchanan', *Table Talk*, October 1911, 22.
71 *Sunday Times* (Perth), 29 June 1919, 4.
72 Alfred Buchanan, *Bubble Reputation: A Story of Modern Life* (Melbourne: George Robertson, 1906); *Australasian*, 13 October 1906, 46.
73 Quoted in a display advertisement for *Bubble Reputation* placed by the publisher, George Robertson & Co., *SMH*, 9 February 1907.
74 *Advertiser*, 27 April 1914.
75 *The Mirror of Australia* (Sydney), 4 December 1915, 4.
76 *Punch*, 23 May 1918, 7.
77 *Sunday Times*, 30 November 1919, 4.
78 Buchanan, *The Real Australia*, 49–50.
79 Buchanan, *The Real Australia*, 66–7.
80 '[T]he biographies of the Prime Ministers will be in their proper home here ... Our future readers will owe thanks to your thoughtfulness.' National Librarian AP Fleming to Capt. AE Buchanan, 28 January 1972, NLA.
81 Memo from AP Fleming, 'AJ Buchanan Manuscripts', 17 January 1973, NLA.
82 Handwritten note by Alec Bolton on memo from AP Fleming, 'AJ Buchanan Manuscripts', 17 January 1973, NLA.
83 Malcolm Booker, *The Great Professional: A Study of WM Hughes* (Sydney: McGraw-Hill, 1980), xi.

2 The Great War to the Great Depression

1 LF Fitzhardinge, *William Morris Hughes: A Political Biography*, vol. 1, *That Fiery Particle, 1862–1914* (Sydney: Angus & Robertson, 1964), 25.
2 Herbert Campbell-Jones, 'The Cabinet of Captains: the romances of Australia's first Federal Parliament', unpublished MS, circa 1935, Papers of Herbert Campbell-Jones, MS 8905, NLA, 73.
3 Clem Lloyd, *Profession: Journalist, A History of the Australian Journalists' Association* (Marrickville: Hale & Iremonger, 1985), 116.
4 Lloyd, *Profession*, 13, 82.
5 WM Hughes, *The Case for Labor* (Sydney: The Work Trustees, 1910); *The Splendid Adventure: A Review of Empire Relations Within and Without the Commonwealth of Britannic Nations* (London: Ernest Benn, 1929); *Australia and war to-day: the price of peace* (Sydney: Angus & Robertson, 1935); *Crusts and Crusades: Tales of Bygone Days* (Sydney: Angus & Robertson, 1947); *Policies and Potentates* (Sydney: Angus & Robertson, 1950).
6 Stanhope W Sprigg, *WM Hughes: The Strong Man of Australia* (London: C Arthur Pearson, 1916); Douglas Sladen, *From Boundary-Rider to Prime Minister: Hughes of Australia, The Man of the Hour* (London: Hutchinson, 1916).
7 Frank C Browne, *They Called Him Billy* (Sydney: Peter Huston, 1946).
8 Cameron Hazlehurst, *Ten Journeys to Cameron's Farm* (Canberra: ANU E Press, 2013), 8.
9 Sprigg, *WM Hughes*; Sladen, *From Boundary-Rider to Prime Minister*.
10 Donald Horne, *In Search of Billy Hughes* (South Melbourne: Macmillan, 1979), 129.
11 Sprigg, *WM Hughes*, 96.
12 Sprigg, *WM Hughes*, 21.
13 James Jupp (ed.), *An Encyclopedia of the Australian People* (Sydney: Angus & Robertson, 1988), 765.

14 Eric Richards, 'An Australian map of British and Irish literacy in 1841', *Population Studies: A Journal of Demography*, 53, 3 (1999), 345.
15 Jean Duparc & David Margolies (eds), *Christopher Caudwell: Scenes and Actions, Unpublished Manuscripts* (London: Routledge & Kegan Paul, 1986), 2.
16 Valentine Cunningham, 'Sprigg, Christopher St John (1907–1937)', *Oxford Dictionary of National Biography*, Oxford University Press, 2004, <www.oxforddnb.com/view/article/59007>, accessed 1 August 2021.
17 EP Thompson, 'Christopher Caudwell', *Critical Inquiry*, 21, 2 (Winter 1995), 306.
18 KJ Cable, 'Sladen, Douglas Brooke (1856–1947)', *Australian Dictionary of Biography*, National Centre of Biography, Australian National University, <adb.anu.edu.au/biography/sladen-douglas-brooke-4590/text7543>, published in hardcopy 1976, accessed online 1 August 2021.
19 Douglas Sladen, *My Long Life: Anecdotes and Adventures* (London: Hutchinson, 1939), 215.
20 Sladen, *My Long Life*, 64–70.
21 'Douglas B. W. Sladen, B.A.', *Cosmopolitan*, II, 4 (February 1888), 72; reprint (London: Williams & Co., 1888).
22 Sladen, *My Long Life*, 190–194.
23 Sladen, *From Boundary-Rider to Prime Minister*, 46–7.
24 Sladen, *From Boundary-Rider to Prime Minister*, 1.
25 Sladen, *From Boundary-Rider to Prime Minister*, 3.
26 Sladen, *From Boundary-Rider to Prime Minister*, 3, 4, 31, 6, 43 & 5 respectively.
27 Sladen, *From Boundary-Rider to Prime Minister*, 46–63.
28 Sladen, *From Boundary-Rider to Prime Minister*, 55.
29 Sladen, *From Boundary-Rider to Prime Minister*, 42.
30 Sladen, *From Boundary-Rider to Prime Minister*, 42.
31 Sladen, *My Long Life*, 215.
32 Sladen, *My Long Life*, 216.
33 *Empire Review*, XXX, 183, April 1916.
34 Vyrnwy Morgan, *The War and Wales* (London: Chapman & Hall, 1916), 373.
35 Anonymous, *Mr Hughes: A Study* (London: T Fisher Unwin, 1918).
36 Anonymous, *Mr Hughes*, 23–4.
37 Frank Owen, *Tempestuous Journey: Lloyd George, His Life and Times* (London: Hutchinson, 1954), 368–9.
38 Browne, *They Called Him Billy*, flyleaf.
39 Horne, *In Search of Billy Hughes*, 129.
40 Browne, *They Called Him Billy*, 7.
41 Browne, *They Called Him Billy*, 225.
42 WM Hughes, House of Representatives, Canberra, 2 January 1946, reproduced in W Farmer Whyte, *William Morris Hughes: His Life and Times* (Sydney: Angus & Robertson, 1957), v.
43 Horne, *In Search of Billy Hughes*, 2.
44 Don Whitington, *Strive to be Fair: An unfinished autobiography* (Canberra: ANU Press, 1977), 82.
45 Malcolm Booker, *The Great Professional: A Study of WM Hughes* (Sydney: McGraw-Hill, 1980), ix–x.
46 Hazlehurst, *Ten Journeys to Cameron's Farm*, 8.
47 LF Fitzhardinge, *The Little Digger 1914–1952: William Morris Hughes, A Political Biography*, vol. 2 (Sydney: Angus & Robertson, 1979), 669, n. W Farmer Whyte's

William Morris Hughes: his life and times (Sydney: Angus & Robertson, 1957) was the other, finished five years after Hughes' death.
48 Frank C Browne, *Things I Hear: For the Confidential Information of Subscribers, A Privately Circulated Digest for Busy People*, periodical, Sydney, 1946–77; Gavin Souter, 'Browne, Francis Courtney (Frank) (1915–1981)', *Australian Dictionary of Biography*, National Centre of Biography, Australian National University, <adb.anu.edu.au/biography/browne-francis-courtney-frank-12259/text21999>, accessed online 1 August 2021.
49 Henry 'Jo' Gullett, interviewed by Mel Pratt, 14–19 November 1970, ORAL TRC 121/1 (transcript), Oral History Collection, NLA, 27.
50 Clem Lloyd, *Parliament and the Press: The Federal Parliamentary Press Gallery 1901–88* (MUP, 1988), 199 & 202.
51 Lloyd, *Parliament and the Press*, 202.
52 Fitzhardinge, *The Little Digger*, 669, n.
53 Letter from William Morris Hughes to W Farmer Whyte, 3 March 1944, Papers of W Farmer Whyte, MS 970, NLA.
54 Letter from William Morris Hughes to W Farmer Whyte, 4 January 1946, Papers of W Farmer Whyte.
55 Letter from William Morris Hughes to W Farmer Whyte, 4 January 1946.
56 Fitzhardinge gives 1940 as the date in the preface to *The Little Digger*, v. However, he gives the date as 1942 in an interview with Tom Molomby, 'Science Bookshop', ABC Radio, 1979; a transcript of the interview is held with Fitzhardinge's Oral History interviews, NLA, 2.
57 LF Fitzhardinge, *That Fiery Particle*, vii.
58 Fitzhardinge, interview with Molomby. The interview transcript is the source for the subsequent story, including quotes.
59 Fitzhardinge, interview with Molomby, 2–3.
60 Fitzhardinge, interview with Molomby, 3.
61 Fitzhardinge, interview with Molomby, 4.
62 Fitzhardinge, interview with Molomby, 5.
63 Cecil Edwards, *The Editor Regrets* (Melbourne: Hill of Content, 1972), 37; *Bruce of Melbourne: Man of Two Worlds* (London: Heinemann, 1965).
64 Letter from Cecil Edwards to Viscount Bruce, 28 November 1962, 1, Papers of Cecil Edwards, MS 4637, NLA.
65 Letter from Stanley Bruce to Cecil Edwards, 11 December 1962, Papers of Cecil Edwards.
66 Letter from Stanley Bruce to Cecil Edwards, 18 February 1963, Papers of Cecil Edwards.
67 Cecil Edwards, submission to the Literature Board of the Australian Council for the Arts concerning a possible grant application to support the writing of a proposed book titled 'The Bruce Papers', 3, Papers of Cecil Edwards.
68 Edwards, submission to the Literature Board.
69 Earle Page, *Truant Surgeon* (Grafton: Examiner, 1959); letter from Stanley Bruce to Cecil Edwards, 22 March 1963, 2, Papers of Cecil Edwards.
70 Letter from Cecil Edwards to Stanley Bruce, 3 April 1963, 1–2, Papers of Cecil Edwards.
71 Letter from Cecil Edwards to Stanley Bruce, 3 April 1963, 2, Papers of Cecil Edwards.
72 Edwards, *The Editor Regrets*, 122.
73 Edwards, *The Editor Regrets*, 123–4.

74 Edwards, *The Editor Regrets*, 187–193, 188.
75 Edwards, *The Editor Regrets*, 190.
76 (London: Continuum Press, 2010).
77 John Robertson, *JH Scullin: A Political Biography* (Nedlands: University of Western Australia Press, 1974), ix.
78 Heather Radi, 'Bruce, Stanley Melbourne (1883–1967)', *Australian Dictionary of Biography*, National Centre of Biography, Australian National University, <adb.anu.edu.au/biography/bruce-stanley-melbourne-5400/text9147>, accessed online 1 August 2021.
79 Lloyd, *Parliament and the Press*, 88.
80 Warren Denning, *Caucus Crisis: The Rise and Fall of the Scullin Government* (Parramatta: Cumberland Argus, 1937). [Denning, *Caucus Crisis*].
81 'Caucus Crisis. Eventful Years in Canberra. Mr W Denning's Book', *Canberra Times*, 21 August 1937, 6.
82 Warren Denning, *James Scullin* (Melbourne: Black Inc., 2000).
83 Paul Keating, personal communication with the author, 1996.
84 Denning, *Caucus Crisis*, 11.
85 Alan Reid, 'Memoir' in Warren Denning, *Caucus Crisis: The rise & fall of the Scullin Government* (Sydney: Hale & Iremonger, 1982), 11 [Reid, 'Memoir'].
86 Reid, 'Memoir'.
87 Denning, *Caucus Crisis*, 77.
88 Denning, *Caucus Crisis*, 79.
89 Denning, *Caucus Crisis*, 66.
90 Stagflation is the contiguous existence of stagnation (low growth) and high inflation in an economy.
91 Denning, *Caucus Crisis*, 22–23.
92 Denning, *Caucus Crisis*, 23–24.
93 Clem Lloyd, 'How Scullin Fell', *Australian Financial Review*, 20 August 1982.
94 Michael Easson, 'Leaders bewildered by crisis', *Catholic Weekly*, 26 September 1982.
95 Easson, 'Leaders bewildered by crisis'.
96 IR Hancock, 'Denning, Warren Edwin (1906–1975)', *Australian Dictionary of Biography*, National Centre of Biography, Australian National University, <adb.anu.edu.au/biography/denning-warren-edwin-9950/text17627>, published first in hardcopy 1993, accessed online 24 January 2015.
97 Reid, 'Memoir', 13.
98 Reid, 'Memoir', 14–15. The Australian Broadcasting Commission has since been renamed the Australian Broadcasting Corporation.
99 Reid, 'Memoir', 15–16.
100 Papers of Warren Denning, MS 5129, NLA.
101 Hancock, 'Denning, Warren Edwin (1906–1975)'.
102 Reid, 'Memoir', 13.
103 Warren Denning, 'Stanley Melbourne Bruce', unpublished MS, Papers of Warren Denning, MS 5129, NLA, 28.
104 CB 'Clem' Christesen, letter to Warren Denning, 13 February 1953, Papers of Warren Denning.

3 Menzies biography mystery

1 AW Martin, *Robert Menzies: A Life*, vol. 2, 1944–1978 (MUP, 1999), xiii.
2 Don Whitington, *Strive to be Fair: An unfinished autobiography* (Canberra: ANU Press, 1977), 72.

3   AW Martin, 'Menzies the Man' in Scott Prasser, JR Nethercote & John Warhurst (eds), *The Menzies Era: A reappraisal of Government, Politics and Policy* (Sydney: Hale & Iremonger, 1995), 20.
4   Martin, 'Menzies the Man', 25.
5   Anne Henderson, *Menzies at War* (Sydney: NewSouth, 2014), 171.
6   Henderson, *Menzies at War*, 170, 183.
7   Cameron Hazlehurst, *Menzies Observed* (Sydney: Allen & Unwin, 1979), 304.
8   'Robert Menzies' in Anna Rothe (ed.), *Current Biography: Who's News and Why* (New York: H. W. Wilson, 1950), 392–4; Ronald Seth, *RG Menzies* (London: Cassell, 1960). A valuable pamphlet by Fred Raven, *History of the Menzies Family in Jeparit* (Jeparit: Jeparit Chamber of Commerce, 1966), covering Menzies' rural Victorian roots and early years, was published in the year of his resignation but after he left office.
9   Liberal Party of Australia, *How Well Do You Know This Man?* (Sydney: Liberal Party, 1949), 2.
10 Communist Party of Australia, *The Calamitous Career of Dictator Bob* (Australia: CPA, 1951), 2 & 7.
11 Ronald Seth, *RG Menzies* (London: Cassell, 1960), 116.
12 Anthony Blond, 'Glory boys', extract from Anthony Blond, *Jew Made in England* (London: Timewell, 2004), London *Sunday Times*, 13 June 2004.
13 Seth, *RG Menzies*, 116–119.
14 Hazlehurst, *Menzies Observed*, 7.
15 Robert Menzies, 'Churchill at Seventy-five', *New York Times Magazine*, 27 November, 1949; reprinted in Robert Menzies, *Speech is of Time* (London: Cassell, 1958), 45–53, 48.
16 Robert Menzies, 'Churchill and his Contemporaries', 22nd Sir Richard Stawell Oration delivered at the University of Melbourne, 8 October 1955; reprinted in Robert Menzies, *Speech is of Time* (London: Cassell, 1958), 54–75.
17 Menzies, 'Churchill and his Contemporaries', 56.
18 Menzies, 'Churchill and his Contemporaries', 62–3.
19 Robert Menzies, *The Measure of the Years* (North Melbourne: Cassell, 1970), 11.
20 Kevin Perkins, *Menzies: Last of the Queen's Men* (Adelaide: Rigby, 1977).
21 Letter from Robert Menzies to Heather Henderson, 15 May 1968, in Heather Henderson (ed.), *Letters to My Daughter: Robert Menzies, letters, 1955–1975* (Millers Point: Murdoch, 2011), 195.
22 Robert Menzies, *The Measure of the Years*, 5.
23 Judith Brett, 'Robert Menzies and England' in Judith Brett (ed.), *Political Lives* (Sydney: Allen & Unwin, 1997), 78.
24 Clem Lloyd, 'The Media' in Scott Prasser, JR Nethercote & John Warhurst (eds), *The Menzies Era: A reappraisal of Government, Politics and Policy* (Sydney: Hale & Iremonger, 1995), 121–122.
25 Letter from Robert Menzies to Heather Henderson, 30 October 1967, in Heather Henderson (ed.), *Letters to My Daughter*, 161.
26 Clem Lloyd, *Parliament and the Press: The Federal Parliamentary Press Gallery 1901–88* (MUP, 1988), 126–7.
27 Stewart Cockburn interviewed by Clem Lloyd, 9 March 1984, ORAL TRC 5253/6, Oral History Collection, NLA.
28 Robert Menzies, *The Measure of the Years*, 11.
29 Robert Menzies, 'Foreword to the First Edition' in John Reynolds, *Edmund Barton* (Sydney: Angus & Robertson, 1979), 2nd edn, x–xi. First published 1948.

30 Judith Brett, *Robert Menzies' Forgotten People* (MUP, 2007) 137, 234. First published 1992.
31 HN Nelson, 'Dawes, Allan Wesley (1900–1969)', *Australian Dictionary of Biography*, National Centre of Biography, Australian National University, <adb.anu.edu.au/biography/dawes-allan-wesley-9924/text17573>, published in hardcopy 1993, accessed online 1 August 2021.
32 Australian Dictionary of Biography, file on Allan Wesley Dawes (1900–1969), ANU Archives, Australian National University, Canberra.
33 Henderson, *Menzies at War*, 21.
34 Paul Hasluck, notes for a review of the Perkins biography of Menzies, attachment to a letter from Nicholas Hasluck to AW Martin, 2 October 1996, Allan Martin Papers, MS 9802, NLA.
35 Tom Frame, *The Life and Death of Harold Holt* (Sydney: Allen & Unwin, 2005), 22. The source of the Dawes–Holt messenger story is not supplied in the footnotes.
36 Whitington, *Strive to be Fair*, 129.
37 'Menzies Biography Mystery', *Daily Telegraph*, 14 September 1969, 20.
38 Papers of Robert Menzies, MS 4936, NLA.
39 Papers of Allan Dawes, MS 8792, NLA.
40 Whitington, *Strive to be Fair*, 55, 60.
41 'Three Press Delegates for Canada', *Sun* (Melbourne), 27 March 1944.
42 Whitington, *Strive to be Fair*, 94–5.
43 Cecil Edwards, *The Editor Regrets*, (Melbourne: Hill of Content, 1972), 37.
44 Edwards, *The Editor Regrets*, n., 38.
45 HN Nelson, 'Dawes, Allan Wesley (1900–1969)', *Australian Dictionary of Biography*, <adb.anu.edu.au/biography/dawes-allan-wesley-9924/text17573>, published first in hardcopy 1993, accessed online 6 June 2022.
46 Edwards, *The Editor Regrets*, n., 38.
47 *SMH*, 2 February 1948.
48 'Allan Dawes Dies at 69', *Melbourne Sun*, 8 September 1969, 11.
49 'New Post For Mr AW Dawes', *SMH*, 25 March 1941, 11.
50 *SMH*, 12 September 1969, 1.
51 Hazlehurst, *Menzies Observed*, 294–296.
52 Hazlehurst, *Menzies Observed*, 308.
53 Ian Hancock, *National and Permanent? The Federal Organisation of the Liberal Party of Australia 1944–1965* (MUP, 2000), 92.
54 Hancock, *National and Permanent?*, 92–3.
55 Hancock, *National and Permanent?*, 93.
56 Whitington, *Strive to be Fair*, 126–7.
57 Cockburn, interviewed by Lloyd. The Australian News & Information Bureau was a federal government agency, founded in 1947 as the Department of Information, renamed ANIB in 1950 and renamed again in 1973 as the Australian Information Service. It was later absorbed into the Department of Foreign Affairs and Trade.
58 Cockburn, interviewed by Lloyd.
59 Cockburn, interviewed by Lloyd, 93.
60 Menzies, 'Foreword to the First Edition' in John Reynolds, *Edmund Barton*, x-xi.
61 Cameron Hazlehurst, *Ten Journeys to Cameron's Farm* (Canberra: ANU Press, 2013), 212.

62 HN Nelson, 'Dawes, Allan Wesley (1900–1969)'.
63 Allan Dawes, *Caesar's Ghost: the journalist, the statesman, the spokesman* (Melbourne: Trustees of the Arthur Norman Smith Memorial, 1946).
64 Transcript of a note from Allan Dawes to Robert Menzies, circa 1950, 7pp., Papers of Allan Dawes, MS 8792, NLA.
65 Note from Dawes to Menzies, 3.
66 Note from Dawes to Menzies, 5.
67 Note from Dawes to Menzies, 5–6.
68 Note from Dawes to Menzies, 7.
69 Allan Dawes, 'Biography of Mr RG Menzies', in Papers of Allan Dawes, MS 8792, NLA, 3–4.
70 Dawes, 'Biography of Mr RG Menzies', 4.
71 Brett, *Robert Menzies' Forgotten People*, 137.
72 Allan Dawes, 'The Sampson Line – Menzies in Parliament', annotated by Menzies, six chapters of biographical manuscript concerning Robert Menzies, Papers of Robert Menzies, MS 4936, Series 10, Box 354, NLA, a.20.
73 Page 46 is missing.
74 Memo from Eileen Lenehan to 'Mr Frank' (likely Frank Menzies), undated, Papers of Robert Menzies, MS 4936, Series 10, Box 354, NLA. NB: The quote has been double-checked and 'taped' is correct, not a typographical error.
75 Anonymous memo, likely to be from Eileen Lenehan to Frank Menzies, undated, Papers of Robert Menzies, MS 4936, Series 10, Box 354, NLA.
76 'Menzies Biography Mystery', *Daily Telegraph*, 14 September 1969, 20.
77 Email communication from NLA staff member Kylie Scroope, 26 June 2014.
78 Hazlehurst, *Menzies Observed*, 345.
79 Dawes, 'The Sampson Line', a.13.
80 Dawes, 'The Sampson Line', a.14.
81 Dawes, 'The Sampson Line', a.20.
82 Dawes, 'The Sampson Line', a.21.
83 Dawes, 'The Sampson Line', a.31.
84 Dawes, 'The Sampson Line', a.41–2.
85 Dawes, 'A Citizen of Two Cities: Menzies Goes to Canberra', annotated by Menzies, six chapters of biographical manuscript, b.14–15.
86 Dawes, 'Citizen of Two Cities', b.16.
87 Dawes, 'Citizen of Two Cities', b.18–19.
88 Dawes, 'Citizen of Two Cities', b.19.
89 Dawes, 'Citizen of Two Cities', b.21.
90 LF Crisp, *Ben Chifley: A Biography* (Croydon: Longmans, 1961).
91 Letter from LF Crisp to Michael Turnbull of Longmans Publishers, 3 July 1961, in Papers of LF Crisp, MS 5243, NLA. Crisp declined to pursue the suggested Menzies biography: '(T)he fact of the matter is that many, many source materials would be shut off from your author. So much indeed as to make it a much harder job than I would care to take on myself in the circumstances – though I admit that some very interesting contemporary biographies have been written on an authorized basis and without access to all the official documentation.'
92 Letter from Robert Menzies to Heather Henderson, 5 July 1967, in Heather Henderson (ed.), *Letters to My Daughter*, 150.
93 'Lady McNicoll met Sir Robert Menzies in 1959 and corresponded with him intermittently in the 1960s. It appears that in 1969 they agreed that she should

write his biography. In 1972 Menzies altered his will to give her exclusive access to his personal papers during his lifetime and for three years after his death. In 1972–73, while she was living in Ankara, Lady McNicoll had an extensive correspondence with Menzies and on her return to Australia she recorded a number of interviews with him. She worked on the biography for several years, but does not appear to have progressed beyond some first drafts. In 1982 the Menzies Family lifted the restriction on most of the Menzies Family Papers and in late 1983 it was decided that Dr Allan Martin should take over as the biographer of Menzies.' Biographical note, Guide to the Papers of Lady Frances McNicoll, NLA, accessed 31 July 2022, <nla.gov.au/nla.obj-299728501/findingaid#biographical-note>.

4 World War II to the end of the Menzies line

1. Gavin Souter, *Company of Heralds: a century and a half of Australian publishing by John Fairfax Limited and its predecessors* (MUP, 1981), 191–2.
2. Alan Reid, 'A Strange Rooftop Sect', *New Journalist*, November 1973, 13–14.
3. Margaret Bridson Cribb, 'Fadden, Sir Arthur William (1894–1973)', *Australian Dictionary of Biography*, National Centre of Biography, ANU, <adb.anu.edu.au/biography/fadden-sir-arthur-william-10141/text17907>, accessed online 1 August 2021.
4. Don Whitington, *Strive to be Fair: An Unfinished Autobiography* (Canberra: ANU Press, 1977), 74.
5. 'He had worked as editor of the West Australian *Worker*, and as a casual on the *West Australian*, the Perth daily newspaper. But frankly, I don't think he could've earned a living as a journalist. But I think he valued his AJA badge, which he wore on his coat.' DK Rogers, press secretary to John Curtin, interviewed by Mel Pratt, 29 April 1971, ORAL TRC 121/14, Oral History Collection, NLA.
6. Lloyd Ross, *John Curtin for Labor and for Australia*, the Inaugural John Curtin Memorial Lecture 1970 (Acton: ANU Press, 1971), 21.
7. John Curtin, *West Australian*, 6 May 1933 quoted in David Black, *In His Own Words: John Curtin's Speeches and Writings* (Bentley: Paradigm, 1995), 119.
8. Black, *In His Own Words*, 119.
9. 'John Curtin', *West Australian*, 6 August 1943, 4.
10. Alan Chester, *John Curtin* (Angus & Robertson: Sydney, 1943), 58 & iii.
11. Chester, *John Curtin*, 53–4.
12. Chester, *John Curtin*, 55.
13. Chester, *John Curtin*, 179–180, 183.
14. Chester, *John Curtin*, 59–60.
15. Chester, *John Curtin*, inscribed copy in the Papers of Philip Whelan, MS 2449, item 134, dated July 1943, NLA.
16. Chester, *John Curtin*, 177.
17. Chester, *John Curtin*, inscribed copy.
18. Lloyd Ross, *John Curtin: A Biography* (South Melbourne: Macmillan, 1977).
19. Alan Chester, *John Curtin* (Angus & Robertson: Sydney, 1943), 177 cited in Ross, *John Curtin*, 130.
20. Ross, *John Curtin*, 130.
21. Melbourne *Advocate*, 2 October 1946.
22. LF Crisp, *Ben Chifley: A Biography* (Croydon: Longmans, 1961), 6.
23. William Dunk, 'Chif', feature by Peter Thompson, ABC, February 1962; script in Papers of LF Crisp, MS 5243, NLA, 6.

24 Jack Fingleton, 'Chif', feature by Peter Thompson, ABC, February 1962; script in Papers of LF Crisp, 6.
25 Letter from LF Crisp to WC Taylor, 6 August 1951, Papers of LF Crisp.
26 AF Davies, review of LF Crisp, *Ben Chifley: A Biography* in *Quadrant*, 6, 2 (Autumn 1962), 94.
27 Don Whitington, 'Canberra has lost all its old zest for living', *Sunday Telegraph*, 11 August 1946.
28 Unsourced note, Papers of LF Crisp.
29 Carbon copy of letter from Ben Chifley to Mr DA Stewart, Manager, Shirt Department, The Myer Emporium, 9 January 1949, Papers of LF Crisp.
30 Carbon copy of letter from Chifley to Stewart, 5 October 1949, Papers of LF Crisp.
31 Victor Courtney, 'I Met Our Prime Minister', *Sunday Times Magazine* (Perth), 12 August 1945.
32 *News* (Adelaide), 5 October 1946.
33 Leicester Webb, 'The Labour Party and the Future', *Australian Quarterly*, 25, 1 (March 1953), 122.
34 Fred Daly, 'Chif', feature by Peter Thompson, ABC, February 1962; script in Papers of LF Crisp, 9.
35 Unsourced note, Papers of LF Crisp.
36 Unsourced note, Papers of LF Crisp.
37 Letter from Ben Chifley to Gil Duthie, 16 August 1949, noted in Papers of LF Crisp.
38 Liberal Party of Australia, 'The Rt. Hon. Harold Holt, CH, MP, Prime Minister – His mid-term record and his approach to government: "Fair, firm, forthright, friendly"' (Canberra: Liberal Party of Australia, 1967), 8pp.
39 Tom Frame, *The Life and Death of Harold Holt* (Sydney: Allen & Unwin, 2005), xvi.
40 Letter from Stanley Melbourne Bruce to Harold Holt, 16 February 1966, National Archives of Australia: M2606, 87.
41 Frame, *The Life and Death of Harold Holt*, xvi.
42 Letter from Stanley Melbourne Bruce to Harold Holt, 16 February 1966, National Archives of Australia: M2606, 87.
43 Paul Keating, widely known for preferring oral briefs to written ones, maintained detailed press cutting scrapbooks of his political career and continues this practice still.
44 Frame, *The Life and Death of Harold Holt*, xii.
45 David McNicoll, *Luck's A Fortune: An Autobiography* (Sydney: Wildcat Press, 1979), 233.
46 See Cameron Hazlehurst, *Ten Journeys to Cameron's Farm* (Canberra: ANU Press, 2013).
47 Henry 'Jo' Gullett, *Good Company: Horseman, soldier, politician* (Brisbane: UQP, 1992), 122.
48 'Menzies, Holt and the Liberals', *Current Affairs Bulletin*, 37, 9, 21 March 1966, 138.
49 Ian Hancock, 'Harold Edward Holt' in Michelle Grattan (ed.), *Australian Prime Ministers* (Sydney: New Holland, 2013), 272–3.
50 *Australian Women's Weekly*, April 1988, 12–13, cited in Frame, *The Life and Death of Harold Holt*, 305.
51 Interview with Sir Robert Menzies in McNicoll, *Luck's A Fortune*, 217.

52 Tom Holt was a business partner of FW Thring, who was the father of both Lola and the actor Frank Thring.
53 Frame, *The Life and Death of Harold Holt*, 7–8.
54 CJ Lloyd, 'McEwen, Sir John (1900–1980)', *Australian Dictionary of Biography*, National Centre of Biography, ANU, <adb.anu.edu.au/biography/mcewen-sir-john-10948/text19455>, published in hardcopy 2000, accessed online 1 August 2021.
55 Peter Golding, *Black Jack McEwen: Political Gladiator* (MUP, 1996), 21.
56 'That, Menzies said once, was when he was in a highbrow mood and only when "I don't want other Country Party men to know what I'm talking about"', Golding, *Black Jack McEwen*, 24.
57 John McEwen, *John McEwen: His Story*, privately published (1982), 80.
58 McEwen, *John McEwen*, 76.
59 McEwen writes in his memoirs that he would have preferred the 'stable team man' Paul Hasluck to have won the Liberal leadership rather than Gorton: 'It is the last description I would think of applying to Gorton.' *John McEwen*, 76–7. In between his election as prime minister and his election as the Member for Higgins, Gorton was Australia's prime minister while being a member of neither house of parliament.
60 Alan Trengove, *John Grey Gorton: An informal biography* (North Melbourne: Cassell, 1969), iv.
61 Graham Freudenberg, interviewed by John Farquharson, 8–9 March 2000, ORAL TRC 3994 (transcript), Oral History Collection, NLA 110.
62 Freudenberg, interviewed by Farquharson, 110.
63 Trengove, *John Grey Gorton*, iv–v.
64 Trengove, *John Grey Gorton*, 53–60.
65 Betty Gorton resumed her abandoned university studies at the ANU after Gorton was appointed Minister for the Navy in December 1958 and they established a permanent home in Canberra. She graduated with a Bachelor of Arts in Asian Studies in 1965 and undertook Masters Qualifying studies the following year, achieving a '2A'. For a while she was employed as research assistant on an English–Malay dictionary being compiled at the ANU. Ian Hancock, *John Gorton: He Did It His Way* (Sydney: Hodder, 2002), 84 & 171.
66 Trengove, *John Grey Gorton*, 64–5.
67 Trengove, *John Grey Gorton*, 66–7.
68 Trengove, *John Grey Gorton*, 89–93.
69 Trengove, *John Grey Gorton*, v.
70 Ian Hancock, 'Liberal Governments, 1966–72' in JR Nethercote (ed.), *Liberalism and the Australian Federation* (Leichhardt: Federation Press, 2001), 205.
71 McEwen, *John McEwen*, 76.
72 Deane Wells, *The Wit of Whitlam* (Melbourne: Outback Press, 1976), 62. The date of the quote is not supplied but is obviously from the time of Gorton's prime ministership.
73 Trengove, *John Grey Gorton*, 243.
74 Allan Barnes, 'Gorton, man of emotions', *Age*, 3 December 1969.
75 Gerard Henderson, 'Sir John Grey Gorton' in Michelle Grattan (ed.), *Australian Prime Ministers* (Sydney: New Holland, 2013), 309.
76 Trengove, *John Grey Gorton*, 23–9.
77 Henderson, 'Gorton', 303.
78 Trengove, *John Grey Gorton*, 25.

79 Henderson, 'Gorton', 303.
80 Hancock, *John Gorton*, 19.
81 Trengove, *John Grey Gorton*, iv.
82 Hancock, *John Gorton*, vii–viii.
83 Wells, *The Wit of Whitlam*, 68.
84 Known as the 'finding aid'.
85 Papers of William McMahon, MS 3926, Series 16, Sub-Series 16/3, Folder 71, NLA.
86 Peter Sekuless, 'Sir William McMahon' in Michelle Grattan (ed.), *Australian Prime Ministers* (Sydney: New Holland, 2013), 314. The opinion of his enemies was not uniformly negative. cf. 'It now tends to be forgotten that McMahon was an extraordinarily skillful, resourceful and tenacious politician. Had he been otherwise, the ALP victory in December 1972 would have been more convincing than it was.' Gough Whitlam, *The Whitlam Government 1972–1975* (Ringwood: Penguin, 1985), 12.
87 Whitlam, *The Whitlam Government*.
88 Mark Latham, 'I'm doing the feminism here', *Australian Financial Review*, 18–19 October 2014, 53.
89 Patrick Mullins, *Tiberius with a Telephone: the life and stories of William McMahon* (Melbourne: Scribe, 2018).
90 Henry Mayer, 'Politician '72', *Current Affairs Bulletin*, 49, 5 (1 October 1972), 143–4.

5 The modern era begins

1 Laurie Oakes, *Whitlam PM: a biography* (Sydney: Angus & Robertson, 1973); Graham Freudenberg, *A Certain Grandeur: Gough Whitlam in Politics* (Melbourne: Macmillan, 1977).
2 Laurie Oakes & David Solomon, *The Making of an Australian Prime Minister* (Melbourne: Cheshire, 1973); Laurie Oakes & David Solomon, *Grab for power: election 74* (Melbourne: Cheshire, 1974).
3 Laurie Oakes, *Crash Through or Crash: The Unmaking of a Prime Minister* (Melbourne: Drummond, 1976).
4 Oakes, *Whitlam PM*, 16.
5 Don Whitington, *Twelfth Man?* (Brisbane: Jacaranda, 1972), 178.
6 Gough Whitlam, 'Foreword' to Irwin Young, *Theodore: His Life and Times* (Sydney: Alpha, 1971), vii–xvi. Others, including HC 'Nugget' Coombs agreed with Whitlam's assessment of Theodore. 'The only (Scullin Government) Minister with a grasp of (economic) issues was "Red Ted Theodore" ... He was a natural "intellectual" and had a background of reading in the socialist classics and surprisingly, in the early writings of JM Keynes including *A Treatise on Money*. But he was soon lost to the government, leaving it intellectually rudderless.' HC Coombs, 'The Predecessors' in Fabian Papers, *The Whitlam Phenomenon* (Fitzroy: McPhee Gribble, 1986), 43.
7 Whitlam, 'Foreword' to Young, *Theodore*, vii.
8 Whitlam, 'Foreword' to Young, *Theodore*, vii–viii. After Young's death, Baiba Irving completed the book and Henry Mayer fact-checked it.
9 Whitlam, 'Foreword' to Young, *Theodore*, viii. This passage has been remarked on by, among others, Clem Lloyd, 'Edward Gough Whitlam' in Michelle Grattan (ed.), *Australian Prime Ministers* (Sydney: New Holland, 2013), 353; and James Walter, *The Leader: A political biography of Gough Whitlam* (Brisbane: UQP, 1980), 130.

10 'The dishonour of Mungana lay not with Theodore but with those of both parties who used Mungana to destroy a great Australian political career and a great Australian.' Whitlam, 'Foreword' to Young, *Theodore*, xiv.
11 Walter, *The Leader*, xiv.
12 Walter, *The Leader*, xix, note 1.
13 Mick Young, 'The Build-Up to 1972' in Fabian Papers, *The Whitlam Phenomenon* (Fitzroy: McPhee Gribble, 1986), 98.
14 Young, 'The Build-Up to 1972', 105. Young would go on to become a minister in the Hawke Government.
15 Laurie Oakes, 'The Years of Preparation' in *Whitlam and Frost: The full text of their TV conversations plus exclusive new interviews* (London: Sundial, 1974), 36–7.
16 Young, 'The Build-Up to 1972', 106.
17 'By 1968, the Gallery doyens whose experience went back to Curtin and Chifley ... were being challenged by a new breed ... the old herd-leaders, like Reid, were being challenged by new ones like ... Oakes'. Freudenberg, *A Certain Grandeur*, 143.
18 Laurie Oakes, 'Foreword' to Ross Fitzgerald & Stephen Holt, *Alan 'The Red Fox' Reid, Pressman Par Excellence* (Sydney: NewSouth, 2010), viii.
19 Alan Reid, 'The Role of the Journalist', Summer School of Professional Journalism, Canberra (1965), 3–4. The poem actually says 'do and die'.
20 Oakes, 'Foreword' to Fitzgerald & Holt, *Alan 'The Red Fox' Reid*, x.
21 SH 'Sydney' Deamer quoted in Don Whitington, *Strive to be Fair: An unfinished autobiography* (Canberra: ANU Press, 1977), 73.
22 Oakes, 'The Years of Preparation', 36–7.
23 Oakes, *Crash Through or Crash*, 10.
24 Oakes, 'The Years of Preparation', 36–7: 'I later learned that Pugh gained his eventual insight into his subject when he watched a television interview in which Whitlam was unusually relaxed and expansive, talking animatedly and gesturing with his hands. Pugh made sketches as he watched, and at the end of the programme went straight to his studio and got to work.'
25 Whitington, *Twelfth Man?*, 11–12. Whitington in his introduction quotes Davies on political fanatics: 'All are lonely people, set severely apart from the common life and mainstream of society... They stand out from other political actors by their will to action, monomania, unscrupulousness and hatred of enemies...a megalomaniac sense of rightness and historic mission; paranoid perceptions of "the enemy" – qualities which stem from deep personal insecurities and which, in certain circumstances, make possible 'unthinkable' swings from one political pole to the other.' – AF Davies, 'Fanaticism in Politics', *Current Affairs Bulletin*, 48, 11 (19 April 1971), 174–5.
26 'Whitlam and Frost', television interview August 1972 in *Whitlam and Frost*, 49.
27 WHITLAM: He had taken two Parliaments – six years – to bring the party on his side of politics from its disaster in 'forty-three to triumph in 'forty-nine. I equated that with our period of disaster – from 'sixty-six to our success in 1972. In 'Looking Ahead', a Whitlam–Frost interview recorded in Canberra 29 November 1973 in *Whitlam and Frost*, 173.
28 Whitington, *Twelfth Man?*, 166.
29 Mungo MacCallum, 'After the Honeymoon' in *Whitlam and Frost*, 102–3.
30 Oakes, 'The Years of Preparation', 37.
31 The crown solicitor is in modern parlance the Australian Government Solicitor.
32 Oakes, *Whitlam PM*, 63.

33 Laurie Oakes, interview with the author, Manuka ACT, 6 November 2014. All Oakes quotes in the rest of this chapter are from that interview unless otherwise specified.
34 Oakes & Solomon, *The Making of an Australian Prime Minister*, 1, 4.
35 Oakes & Solomon, *The Making of an Australian Prime Minister*, 311–314. '"Replying to a telegram of good wishes from Menzies, Whitlam said: 'I was profoundly moved by your magnanimous message on my election to this great office. No Australian is more conscious than I how much the lustre, honor and authority of that office owes to the manner in which you held it with such distinction for so long. No Australian understands better than you the private feelings of one now facing the change from the years of leading the Opposition to the burdens and rewards of leading our nation. You would, I think, be surprised to know how much I feel indebted to your example, despite the great differences in our philosophies. In particular, your remarkable achievement in rebuilding your own party and bringing it so triumphantly to power within six years has been an abiding inspiration to me.'"
36 Cf. Whitington, *Twelfth Man?*, 166; Oakes, 'The Years of Preparation', 37.
37 Oakes & Solomon, *The Making of an Australian Prime Minister*, 312, 318.
38 Oakes, interview with the author.
39 Oakes, *Whitlam PM*, 1.
40 Oakes, *Whitlam PM*, 2–3 and 50. Chifley would discuss Whitlam's quiz performances with Whitlam's father, Fred Whitlam.
41 Oakes, *Whitlam PM*, 99.
42 'I, Crean and Pollard are better than any three in Cabinet today,' Whitlam said, for example, in a media interview in October 1965. Oakes, *Whitlam PM*, 115.
43 Edward St John, 'Portrait of a great PM', *Canberra Times*, 28 February 1974, 2.
44 Freudenberg, *A Certain Grandeur*, 405.
45 Oakes, *Whitlam PM*, 246.
46 Oakes & Solomon, *Grab for Power*, 510–513.
47 Oakes, *Crash Through or Crash*, 33.
48 Oakes, *Crash Through or Crash*, 295.
49 Boswell, James, *The Life of Samuel Johnson, LLD. Comprehending an Accout of his Studies, and Numerous Works, in Chronological Order; A Series of his Epistolary Correspondence and Conversations with Many Eminent Persons; and Various Original Pieces of his Composition, Never Before Published: the Whole Exhibiting a View of Literature and Literary Men in Great-Britain, for Near Half a Century During Which He Flourished* (London: Charles Dilly, 1791), 2 vols. Vol. 1 is 516 pages, and vol. 2 is 588 pages.
50 'The Canberra Press Gallery, past and present, teems with published authors. Its output in recent years, for both quality and quantity, has been unexcelled in any of the democracies. I spawned a great many of the books myself. Indeed, for a number of years up to 1983, the Whitlam book industry was our largest growth industry after tax avoidance.' Gough Whitlam, 'The Second Coming' in Fabian Papers, *The Whitlam Phenomenon* (Fitzroy: McPhee Gribble, 1986), 9.
51 'He was kind enough to say that one of the reasons he had to do it was because of the dedication.' Laurie Oakes, interview with the author. The resulting book was Freudenberg, *A Certain Grandeur*.
52 Freudenberg, *A Certain Grandeur*, xi.
53 Susan Mitchell, *Margaret Whitlam, a biography* (North Sydney: Random House, 2007), 283–4.

54 'Book on Whitlam Launched', *Canberra Times*, 25 October 1977, 7.
55 LF Crisp, 'A new perspective on Gough Whitlam', *Age*, 3 December 1977.
56 Graham Freudenberg, interviewed by John Farquharson, 8–9 March 2000, ORAL TRC 3994 (transcript), Oral History Collection, NLA, 7.
57 Freudenberg, *A figure of speech*, 1. He dates this to 1946 when he was 12 years old, see Freudenberg, interviewed by Farquharson, 4.
58 Freudenberg, interviewed by John Farquharson, 5.
59 Freudenberg, interviewed by Farquharson, 266.
60 Freudenberg, *A figure of speech*, 13–14.
61 Freudenberg, interviewed by Farquharson, 7, 9.
62 Rob Chalmers, *Inside the Canberra Press Gallery: Life in the Wedding Cake of Old Parliament House*, Sam Vincent & John Wanna (eds), (Canberra: ANU E Press, 2011), 205.
63 Freudenberg, interviewed by Farquharson, 10.
64 Freudenberg, interviewed by Farquharson, 10
65 Freudenberg, interviewed by Farquharson, 11–12.
66 Freudenberg, interviewed by Farquharson, 12–13.
67 Freudenberg, *A figure of speech*, 27.
68 Freudenberg, interviewed by Farquharson, 266.
69 Freudenberg, *A Certain Grandeur*, 13.
70 Freudenberg, *A Certain Grandeur*, 14.
71 Freudenberg, interviewed by Farquharson, 79.
72 Whitlam interview with Peter Westerway cited in Freudenberg, *A figure of speech*, 69–70.
73 Freudenberg, interviewed by Farquharson, 84.
74 Freudenberg, interviewed by Farquharson, 85.
75 Freudenberg, *A figure of speech*, 73.
76 John Menadue, *Things You Learn Along the Way* (Ringwood: David Lovell Publishing, 1999), 82.
77 Freudenberg, *A figure of speech*, 87–91.
78 Freudenberg, interviewed by Farquharson, 88.
79 Freudenberg, interviewed by Farquharson, 133.
80 Oakes, interview with the author.
81 Oakes, *Whitlam PM*, 165.
82 Oakes, *Whitlam PM*, 165.
83 James Walter, *The Leader*, 102.
84 Oakes, *Whitlam PM*, 165–6.
85 Graham Freudenberg, speech at Memorial Service for Gough Whitlam (1916–2014), Sydney Town Hall, 5 November 2014, <www.youtube.com/watch?v=yZbzQ3qymUM>, accessed 1 August 2021. 'Blacktown' refers to Whitlam's 1972 campaign launch speech at Bowman Hall, Blacktown, 13 November 1972. It was noted by Donald Horne: 'It is 8.30... he touches his speech writer Graham Freudenberg for luck and walks down past the cheering people and the waving signs to the lectern and begins with the words John Curtin had used in wartime: "Men and women of Australia..."' Donald Horne, *Time of Hope: Australia 1966–72* (Sydney: Angus & Robertson, 1980), 4.
86 Graham Freudenberg, *A figure of speech: A political memoir* (Brisbane: Wiley, 2005).
87 Freudenberg, *A Certain Grandeur*, viii.
88 Freudenberg, *A figure of speech*, 193.

89 Freudenberg, interviewed by Farquharson, 104–5.
90 Freudenberg, interviewed by Farquharson, 258.
91 Walter, *The Leader*, 163, n. 5.
92 Oakes, *Whitlam PM*, 215–6.
93 Craig McGregor, *Left Hand Drive* (Melbourne: Affirm, 2013), 170–181.
94 Barnett would later write a contemporary political biography of John Howard, *John Howard: Prime Minister* (Ringwood: Viking, 1997).
95 McGregor, *Left Hand Drive*, 174.
96 McGregor, *Left Hand Drive*, 179.
97 Recent Whitlam biographer Jenny Hocking says that Freudenberg taking, and quickly regretting, an office in West Block after the 1972 win because of tight space in the prime minister's office was a factor: 'When he came to Whitlam's office, it was no longer as a critical member of Whitlam's loyal entourage, but as a visitor', Hocking writes. 'For the first time in their intense, intuitive relationship, Freudenberg felt excluded and, more significantly, Whitlam found himself apart from the core band of advisers who had served him so well in opposition.' Jenny Hocking, *Gough Whitlam: His Time*, vol. 2 (Carlton: Miegunyah Press, 2012), 11.
98 Hocking, *Gough Whitlam*, 384.
99 Hocking, *Gough Whitlam*, 388. Freudenberg does not refer to these conversations with McGregor in *A Certain Grandeur*.
100 Freudenberg, interviewed by Farquharson, 211.
101 Freudenberg, *A Certain Grandeur*, vii, viii.
102 CJ Lloyd & GS Reid, *Out of the Wilderness* (1974) cited in Freudenberg, *A Certain Grandeur*, 1.
103 Freudenberg, interviewed by Farquharson, 222.
104 Freudenberg, *A Certain Grandeur*, flyleaf.
105 Freudenberg, *A Certain Grandeur*, xiii.
106 Freudenberg, *A Certain Grandeur*, xiii
107 Freudenberg, *A Certain Grandeur*, 77.
108 'The present world-wide inflation wave had its origin in the economic policies pursued by the United States government during the Vietnam war, and the associated mismanagement of aggregate demand after 1965. The spread to the rest of the world operated through a variety of transmission channels. Of particular importance were the liquidity effects of the very large increase of world international reserves produced both by record US government deficits and record US balance of payments deficits. The increase in the prices of internationally traded foodstuffs, raw materials and manufactured products, the permissive climate created by these developments generally and by the remove of the threat of balance of payments crises were supplementary channels of transmission of inflation.' Fred Gruen, *Australian Quarterly*, December 1976, quoted in Freudenberg, *A Certain Grandeur*, 276.
109 Stagflation is the term used to describe economies simultaneously subject to stagnation (that is, low growth) and high inflation.
110 Whitlam's own book *The Whitlam Government 1972–1975* was in part an attempt to dispel 'certain myths' including 'that preoccupation with the program precluded proper attention to the problems of economic management'. Gough Whitlam, 'The Second Coming' in Fabian Papers, *The Whitlam Phenomenon* (Fitzroy: McPhee Gribble, 1986), 10.

111 Australian Government, *Mid-Year Economic and Fiscal Outlook 2013–14*, Appendix D: Historical Australian Government Data, Table D1: Australian Government general government sector receipts, payments, net Future Fund earnings and underlying cash balance, 264, <archive.budget.gov.au/2013-14/myefo/2013_14_MYEFO.pdf>, accessed 1 August 2021.
112 Australian Government, *Mid-Year Economic and Fiscal Outlook 2013–14*, Table D1.
113 Freudenberg, *A Certain Grandeur*, 409.
114 Freudenberg, *A Certain Grandeur*, xii.
115 Freudenberg, *A Certain Grandeur*, xi.
116 Freudenberg, *A Certain Grandeur*, 410.
117 Freudenberg, *A Certain Grandeur*, 410.
118 Freudenberg, *A Certain Grandeur*, 413.
119 Freudenberg, *A Certain Grandeur*, 318.
120 Freudenberg, interviewed by Farquharson, 266.
121 Graham Freudenberg, 'The Program' in Fabian Papers, *The Whitlam Phenomenon* (Fitzroy: McPhee Gribble, 1986), 130–1.
122 Mark McKenna, *An Eye for Eternity: The life of Manning Clark* (Carlton: Miegunyah Press, 2011), 571–2.
123 Freudenberg, Speech at Memorial Service.
124 Opinion polls pointed to the high probability of a win for Labor opposition leader Bill Hayden until, a week out from polling day, Labor frontbencher Senator Peter Walsh made careless comments on the issue of capital gains tax, which were seized on by Fraser who parlayed them into a third consecutive election win.
125 Patrick Weller, *Malcolm Fraser PM: A Study in Prime Ministerial Power in Australia* (Ringwood: Penguin, 1989), xvii.
126 John Edwards, *Life wasn't meant to be easy: a political profile of Malcolm Fraser* (Mayhem: Sydney, 1977).
127 Russell Schneider, *War Without Blood: Malcolm Fraser in Power* (Sydney: Angus & Robertson, 1980).
128 Laurie Oakes, interview with the author, Manuka ACT, 6 November 2014.
129 John Edwards, email communications with the author, 1 December 2014 & 3 May 2015. Edwards later did a doctorate in economics at George Washington University.
130 Edwards, email communications with the author.
131 Edwards, email communications with the author.
132 Edwards, email communications with the author. 'They had been after (Alan) for a while. I was sacked for various political errors during the 1974 campaign, plus what they probably saw as a general unreliability. Actually I wasn't entirely sacked – they wanted me to come to Sydney and write features. I don't find News Ltd congenial. It was a period in which the paper was shifting right under the influence of a new editor who came from the production side ... Jim Hall was the nominal editor, but cowed by the new man.'
133 Edwards, email communications with the author.
134 Edwards, email communications with the author.
135 Philip Ayres, *Malcolm Fraser, a biography* (Port Melbourne: Mandarin, 1989), 218.
136 Weller, *Malcolm Fraser PM*, 182, 185.
137 Ayres, *Malcolm Fraser*, 208–9.

138 Ayres, *Malcolm Fraser*, 208–9.
139 Ayres, *Malcolm Fraser*, 239–240.
140 Malcolm Fraser & Margaret Simons, *Malcolm Fraser: The Political Memoirs* (Carlton: Miegunyah Press, 2010), 345.
141 Geoff Pryor, 'Malcolm Fraser as an Easter Island statue with a tear rolling down his cheek', *Canberra Times*, 6 March 1983; Pryor collection of cartoons and drawings, NLA.
142 Beckett Green Publishing, *Great Frasers of Our Time* (Sydney: Hodder & Stoughton, 1977), 1. According to the imprint page, the book was created and produced by Beckett Green Publishing who thanks 'friends who helped them caption their photographs: Kevin Childs, Don and Sheila Drummond, Libby and Alan Foreth, John Hindle, John Jost, John Larkin, Vane Lindesay, John Matheson, Peter Nicholson and Anders Ousback'.
143 Steve Crabb, *The Prefect* (Camberwell: Widescope, 1975).
144 Allan Langoulant, *A Mal for all seasons: The Book of Mal* (Perth: Panorama, 1981); Kevin Pappas & Dennis Welsh, *The Mal Book* (Melbourne: Samsbooks, 1980); Patrick Cook, *Fraser Country* (Melbourne: Fontana, 1980).
145 Edwards, *Life wasn't meant to be easy*, xi.–xii
146 Edwards, *Life wasn't meant to be easy*, 7.
147 Edwards, *Life wasn't meant to be easy*, 8.
148 Edwards, *Life wasn't meant to be easy*, 14–15. Neville Fraser would subsequently tire of the frequent drought in the Riverina, purchase 'Nareen' in Victoria's Western District and relocate there.
149 Edwards, *Life wasn't meant to be easy*, 15.
150 Edwards, *Life wasn't meant to be easy*, 100, 122.
151 Edwards, *Life wasn't meant to be easy*, 14, 14, 26.
152 Edwards, *Life wasn't meant to be easy*, 27.
153 Beazley refers to Kim Beazley Snr (1917–2007); Henry 'Jo' Gullett, *Good Company: Horseman, soldier, politician* (Brisbane: UQP, 1992), 239–240.
154 Schneider, *War Without Blood*, ix.
155 Schneider, *War Without Blood*, 7, 10–11, 2.
156 Schneider, *War Without Blood.*, 6 & 3–4.
157 Russell Schneider, *The Colt From Kooyong: Andrew Peacock, a political biography* (Sydney: Angus & Robertson, 1981).

6 Bob Hawke, writ large

1 Bob Hawke, interview with the author, Northbridge NSW, 18 January 2014.
2 Hawke, interview with the author.
3 Stephen Mills, *The Hawke Years: The Story from the Inside* (Ringwood: Penguin, 1993), 204.
4 Stan Anson, *Hawke: An Emotional Life* (Ringwood: McPhee Gribble, 1991); Blanche d'Alpuget, *Robert J Hawke: a biography* (Melbourne: Schwartz, 1982); John Hurst, *Hawke, the definitive biography* (Sydney: Angus & Robertson, 1979); Robert Pullan, *Bob Hawke: A Portrait* (Sydney: Methuen, 1980).
5 Harold Holt was a parliamentarian for 30 years before becoming prime minister, John Gorton for 18 years, William McMahon for 22 years, Gough Whitlam for 20 years, Malcolm Fraser for 21 years, Paul Keating for 22 years and John Howard for 22 years.
6 Hurst, *Hawke*, flyleaf.
7 Hurst, *Hawke*, vii.

8   Hurst, *Hawke*, vii–viii.
9   Hurst, *Hawke*, 167.
10 Hurst, *Hawke*, 167–8.
11 Hurst, *Hawke*, 241.
12 Hurst, *Hawke*, 241–2.
13 Hurst, *Hawke*, 251.
14 Pullan, *Bob Hawke: A Portrait*.
15 McMullan later became a factional independent.
16 Robert Pullan, interview with the author, Camperdown NSW, 31 January, 2014.
17 'This is the height of my journalistic hypocrisy. On the Springboks' tour in '69, I demonstrated – "Paint them black and send them back" – and when I was writing editorials for the reactionary *West Australian*, I wrote an editorial – I promise you I did, because I still feel a certain degree of dread and shame – denouncing the demonstrators. Why? Because I persuaded myself that it would have been less silly and unjustified if I wrote it than if one of the others [did]. That, of course, is just a rationalization. I wouldn't have done it twice, I like to think.' Pullan, interview with the author.
18 Pullan, interview with the author.
19 Pullan, interview with the author.
20 Pullan, interview with the author.
21 Pullan, interview with the author.
22 Pullan, interview with the author.
23 The convention in Australian political reporting is that peccadillos are not reported unless there are public policy implications. Laurie Oakes did not report on the cache of emails between lovers Senator Cheryl Kernot and Hon. Gareth Evans MP at the time they were leaked to him. However, when Kernot later wrote a memoir and omitted the relationship which was material to the story of Kernot's move to the ALP, Oakes drew on some of the emails and made the relationship public knowledge, thereby correcting the gap in what was a significant event in ALP history. Kernot's memoir was *Speaking for Myself Again: Four years with Labor and beyond* (Pymble: HarperCollins, 2002).
24 Pullan, interview with the author.
25 Pullan, interview with the author. Hazel Hawke subsequently wrote about the termination in her own memoir published after Hawke left office.
26 Blanche d'Alpuget, interview with the author, Northbridge NSW, 18 January 2014.
27 d'Alpuget, interview with the author.
28 'It is not a biography ... Nor is it a political and industrial history ... Nor is it an attempt to evaluate academically the ideas he embraced at Oxford and articulated with such force before the Arbitration Commission. I have made no attempt at prophecy, believing such attempts to be dangerous and valueless.' Pullan, *Bob Hawke: A Portrait*, 9.
29 Pullan, interview with the author.
30 Pullan, interview with the author.
31 Pullan, *Bob Hawke: A Portrait*, 219.
32 Pullan, *Bob Hawke*, 220–221.
33 d'Alpuget, *Robert J Hawke*; Anson, *Hawke: An Emotional Life*.
34 Jennifer Ellison, *Rooms of Their Own* (Ringwood: Penguin, 1986), 17; Anson, *Hawke: An Emotional Life*, author note.

35 Anson, *Hawke: An Emotional Life*, viii.
36 Joy Damousi, 'Freud in the Antipodes: A Cultural History', Trevor Reese Memorial Lecture, Menzies Centre for Australian Studies, Kings College London (London: Menzies Centre, 2001), 9.
37 Stephen Garton, 'Freud and Psychiatrists: The Australian Debate 1900–1940' in Brian Head and James Walter (eds), *Intellectual Movements and Australian Society* (Melbourne: Oxford UP, 1988), 184, cited in Damousi, 'Freud in the Antipodes', 9–10.
38 Joy Damousi, 'Freud in the Antipodes', 19–20.
39 Damousi, 'Freud in the Antipodes', 6.
40 Damousi, 'Freud in the Antipodes', 21.
41 Michael Crozier, 'Obituary – Graham Little', *Australian Journal of Political Science*, 35, 2 (2000), 313.
42 Crozier, 'Obituary – Graham Little'.
43 'Davies, Alan' in Brian Galligan & Winsome Roberts (eds), *Oxford Companion to Australian Politics* (Oxford University Press, 2007), <www.oxfordreference.com/view/10.1093/acref/9780195555431.001.0001/acref-9780195555431-e-97>, accessed 1 August 2021.
44 AF Davies, *Private Politics: a study of five political outlooks* (Melbourne: MUP, 1966); AF Davies, *Images of Class: an Australian study* (Sydney: Sydney University Press, 1969); James Walter, 'Davies, Alan Fraser (1924–1987)', *Australian Dictionary of Biography*, National Centre of Biography, ANU, <adb.anu.edu.au/biography/davies-alan-fraser-12406/text22303>, accessed 1 August 2021.
45 AF Davies, 'The Task of Biography' in *Essays in Political Sociology* (Melbourne: Cheshire, 1972), 109–117.
46 Walter, 'Davies, Alan Fraser (1924–1987)', *Australian Dictionary of Biography*. cf. Joy Damousi, *Freud in the Antipodes: A cultural history of psychoanalysis in Australia* (Sydney: UNSW Press, 2005), 308–9.
47 Graham Little, *The Public Emotions: from mourning to hope* (Sydney: ABC Books, 1999); Michael Crozier, 'Obituary – Graham Little', 314.
48 Crozier, 'Obituary – Graham Little', 313.
49 Graham Little, *Political Ensembles: A psychosocial approach to politics and leadership* (Melbourne: Oxford University Press, 1985), vii.
50 Douglas Kirsner, 'The Freud Conference', *Australasian Journal of Psychotherapy*, 18, (2), 1999: 102–113.
51 cf. Photocopy of 'Running comments' by AF 'Foo' Davies, 7pp., attached to a letter from James Walter to Graham Little, 31 October 1978, in Box 4, Papers of James Walter, MS 7846, NLA; note attached to thesis excerpt (Draft, Part One) from Graham Little to James Walter, 15 December 1978, and subsequent undated notes.
52 James Walter, '(Draft Only: Confidential) EG Whitlam: An Essay in Political Biography ... A thesis submitted in fulfillment of the requirements for the degree of Doctor of Philosophy in the Department of Political Science, University of Melbourne, July 1979', Preface, Papers of James Walter.
53 d'Alpuget, *Robert J Hawke*, ix.
54 Stan Anson, 'Representing RJ Hawke', thesis submitted in fulfilment of the requirements of the degree of Master of Arts, University of Melbourne, 1988.
55 Judith Brett, 'Introduction' in Judith Brett (ed.), *Political Lives* (Sydney: Allen & Unwin, 1997), vii.

56 Judith Brett, *Robert Menzies' Forgotten People* (Sydney: Sun, 1992); James Walter, *The Leader: A Political Biography of Gough Whitlam* (Brisbane: UQP, 1980); Angus McIntyre, 'Soeharto's composure' in Judith Brett (ed.), *Political Lives*.
57 Denis Fisk, 'A journalist who knew his onions: Louis d'Alpuget 1915–2006', *SMH*, 9 June 2006, <www.smh.com.au/news/obituaries/a-journalist-who-knew-his-onions/2006/06/08/1149359881272.html>, accessed 1 August 2021.
58 d'Alpuget, interview with the author.
59 d'Alpuget, interview with the author.
60 Hawke, interview with the author.
61 Candida Baker, 'Blanche d'Alpuget', interview at Springwood NSW, June 1985, in *Yacker: Australian Writers Talk About Their Work* (Sydney: Picador, 1986), 91.
62 Blanche d'Alpuget, *On Longing* (MUP, 2008), 9–10.
63 d'Alpuget, *On Longing*, 18.
64 Baker, 'Blanche d'Alpuget', 97.
65 Susan Ryan, *Catching the Waves: Life In and Out of Politics* (Pymble: Harper Collins, 1999), 194.
66 d'Alpuget, *On Longing*, 15.
67 d'Alpuget, *On Longing*, 18–19.
68 Blanche d'Alpuget, *Mediator: A Biography of Sir Richard Kirby* (MUP, 1977), xi.
69 'For him, the preparation of a biography was often painful. At times he said plaintively, "Oh God. I feel like a full frontal nude!" At other times he reproved me, "Not enough warts, Boyo!"' d'Alpuget, *Mediator*, xi.
70 d'Alpuget, interview with the author.
71 Blanche d'Alpuget, book launch, *Robert J Hawke: a biography*, speakers Blanche d'Alpuget, Bob Hawke, Sir Richard Kirby & Morry Schwartz, Lakeside Hotel, Canberra, 5 October 1982, sound recording, NLA.
72 Blanche d'Alpuget, *Monkeys in the Dark* (Sydney: Aurora, 1980).
73 Blanche d'Alpuget, 'Lust' in Ross Fitzgerald (ed.), *The Eleven Deadly Sins* (Port Melbourne: Minerva, 1993), 113.
74 d'Alpuget was one of two *Mirror* journalists who taught Canberra Press Gallery journalist Laurie Oakes, when he was a cadet in Sydney, how to cover courts; the other was Anna Torv (later Anna Murdoch).
75 d'Alpuget, interview with the author.
76 d'Alpuget, *Mediator*, 156–7.
77 d'Alpuget, *Mediator*, 157–8.
78 d'Alpuget, *Mediator*, 158.
79 Blanche d'Alpuget, *On Longing*, 20–1.
80 d'Alpuget, interview with the author.
81 d'Alpuget, *On Longing*, 20–1, 23–4.
82 'Christ yes, because I was married ... but they're written in this little secret code.' d'Alpuget, interview with the author.
83 d'Alpuget, *On Longing*, 24.
84 d'Alpuget, *On Longing*, 31–32.
85 d'Alpuget, *On Longing*, 34–35.
86 Blanche d'Alpuget, *Turtle Beach* (Ringwood: Penguin, 1981).
87 d'Alpuget, *On Longing*, 25–6 & 36.
88 d'Alpuget, *On Longing*, 36, 46, 37.
89 Hazel Hawke, *My Own Life* (East Melbourne: Text, 1992), 199.
90 d'Alpuget, *On Longing*, 37–43.
91 d'Alpuget, interview with the author.

92 d'Alpuget, interview with the author.
93 d'Alpuget, *On Longing*, 28.
94 Mrs Monk did not want attention drawn to the fact she was Albert's second wife: d'Alpuget, interview with the author.
95 Baker, 'Blanche d'Alpuget', 102; Blanche d'Alpuget, book launch *Robert J Hawke*.
96 d'Alpuget, interview with the author.
97 d'Alpuget, *On Longing*, 44–5.
98 Ellison, *Rooms of Their Own*, 10.
99 Baker, 'Blanche d'Alpuget', 95.
100 Ellison, *Rooms of Their Own*, 17.
101 Baker, 'Blanche d'Alpuget', 102.
102 Blanche d'Alpuget, *Canberra Times* Literary Luncheon, speech, Lakeside Hotel, Canberra, 27 October 1982, sound recording, NLA.
103 d'Alpuget, *Canberra Times* Literary Luncheon.
104 d'Alpuget, *Canberra Times* Literary Luncheon.
105 d'Alpuget, *Canberra Times* Literary Luncheon. It was a financial success. Three years after *Robert J Hawke: A Biography* was published, d'Alpuget told Candida Baker: 'I did that book for a mass of practical reasons. One of the most practical was that I knew I'd make dough out of it, but I had no idea how much I'd make. I ended up making a hell of a lot, enough to give me a tax problem ... but I've spent it all now and I still have the tax problem.' Baker, 'Blanche d'Alpuget', 95.
106 d'Alpuget, interview with the author.
107 Hawke, interview with the author.
108 Hawke, interview with the author.
109 d'Alpuget, interview with the author.
110 Peter Ryan, letter to Blanche d'Alpuget, 3 May 1982, 1, Papers of Peter Ryan, MS9897, NLA.
111 Kate Jennings, *Come to Me, My Melancholy Baby* (Melbourne: Outback Press, 1975); Carol Jerrems & Virginia Fraser, *A book about Australian women* (Melbourne: Outback Press, 1974).
112 Kate Jennings (ed.), *Mother I'm Rooted: An anthology of Australian women poets* (Melbourne: Outback Press, 1975).
113 d'Alpuget, interview with the author.
114 d'Alpuget, commentary on *Robert J Hawke*.
115 d'Alpuget, commentary on *Robert J Hawke*. Schwartz maintains it was a straight commercial decision.
116 Ellison, *Rooms of Their Own*, 18.
117 Hawke, interview with the author.
118 Blanche d'Alpuget, letter to Peter Ryan, 21 April 1982, 2, Papers of Peter Ryan.
119 Graham Richardson, *Whatever It Takes* (Moorebank: Bantam, 1994), 123. Richardson, a Hawke ally, is unusual in revealing some of the detail of Hawke's campaign: 'When, on the night of his accession to the leadership Hawke denied to ABC TV's Richard Carleton that he had "blood on his hands", this served to underline his ability to absolve himself of responsibility for any acts that history might not record as wholly desirable. Being prepared to deny Hayden the right to announce the economic policy he had laboured over for so long was certainly the correct political decision for the challenger – it was also one of the most ruthless political acts I have ever witnessed. There was a smell of blood about it. 'Some six months earlier, he had conspired with Bob McMullan and me to

ensure the release of poll information damaging to Hayden. Right down to the timing during a national executive meeting when I would ask McMullan to pass on the details of Rod Cameron's latest research, Hawke was involved. When stories were to be leaked to journalists, he often chose which one would be the beneficiary of the leak. So, while much of the blood was seen to be on my hands, you may rest assured that I was in the best of company.' *Whatever It Takes*, 116–7.

120 Mills, *The Hawke Years*, 204.
121 d'Alpuget, *Robert J Hawke*, 127.
122 Laurie Oakes cited in Paul Kelly, *The Hawke Ascendancy* (North Ryde: Angus & Robertson, 1984), 148.
123 Ryan, *Catching the Waves*, 194–5.
124 Tom Uren, *Straight Left* (Milsons Point: Random House, 1994), 33–4.
125 Ellison, *Rooms of Their Own*, 18.
126 Hawke, interview with the author.
127 d'Alpuget, interview with the author.
128 d'Alpuget, interview with the author. d'Alpuget identified the person as Susan Ryan in an email to the author, 5 March 2014.
129 'from what I already knew as an insider in the Hawke camp', author note dated 31 March 2010, Blanche d'Alpuget, *Hawke: The early years* (Melbourne: MUP, 2010) which is the 2nd edn of *Robert J Hawke: A Biography* (Melbourne: Schwartz, 1982).
130 d'Alpuget, interview with the author.
131 d'Alpuget, interview with the author.
132 cf. the later comments of Hawke's daughter, Sue Pieters-Hawke: 'This ugly behaviour had been going on for years. Speaking for myself at least, it was, at root, the underlying reason for the level of cynicism and estrangement we kids too often felt then towards our father, even though we knew there was a strong and mutual love between us all. We simply could not stomach some of his behaviour towards our mother, especially in the seventies and early eighties. Friends who witnessed the worst of it were deeply appalled – Mick Young, an ex-shearer who'd seen a lot of rough stuff in his time, was one who commented on it after witnessing an outburst, expressing his shock and saying he'd "never heard a man speak to a woman like that". Hazel was by now capable of striking back when she, too, had been drinking, but friends and witnesses are somewhat skeptical of her own assessment that she gave as good as she got.' Sue Pieters-Hawke, *Hazel: My Mother's Story* (Sydney: Macmillan, 2011), 185–6.
133 d'Alpuget, interview with the author.
134 d'Alpuget, interview with the author.
135 d'Alpuget, *Robert J Hawke*, ix, 328.
136 d'Alpuget, *Robert J Hawke*, 223–4.
137 d'Alpuget, *Robert J Hawke*, 392–3.
138 d'Alpuget, *On Longing*, 62.
139 Letter reproduced in Hazel Hawke, *My Own Life*, 128–9.
140 d'Alpuget, *Robert J Hawke*, xi.
141 Hazel Hawke, *My Own Life*, 133–4.
142 Pieters-Hawke, *Hazel: My Mother's Story*, 157, 185. Pieters-Hawke writes that her parents' 'connection was sorely tested by Bob's drinking and his other relationships. These were not just casual flings but included more than one ongoing relationship. The best known of these was with the writer Blanche

d'Alpuget. It began after she came to interview him about his ACTU work in 1976; Bob and Blanche's attraction to one another was intense then, as now. Hazel knew about the affair and was distressed and angry, but work and her own social life provided a much-needed outlet and focus away from family dilemmas.'

143 Hazel Hawke, *My Own Life*, 141.
144 Pieters-Hawke, *Hazel: My Mother's Story*, 157 & 186.
145 d'Alpuget, interview with the author.
146 Blanche d'Alpuget, letter to Peter Ryan, 21 April 1982, Papers of Peter Ryan.
147 Blanche d'Alpuget, letter to Peter Ryan, 26 April 1982, Papers of Peter Ryan.
148 'There was great pressure of time in producing the book: chapter by chapter, in the later stages, it was edited and marked up as it was written. This speedy delivery caused in me a sort of post-natal depression during the fortnight's break between finishing writing and waiting for typesetting to begin, and I was overcome with doubts. Peter Ryan's encouragement arrived like a basket of flowers in winter.' d'Alpuget, *Robert J Hawke*, ix–x.
149 Blanche d'Alpuget, letter to Peter Ryan, 26 April 1982, Papers of Peter Ryan.
150 Blanche d'Alpuget, email to the author, 7 April 2014.
151 Blanche d'Alpuget, book launch, *Robert J Hawke*.
152 Hawke, interview with the author.
153 d'Alpuget, interview with the author.
154 Blanche d'Alpuget, *SMH*, 15 March 1986, cited in Paul Kelly, *The End of Certainty: Power, Politics & Business in Australia* (Sydney: Allen & Unwin, 1994), 210–211; first published 1992.
155 d'Alpuget, *On Longing*, 59–60.
156 Ellison, *Rooms of Their Own*, 20.
157 d'Alpuget, *Robert J Hawke*, 198.
158 Baker, 'Blanche d'Alpuget', 98.
159 Blanche d'Alpuget, *Canberra Times* Literary Luncheon.
160 d'Alpuget, interview with the author.
161 d'Alpuget, interview with the author.
162 d'Alpuget, interview with the author.
163 d'Alpuget, interview with the author.
164 Graham Little, *Friendship: Being Ourselves With Others* (Melbourne: Text, 1993), 7.
165 Ellison, *Rooms of Their Own*; Baker, 'Blanche d'Alpuget'.
166 Leslie Stephen, *Samuel Johnson* (1878), Kindle edition, Loc 1099.
167 d'Alpuget, interview with the author.
168 Robert Haupt & Michelle Grattan, *31 Days to Power: Hawke's Victory* (Sydney: Allen & Unwin, 1983), 14.
169 Blanche d'Alpuget, email to the author, 5 March 2014.
170 Alan Davies, *Skills, outlooks and passions: a psychoanalytic contribution to the study of politics* (Cambridge: Cambridge University Press, 1980).
171 Blanche d'Alpuget, book launch, *Robert J Hawke*.
172 Anson, *Hawke: An Emotional Life*.
173 Stan Anson, 'Representing R.J Hawke', i.
174 Anson, *Hawke: An Emotional Life*, viii.
175 Anson, *Hawke: An Emotional Life*, 158–9.
176 Blanche d'Alpuget, email to the author, 5 March 2014.
177 Brett, *Political Lives*, ix.

178 Caroline Wilson, 'Chapter closes on bitter battle of the publishers', *Sunday Age*, 1 March 1992.
179 Anson, *Hawke: An Emotional Life*, updated edn (Ringwood: McPhee Gribble, 1992), viii.

7 Polaroids of a busy life

1 Edna Carew, *Keating, a biography* (Sydney: Allen & Unwin, 1988); Michael Gordon, *A Question of Leadership: Paul Keating, Political Fighter* (Brisbane: UQP, 1993).
2 Paul Keating, interview with the author, 'Tusculum', Potts Point, 26 November 2014.
All Keating quotes otherwise unattributed in this chapter are from this source.
3 Paul Keating, interview with the author. American literary critic Richard Ellman (1918–1987) was the biographer of James Joyce, Oscar Wilde and William Butler Yeats.
4 Don Watson, *Recollections of a Bleeding Heart: A Portrait of Paul Keating PM* (Sydney: Random House, 2002), 49.
5 Keating, interview with the author.
6 Fia Cumming, *Mates: Five Champions of the Labor Right* (Sydney: Allen & Unwin, 1991), i.
7 Cumming, *Mates*, 121.
8 Watson, *Recollections of a Bleeding Heart*, 75–6. Barbara Tuchman, *The Guns of August* (London: Constable,1962); William Manchester, *The Caged Lion: Winston Spencer Churchill 1932–1940* (London: Michael Joseph, 1988).
9 Keating quoted in John Edwards, *Keating, The Inside Story* (Viking: Ringwood, 1996).
10 Keating quoted in Edwards, *Keating*. Keating did, indeed, lose the first ballot 66 votes to 44 on 3 June 1991; he beat Hawke in a second ballot on 19 December 1991, 56 votes to 51.
11 Edna Carew, email communications with the author, November 2014. All Carew quotes otherwise unattributed are from this source.
12 Carew, email communications with the author.
13 Carew, email communications with the author.
14 Edna Carew, *Fast Money: The Money Market in Australia* (Sydney: Allen & Unwin, 1983), vii.
15 Carew, *Fast Money*, 59, 55.
16 Carew, email communications with the author.
17 Carew, email communications with the author.
18 Edna Carew, *The Language of Money* (Sydney: Allen & Unwin, 1985); *New Zealand's money revolution: a comprehensive, up-to-the-minute guide to New Zealand's rapidly changing financial system* (Sydney: Allen & Unwin, 1987).
19 Carew, email communications with the author.
20 Carew, email communications with the author.
21 Carew, email communications with the author.
22 Carew, email communications with the author.
23 Keating, interview with the author.
24 Carew, email communications with the author.
25 Carew, email communications with the author.
26 Carew, email communications with the author.
27 Keating, interview with the author.

28 Edna Carew, *Paul Keating, Prime Minister*, 2nd edn (Sydney: Allen & Unwin, 1992), 2nd edn; originally published as *Keating, a biography*, 226–7.
29 Carew, *Keating*, 305–6.
30 Keating, interview with the author.
31 Keating, interview with the author.
32 Gordon, interview with the author, Parliament House, Canberra, 17 July 2014.
33 Keating, interview with the author.
34 Michael Gordon, interview with the author.
35 Michael Gordon, interview with the author.
36 Keating, interview with the author.
37 Christine Wallace, *Hewson, A Portrait* (Port Melbourne: Pan Macmillan, 1993).
38 Liberal Party of Australia, *Fightback!: fairness and jobs* (Barton: Liberal Party, 1992).
39 Don Watson, *Recollections of a Bleeding Heart*, 299.
40 Gordon, interview with the author.
41 Gordon, interview with the author.
42 Gordon, interview with the author.
43 Gordon, interview with the author.
44 Gordon, interview with the author. Keating has no recollection of reading the Gordon biography in manuscript form but does say he read the published version: Keating, interview with the author.
45 Gordon, interview with the author; Warren Denning, *Caucus Crisis: the rise and fall of the Scullin Government* (Parramatta: Cumberland Argus, 1937).
46 Keating, interview with the author.
47 Gordon, interview with the author.
48 The first occasion was the 1977 election with Freudenberg's biography of Whitlam and Edwards' brief biography of Fraser.
49 Watson, *Recollections of a Bleeding Heart*, 299.
50 Watson, *Recollections of a Bleeding Heart*, 304–5.
51 Amanda Buckley, 'Author casts new light on PM', *Daily Telegraph*, 30 January 1993, 25.
52 John Howard, telephone interview with the author, 13 November 2014. Howard quotes in the rest of this chapter not otherwise attributed are from this source.
53 John Howard, telephone interview with the author.
54 David Barnett with Pru Goward, *John Howard, Prime Minister* (Ringwood: Viking, 1997); Wayne Errington & Peter van Onselen, *John Winston Howard* (MUP, 2007), rev. edn, *John Winston Howard: The Definitive Biography* (MUP, 2008).
55 David Barnett, interview with James Walter for his 'Political advisors project', Canberra, 6 October 1982, transcript, 18–19, Papers of James Walter, MS 7846, NLA.
56 Barnett, interview with James Walter, 13.
57 Barnett, *John Howard*, viii–ix.
58 Barnett, *John Howard*, 1–2.
59 Laurie Oakes, Speech at the launch of the book *Backroom Briefings: John Curtin's War* by Clem Lloyd & Richard Hall, Old Parliament House, 1 December 1997 Papers of Laurie Oakes, MS 9159, NLA, 1.
60 Howard, telephone interview with the author.
61 Howard, telephone interview with the author.

62 Peter van Onselen, email communication with the author, January 2015. All further van Onselen quotes not otherwise attributed are from this source.
63 Errington & van Onselen, *John Winston Howard,* vii.
64 Wayne Errington, email communication with the author, 17 November, 2014. All further Errington quotes not otherwise attributed are from this source.
65 van Onselen, email communication with the author.
66 Errington, email communication with the author.
67 Errington & van Onselen, *John Winston Howard,* 384. Wayne Errington, email communication: 'I mentioned that Peter and I did the key interviews together but he thought knowing Mrs Howard ... would be helpful so they went one on one – a little less formal, I guess. She said some interesting things which Howard was unwilling to contradict but wouldn't have said himself.'
68 Errington & van Onselen, *John Winston Howard,* 386.
69 Errington & van Onselen, *John Winston Howard,* 387–8.
70 Kerry O'Brien, 'Costello, Howard try to hose down biography comments', *7.30 Report,* ABC-TV, 19 July 2007, <www.abc.net.au/7.30/content/2007/s1983190.htm>, accessed 1 August 2021.
71 O'Brien, 'Costello, Howard try to hose down biography comments'.
72 Shaun Carney, 'Authors mine literary gold at the Treasury', *Age,* 20 July 2007, <www.theage.com.au/news/national/authors-mine-literary-gold-at-the-treasury/2007/07/19/1184559956590.html>, accessed 1 August 2021.
73 Errington & van Onselen, *John Winston Howard,* 317. The Costellos had dined with John and Janette Howard at 'leadership dinners with a larger group'.
74 Howard, interview with the author.
75 Howard, interview with the author.
76 Errington, email communication with the author.

8 Political biography as political intervention

1 Ludwig Wittgenstein, *Philosophical Investigations,* trans. GEM Anscombe, PMS Hacker & Joachim Schulte, rev. 4th edn by PMS Hacker & Joachim Schulte (Chichester: Wiley-Blackwell, 2009), 115, 53e; first published 1953.
2 Alan Jones, speech to the Sydney University Liberal Club, 23 September 2012.
3 Roy Morgan, Australia's Most Trusted and Distrusted Brands and Politicians, webinar report, March 2022, <www.roymorgan.com/~/media/files/findings%20pdf/2020s/2022/april/australiasmosttrusteddistrustedbrandsandpoliticianswebinarreportmarch2022.pdf?la=en>, accessed 7 June 2022.
4 Cecil Edwards, *The Editor Regrets* (Melbourne: Hill of Content, 1972), 206.
5 Graham Freudenberg, *A Certain Grandeur: Gough Whitlam in Politics* (South Melbourne: Macmillan, 1977), 415.
6 Paul Keating, interview with the author, 'Tusculum', Potts Point, 26 November 2014.
7 Cameron Hazlehurst, *Menzies Observed* (Sydney: Allen & Unwin, 1979), 7.
8 Karen Middleton, *Albanese: Telling It Straight* (Sydney: Random House, 2017); Margaret Simons, *Penny Wong: Passion and Principle* (Collingwood: Black Inc, 2019); Annika Smethurst, *The Accidental Prime Minister* (Sydney: Hachette, 2021); Jacqueline Kent, The Making of Julia Gillard (Melbourne: Viking, 2009).
9 John Howard, telephone interview with the author, 13 November 2014.
10 This does not include the unfinished biography of George Reid by an unidentified biographer, nor the unfinished biography of Menzies by Allan Dawes.

11 Stanhope W Sprigg, *WM Hughes: The Strong Man of Australia* (London: C Arthur Pearson, 1916); Douglas Sladen, *From Boundary-Rider to Prime Minister: Hughes of Australia, The Man of the Hour* (London: Hutchinson, 1916).
12 Alan Chester, *John Curtin* (Angus & Robertson: Sydney, 1943).
13 Frank C Browne, *They Called Him Billy* (Sydney: Peter Huston, 1946).
14 Ronald Seth, *RG Menzies* (London: Cassell, 1960).
15 Alan Trengove, *John Grey Gorton: An informal biography* (North Melbourne: Cassell, 1969).
16 Laurie Oakes, *Whitlam PM: a biography* (Cremorne: Angus & Robertson, 1973); Freudenberg, *A Certain Grandeur*; John Edwards, *Life wasn't meant to be easy: a political profile of Malcolm Fraser* (Mayhem: Sydney, 1977).
17 On Hawke: John Hurst, *Hawke, the definitive biography* (Sydney: Angus & Robertson, 1979); Robert Pullan, *Bob Hawke: A Portrait* (Sydney: Methuen, 1980); Blanche d'Alpuget, *Robert J Hawke: A Biography* (Melbourne: Schwartz, 1982); and Stan Anson, *Hawke: An Emotional Life* (Ringwood: McPhee Gribble, 1991). On Keating: Edna Carew, *Keating, a biography* (Sydney: Allen & Unwin, 1988); Michael Gordon, *A Question of Leadership: Paul Keating, Political Fighter* (Brisbane: UQP,1993). On Howard: David Barnett with Pru Goward, *John Howard, Prime Minister* (Ringwood: Viking, 1997); Wayne Errington & Peter van Onselen, *John Winston Howard* (MUP, 2007).
18 Lisa Visentin, '"Don't trust in governments": Scott Morrison delivers Pentecostal church sermon', 18 July 2022, <www.smh.com.au/politics/federal/don-t-trust-in-governments-the-un-scott-morrison-delivers-pentecostal-church-sermon-20220718-p5b2i2.html>, accessed 31 July 2022.

Bibliography

The biographies
Anson, Stan, *Hawke: An Emotional Life* (Ringwood: McPhee Gribble, 1991).
Barnett, David, with Pru Goward, *John Howard, Prime Minister* (Ringwood: Viking, 1997).
Browne, Frank C, *They Called Him Billy* (Sydney: Peter Huston, 1946).
Carew, Edna, *Keating, a biography* (Sydney: Allen & Unwin, 1988); 2nd edn, *Paul Keating, Prime Minister* (Sydney: Allen & Unwin, 1992).
Chester, Alan, *John Curtin* (Angus & Robertson: Sydney, 1943).
d'Alpuget, Blanche, *Robert J. Hawke: a biography* (Melbourne: Schwartz, 1982); 2nd edn, *Hawke: the early years* (Melbourne: MUP, 2010).
Edwards, John, *Life wasn't meant to be easy: a political profile of Malcolm Fraser* (Mayhem: Sydney, 1977).
Errington, Wayne & Peter van Onselen, *John Winston Howard* (Melbourne: MUP, 2007); revised edition, *John Winston Howard: The Definitive Biography* (Melbourne: MUP, 2008).
Freudenberg, Graham, *A Certain Grandeur: Gough Whitlam in Politics* (Melbourne: Macmillan, 1977).
Gordon, Michael, *A Question of Leadership: Paul Keating, Political Fighter* (Brisbane: QUP, 1993).
Hurst, John, *Hawke, the definitive biography* (Sydney: Angus & Robertson, 1979); rev. edn *Hawke PM* (Sydney: Angus & Robinson, 1983).
Oakes, Laurie, *Whitlam PM: a biography* (Sydney: Angus & Robertson, 1973).
Pullan, Robert, *Bob Hawke: A Portrait* (Sydney: Methuen, 1980).
Seth, Ronald, *RG Menzies* (London: Cassell, 1960).
Sladen, Douglas, *From Boundary-Rider to Prime Minister: Hughes of Australia, The Man of the Hour* (London: Hutchinson, 1916).
Sprigg, Stanhope W, *WM Hughes: The Strong Man of Australia* (London: C Arthur Pearson, 1916).
Trengove, Alan, *John Grey Gorton: An informal biography* (Melbourne: Cassell, 1969).

Other works
Anson, Stan, 'Representing RJ Hawke', thesis submitted in fulfilment of the requirements of the degree of Master of Arts, University of Melbourne, 1988.
Arklay, Tracey, John Nethercote & John Wanna (eds), *Australian Political Lives: Chronicling political careers and administrative histories* (Canberra: ANU Press, 2006)
Australian Fabian Society, *The Whitlam Phenomenon: Fabian Papers* (Fitzroy: McPhee Gribble, 1986).
Ayres, Philip, *Malcolm Fraser, a biography* (Melbourne: Mandarin, 1989).
Baker, Candida, 'Blanche d'Alpuget', interview at Springwood NSW, June 1985, in *Yacker: Australian Writers Talk About Their Work* (Sydney: Picador, 1986), 78–103.
Barnett, David, interview with James Walter for his 'Political advisors project', Canberra, 6 October 1982, Papers of James Walter, MS 7846, NLA.

Bibliography

Bastian, Peter, *Andrew Fisher: An underestimated man* (Sydney: UNSW Press, 2009).
Bebbington, G., *Pit boy to prime minister: the story of the Rt. Hon. Sir Joseph Cook, PC, GCMG* (Keele: University of Keele, 1988).
Beckett Green Publishing, *Great Frasers of Our Time* (Sydney: Hodder & Stoughton, 1977).
'Biography of the Hon. George Houston Reid', manuscript, 24pp., Papers of Sir George Reid, MS 2242, NLA.
Black, David, *In His Own Words: John Curtin's Speeches and Writings* (Bentley: Paradigm, 1995).
Blond, Anthony, 'Glory boys', *Sunday Times* (London), 13 June 2004, extract from *Jew Made in England* (London: Timewell, 2004).
Bolton, Geoffrey, *Edmund Barton* (Sydney: Allen & Unwin, 2000).
Booker, Malcolm, *The Great Professional: A Study of WM Hughes* (Sydney: McGraw-Hill, 1980).
Brett, Judith, *Robert Menzies' Forgotten People* (Melbourne: MUP, 2007); first published 1992.
Brett, Judith (ed.), *Political Lives* (Sydney: Allen & Unwin, 1997).
Browne, Frank C, *Things I Hear: For the Confidential Information of Subscribers, A Privately Circulated Digest for Busy People*, periodical, Sydney (1946–77).
Buchanan, Alfred, *Bubble Reputation: A Story of Modern Life* (Melbourne: George Robertson, 1906).
——'The Prime Ministers of Australia', unpublished manuscript, 1940, Papers of Alfred Buchanan, MS 3034, NLA.
——*The Real Australia* (London: T Fisher Unwin, 1907), Colonial Edition.
Caine, Barbara, *Biography and History* (Basingstoke: Palgrave Macmillan, 2010).
Campbell-Jones, Herbert, *The Cabinet of Captains: the romances of Australia's first Federal Parliament*, unpublished manuscript, circa 1935, Papers of Herbert Campbell-Jones, MS 8905, NLA.
Cannon, Michael, *The Land Boomers: The Complete Illustrated History* (Melbourne: Lloyd O'Neill, 1986), originally published 1972.
Carew, Edna, *Fast Money: The Money Market in Australia* (Sydney: Allen & Unwin, 1983).
——*The Language of Money* (Sydney: Allen & Unwin, 1985).
——*New Zealand's money revolution: a comprehensive, up-to-the-minute guide to New Zealand's rapidly changing financial system* (Sydney: Allen & Unwin, 1987).
Chalmers, Rob, *Inside the Canberra Press Gallery: Life in the Wedding Cake of Old Parliament House*, eds Sam Vincent & John Wanna (Canberra: ANU Press, 2011).
Churchill, Winston, *The World Crisis* (London: Butterworth, 1923).
Clark, Colin, *Australian Hopes and Fears* (London: Hollis & Carter, 1958).
Cobden Club, *A History of the Cobden Club by Members of the Club* (London: Cobden-Sanderson, 1939).
Cockburn, Stewart, interviewed by Clem Lloyd, 9 March 1984, ORAL TRC 5253/6, Oral History Collection, NLA.
Communist Party of Australia, *The Calamitous Career of Dictator Bob* (Australia: CPA, 1951).
Cook, Patrick, *Fraser Country* (Melbourne: Fontana, 1980).
Crabb, Steve, *The Prefect* (Camberwell: Widescope, 1975).
Crawford, RM, 'History', 10 October 1947, 15pp., in 'Research in the Social Sciences in Australia: Reports prepared at the request of Professor WK Hancock', January 1948, roneoed copy.

Crisp, LF, *Ben Chifley: A Biography* (Croydon: Longmans, 1961).
——'A new perspective on Gough Whitlam', *Age*, 3 December 1977.
——Papers of LF Crisp, MS 5243, NLA.
Crozier, Michael, 'Obituary – Graham Little', *Australian Journal of Political Science*, 35, 2 (2000), 313–6.
Cumming, Fia, *Mates: Five Champions of the Labor Right* (Sydney: Allen & Unwin, 1991).
d'Alpuget, Blanche, Book launch: *Robert J Hawke: a biography*, speakers Blanche d'Alpuget, Bob Hawke, Sir Richard Kirby & Morry Schwartz, Lakeside Hotel, Canberra, 5 October 1982, sound recording, NLA.
——*Canberra Times* Literary Luncheon, speech, Lakeside Hotel, Canberra, 27 October 1982, sound recording, NLA.
——Letters to Peter Ryan, 1982, in Papers of Peter Ryan, MS 9897, NLA.
——'Lust' in Fitzgerald, Ross (ed.), *The Eleven Deadly Sins* (Port Melbourne: Minerva, 1993).
——*Mediator: A Biography of Sir Richard Kirby* (Melbourne: MUP, 1977).
——*Monkeys in the Dark* (Sydney: Aurora, 1980).
——*On Longing* (Melbourne: MUP, 2008).
——*Robert J. Hawke: a biography* (Melbourne: Schwartz, 1982); 2nd edn, *Hawke: the early years* (Melbourne: MUP, 2010).
——*Turtle Beach* (Ringwood: Penguin, 1981).
Damousi, Joy, 'Freud in the Antipodes: A Cultural History', Trevor Reese Memorial Lecture, Menzies Centre for Australian Studies, Kings College London (London: Menzies Centre, 2001).
——*Freud in the Antipodes: a cultural history of psychoanalysis in Australia* (Sydney: UNSW Press, 2005).
Davies, AF, 'Fanaticism in Politics', *Current Affairs Bulletin*, 48, 11 (19 April 1971), 163–76.
——*Images of Class: an Australian study* (Sydney University Press, 1969).
——*Private Politics: a study of five political outlooks* (Melbourne: MUP, 1966).
——Review of LF Crisp, *Ben Chifley: A Biography* in *Quadrant*, 6, 2 (Autumn 1962), 94–6.
——*Skills, outlooks and passions: a psychoanalytic contribution to the study of politics* (Cambridge: CUP, 1980).
——'The task of biography' in *Essays in Political Sociology* (Melbourne: Cheshire, 1972), 109–17.
Dawes, Allan, 'Biography of Mr RG Menzies', in Papers of Allan Dawes, MS 8792, NLA.
——*Caesar's Ghost: the journalist, the statesman, the spokesman* (Melbourne: Trustees of the Arthur Norman Smith Memorial, 1946).
Day, David, *Andrew Fisher, Prime Minister of Australia* (Sydney: HarperCollins, 2008).
Deakin, Alfred, *'And Be One People': Alfred Deakin's Federal Story* (Melbourne: MUP, 1995).
——'Books and a Boy' (1910?), manuscript, Papers of Alfred Deakin, MS 1540, Series 4, 112–149, NLA.
——Notebook with newspaper clippings, (c 1883–4), Papers of Alfred Deakin, MS 1540, 1540/4/585, NLA.
Denning, Warren, *Caucus Crisis: The rise and fall of the Scullin government* (Parramatta: Cumberland Argus, 1937); new edn with a memoir of the author by Alan Reid (Sydney: Hale & Iremonger, 1982); republished with an

Bibliography

introduction by Frank Moorhouse as *James Scullin* (Melbourne: Black Inc., 2000).

——'Stanley Melbourne Bruce', unpublished manuscript, Papers of Warren Denning, MS 5129, NLA.

Duparc, Jean & David Margolies (eds), *Christopher Caudwell: Scenes and Actions, Unpublished Manuscripts* (London: Routledge & Kegan Paul, 1986).

Easson, Michael, 'Leaders bewildered by crisis', *Catholic Weekly*, 26 September 1982.

Edwards, Cecil, *Bruce of Melbourne: Man of Two Worlds* (London: Heinemann, 1965).

——*The Editor Regrets* (Melbourne: Hill of Content, 1972).

——Papers of Cecil Edwards, MS 4637, NLA.

Edwards, John, *Keating, The Inside Story* (Viking: Ringwood, 1996).

Ellison, Jennifer, 'Blanche d'Alpuget' in *Rooms of Their Own* (Ringwood: Penguin, 1986), 8–27.

English, John, *'Reid the Wriggler' or the False Prophet of Freetrade Tried and Convicted on his Professions, Promises and Performances* (Sydney: TJ Houghton & Co, Printers, 1895).

Fisk, Denis, 'A journalist who knew his onions: Louis d'Alpuget 1915–2006', *Sydney Morning Herald*, 9 June 2006, <www.smh.com.au/news/obituaries/a-journalist-who-knew-his-onions/2006/06/08/1149359881272.html>, accessed 1 August 2021.

Fitzhardinge, LF, interviewed by Tom Molomby, 'Science Bookshop', ABC Radio, 1979.

——*William Morris Hughes: A Political Biography*: vol. 1, *That Fiery Particle, 1862–1914* (Sydney: Angus & Robertson, 1964); vol. 2, *The Little Digger 1914–1952* (Sydney: Angus & Robertson, 1979).

Frame, Tom, *The Life and Death of Harold Holt* (Sydney: Allen & Unwin, 2005).

Fraser, Malcolm & Margaret Simons, *Malcolm Fraser: The Political Memoirs* (Melbourne: Miegunyah Press, 2010).

Freudenberg, Graham, *A figure of speech: A political memoir* (Brisbane: Wiley, 2005).

——interviewed by John Farquharson, 8–9 March 2000, ORAL TRC 3994 (transcript), 269pp., Oral History Collection, NLA.

——Speech at Memorial Service for Gough Whitlam (1916–2014), Sydney Town Hall, 5 November 2014, <www.youtube.com/watch?v=yZbzQ3qymUM>, accessed 1 August 2021.

Garton, Stephen, 'Freud and Psychiatrists: The Australian Debate 1900–1940' in Brian Head & James Walter (eds), *Intellectual Movements and Australian Society* (Melbourne: OUP, 1988).

Golding, Peter, *Black Jack McEwen: Political Gladiator* (Melbourne: MUP, 1996).

Grattan, Michelle (ed.), *Australian Prime Ministers* (Sydney: New Holland, 2013).

Grassby, Al & Silvia Ordonez, *The Man Time Forgot: The life and times of John Christian Watson, Australia's first Labor Prime Minister* (Annandale: Pluto Press, 1999).

Gullett, Henry 'Jo', *Good Company: Horseman, soldier, politician* (Brisbane: QUP, 1992).

——interviewed by Mel Pratt, 14–19 November 1970, transcript, ORAL TRC 121/1, Oral History Collection, NLA.

Hancock, Ian, *John Gorton: He Did It His Way* (Sydney: Hodder, 2002).

——'Liberal Governments, 1966–72' in JR Nethercote (ed.), *Liberalism and the Australian Federation* (Sydney: Federation Press, 2001), 196–213.

—— *National and Permanent? The Federal Organisation of the Liberal Party of Australia 1944–1965* (Melbourne: MUP, 2000).
Haupt, Robert & Michelle Grattan, *31 Days to Power: Hawke's Victory* (Sydney: Allen & Unwin, 1983).
Hawke, Hazel, *My Own Life* (Melbourne: Text, 1992).
Hazlehurst, Cameron, *Menzies Observed* (Sydney: Allen & Unwin, 1979).
—— *Ten Journeys to Cameron's Farm* (Canberra: ANU Press, 2013).
Henderson, Anne, *Menzies at War* (Sydney: NewSouth, 2014).
Henderson, Heather (ed.), *Letters to My Daughter: Robert Menzies, letters, 1955–1975* (Sydney: Murdoch, 2011).
Hocking, Jenny, *Gough Whitlam: His Time*, vol. 2, (Melbourne: Miegunyah Press, 2012).
Horne, Donald, *In Search of Billy Hughes* (Melbourne: Macmillan, 1979).
—— *Time of Hope: Australia 1966–72* (Sydney: Angus & Robertson, 1980).
Hughes, WM, *Australia and war to-day: the price of peace* (Sydney: Angus & Robertson, 1935).
—— *The Case for Labor* (Sydney: The Work Trustees, 1910).
—— *Crusts and Crusades: Tales of Bygone Days* (Sydney: Angus & Robertson, 1947).
—— *Policies and Potentates* (Sydney: Angus & Robertson, 1950).
—— *The Splendid Adventure: A Review of Empire Relations Within and Without the Commonwealth of Britannic Nations* (London: Ernest Benn, 1929).
Humphreys, Edward W, *Andrew Fisher: The forgotten man* (Teesdale: Sports & Editorial Services, 2008).
Jupp, James (ed.), *An Encyclopedia of the Australian People* (Sydney: Angus & Robertson, 1988).
Kelly, Paul, *The End of Certainty: Power, Politics & Business in Australia* (Sydney: Allen & Unwin, 1994).
—— *The Hawke Ascendancy* (Sydney: Angus & Robertson, 1984).
Kirsner, Douglas, 'The Freud Conference', *Australasian Journal of Psychotherapy*, 18, (2), 1999: 102–113.
La Nauze, JA, *Alfred Deakin: A Biography* (Melbourne: MUP, 1965), 2 vols.
—— *Alfred Deakin: Two Lectures*, the John Murtagh Macrossan Memorial Lectures, 1958 (Brisbane: UQP, 1960).
—— interviewed by Neville Meaney, 26 August 1986, ORAL TRC 2053/2 (transcript), Oral History Collection, NLA.
—— & Nurser, Elizabeth (eds.), *Walter Murdoch and Alfred Deakin on Books and Men: Letters and Comments 1900–1918* (Melbourne: MUP, 1974).
Langoulant, Allan, *A Mal for all seasons: The Book of Mal* (Perth: Panorama, 1981).
Liberal Party of Australia, *Fightback!: fairness and jobs* (Barton: Liberal Party, 1992).
—— *How Well Do You Know This Man?* (Sydney: Liberal Party, 1949).
—— 'The Rt Hon. Harold Holt, CH, MP, Prime Minister: His mid-term record and his approach to government: "Fair, firm, forthright, friendly"' (Canberra: Liberal Party of Australia, 1967), 8pp.
Little, Graham, *Friendship: Being Ourselves With Others* (Melbourne: Text, 1993).
—— *Political Ensembles: A psychosocial approach to politics and leadership* (Melbourne: OUP, 1985).
—— *The Public Emotions: from mourning to hope* (Sydney: ABC Books, 1999).
Lloyd, Clem, *Parliament and the Press: The Federal Parliamentary Press Gallery 1901–88* (Melbourne: MUP, 1988).

Bibliography

——*Profession: Journalist, A History of the Australian Journalists' Association* (Sydney: Hale & Iremonger, 1985).
Loveday, Peter, 'Political History and Political Biography' in Don Aitken (ed.), *Surveys of Australian Political Science* (Sydney: George Allen & Unwin, 1985), 86–118.
McEwen, John, *John McEwen: His Story*, privately published and circulated (1982).
McGregor, Craig, *Left Hand Drive* (Melbourne: Affirm, 2013).
McKenna, Mark, *An Eye for Eternity: The life of Manning Clark* (Melbourne: Miegunyah Press, 2011).
McMinn, WG, 'The Making of a Politician: The Early Career of GH Reid', *Journal of the Royal Australian Historical Society*, 67, 1 (June 1981), 1–17.
——*George Reid* (MUP, 1989).
McNicoll, David, *Luck's A Fortune: An Autobiography* (Sydney: Wildcat Press, 1979).
Manchester, William, *The Caged Lion: Winston Spencer Churchill 1932–1940* (London: Michael Joseph, 1988).
Marsden, Susan & Roslyn Russell, *Our First Six: Guide to Archives of Australia's Prime Ministers*, (Canberra: National Archives of Australia, 2002).
Martin, AW, *Robert Menzies: A Life*, vol. 2, 1944–1978 (Melbourne: MUP, 1999).
Mayer, Henry, 'Politician '72', *Current Affairs Bulletin*, 49, 5 (1 October 1972), 143–5.
Menadue, John, *Things You Learn Along the Way* (Ringwood: David Lovell Publishing, 1999).
Menzies, Robert, *The Measure of the Years* (Melbourne: Cassell, 1970).
——Papers of Robert Menzies, MS 4936, NLA.
——*Speech is of Time* (London: Cassell, 1958).
Mills, Stephen, *The Hawke Years: The Story from the Inside* (Ringwood: Penguin, 1993).
Mitchell, Susan, *Margaret Whitlam, a biography* (Sydney: Random House, 2007).
Morgan, Vyrnwy, *The War and Wales* (London: Chapman & Hall, 1916).
Mr Hughes: A Study (London: T Fisher Unwin, 1918.
Murdoch, Walter, *Alfred Deakin: A Sketch* (London: Constable, 1923).
Nolan, Melanie, *Biography: An Historiography* (Abingdon: Routledge, 2022)
——'Country and Lives: Australian Biography and Its History', *Cercles*, 35 (2015), 96–117.
Oakes, Laurie, *Crash Through or Crash: The Unmaking of a Prime Minister* (Melbourne: Drummond, 1976).
——'Foreword' to Ross Fitzgerald & Stephen Holt, *Alan 'The Red Fox' Reid, Pressman Par Excellence* (Sydney: NewSouth, 2010), vii–xii.
——Speech at the launch of the book *Backroom Briefings: John Curtin's War* by Clem Lloyd & Richard Hall, Old Parliament House, 1 December 1997, in Papers of Laurie Oakes, MS 9159, NLA, 8pp. Oakes, Laurie & David Solomon, *Grab for power: election 74* (Melbourne: Cheshire, 1974).
——*The Making of an Australian Prime Minister* (Melbourne: Cheshire, 1973).
Owen, Frank, *Tempestuous Journey: Lloyd George, His Life and Times* (London: Hutchinson, 1954).
Page, Earle, *Truant Surgeon* (Grafton: Examiner, 1959).
Pappas, Kevin & Dennis Welsh, *The Mal Book* (Melbourne: Samsbooks, 1980).
Penrose, Elizabeth, *A history of England: from the first invasion by the Romans to the 14th year of the reign of Queen Victoria* (London: Murray, 1857).
Perkins, Kevin, *Menzies: Last of the Queen's Men* (Adelaide: Rigby, 1977).
Pieters-Hawke, Sue, *Hazel: My Mother's Story* (Sydney: Macmillan, 2011).

Prasser, Scott, JR Nethercote & John Warhurst, (eds), *The Menzies Era: A reappraisal of Government, Politics and Policy* (Sydney: Hale & Iremonger, 1995).
Pryor, Geoff, 'Malcolm Fraser as an Easter Island statue with a tear rolling down his cheek', *Canberra Times*, 6 March 1983; Pryor collection of cartoons and drawings, NLA.
Raven, Fred, *History of the Menzies Family in Jeparit* (Jeparit: Jeparit Chamber of Commerce, 1966).
Reid, Alan, 'The Role of the Journalist', Summer School of Professional Journalism, Canberra (1965), 16pp.
——'A Strange Rooftop Sect', *New Journalist*, November 1973, 11–14.
Reid, George, *The Diplomacy of Victoria on the Postal Question, and the True Policy of New South Wales* (Sydney: W Maddock, 1873).
——*An Essay on New South Wales, The Mother Colony of the Australias* (Sydney: Thomas Richards, Government Printer, 1876).
——*Five Free Trade Essays* (Melbourne: Gordon & Gotch, 1875).
——*My Reminiscences* (London: Cassell, 1917).
——'Opinions of the Press', [*An Essay on New South Wales, The Mother Colony of the Australias* by GH Reid]: (1877), pamphlet, 12pp.; Papers of George Reid, MS 7842/4, 'Sir George Reid, Publications', NLA.
Reynolds, John, *Edmund Barton* (Sydney: Angus & Robertson, 1948).
Richards, Eric, 'An Australian map of British and Irish literacy in 1841', *Population Studies:*
A Journal of Demography, 53, 3 (1999), 345–59.
Richardson, Graham, *Whatever It Takes* (Sydney: Bantam, 1994).
Robertson, John, *JH Scullin: A Political Biography* (Perth: UWA Press, 1974).
Roe, Jill, 'Biography Today: A Commentary', *Australian Historical Studies,* Special Issue on Biography and Life-Writing, 1, 43 (March, 2012), 107–18.
Rogers, DK, press secretary to John Curtin, interviewed by Mel Pratt, 29 April 1971, ORAL TRC 121/14, Oral History Collection, NLA.
Ross, Lloyd, *John Curtin: A Biography* (Melbourne: Macmillan, 1977).
——*John Curtin for Labor and for Australia*, the Inaugural John Curtin Memorial Lecture 1970 (Acton: ANU Press, 1971).
Rothe, Anna (ed), 'Robert Menzies', *Current Biography: Who's News and Why* (New York: HW Wilson, 1950), 392–4.
Ryan, Peter, Papers of Peter Ryan, MS 9897, NLA.
Ryan, Susan, *Catching the Waves: Life In and Out of Politics* (Sydney: Harper Collins, 1999).
Schneider, Russell, *The Colt From Kooyong: Andrew Peacock, a political biography* (Sydney: Angus & Robertson, 1981).
——*War Without Blood: Malcolm Fraser in Power* (Sydney: Angus & Robertson, 1980).
——*My Long Life: Anecdotes and Adventures* (London: Hutchinson, 1939).
Seth, Roland, *RG Menzies* (London: Cassell, 1960).
Souter, Gavin, *Company of Heralds: a century and a half of Australian publishing by John Fairfax Limited and its predecessors* (Melbourne: MUP, 1981).
Stephen, Leslie, *Samuel Johnson* (1878), Kindle edition.
St John, Edward, 'Portrait of a great PM', *Canberra Times*, 28 February 1974, 2.
Thompson, EP, 'Christopher Caudwell', *Critical Inquiry*, 21, 2 (Winter 1995), 305–53.
Thompson, Peter, 'Chif', Australian Broadcasting Commission, February 1962; script in Papers of LF Crisp, MS 5243, NLA.
Tuchman, Barbara, *The Guns of August* (London: Constable, 1962).

Bibliography

Turner, Henry Gyles, *The First Decade of the Australian Commonwealth: A Chronicle of Contemporary Politics, 1901–1910* (Melbourne: Mason, Firth & McCutcheon, 1911).
Uren, Tom, *Straight Left* (Sydney: Random House, 1994).
Wallace, Chris, *Hewson, A Portrait* (Melbourne: Pan Macmillan, 1993).
Walter, James, 'The Biography of a Contemporary Figure and Its Pitfalls' in James Walter & Raija Nugent (eds.), *Biographers at Work* (Brisbane: Institute for Modern Biography, 1984), 59–62.
——'Biography, Psychobiography, and Cultural Space' in Ian Donaldson, Peter Read & James Walter (eds), *Shaping Lives: Reflections on Biography* (Canberra: Humanities Research Centre ANU, 1992), 260–86.
——'(Draft Only: Confidential) EG Whitlam: An Essay in Political Biography ... A thesis submitted in fulfillment of the requirements for the degree of Doctor of Philosophy in the Department of Political Science, University of Melbourne, July 1979', Papers of James Walter, MS 7846, NLA.
——*The Leader: A political biography of Gough Whitlam* (Brisbane: UQP, 1980).
——'Studying Political Leaders from a Distance: the Lessons of Biography' in James Walter (ed.), *Reading Life Histories*, Griffith Papers on Biography (Brisbane: Institute for Modern Biography, 1981), 29–38.
Watson, Don, *Recollections of a Bleeding Heart: A Portrait of Paul Keating PM* (Sydney: Random House, 2002).
Webb, Leicester, 'The Labour Party and the Future', *Australian Quarterly*, 25, 1 (March 1953), 122–7.
Weller, Patrick, *Malcolm Fraser PM: A Study in Prime Ministerial Power in Australia* (Ringwood: Penguin, 1989).
Wells, Deane, *The Wit of Whitlam* (Melbourne: Outback Press, 1976).
Whitington, Don, *Strive to be Fair: An unfinished autobiography* (Canberra: ANU Press, 1977).
——*Twelfth Man?* (Brisbane: Jacaranda, 1972).
Whitlam, Gough, 'Foreword' to Irwin Young, *Theodore: His Life and Times* (Sydney: Alpha Books, 1971), vii–xiv.
——*The Whitlam Government 1972–1975* (Ringwood: Penguin, 1985).
Whitlam, Gough & David Frost, *Whitlam and Frost: The full text of their TV conversations plus exclusive new interviews* (London: Sundial, 1974).
Whyte, W Farmer, Papers of W Farmer Whyte, MS 970, NLA.
——*William Morris Hughes: His Life and Times* (Sydney: Angus & Robertson, 1957).
Wilson, Caroline, 'Chapter closes on bitter battle of the publishers', *Sunday Age*, 1 March 1992.
Wittgenstein, Ludwig, *Philosophical Investigations*, trans. GEM Anscombe, PMS Hacker & Joachim Schulte rev. 4th edn by PMS Hacker & Joachim Schulte (Chichester: Wiley-Blackwell, 2009); first published 1953.

Index

Abbott, Tony x, 243
Adler, Louise 249
Advocate (Melbourne) 101
The Age 22, 206, 252
Albanese, Anthony x, 258
Allen & Unwin x, xii, 227, 229
Angus & Robertson 96, 130, 157
Anson, Stan 169, 217, 261, 262
    Hawke biography *see Hawke:*
      An Emotional Life
    MA thesis on Hawke 217–18
Anthony, Doug 116
Argus 2, 5, 18, 20, 22
Arndt, Bettina 227
The Australian 156, 170, 175, 176–77
Australian Associated Press (AAP) 244
Australian Broadcasting Commission
    (ABC) 53
Australian Council of Trade Unions
    (ACTU) 168, 169, 173, 186, 191, 202, 205
Australian Dictionary of Biography (ADB)
    67, 68, 91
Australian Financial Review (AFR) 155–56,
    160, 227, 228–29
Australian Journalists' Association (AJA)
    27–28, 95
Australian Labor Party (ALP) 4, 5, 74,
    140–41
    1979 federal conference 173, 193
Australian National University (ANU)
    40, 41, 43, 67, 92, 150, 156, 168, 172, 182,
    190, 247
Australian Parliament colonial
    environment 3
Ayres, Philip 157, 158

Baird, Mike 243
Baker, Candida 195, 216
Baldwin, Stanley 62
Barnard, Lance 141
Barnes, Allan 114
Barnes, Roger 157
Barnett, David 145–46, 242–43, 261
    Howard, belief in 244–45
    John Howard, Prime Minister 242–46,
      261
    journalism 243–44
Barton, Edmund 'Toby' 1, 3, 5–7
    first biography 2
    privacy 6
    The Real Australia 5–6, 9, 22
Bastian, Peter 19
    Andrew Fisher: An underestimated
      man 19
Bavin, Tom 6–7
Beasley, 'Stabber Jack' 48
Beaverbrook, Lord 30
Beazley, Kim ix
Beckett Green Publishing 159–60
    Great Frasers of Our Time 159–60
Ben Chifley: A Biography 101, 242
Bevan, Aneurin 139
Bishop, Julie 243
Black, Adam 32
Black Inc. 49, 155
    James Scullin 49
    Quarterly Essay 155
Blamey, Thomas 78–79
Blond, Anthony 60
Bob Hawke: A Portrait 174, 175–81, 200, 261
    cooperation from Hawke and family,
      lack of 176–77, 178
    Hawke interview 177–78
    inherent modesty 179–80
    insight 180
    research 176–77
    sources and information confirmation
      178–79
Bolton, Alec 25
Bolton, Geoffrey 6, 106
Booker, Malcolm 26, 37
Bowen, Lionel 225
Bradman, Donald 59
Brennan, WA 88
Brereton, Laurie 224
Brett, Judith 2, 64, 67, 68, 70, 184, 185, 219

Index

The Enigmatic Mr Deakin 2
Political Lives 219
Robert Menzies' Forgotten People 67, 70, 185
Brisbane Telegraph 138
British Broadcasting Corporation (BBC) 46
British Colonist 16
   'fifty most illustrious names in British history' 16
British Labour Party 139
Brown, Henry 111
Browne, Frank C 35, 38, 39, 260, 261
   'Browne and Fitzpatrick Case' 38
   Hughes biography *see They Called Him Billy*
   journalism 38
Bruce of Melbourne 42–47
Bruce, Stanley Melbourne 42–47, 71, 105
   attitudes to biography 43–44
   non-contemporaneous biography of 42–47
   unconfirmed assertions and 45–47
Buchan, John 111
Buchanan, Alfred 1, 8, 10, 18–19, 20, 21–24, 52, 260
   Bubble Reputation: A Story of Modern Life 22
   The Image Breaker 22
   'The Prime Ministers of Australia' 25–26
   The Real Australia 1, 5–6, 20, 22, 24–25
   She Loved Much 22
   Where the Day Begins 22
Buchanan, Captain AE 25
Buckley, Amanda 240
Bulletin 175, 176, 233
Burke, Edmund 137–38
Burns, James MacGregor 242

C Arthur Pearson 29
   'Books for War Time' 29
Cable, KJ 31
Cairns, Jim 152
Calwell, Arthur 128, 139–41
Cameron, Archie 53
Cameron, Clyde 152, 156
Campbell Committee of Inquiry into the Australian Financial System 227
Campbell, Jean 111
Campbell-Jones, Herbert 2–3, 5, 18, 20–21, 52, 260
   'The Cabinet of Captains: the romance of Australia's first Federal Parliament' 20–21
Canberra Air Disaster 68, 71, 106
Canberra Press Gallery 37, 48, 74, 95, 102, 120, 157–58, 165, 201, 235, 242
   assumptions about d'Alpuget Hawke biography 210
   'Chatham House' rules 238
   National Press Club end of year dinner 238
Canberra Times 120, 159
   Literary Luncheon 1982 195–96
Cannon, Michael 162
Carew, Edna 222–23, 227–28, 261
   Fast Money: The Money Market in Australia 228
   Fast Money 2 229
   financial background 227–28
   Keating biography *see Keating, a biography*
   The Language of Money 229
   New Zealand's money revolution 229
   writing 227–28
Carlton, Jim 224
Carr, Bob 176, 224
Carroll, Vic 155–56
Casey, Richard 'Dick' 73, 163
Cassell's 'Red Lion Lives' series 59–60, 93
Caudwell, Christopher (Christopher Sprigg) 30
A Certain Grandeur: Gough Whitlam in Politics 120, 135–36, 140, 143, 147–54, 260, 261, 262
   The Age Book of the Year award 148
   Australians' attitude to themselves 152
   economy role in Dismissal 149–51
   Fraser/Whitlam contrast 152–53
   Menzies to Whitlam framework 148–49
   progressive change by parliamentary means 151–52
   title origins 148
   trauma surrounding the Dismissal 136–37

Chalmers, Jim 256
Chamberlain, Joe 141
Chamberlain, Neville 46, 62
Cheshire 130
Chester, Alan 96–100, 259, 261
   biography of Curtin *see* John Curtin
   novelistic skills 98
Chifley, Ben 72, 73, 92, 95, 101–104, 115, 132
   appearance 102–103, 104
   biography, opinion on 104
   contemporary biography, lack of 101
   first posthumous biography 101
   political method 102–104
   public perceptions 103
   self-education 101
Chifley, Elizabeth (nee McKenzie) 115
Chisholm, Alec 42
Churchill, Winston 61, 106, 121, 148, 225, 226
Christesen, Clem 54
Cinematic Exhibitors' Association 107
Clark, Colin 4
Clark, Manning 122, 137, 152, 153
climate change vii, viii
Coalition 4
Cobden, Richard 16, 17
Cockburn, Stewart 64, 74–75, 81, 82, 83, 84, 87, 91
Cold War 84, 139
Coles, Arthur 95
Combe, David 133
Commonwealth Arbitration Court 47
Commonwealth Conciliation and Arbitration Commission 188, 190
Communist Party of Australia 59
   publication against Menzies 59
Connor, Rex 152
Conway, Ronald 106
Cook, Joseph 'Joe' 1, 20
   first biography 2
Cook, Patrick 160, 162
   Fraser Country 160
Coombs, Nugget 191
Copenhagen Climate Change Conference (COP 15) viii
Copland, Douglas 41
Costello, Peter 241, 249–51
Costello, Tanya 252
Country Party 56, 87–88, 94, 109, 116, 141

Courier Mail 170
Courtney, Victor 103
Crabb, Steve 160
   The Prefect 160
Craig, Helen 60
Creswell, Rose 198, 199
Crisp, LF 'Fin' 92, 101, 102, 137
   Chifley posthumous biography 101, 242
   research files 102–103, 104
Crosland, Anthony 139
Crossman, Richard 139
Crozier, Michael 183
Cumming, Fia 224–25
   Mates: Five Champions of the Labor Right 224–25
Cunningham, Col 173
Current Affairs Bulletin 107
Current Biography 58
Curtin, Elsie 98
Curtin Government 99
Curtin, Jack 98
Curtin, John 52–53, 54, 56, 70, 72, 94, 95–100, 180
   achievements 97
   biography and history, view of 95–96
   contemporary political biography 95, 96–100
   historic appeal to US 99
   journalism 95
   Ross biography 100
   wartime leadership 97

Daily Express (London) 28, 29–30
Daily Mirror 138, 185, 186, 190, 193
Daily News (Perth) 160
Daily Telegraph 69, 83, 138, 240
   'Menzies Biography Mystery' 69–70, 83, 91, 259
Dalrymple, Rawdon 186
Daly, Fred 103, 152
Daly, General 162
d'Alpuget, Blanche 114, 169, 179, 185–86, 261, 262
   Anson biography of Hawke and 218–19
   Canberra 187
   as diplomatic wife as 186
   Fellowship of Australian Writers' prizes 188

Index

first marriage 186–88
Hawke biography *see Robert J Hawke: A Biography*
Hawke, relationship with 186–87, 191–94, 198, 200–212, 215, 216–17
journalism 185–86
Literature Board grant 198, 199
Mediator: A Biography of Sir Richard Kirby 188–91, 194, 195
Monkeys in the Dark 189, 194, 197
newspaper profile of Hawke 210–11
novels 188, 189, 192
On Longing 192, 193, 195
rivals 204–208
South-East Asia 186–87
Turtle Beach 192, 197
d'Alpuget, Lou 185–86
Damousi, Joy 182
Davies, AF 'Foo' 102, 127, 183, 184, 217, 262
  Images of Class 183
  Private Politics 183
  Skills, outlooks and passions: a psychoanalytic contribution to the study of politics 217
  'The Tasks of Biography' 183
Dawes, Allan 66–70, 76
  AN Smith Lecture 76
  biography of Menzies 66, 67–70, 76–93, 259
  excessive drinking allegation 67–69, 83, 91–92, 93
  government press work 71–72
  image-making 76
  Liberal Party work 71, 76
  reputation as journalist 70–72
  sources for Menzies biography 78, 80
Day, David 19
  Andrew Fisher, Prime Minister of Australia 19
  biographies of Chifley and Curtin 242
de Beauvoir, Simone 212
  The Second Sex 212
Deakin, Alfred 1, 4, 5, 7
  Alfred Deakin: A Biography 2
  Alfred Deakin: A sketch 2
  attitude to press 8
  biography, relationship with 7–8
  The Enigmatic Mr Deakin 2

first biography 2
Deakin University 184
Deamer, Sydney 126
Denning, Warren 48–53
  Caucus Crisis: The rise and fall of the Scullin Government 48–52, 239
  contemporary biographical works 53–54, 55
  journalists and politicians, relationship 49–50, 53
  writerly ambitions 53
Dixon, Owen 57, 80, 81
Dollard, John 183
  Criteria for the Life History 183
Downer, Alexander 224, 240
Downing, Dick 191
Drysdale, Alister 158, 159
Dunk, Sir William 101
Dunstan, Albert 87–88
Duthie, Gil 104

Easson, Michael 51, 52
Eden, Anthony 106
Edith Cowan University 247
Edwards, Cecil 42–47, 70–71, 105, 256
  Bruce of Melbourne 42–47
  ground rules for biography 44–45
Edwards, John 155–56, 260
  Fraser biography *see Life wasn't meant to be easy: a political profile of Malcolm Fraser*
  journalism 155–56
  Keating biography 225–26, 233
Eggleston, Richard 190
Ellison, Jennifer 195, 216
Ennor, Sir Hugh 162
Epstein, Michael 184, 194, 213
Errington, Wayne 242, 243, 246–53, 261
  Howard biography *see John Winston Howard*
Evatt, HV 'Doc' 38, 74, 129

Fadden, Arthur 56, 94–95
Fadden Government 95
federal elections
  1919 23
  1925 70
  1937 98
  1943 100
  1946 72, 103

1949 58, 73–74, 104
1954 74, 84
1961 140
1969 110
1972 117, 119, 123, 126, 130–31
1974 134, 156
1975 154
1977 153, 154
1980 154, 174
1983 159, 167, 168
1993 234, 239–40
1996 239
2010 x
Federation 1, 13, 18
  political parties 4
  rise of ALP 4
Fell, James 108
Ferrier, Kathleen 59
Fingleton, Jack 101
First Nations peoples
  dispossession 3
  massacres 3
Fisher, Andrew 1, 5, 19, 32, 167
  biographies 19
  early political career 19
  first biography 2
Fitzhardinge, LF 38, 39–40
  Hughes, relationship with 39–42
  political biography of Hughes 39–42
Fleming, AP 25
Forde, Frank 96, 100–101
Forum 227
Foster, Alf 191
Frame, Tom 68, 105, 107
  The Life and Death of Harold Holt 105
Fraser Government 228, 241, 244, 246, 250
Fraser, Lori 163
Fraser, Malcolm 120, 134, 137, 145, 146, 152–53, 154, 156–57, 174, 175, 199, 201, 244, 245
  cartoons 159, 160–61, 162
  competitors, struggles with 162–63
  contemporary biographical accounts 155–66
  controversy surrounding first office 154, 157–58, 161
  'Easter Island statue' cartoons 159
  family history 161–62
  later criticism of Liberal Party 154–55
  post-retirement biography 157
  press gallery, relationship with 157–59
  public image 154–55, 157–58
  satirical treatments 159–60
  two-dimensionality 164
Fraser, Neville 164
Fraser, Simon 161–62
Free Trade Party 4, 11
Freer, Mabel 90
'Freud Conference' 184
Freud, Sigmund 183, 212–13
  The Interpretation of Dreams 212–13
Freudenberg, Graham 111, 120, 133, 135–54, 257, 260, 261, 262
  ALP and 139–47
  London 139
  journalism 138–39
  political engagement 137–38
  relationship with Whitlam 141–48
  Whitlam biography *see A Certain Grandeur: Gough Whitlam in Politics*
  Whitlam's speeches 142–45
From Boundary Rider to Prime Minister: Hughes of Australia, The Man of the Hour 28, 30, 32, 261
  hagiography 33
  Hughes and personality 32–33
  political agenda 30–31, 32, 35
Frost, David 126–27
Froude, James 8
  biography of Carlyle 8

Gaddis, John Lewis 242
  George Kennan biography 242
Gaitskell, Hugh 139
Gallagher, Patrick 227–28
Gallup Poll data 57, 72, 73
Garton, Stephen 182
George, AL 142
Georgiou, Petro 165
Gillard, Julia vii, ix–x, 254–55, 258
  'Misogyny speech' x, 254
  Wallace biography vii, ix–xii
Gillespie, Marjorie 107
Gladstone, William 12–13
Golding, Peter 109

Index

Gollan, Ross 95
Goodwin, Doris Kearns 242
Gordon, Adam Lindsay 32
Gordon, Harry 237
Gordon, Michael 222–23, 234–38, 261
   journalism 235
   Keating biography *see A Question of Leadership: Paul Keating, Political Fighter*
Gorton, Bettina 'Betty' (nee Brown) 111
Gorton, John 38, 108, 109–10, 157, 159, 160, 162, 255–56, 260
   Abraham Lincoln, influence 112
   contemporary biography 110–15
   father's death 112
   illegitimacy 114–15
   literary hero 111
   Oxford University 111
   scrutiny/commentary 113
   'unorthodoxy' 114
   World War II experience 112
Goward, Pru 242–43
   ABC-TV series *The Liberals* 243
   John Howard, Prime Minister 242–43
   Office of the Status of Women appointment 242–43
Grassby, Al 9–10
   The Man Time Forgot: The life and times of John Christian Watson, Australia's first Labor Prime Minister 9–10
Grattan, Michelle 217
Great Depression 47–50, 55, 121
Greenwood, Gordon 138
Greens 154
Greer, Germaine 177
Griffin, Walter Burley 54
Griffith University 184
Groom, Littleton 39
Groser, Horace G 29
   Lord Kitchener: The Story of his Life 29
Gruen, Fred 150
GTV9 138
Gullett, Henry 'Jo' 38, 106–107, 164–65
Gullett, Sir Henry 106
Guthrie, Bruce 237–38

Hackett, Winthrop 22
Hale & Iremonger 49, 50, 157

Hale, Sylvia 157
Hall, Richard 130
Hancock, Ian 52, 53, 73–74, 107, 115
   John Gorton: He Did It His Way 115
Hancock, Keith 43–44
Hansen-Rubensohn Company 73
Hanson, Pauline 255
Harrison, Eric 60
Hasluck, Paul 67–68, 83, 113
Haupt, Robert 217
Hawke, Bert 172
Hawke: the definitive biography 170–74, 180, 195, 200, 202, 221, 261
   leadership credentials 171–72
   personal dimension 172–73
   preconceptions on subject, confirmation 170–71
   research 170
Hawke, Ellie 193, 196–97, 213
Hawke: An Emotional Life 181, 217–20, 253, 261, 262
   dependency on d'Alpuget 181, 218–19, 220
   impact 218–21
   'passing off' accusation 218–19
   political polemic 219–20
   Political Science influence 182, 184
   psychobiography 181, 185, 218
   research 184
Hawke, Hazel (nee Masterson) 172, 177, 179, 193, 196, 204, 206, 207–209, 216
   views on d'Alpuget biography 206–207
Hawke, Neil 172
Hawke, Robert James Lee 'Bob' 114, 120, 138, 166, 167–70, 238, 260–61
   ACTU 169–70, 172, 173, 186, 191, 202, 205
   alcohol 169, 173, 193, 199, 207, 212, 213, 215
   ALP leadership 200, 203–204, 211
   Boyer Lectures 1979 218
   Canberra Press Gallery opinions of 201
   career phases 168, 172
   children 206
   Curtin and 180, 218
   d'Alpuget, relationship with 186–87, 191–94, 198, 200–212, 215, 216–17
   economic literacy 168

education 168
evocation of Curtin 180–81
health problems 174
Kirby, relationship with 190–91
Kirribilli Agreement 231–32, 233
Labor caucus opinions 201–202
major economic reform under 168, 229
personal impact of d'Alpuget biography 211–12
potential for biographers 169, 170
Rhodes Scholarship 172, 178
success as federal Labor leader 167–68
Wills, candidature for 174, 180–81, 192–93, 200
'womanising' 169, 170, 173, 192, 204
Hawkins, Trevor 158–59
Hayden, Bill 151, 152, 168, 173, 202, 203
Hazlehurst, Cameron 28, 57–58, 61, 72, 73, 84–85, 258
Hazlitt, William 223–24
Henderson, Anne 57, 67, 68
Menzies at War 67–68
Henderson, Gerard 114, 115
Henderson, Heather 63, 64
Herald (Melbourne) 42, 71
Herald & Weekly Times group 110, 116, 175
Hetherington, Jack 71
Hewson, John 224, 236–37
Keating's attack on 239–40
Wallace biography 236–37, 239–40
Higgins, Roy 174
Hitler, Adolf 46
Hoffer, Hedwig 183
Hollings, Les 176
Holt, Harold 68, 94, 105, 166
biography, alleged indifference 105–106
chronic infidelity 107–108
contemporary biography, lack of 105, 107–108
family history 107–108
image problem 106
posthumous biography 105
public image 107
Holt, Tom 108
Holt, Zara (nee Dickens) 107–108
Horne, Donald 28, 35–36, 37

Howard, Janette 247, 248, 249, 250, 252
Howard, John 168, 222, 240–53, 261
biography, views on 222, 241–42, 259
contemporary biographies 242–53
Costello, relationship with 249–52
'plain man' persona 246, 247
political dramas 245–46
Treasurer, as 245, 250
Howard, Richard 243, 247
Howard, Stewart 74
Hughes, William Morris 'Billy' 23, 27–42, 77
attack on 35
biographical writing, opinion 36–37, 38–39, 258, 259
biographies 38–40, 259–60
birth certificate 42
books 28
Britain 28, 34–35
'Imperial Preference' tariff policy 30, 35
journalism connection 27–28
Mr Hughes: A Study 35
political life 28
praise for 34–35
three contemporary biographies 28
World War I presence 35
Hurst, John 169, 170, 180, 261
Hawke biography *see Hawke: the definitive biography*
journalism 170
Hutchison 111

Immigration Restriction Act 'language test' 89
International Labour Organisation (ILO) 186, 187
International Public Relations (IPR) 158
Iremonger, John 156–57, 227, 229
Isaac, Joe 191

Jennings, Kate 198
John Curtin 96–100, 259, 261
Curtin's achievements 97
intended impact 97–100
novelistic skills 98
John Grey Gorton: An informal biography 110–15, 260, 261
advocacy 113–14
candour 261

Index

journalistic approach 110
origins 110
review 114
John Winston Howard 242, 246–53, 261
  interviews 249–50
  modernity 248
  on-the-record comments 248, 250–51
Johnston, George 175
Jones, Alan 254
Jupp, James 29

Keating, Anne 230
Keating, Annita 230
Keating, a biography 229–34, 261
  interviews 230–32
  second edition *Paul Keating, Prime Minister* 233–34
Keating, The Inside story 225–26, 233
Keating, Min 230
Keating, Paul 49, 106, 167, 210, 211, 218, 222–40, 261
  attack on Hewson 239–40
  biography, views and use of 222, 223–26, 230–33, 257, 258–59
  contemporary biographies 222–23
  cooperation with biographers 223
  epithets aptitude 224
  Kirribilli Agreement 231–32, 233
  leadership challenges 169, 220, 226, 233, 238
  major economic reform under 168, 229
  'Placido Domingo' speech 238
  private person 234
Kelly, Paul 201
  The Hawke Ascendancy 201
Kelty, Bill 234
Kent, Jacqueline 258
Kerr, Sir John 120, 134, 145–47, 151, 152, 245
Kirby, Sir Richard 188–90, 193, 194
Kirby, Sue 188–89
Kirsner, Douglas 184
Kisch, Egon 89
Knowles, George 39

La Nauze, JA 2, 7, 8, 25
  Alfred Deakin: A Biography 2
Lane, Robert 183

Lang, Jack 48, 101, 121
Lang, John Dunmore 11–12
Langoulant, Allan 160
Lasswell, Harold 182–83
Latham, Mark ix, x, 117, 248
Latham, Sir John 80, 89
Lee, David 47
  Stanley Melbourne Bruce: Australia's Internationalist 47
Leggett, William 60
Lenihan, Eileen 'Lennie' 82–83
Liberal Party 4, 56, 57–58, 109, 116, 154–55
  1949 election campaign 58–59, 73–74
Life wasn't meant to be easy: a political profile of Malcolm Fraser 155, 156–57, 160–63, 260
  class privilege motif 163–64
  Fraser's childhood 162
  Fraser's family history 161–62
  long-form journalism 155
  psychological insights 163
Little, Graham 182–84, 194, 215, 217, 218
  The Public Emotions 183
Lloyd, Clem 19, 38, 51, 64
  Out of the Wilderness 148
Lloyd George, David 28, 34, 35
Longmans 92
Lynch, Phillip 244
Lyons Government 53, 71, 72, 84, 88–89
Lyons, Joseph 46, 55, 77, 84
  contemporary biography, lack of 55

MacCallum, Mungo 128–29
McClelland, Jim 233
MacDonald, Ramsay 62
McEwen, John 'Black Jack' 108, 113, 116
  acting prime ministership 109
  contemporary biography, lack of 109
  posthumous biography 109
  protectionist economic policies 109
McGregor, Craig 106, 145–47
McIndoe, Archibald 59
McIntyre, Angus 184, 185, 194
Macintyre, Stuart 9
McKenna, Mark 153–54
Macklin, Jenny viii, ix
McLeay, Leo 224
McMahon, Gregan 22

McMahon, William 'Billy' 109, 113, 116–18, 130
   biography, desire for 116–17, 259
   contemporary biography, lack of 116
Macmillan 147
Macmillan, Harold 59
McMinn, WG 16–17
   George Reid 16–17
McMullan, Bob 174, 178
McNicoll, David 106
McNicoll, Lady (Frances) 93
McPhee Gribble 218
McPhee, Hilary 236
Manchester, William 225
   Churchill biography 225, 226
Marr, David 242
   Patrick White biography 242
Martin, Allan 56
Marxism 30
Mayer, Henry 117
Meanjin 54
Medibank 134
Meeking, Charles 72
Melbourne Club 163–64
Melbourne University Press 189, 198, 208, 249
Menadue, John 141
Menzies, Douglas 80, 94
Menzies, Frank 60, 67, 81, 82, 83
Menzies, Isabel 67
Menzies, Pattie 60
Menzies, Robert Gordon 28, 37, 53, 55, 56–58, 104, 107, 108, 109, 127, 148–49, 168, 169
   Afternoon Light 69, 93
   annotations of Dawes' biography 85–89, 93
   anti-communism 73, 74
   biography, attitude to 61–66, 75–76, 93, 259
   Calamitous Career of Dictator Bob 59
   Central Power in the Australian Commonwealth 92–93
   'Churchill and his Contemporaries' 61–62
   'Churchill at Seventy-five' 61
   contemporary biography, lack of 58, 63–66, 92–93
   cooling off on Dawes' biography 84–85, 91, 93
   Dawes' biography of 66, 67–70, 75–93
   fluctuating public approval of 72, 73, 74–75, 84–85, 93
   How Well Do You Know This Man? 58–59, 74, 75
   journalists, opinion of 64–65
   Liberal Party election campaign 1949 73–74
   The Measure of the Years 93
   'Pig Iron Bob' 90
   politics as *performance* 64
   popular perception of 57, 73–74
   public speaking skill 64
   retainers from companies, cancellation of 90
   Speech is of Time 60, 61, 92
   two prime ministerships 56–57
   unpopularity within party 56–58
Methuen 174, 176
Middleton, Karen 258
The Mike Walsh Show 201
Millais, Sir John 162
Mills, Stephen 169
Mitchell, Susan 136
Mockridge, Tom 235
Molomby, Tom 39
Monash University 184
Monk, Albert 191, 194, 197, 216
Montgomery, Field Marshal 59
Moore, Charles 242
   biography of Thatcher 242
Moorhouse, Frank 49
Morgan, Vyrnwy 34–35
   The War and Wales 34–35
Morrison, Scott 258, 262
Mountbatten, Lord Louis 59
Muirhead, Margaret 31
Muller, Laurie 237
Mullins, Patrick 117
   Tiberius with a Telephone: The Life and Stories of William McMahon 117
'Mungana Affair' 121, 123
Munich Agreement 46
Murdoch, Sir Keith 33, 42, 100
Murdoch, Walter 2, 8, 9
   Alfred Deakin: A sketch 2, 9
Murphy, Denis 19
Murphy, Lionel 152

Index

Nation Review 170
National Disability Insurance Scheme (NDIS) x
'National Insurance' scheme 71
National Library of Australia (NLA) 14, 25
  Allan Dawes papers 70, 76–91
  McMahon Papers 116–17
  Menzies papers 70, 83–84, 91
  Reid Papers 14, 17
National Party 4
National Times 156–57, 158, 160
Nelson, HN 'Hank' 67, 83, 91
New York Times 61
Niemeyer, Sir Otto 50
Nuffield, Lord 59

Oakes, Laurie 120, 123–26, 129–30, 134–35, 138, 141–42, 145, 155, 201, 245, 260, 261, 262
  Crash Through or Crash: The Unmaking of a Prime Minister 120, 134–35, 161, 262
  Grab for Power: Election 74 120, 134, 262
  The Making of an Australian Prime Minister 120, 130–31, 262
  new generation of journalists 124–25, 129
  research on Whitlam 126, 129–30
  university 124
  Whitlam biography see Whitlam PM: A biography
  Whitlam's psychology 126–28, 131
O'Brien, Kerry 251
O'Farrell, Barry 243
O'Malley, King 10
Ordonez, Silvia 9–10
  The Man Time Forgot: The life and times of John Christian Watson, Australia's first Labor Prime Minister 9–10
Outback Press 198–99
Owen, Frank 35
  Tempestuous Journey: Lloyd George, His Life and Times 35

Page, Earle 44, 55
  Truant Surgeon 44
Palaszczuk, Annastacia 255

Pan Macmillan 236
Pappas, Kevin 160
Parkes, Henry 13
Peacock, Andrew 162, 166, 174, 240, 246
Pearson, (Cyril) Arthur 29–30
Penguin 198, 218
Penrose, Elizabeth 7
  'Mrs Markham's History' 7
Penton, Brian 138
Perkins, Kevin 63, 67–68
  biography of Menzies 67–68
Petrov Affair 84
Pieters-Hawke, Sue 207, 208
Pilger, John 186
Plibersek, Tanya 256
political analysis 184–85
political biography
  academic approach 248
  admired subject 44–45
  'attack culture' 262
  biographer as political player 203–204
  candour 261
  collaborative 77–78
  confessional culture 182
  contemporary biography 46–47, 257, 259–61
  contextualisation of events 153–54
  disclose-and-rebut approach 88–91, 93
  diversity in authors and subjects 256–58, 262
  emotional appeal and wide readership 99
  historians as authors 257–58
  journalistic background of authors 256–57
  less to subject than meets the eye 164–65
  Menzies 61–66
  modern era 120
  motivations 261–62
  observational and writing style 54
  potential exploitation by 'bad actors' x–xii, 220, 254
  psychobiographical works 127, 169, 181–85, 210, 212–14, 216–17, 220–21, 262
  reputational impact xi, xiii, 220, 236–237, 239–40, 263

revelatory 113–15
scholar-journalist/writer-journalist
    44–45, 52, 78–79
unconfirmed assertions 45–47
political journalism 185
political parties
    early Federation years 4–5
    leaders 4–5
Pratt, Tony 186, 187
prime ministers
    contemporary biographies, views on
        258–59
    early, environmental context 3
    ethnicity 255
    political party affiliations 1
    state of origin 1
    women 254–55
Protectionist Party 4
Pryor, Geoff 159
psychoanalysis 182–83
Pugh, Clifton 126
Pullan, Robert 169, 174–75, 261
    ALP, identification with 176
    biographical sketches 175
    Hawke biography *see Bob Hawke:
        A Portrait*
    journalism 175, 176

Queen Victoria 13
*A Question of Leadership: Paul Keating,
    Political Fighter* 234–40, 261
    interviews 235–36
    Keating's opinion of 239
    process of writing 237
Quiller-Couch, Arthur 186

Ramsay, Alan 156
Reader's Digest 175
Reid, Alan 'The Red Fox' 49, 52, 53, 95,
    124, 125–26
    powerlessness of journalists 125
Reid, George 1, 5, 11–19, 94
    anonymous contemporary biography
        13–17, 52
    first biography 2, 13–16
    memoir 11
    'Reid the Wriggler' 17–18
    writing as career advancement 11–13
    'Yes–No Reid' 18
Reid, Gordon 148

Out of the Wilderness 148
Reynolds, John 65
    Edmund Barton 65
Richards, Eric 29
Richardson, Graham 224
Riesman, David 183
Robert J Hawke: A Biography 181, 194,
    200–217, 261, 262
    author engagement with subject 216
    cover photograph 204
    effect of process on Hawke 211–12
    events during writing 200–204, 211
    Hawke's childhood 213–14
    initial reactions from press and
        politicians 210
    interviews 198, 199–200
    motives for writing 194–98, 202, 216
    Political Science influence 182, 184
    psychobiography 181, 184–85, 210,
        212–14, 216–17
    quest narrative 215
    use by Anson 218
    'warts and all portrayal' 203, 206–
        207, 261
Roberts, Andrew 242
    biography of Halifax 242
Robertson, John 47
Robinson, Hercules 11
Ross, Lloyd 95, 100
    awareness of previous Curtin
        biography 100
    John Curtin: A Biography 100
Rowley, Hazel 177
Royal Australian Historical Society
    (RAHS) 40–41
Royce PR 158
Rudd Government vii–ix
Rudd, Kevin vii–x
Russell, Bertrand 139
Russell, Don 236
Ryan, Lyndall 3
Ryan, Mark 235, 236, 238
Ryan, Peter 189, 198, 200, 208
Ryan, Susan 187–88, 201–202, 203

Salisbury, Lord 13
Samuel, Saul 11–12
Santamaria, Cathy 84
Schieffer, Tom 242
Schneider, Russell 155, 165–66

Index

The Colt From Kooyong: Andrew Peacock, a political biography 166
Fraser biography *see War Without Blood: Malcolm Fraser in Power*
Schultz, Julianne 3–4
  The Idea of Australia 3–4
Schwartz, Morry 198–99, 203–204, 208
Scott, Professor Ernest 10
Scullin, James 'Jim' 47–54, 96, 119
  contemporary history 48–54
  journalism 48, 51
Sekuless, Peter 116
Seth, Ronald 58, 67, 260, 261
  pseudonym 59
  RG Menzies 59–60, 92, 260, 261
  sources for Menzies biography 60
  works 59–60
Shorten, Bill ix
Simons, Margaret 255, 258
Sinclair, Ian 224
Sinclair, Jean 200–201, 204–206, 207
Skidelsky, Robert 241–42
  John Maynard Keynes biography 242
Sladen, Charles 31
Sladen, Douglas 28, 30, 261
  Australian connection 31
  Hughes biography *see From Boundary Rider to Prime Minister: Hughes of Australia, The Man of the Hour*
  Hughes, meeting with 33–34
  non-journalist 31
  Oxford education 31
  Who's Who 32
  writing 31–32
Smethurst, Annika 258
Snedden, Billy 133, 134, 158, 159, 160, 162, 244
Solomon, David 120, 130, 135
  Grab for Power: Election 74 120, 134
  The Making of an Australian Prime Minister 120, 130–31
Somare, Michael 175
Souter, Gavin 95
Spanish Civil War 30
Sprigg, Christopher 30
Sprigg, Stanhope W 28–29, 261
  publishing record 30
  Hughes biography *see WM Hughes: The Strong Man of Australia*
  Yorkshire Observer editor 30
  views on Australia 29
Staley, Tony 244
Stephen, Leslie 216–17
Stephenson, Josie 185
Stoyles, Megan 156
Street, Geoffrey 68, 71, 76
Stubbs, John 141
Suez Crisis 139
Suharto, President 187
Suich, Max 156, 189, 199
Sukarno, President 188
Sun 185, 186, 243
Sun News-Pictorial 110, 123, 124, 138
Sunday Age 220, 234, 237–38
Sunday Telegraph 102, 156
Sunday Times Magazine 103
Sunraysia Daily 138
Swan, Wayne vii
Sydney Morning Herald 72, 94–95, 145, 210, 239, 243

T Fisher Unwin Ltd 35
Tanck, Johan Cristian *see* Watson, John Christian 'Chris'
Tange, Sir Arthur 162
Taylor, Bill 102
Taylor, Peter 175–76
Theodore, EG 'Red Ted' 48, 50–51, 121–23
They Called Him Billy 35, 37, 39, 260, 261
  hagiography 35–36
Thompson, EP 30
Thring, Viola 'Lola' 108
Trengove, Alan 110–15, 260, 261
  Gorton biography *see John Grey Gorton: An informal biography*
Triple A 229
Truman, Tom 138
Tuchman, Barbara 225
Turnbull, Malcolm 176, 243
Turner, Henry Gyles 4
  The First Decade of the Australian Commonwealth: A Chronicle of Contemporary Politics, 1901–1910 4

United Australia Party (UAP) 28, 55, 56
University of Melbourne 182, 217
  Melbourne Psychosocial Group 184, 185, 217, 262
  Political Science program 182–83

University of New South Wales (UNSW) 247
University of Oxford 168, 172
University of Queensland Press (UQP) 236, 237
University of Sydney 124, 185
University of Western Australia 168, 172, 174, 246, 247
Uren, Tom 152, 202

van Onselen, Peter 242, 243, 247–53, 261
   Howard biography *see John Winston Howard*
   Howard family, association with 247, 249, 252
   journalism 243
van Sommers, Tess 189
Vietnam War 149–50, 155

Walter, James 123, 142, 183, 184, 185, 219, 243, 253
Walsh, Eric 133, 141
Walsh, Richard 130, 157, 188
War Without Blood: Malcolm Fraser in Power 155, 165–66
   Fraser's style of governing 165–66
Ward, Eddie 140
Watson, Don 223–24, 225, 236, 239
   Recollections of a Bleeding Heart 236–37
Watson, George 9
Watson, John Christian 'Chris' 1, 5, 9, 45, 94
   evasiveness 10
   first biography 2, 9–10
   heritage 9–10
Webb, Leicester 103
Weller, Patrick 154, 157–58
Welsh, Dennis 160
West Australian 95–96, 175
Westralian Worker 95
Whelan, Philip 99
White, Charles 29
   Our Regiments and Their Glorious Deeds 29
White, Patrick 242
Whitington, Don 37, 57, 68, 70, 74, 95, 121
   Canberra Press Gallery memoir 37
   Strive To Be Fair 70

Twelfth Man? 126–28
Whitlam, Freda 129
Whitlam, Gough 110–11, 113, 116, 117, 118, 119–20, 140–54, 160, 162, 243
   biography, interest in 120–23
   contemporary biographies 120–54
   disinformation campaign against 136–37
   'The Dismissal' 119, 134, 136, 143, 145–52, 158, 165
   double dissolution election 134
   foreword to Theodore biography 121–22
   'Impotent are Pure' speech 144
   'It's time' 131
   journalists, relationship with 124
   key legislative reforms 234
   middle-class background 129
   oratory style 142
   polling 123–24, 128, 131, 133
   Victorian ALP executive 143–44
   voters' views 123–24, 128–25, 131
Whitlam Government 244
Whitlam, Margaret 129, 136–37, 143
Whitlam PM: A biography 120, 123, 131–35, 260, 261
   hard truths 132
   leadership 133
   revelatory details 131–32
Whitlam, Tony 130
Whyte, W Farmer 38–39
Willesee, Mike 163–64
Wilson, Alec 95
Wilson, Caroline 220
Withers, Reg 'The Toecutter' 165, 166
WM Hughes: The Strong Man of Australia 28–29, 261
   hagiography 34, 35
   migration and literacy link 29
Wong, Penny 255–56, 258
Wran, Neville 143
Wren, John 22

Yale's 'Psychology and Politics' program 183
Young, Irwin 121, 124
   biography of EG 'Ted' Theodore 121–22
Young, Mick 170–71, 202

www.ingramcontent.com/pod-product-compliance
Lightning Source LLC
Chambersburg PA
CBHW030607230426
43661CB00053B/1871